THE CHRISTIAN STATE OF LIFE

HANS URS VON BALTHASAR

THE CHRISTIAN STATE
OF LIFE

TRANSLATED BY
SISTER MARY FRANCES MCCARTHY

IGNATIUS PRESS　　SAN FRANCISCO

Title of German original:
Christlicher Stand
© 1977 Johannes Verlag, Einsiedeln

Cover by Victoria Hoke Lane

TABLE OF CONTENTS

CONTENTS

PART III
THE CALL

CONTENTS

PREFACE ON THE SCOPE OF THIS BOOK

WHAT IS INTENDED

The sole purpose of this book is to provide a comprehensive meditation on the foundations and background of St. Ignatius' contemplation on the "Call of Christ",[1] on the answer we must give if we want "to give greater proof of [our] love" (*Sp Ex*, 97), and on the choice explicitly demanded of us: either to follow Christ our Lord to "the first state of life, which is that of observing the commandments", of which he has given us an example by his obedience to his parents; or to follow him to "the second state, which is that of evangelical perfection", of which he has given us an example by leaving his family "to devote himself exclusively to the service of his eternal Father". And this so that we can "arrive at perfection"—which is, of course, the perfection of Christian love—"in whatever state or way of life God our Lord

Unless otherwise specified, all translations from the Bible are from the *New Catholic Edition of the Holy Bible* (New York: Catholic Book Publishing Co., 1953). However the psalm numbering follows the modern convention.

Unless otherwise specified, all quotations from Latin, Greek and French, as well as from German, have been newly translated from the original text. Wherever possible, however, I have indicated the existence of an English translation of the whole text of these works. [Translator's note.]

[1] The reference here is to the *Spiritual Exercises* of St. Ignatius Loyola, which von Balthasar quotes in German. To avoid doing violence to his thought, which is often based on the wording of St. Ignatius' text, I have translated from the German text as quoted by von Balthasar rather than from the original. The reference to the contemplation on the "Call of Christ" will be found in paragraph 91 of the *Spiritual Exercises*, where the more usual designation is "The Kingdom of Christ". Further references to the *Spiritual Exercises* (henceforth *Sp Ex*) will be given in parentheses in the text, using the traditional paragraph numeration. For an English translation, see *The Spiritual Exercises of St. Ignatius Loyola*, trans. Louis J. Puhl, S.J. (Chicago: Loyola University Press, 1951). [Tr]

9

may grant us to choose" (*Sp Ex*, 135). In his Directory,[2] St. Ignatius adds that clearer signs are needed for entering upon the first than upon the second of these ways.

The goal of our meditation is to understand why this act of choosing a "state or way of life" "within our Holy Mother, the hierarchical Church" (*Sp Ex*, 170) is possible and necessary in the first place, and why there should be any either-or since both ways are capable of leading us to the same "perfection of love", just as the same act, viewed from different perspectives, can be either absolute or relative.

We begin, then, by affirming in its totality the significance conferred by the Spiritual Exercises on the practice of the principal act of the Christian life—a significance we recognize as emanating from the Gospel itself, from the personal meeting of the believer with Jesus Christ. Far from attempting to undermine this significance, we seek to understand it more fully, particularly within the structural and historical realities of the Church, for it is only within these realities—which, as they relate to calling, state and choice, have remained essentially unchanged since the Spiritual Exercises were composed—that the Christian is able to meet Christ concretely.

If this acceptance of the Church's interpretation of the Gospel makes our meditation seem naive and vulnerable, it is well to remember that there is no aspect of this interpretation that has not been contested and the "scientific" refutation of which has not elicited long treatises which, in the end, have also failed to satisfy those who reject the Church's viewpoint.

---

[2] St. Ignatius died in 1556. In 1559, the first edition of the "Directorium Exercitiorum SPN Ignatii" was published by early members of the Society of Jesus. Apart from a few passages actually written by Ignatius himself or collected by one of his followers, the text was dictated by him in the year 1555. For the full text, see "Exercitia Spiritualia Sancti Patris Ignatii de Loyola et eorum Directoria", *Monumenta Ignatiana*, series secunda, tomus unicus, in *Monumenta historica Societatis Jesu* (Madrid, 1919). Ignatius' actual comment is as follows: "Without doubt, it requires more obvious signs to determine that God's will would have us remain in a state of life that demands only the observance of the commandments than that it would have us enter upon the way of the counsels; for

WHAT IS PRESUPPOSED

1. We presuppose, in the first place, that there exist within the Church, in which all Christians are called by God to take their stand[3] and where there is room for all to stand, many contrasting and mutually supplementary states of life.[4] Our concern is with the concept of "state of life", not with the antiquity of the expression[5] or its (alleged) relationship to a medieval world

---

the Lord clearly exhorts us to the keeping of the counsels, whereas of the other state of life he says only that it is fraught with great dangers" (chap. 23, 4). [Tr]

[3] Here and elsewhere throughout the text, von Balthasar has opposed the dynamism of *stehen* (verb) and *Stehen* (noun) to the more static quality of *Stand*. I have attempted to preserve the etymological relationship as well as the semantic emphasis by translating these words, respectively, as "take a stand", "stand" (cf. the dictionary meaning: "a position especially with respect to an issue"), and "state of life" (cf. Lat. *status*). It is unfortunate, but unavoidable, that English "stand" more accurately conveys the meaning of German *Stehen* than of German *Stand*. [Tr]

[4] For a comprehensive study of this theme, see Barbara Albrecht, *Stand und Stände. Eine theologische Untersuchung* (Paderborn: Bonifatius, 1962). This very detailed analysis demonstrates the polyvalence of the term "state" not only outside the Church (e.g., in sociology, philosophy), but also in the Church's theology. On this analogy, cf. also Gustav Gundlach, S.J., "Stand" in *Staatslexikon* V (Freiburg: Herder, 1932), 45–62; Gundlach, "Stand" in *Lexikon für Theologie und Kirche* (henceforth LTK) IX, 1st ed. (Freiburg: Herder, 1937), 768–69; Bernard Häring, "*Stand*" in LTK IX, 2nd ed. (Freiburg: Herder, 1964), 1009–11. Barbara Albrecht's study may owe its inspiration in some instances to the lectures of Hermann Volk, who later as bishop seems to have drawn upon her work: Cf. his "Christenstand—Ordensstand" in *Ordenskorrespondenz* 7 (1966), 66–92 (also contained in his *Gesammelte Schriften* II [Mainz: Matthias Grünewald, 1966], 229–36).

[5] The word was in use even before Thomas Aquinas (*Summa Theologiae*, 60 vols. [New York: McGraw-Hill, 1964–1975], vol. 47, *The Pastoral and Religious Lives*, 2a 2ae 183). Cf. Willibald Maria Pöchl, *Geschichte des Kirchenrechts*, 2nd ed. (Wien-München: Herold, 1960), vol. I, 63 (quoted in B. Albrecht, p. 94): "The ancient Church spoke of the *status*, the state, of the laity, whereas members of the religious state belonged to the *ordo*. This distinction was borrowed from the Roman social structure. Opposed to the *status* of the Roman citizen was the *ordo*, a

view,[6] but with the concept that is (and that Ignatius considered to be) synonymous with "life", *vita*.[7] We shall investigate the theological origin of this differentiation of states as it appears and is reconciled in the life of Jesus (and Mary) and shall attempt to locate it in the "state of fallen nature" in which the originally intended synthesis was shattered. This topic is discussed at greater length in Part II, where we speak of "The Christian States of Life".

2. We presuppose also that to ensure the unity of his Church Jesus Christ, in calling the Twelve and challenging them to a radical following of himself, intended a primary election in which the personal element—the decision to share his life—was the definitive one and the element of ministerial calling (the call to the "priestly" as opposed to the lay state as the Church later distinguished them) was a secondary stage. This sentence contains a fundamental presupposition of our whole train of thought. In summary, it recognizes in those who are "specially" called to follow Christ (the word "specially" cannot be avoided here) a personal union of the state of evangelical perfection and the priestly state, but postulates within the Church itself a temporal, and even a qualitative, preeminence of the state of evangelical perfection over that of the ecclesiastical ministry.[8] Christ's primary intention was not to form a hierarchy, but to win men to that personal following of himself that leads to the reconciliation of the world with God by a renunciatory, even a crucified, love: with him, they are to be "the light of the world".

---

formal state that, by reason of the office or privileged position it entailed, brought with it greater rights and special duties. It was customary, for instance, to speak of the *ordo senatorius*. Similarly, the Church designated members of the religious state as belonging to the *ordo clericalis*."

[6] Wilhelm Schwer, *Stand und Ständeordnung im Weltbild des Mittelalters* (Paderborn: Schöningh, 1934).

[7] See below, pp. 238–40.

[8] Cf. the emphasis on the primacy of the Marian over the Petrine calling in Hans Urs von Balthasar, *Der antirömische Affekt* (Freiburg: Herder, 1974).

Early theologians saw this fact clearly;[9] Vatican Council II took it for granted.[10] Since Martin Hengel's *Nachfolge und Charisma* [Discipleship and charisma],[11] it is no longer necessary to refute those minimalist exegetes who claim that Jesus was merely a kind of rabbi, who, like so many, accepted disciples "for the time being", but that it was only after Easter that the relationship came to be understood as an election that was absolute and binding for life. For this reason, Heinz Schürmann's foundational study, the frequently quoted and frequently attacked "Der Jüngerkreis Jesu als Zeichen für Israel und als Urbild des kirchlichen Rätestandes" [Jesus' disciples as a sign for Israel and as a prototype of the Church's state of evangelical perfection][12] continues to be valid in all that is essential.

There are two corollaries to this line of thought. 1) In addition to the total personal calling of those on whom Jesus, in his lifetime, expressly bestowed the full powers of ecclesial office, there was also established a permanent bond between official priesthood and personal sharing in the priesthood of Christ (in the "state of evangelical perfection"), however flexibly and variably the Church may have interpreted this bond throughout

[9] Cf. below, pp. 290–92.

[10] This is evidenced by its teaching that "the pursuit of perfect charity by means of the evangelical counsels traces its origin to the teaching and the example of the Divine Master. . . ." For the text of the "Decree on the Up-to-Date Renewal of Religious Life" [*Perfectae Caritatis*], see *Vatican Council II. The Conciliar and Post Conciliar Documents*, gen. ed. Austin Flannery, O.P. (Northport, N.Y.: Costello Publishing Co., 1975), 611–23. The above quotation will be found on page 611. For a commentary on the decree *Perfectae Caritatis*, see Gustave Martelet, S.J., "Réflexion théologique sur le décret 'Perfectae Caritatis' ", in *Vie Consacrée* 38 (1966), 32–46.

[11] Published by Alfred Töpelmann (Berlin, 1968).

[12] First appeared in *Erbe und Auftrag. Festschrift zum hundertjährigen Bestehen der Armen Franziskanerinnen von der Ewigen Anbetung zu Olpe* (Werl, 1963); then in *Ursprung und Gestalt. Erörterungen und Besinnungen zum Neuen Testament* (Düsseldorf: Patmos, 1970), 46–60.

her history. 2) When the two *ordines*[13] are ordered functionally—
as "services"—to the fundamental state (Lat. *status*) within the
Church as such (i.e., to the *laos*, the "people"), they thus become
both the determinant and the support of this *status*—and this in
such a way that the Church is first founded upon (Eph 2:20) and
endures by reason of (Rev 21:14) the office, but the office itself,
in its turn, is founded upon the total self-giving of the *ecclesia
immaculata* (Eph 5:27), on the state of life of those who are at least
supposed to represent perfect love.[14]

3. We are not concerned, then, with exegetical theorizing about
the origin of the "three evangelical counsels". Unquestionably,
they—like the "seven" sacraments—were "counted" at a later
date and singled out as the constitutive elements of the "life
of evangelical perfection"—without, of course, losing their
meaning in relation to Christ as the approximation of his loving
gift of himself to the Father and to men. Admittedly, too, the
three "counsels" are rooted differently in the Gospel and in Paul.
But that does not alter the fact that together they so completely
exhaust the possibilities of what can be given[15] that they are in no
way subordinate to any of Jesus' other counsels.

If the evangelists and the primitive Church extend their literal

[13] Cf. note 5.

[14] Cf. the scene in Job 21, where this state is symbolized, and the comments
below, pp. 281–87.

[15] Some of the many works on this theme are: Albert van Gansewinkel,
Die Grundlage für den Rat des Gehorsams in den Evangelien (Mödlingen: Missions-
druckerei St. Gabriel, 1937); Franz Mussner, "Die evangelischen Räte und das
Evangelium" in *Benediktinische Monatschrift* 30 (1954), 485–93; Heinrich Zimmer-
mann, "Christus nachfolgen. Eine Studie zu den Nachfolgeworten der synop-
tischen Evangelien" in *Theologie und Glaube* 53 (1963), 244–55; Wilhelm Pesch,
"Die evangelischen Räte und das Neue Testament" in *Ordenskorrespondenz* 4
(1963), 86–96; Paul Lamarche, "Les fondements scripturaires de la vie religieuse"
in *Vie Consacrée* 41 (1969), 323–27; Rudolf Schnackenburg, *Die sittliche Botschaft
des Neuen Testaments* (München: Huber, 1954), 22–29; Schnackenburg, *Christliche
Existenz nach dem Neuen Testament*, vol. I (München: Kösel, 1967), 147–55;
Schnackenburg, "Evangelische Räte", in LTK III, 2nd ed., 1245–46.

understanding of the counsels analogously and with full justification to one that is (purely) spiritual (cf. *Sp Ex*, 98), this does not
prevent them from retaining the literal interpretation as well.[16]
Only exegetical prejudice (which minimalizes Jesus' call to discipleship) can reject as unbiblical the concept of a "special"
(or, we might say, a "qualitative") discipleship.[17] And even
if the primitive Church as a whole actually inclined to an
understanding of the "counsels" that was, in fact, spiritual (the
vita apostolica), its unquestioning acceptance of the presence of
"virgins" and "ascetics" in its midst proves that it did not attempt
to interpret spiritually the way of life of "special" discipleship.[18]
The *duae vitae* [two ways of life], neither of which excludes

---

[16] Cf. Paul Lamarche, op. cit., 327: "La généralisation opérée par les évan-
gelistes ne détruit pas ce qu'il y avait de particulier dans les récits de vocation."

[17] P. Lippert, C.SS.R., writes, for instance: "Certainly the words of discipleship retain their validity even after Easter, but they are presented to us in an
authorized contemporary version (!) of the evangelists that has been edited to
reflect a post-Easter point of view. This means, in practice, that we can no longer
speak of the perpetuation of a pre-Easter disciple-relationship (!) as a model (e.g.,
for members of a religious order), but rather of a commonly held Christian ideal,"
Ordenskorrespondenz 10 (1969), 401.

[18] On this subject, see René Carpentier's article: "Etats de vie" in *Dictionnaire
de Spiritualité* IV/2 (Paris: Beauchesne, 1961), 1406–28. The author rightly shows
that the original concept of the *communio sanctorum* hardly admitted of a thematic
exposition of the various "states of life" within the Church, and suggests that this
was undoubtedly an advantage in view of the rigidity of many of the theoretical
and practical formulations in the later life of the Church. Nevertheless, differences
did exist—in the sense of Paul's teaching on the body and its members—and the
emergence of monasticism in the fourth century was not primarily, as we might
have expected, the accenting of one particular state, but rather an attempt to
perpetuate the ideal of the *vita apostolica* as it was accepted in the beginning by the
whole Church. Cf. also Louis Bouyer, *La vie de S. Antoine* (Paris: Editions de
Fontenelle, 1950); Dom Germain Morin, *L'idéal monastique et la vie chrétienne des
premiers jours*, 3rd ed. (Paris: Lethielleux, 1921). ". . . Such as the Church of
those believing in Christ was in the beginning, so monks now strive to be,"
says St. Jerome and the whole Christian tradition (St. Jerome, "De Viris Il-
lustribus", in *Texte und Untersuchungen*, vol. XIV [Leipzig: J. C. Hinrichs'sche
Buchhandlung, 1896], no. XI [addressed to Philon Judaeus], 14). (For texts,

the other, existed in the Church from the beginning, as did the priestly office, which throughout history has sought in often dramatic ways to define its relationship to the *duae vitae*. This point will be treated more fully in later pages.

Many will no doubt find it naive that, in accordance with tradition, we trace the distinctive character of the life of the evangelical counsels to Jesus, just as they will find naive our "uncritical" treatment of Holy Scripture, which we have frequently cited in support of our basic thesis. Be that as it may. We regard Holy Scripture as an inspired whole—one that is, moreover, interpreted in the essential tradition and history of the Church.

---

see Fr. Bivarius, *Opus de veteri Monachatu et regulis monasticis in duas partes distributum* [Lyons, 1662] and below, pp. 290–91 and Pt. II, note 28.) The concept is evidenced throughout the whole tradition and has been treated again by René Carpentier in *Témoins de la Cité de Dieu* (Paris: Coll. Museum Lessianum, 1956), where he describes the life of the evangelical counsels as a "summary of the Church's ideal" not only (as is usually emphasized) as an eschatological sign of the Church that will reach its perfection in the hereafter, but as an attempt to express as completely as possible the holiness of the present Church. A similar theme is developed by L. Holtz, "Ordensleben als Zeichen des Endzustandes", in *Ordenskorrespondenz* 9 (1968), 26 ff.; Giuliano Ligabue, *La testimonianza escatologica della vita religiosa* (Paris: Vrin, 1968).

On the other hand, our whole study resists the tendency to eradicate, or even to weaken, the fruitful variety that has, from the beginning, characterized the states of life within the Church by identifying it with what some would regard as the original formlessness of a "democratic people of God". The structure of *Lumen Gentium* makes it abundantly clear that such a concept is far from the intention of Vatican Council II, which emphasized the notion of "people" as a name for the Church itself. The popular attempts being made in France and elsewhere to remove the distinction between laity and clergy by a continual interchange of services, ministries and even "offices" and "functions" (for instance, the attempts to smuggle in here the demands for the admission of women to the priesthood) seem to me to be just as unbiblical as the obliteration of the distinction between virginity and marriage in a ridiculous "third way".

THE LIMITS TO WHAT IS INTENDED

1. We have not yet named the central theme of our study. The fruitful complementarity of states of life within the Church, which on the one hand refer each to the other (and therefore, depending on perspective, can each claim for itself the primacy),[19] and which on the other hand are admissible of certain higher or lower rankings that it is anathema to gainsay,[20] points in the last analysis to the mystery of the Church itself, not, indeed, as an external organization, but as an extension of Jesus Christ, who, in order to heal human nature, chooses as his state of life precisely the mission ordained for him by the Father, who sends him into the world to do there the will of the Father "on earth as . . . in heaven", and so to let the "kingdom of God come" on earth. Compared with man's sociological "stand" [*Stehen*][21] in relation to the world, the stand taken by Jesus is eccentric (i.e., having its center elsewhere) because it is, in a deeper sense, concentric in relation to God. The primitive ecclesiological echo of such a stand is the stand of Mary (as prototype of the Church), whose obedient-poor virginity earned for her the fecundity of motherhood.

2. This eccentric-concentric stand taken by Christ for the healing of human nature seems, however, to reflect man's primitive stand: concentric in relation to God, but not for that reason

[19] Cf. below, Pt. II, Ch. III, sec. 5: *Evangelical State, Priestly State, Lay State*, as well as the subtle analysis of the "complementarity" of the states of life in Barbara Albrecht, op. cit., 113–29.

[20] "If anyone says that the conjugal state is to be preferred to the state of virginity or celibacy, and that it is not better and more blessed to remain in virginity or celibacy than to be joined in matrimony, let him be anathema," *Concilium Tridentinum: Diariorum, Actorum, Epistularum, Tractatuum*, Nova Collectio, vol. 9, "Concilii Tridentini Actorum", pars sexta, ed. Stephanus Ehses (Freiburg: Herder, 1924), sessio XXIV (11 novembris 1563), canon decimus, 968.

[21] Cf. note 3.

eccentric to the cosmos. Indeed, as we turn our gaze from the mystery of Christ/Church to man in his original state, in which he was not yet in need of healing or salvation, we become aware of an equally great mystery that the Fathers of the Church contemplated with wonder, but that we either fail to see at all or look away from in embarrassment. We cannot doubt that God created man, not in a state of alienation, but in *rectitudo*. As befits his nature and his supernatural orientation to God, he was "very good". Because man's primitive state was a simple one in which those characteristics had not yet been differentiated (rich-poor, free-obedient, fruitful-virginal) that would later split it into a multiplicity of states, it resists every attempt to reconstruct it clearly. Yet it realizes in itself that original synthesis of love that is the ultimate norm: God's love as it is in itself and as it is revealed in his creation. Our meditation begins with this love.

But if we meet our first obstacle in attempting to reconstruct this primitive state (since it is impossible to describe it as it was), we meet a second one here: Where do we find the criteria for such a description of the essence of love if not in revelation, especially in that of the New Testament? Thus, all chronology to the contrary notwithstanding (1 Cor 15:46), Christ comes before Adam: As the true omega, he is also the true alpha. This can be seen most clearly in the fact that the synthesis man enjoyed in paradise continued to be a fragile one (*posse non peccare*) so long as Adam did not ratify it for himself by his own free choice.[22] This primitive election (as a preference of God over self) has nothing to do with the choice (of a state of life within the Church) that is referred to in the Exercises. For that reason, no "calling" analogous to the Christian one can come before it.

It follows then—*qui legit intelligat!* (Mk 13:14)—that we will be able to contemplate man's state in paradise in relation to the differentiated states of life within the Church only as a symbol of unity—a symbol, however, that must be regarded as indis-

[22] See Henri de Lubac's treatment of this subject in *Surnaturel* (Paris: Aubier, 1946).

pensable since the final synthesis in Christ is consequent upon man's fall from this unity, upon his state as sinner. Thus our introductory description of the unity of love that must precede every synthesis cannot be other than abstract; it becomes full-bloodedly concrete only as it proceeds through the bloody "choice" of the Cross (cf. Heb 12:2) in which love wins back in total renunciation the total "joy" of wholeness in God and in the world.[23]

3. It is only in the course of salvation history that the differentiating "call" examined (still in Ignatian terms) in the third part of this book makes its appearance. Nevertheless, the introductory description of the "background" (pt I), however abstract it may be (but Ignatius' "Principle and Foundation" is also relatively abstract), will help us to understand the objective norm that is operative in every call to discipleship and the subjective norms of value that must be operative in our answer to this call. "Whatever state or way of life" the call offers for our choice, its purpose, according to St. Ignatius, is always "to achieve the perfection of love".[24] We are speaking here of an absolute that engages our

[23] This brings us formally close to Hegel, insofar as his original synthesis remains abstract and without passage through the tragedy of history and the possibility of a Good Friday. However, we are not interested in world history, but in the structure of the states of life within the Church. Moreover, Christ is not for us a "principle", but a unique person whose free and loving gift of himself to the Creator is the primary and only adequate explanation for the creation of the world.

[24] From this perspective, Luis de la Puente composed the great work that has been translated into many languages: *Tratado de la perfección en todos los estados de la vida del cristiano*, 3 vols.: Secular State, Ecclesiastical State, Religious State (Valladolid: Francisco Fernandez de Cordova, 1613); cf. Carlos Sommervogel, S.J., *Bibliothèque de la Compagnie de Jésus*, vol. VI (Paris: Picard, 1895), cols. 1285–86. On the "call [to a state of life]" as Vatican Council II viewed it, see *La Vocation et les vocations à la lumière de l'ecclésiologie de Vatican II* (Brussels: Centre national des vocations, 1966), in which Pierre de Locht clearly demonstrates the complementarity of vocations within the Church. On the basis of this complementarity, we consider the dichotomy between the view that the evangelical state

whole existence, hence the call to a state of life is "once and for all".[25]

WHAT IS EXCLUDED

In the preceding pages, we have outlined the scope of our study. The reader will perhaps note with disappointment that most of the issues that are (for the most part rightly) of concern to men today find no resonance here. There is no direct reference to the *aggiornamento* of the states of life that was inaugurated by Vatican Council II (for example, with regard to the contemporary practice of the evangelical counsels; the relationship of the various states of life within the Church to the great world movements of today; the philosophical basis on which ideals regarding a Christian state of life must rest); no direct reference to the immense casuistry in religious life as it is presently lived, to the problems arising from the confrontation of the general norms for this state of life with the actual problems that occur in the lives of its individual members; no direct reference to the mode of transfer from one state to another.

In the theological sphere, too, much has been excluded—the Old Testament, for example. Our interest has been focused on the Catholic Church of Christ. Questions relating to the "state of grace" (which is here mentioned only briefly) do not belong to our theme.

---

is normative for all states of life within the Church—as advanced, for instance, by René Carpentier, *Témoins de la Cité de Dieu*; Fernando Sebastién Aguilar, *Vida Evangelica* (Bilboa: Desclée, de Brouwer, 1966); Aguilar, *Secularisazión y vida religiosa* (Salamanca, 1970)—and the concept that evangelical state and lay state are necessary complements within the Church militant (cf. Karl Rahner) to be no true dichotomy (cf. Victor Codina, S.J., *Teología de la vida religiosa*, Biblioteca "Razón y Fe" de Teología, 17 (Madrid: Razón y Fe, 1968). It is to be hoped that our whole study will be instrumental in destroying even the appearance of such a dichotomy.

[25] Cf. Klaus Demmer, *Die Lebensentscheidung. Ihre moraltheologischen Grundlagen* (München: Schöningh, 1974); idem., "Die unwiderrufliche Entscheidung. Überlegungen zur Theologie der Lebenswahl", in *Internationale katholische Zeitschrift "Communio"* 3 (1974), 385–98.

The whole is intended as a prelude to meditation; hence our avoidance, so far as possible, of a multiplicity of annotations.[26] The excursions into the history of theology (in smaller print) are intended to be merely illustrative; they never attempt an exhaustive presentation.

If this book can claim any distinction, it is as a reflection on the one thing necessary (the *unum necessarium*) by the persistent factual exposition of the *structura amoris*. But singleness of purpose does not mean one-sidedness. Whoever takes the trouble to read the book in its entirety will discover that every element in its place presupposes all other elements in their places; the movement is consistently cyclic, increasingly integrated, as befits Catholic thought.

[26] Abundant literature on this subject may be found in such periodicals as: *Zeitschrift für Aszese und Mystik* (now *Geist und Leben*); *Revue d'Ascétique et de Mystique* (now *Revue d'Histoire de la Spiritualité*); *Ordenskorrespondenz*; *Vie Consacrée*; *The Way*; *Revista di Vita Spirituale*; *Bibliographia Internationalis Spiritualitatis* (since 1966). Also worth noting is Johannes Baptist Metz, *Zeit der Orden? Zur Mystik und Politik der Nachfolge* (Freiburg: Herder, 1977).

PART ONE

BACKGROUND

CHAPTER ONE

THE CALLING TO LOVE

I. THE GREAT COMMANDMENT

"Master, which is the great commandment in the law?" He answers them, "Thou shalt love the Lord thy God with thy whole heart, with all thy soul, and with all thy mind. This is the greatest and the first commandment. And the second is like it. Thou shalt love thy neighbor as thyself. On these two commandments depend the whole law and the prophets" (Mt 22:36–40).

In these words, Jesus summarizes the ultimate goal—and indeed the very meaning—of existence. If we will enter into life, if we will fulfill our calling, we must keep the commandments (Mt 19:17). But the commandments are so completely contained in the dual commandment of love of God and love of neighbor that whoever keeps this commandment, on which the whole law and the prophets depend, has done all that is necessary (Rom 13:10). Without love, on the other hand, even the perfect observance of the commandments is meaningless and useless (1 Cor 13:1–3). Yet this commandment is so unconditional and inflexible in its formulation, so transcendent of time and so apparently immutable in the face of every human ability or inability to observe it, every hope and doubt, every striving and failure, even every conviction, that no one on earth can seriously claim to have observed it in its entirety; that we are, in fact, more likely to regard it as an expression of wishful thinking, of an ideal but unattainable polestar riding high above the lowlands of human wretchedness, than as the commandment it actually is.

But the Lord does not call this commandment a wish on the part of God or a recommendation that we can safely ignore and still fulfill our calling, albeit with difficulty; he does not speak of it as a steep path beside which there are other—easier—ones. On the contrary, he is so unwilling to leave in doubt love's status as a commandment that he appropriates this great commandment of the Old Testament (Dt 6:5; Lev 19:18) not only as something already decreed, but also, with intensified and deepened meaning, as his own commandment: "A new commandment I give you, that you love one another: that as I have loved you, you also love one another. By this will all men know that you are my disciples, if you have love for one another" (Jn 13:34–35). The command to love one's neighbor, which, in the Old Testament, may have seemed to take second place to the command to love God, now moves firmly into the foreground. Because its measure is none other than the love of the incarnate God for us: "This is my commandment, that you love one another as I have loved you" (Jn 15:12), it has also become the criterion of our love of God: "He who has my commandments and keeps them"—precisely these commandments of love—"he it is who loves me" (Jn 14:21). If we do not love, we have so completely failed to fulfill our calling that we are dead even though our bodies are still alive: "He who does not love abideth in death" (1 Jn 3:14). We have condemned ourselves. For there will be no other standard of judgment on the last day than the standard of love—a fact that will take both good and bad by surprise. To the very end they will not have understood how seriously, how literally, the oneness of love of God and love of neighbor was intended by the Lord who now judges them. The just no less than the unjust will respond to the pronouncement of the Lord with the astonished query: "Lord, when did we see thee hungry, and feed thee; or thirsty, and give thee drink?" And the Lord will answer them: "Amen I say to you, as long as you did it for one of these, the least of my brethren, you did it for me" (Mt 25:34–40). If we love our neighbor in a Christian way, we love God in him, for in Christ both natures are joined in one person. Therefore, in loving our neighbor we love God in him without knowing that we do so, for "God is love, and he who abides in love abides in God, and God in him" (1 Jn 4:16). Whoever loves in this way has fulfilled the commandment of love and of the New Testament and will enter into eternal life.

Thus the principle is affirmed that the calling to love is an absolute one, admitting of no exception, and so ineluctable that failure to observe it is tantamount to total corruption. Let there be no doubt. We are here to love—to love God and to love our neighbor. Whoever will unravel the meaning of existence must accept this fundamental principle from whose center light is shed on all the dark recesses of our lives. For this love to which we are called is not a circumscribed or limited love, not a love defined, as it were, by the measure of our human weakness. It does not allow us to submit just one part of our lives to its demands and leave the rest free for other pursuits; it does not allow us to dedicate just one period of our lives to it and the rest, if we will, to our own interests. The command to love is universal and unequivocal. It makes no allowances. It encompasses and makes demands upon everything in our nature: "with thy whole heart, with all thy soul, and with all thy mind".

As it is stated, this commandment takes no heed of our human potential for observing it. All that is important is *that* it be observed; *how* this is to be done is a second question with which the first is not concerned. If we are unable to observe it by our own strength, God will not fail to give us the means to do so. But one thing God will not do: He will not accommodate his great commandment to our human insufficiency. For he knows there is only one thing that love cannot endure: to have limits set to it. Love cannot survive unless it is active; if its activity is constrained, it withers and dies. Love has its origin in God, who is eternal and boundless life. A love that is not active, that is not ready to prove itself in ever new and different ways, is not love. Love can breathe only in the spaciousness of the beloved and in its own unlimited capacity for growth. For love "with all thy soul" can never mean that it has given all it is capable of giving and is now condemned to remain forever at this level of fulfillment. It can never mean that it has reached the limit of its capacity to love (perhaps because the human soul, spirit, strength are, in the last analysis, finite) and can now find comfort in the thought that it has fulfilled its obligation to love. If such a thought enters the love of two individuals, their love is already growing cold. The inner life of love is inconceivable without the rhythm of growth, of ever new openness and spontaneity. Love can never give itself sufficiently, can never exhaust its ingenuity in preparing new joys for the beloved, is never so satisfied with itself and its deeds that it does not look for new proofs of love, is never so familiar with the person of the beloved that it does not crave the wonderment of new knowledge. And if, for outsiders, the daily protestations of those who love seem to have an essential sameness, for the lovers themselves they are always new and always different so long as their love remains alive.

"Obligation", then, is a word that pure love does not know. Or rather: its "obligation" is always a "choice". It experiences the necessity it is under of loving the beloved as the highest and most perfect freedom—a freedom not to be exchanged for all the goods of this world. What appears as cold duty to one who does not love is for love a joy: Love "bears all things, believes all things, hopes all things, endures all things" (1 Cor 13:7). Faith and hope are its characteristic modes of behavior; patience and endurance are not undesirable burdens for it, but the elements by which it lives. Love is ready for any sacrifice so long as the one thing necessary is not forbidden it: to love. Love is so precious that there is no price love will not pay for love. It knows no greater privilege than to be allowed to love. Far from comprehending one who would speak to it of the boundary between "obligation" and "choice", duty and supererogation, it regards such a one with astonishment and incomprehension: A person who says such things is not of the company of those who love. If we are convinced that everything—more, indeed, than we are able to give—belongs to the beloved, the word supererogation has no meaning for us. What lover would not gladly lay the whole world at the feet of the beloved? If we love, we do not know the difference between command and wish. The wish of the beloved is our command. We forestall every unspoken desire on the lips of the beloved and fulfill it as meticulously as one who does not love performs the strictest commands.

We are not asking here whether this is the nature of human beings or whether and to what extent they are capable of loving in this way. Our concern is with the nature, *the pure essence*, of love itself. And in every purest expression of it, we encounter anew the mystery of self-giving. For the sake of the beloved, love would gladly renounce all its possessions if it could thereby enrich the beloved. It would gladly *accept* gifts if it knew the beloved would find happiness in the act of giving. For love, even receiving is a form of self-giving. Love adorns itself, not to be beautiful for its own sake, but to appear beautiful to the beloved. Hence it will just as readily deprive itself of all adornment if by this means it can adorn the beloved. Love chooses to forget itself for the sake of the beloved and to remain present to the beloved only so long as the beloved desires the presence of a living and personal other. If we truly love, if we live only for love, we set apart in ourselves no private domain that is withdrawn from love and the service of love. We cannot perceive of love as a merely penultimate good of our spirit, cannot reserve for it a circumscribed place in our soul, cannot assign to it but a limited portion of our strength. We have only one desire: to bestow on the beloved our whole person and all our powers. We will henceforth have no other rule or law of life than that which we receive from the beloved. We will regard it as our greatest *freedom* to do, not our own will, but the will of the beloved. We will treasure it as our greatest *riches* to possess nothing but what the beloved bestows upon us. We will esteem it our greatest *fecundity* to be but a vessel held in readiness for every fructifying seed of the beloved.

The spirit of love is a spirit of self-giving and, consequently, of "choice". If love is pure, it gives itself to God and man by an interior movement that is wholly proper to it. It is nothing *but* self-giving. For this reason, it needs no other law than itself; all other laws are subsumed, fulfilled, transcended in the one law of love. Love does not have to be incited or encouraged to self-giving as to something higher than itself, as to a model it must emulate if it is not to stray from the right path. Love is itself the greatest commandment. Whoever observes it in its entirety has done all that is necessary. There is no authority higher than love. On the contrary, it is itself the highest authority, holding all else under its sway. Because it is compelled by no necessity, *necessity and freedom are conjoined in it*. When in all freedom it makes its decision to love, it fulfills all that is required. For love is the one thing necessary.

But all this changes if we fall away from love. As love cools, the glowing lava of its immense spontaneity hardens into the fixed and narrow molds of individual commandments. "Where love grows sluggish, law flourishes." By withdrawing from the innermost core of love, we place distance between ourselves and the beloved, whom we soon come to regard with an "objective", "impartial" gaze. This does not mean that the former object of our love has no further attraction for us. On the contrary, it may still appear beautiful, attractive, even desirable. But it is now only one of many possible objects of our free choice. When we live at the innermost core of love, we no longer choose. Our choice lies behind us and has not changed from the time we first came to know love. Even if we subsequently reaffirm our choice at every moment of our lives, it is not because we have reconsidered it and found it good. The lover as such *never stands at the point of indifference between loving and not loving*—is not even tempted to stand there. To one who loves, it would seem the rankest disloyalty to set beside the beloved a second possible object of choice in order, by a kind of qualitative analysis, to give preference to the first. Such indifference about the object of its choice may be an initial stage on the road to love; but within love itself it has no place. Love is so steadfast that it never reverts to the point of indifference that precedes choice. It rejects "freedom of choice" in favor of freedom of love.[1] Only when love grows cold does it

---

[1] No one has expressed this more cogently than Maximus the Confessor, who teaches that "true freedom of choice" (γνώμη) could exist only after the Fall. Until

again approach the zone of indifferent freedom. But the nearer it comes to this "middle point" between loving and not loving, the more it ceases to be a choice and becomes an obligation. It comes to be a duty. And the one commandment of love in which all the rest are contained is split thereby into its component parts. But if these parts are signs that we have fallen out of the unity of love, they are also guideposts by which we can find our way back again. The content of the commandments is positive to the extent that they point to love and live from the love that finds its expression in them. Their content is negative insofar as they reveal only a partial view of love and, far from proclaiming the wondrous unity of freedom and "inevitability" that is love's hallmark, assume the character of prohibitions that lay claim to obligatory observance. The very existence of such commandments is, then, a sign that man does not live in perfect love. "But we know that the law is good, if a man uses it rightly, knowing that the law is not made for the just, but for the unjust and rebellious, for the ungodly and sinners, for criminals and the defiled . . ." (1 Tim 1:8–9). The more we remove ourselves from the innermost core of love, the more the commandment to love acquires for us a negative character and becomes a prohibition. In this way, the sweet inevitability of the lover's free choice to love is transformed into the harsh compulsion of an obligation—a compulsion that becomes so much the harsher when the one who is so commanded no longer knows intuitively that love is the goal and end of every commandment.

There are no sanctions in perfect love because it is unthinkable

---

then, man had only to follow the "*logos* of his own nature" to attain to the "*logos* of well-being" (*Ambigua* in J. P. Migne, ed. *Patrologiae Cursus Completus*, Series Graeca, 161 vols. [Paris, 1857–1866], vol. 91, col. 1353. Further references to this series [henceforth PG] will be given in parentheses in the text.) Even in the case of the tempted Christ, however, *gnome* presumes a "false indifference" that we cannot accept (cf. von Balthasar, *Kosmische Liturgie, das Weltbild Maximus des Bekenners*, 2nd ed. [Einsiedeln: Johannes Verlag, 1961], 261–69; Lars Thunberg, *Microcosm and Mediator, The Theological Anthropology of Maximus the Confessor* [Lund: C. W. K. Gleerup, 1965], 226).

that one who truly loves would turn aside from the will of the beloved, which for the lover is a command. "In this is love perfected with us, that we may have confidence in the day of judgment; because as he is, even so are we also in this world. There is no fear in love; but perfect love casts out fear" (1 Jn 4:17–18). It is only when love grows cold that there must be sanctions for not loving. For the urgency of the command to love is so absolute that it necessarily demands such a sanction for all who do not know this urgency.

2. OBLIGATION AND CHOICE

It will be useful to pursue this general and very basic consideration of love a bit further before inquiring how its concrete premises and stipulations relate to the human person both as a creature composed of body and soul and as a social being. Even though laws and commands tend to become more individualized and negative, to assume the character of duties, as one moves away from the innermost core of love, it must not therefore be assumed that pure love is in any way lawless. On the contrary, it is "the fulfillment of the law" (Rom 13:10), "for the whole law is fulfilled in one word: Thou shalt love thy neighbor as thyself" (Gal 5:14). But this fulfillment is more than the sum of all individual commandments; it is likewise their transcendence: ". . . If you are led by the Spirit, you are not under the law. . . . The fruit of the Spirit is: charity, joy, peace, patience, kindness, goodness, faith, modesty, continency. Against such things there is no law" (Gal 5:18, 22–23).

There exists, then, the possibility of fulfilling the law even while at the same time living beyond the law. If we live in love, we do not live partly under the law and its duties and partly outside the sphere of the law, in a region where duty ceases and counsels, recommendations, and free choice begin. On the contrary, we "have been made to die to the law . . . we have been set free from the law . . . by which we were held down" (Rom 7:4, 6). If we live by the law of love, we do not have to live simultaneously under the laws of duty—on the one hand, because in loving we automatically fulfill the laws of duty; on the other hand, because these laws are in themselves only the objective corollary of a subjective state outside of perfect love. If there were no departures from the law of love, if sin did not exist, there would be no law that was not identical with the law of love. We would have fulfilled—and more than fulfilled—every law when, in all things, we followed the one law of love.

The form of the law changes, then, in the measure in which we approach or withdraw from love. Indeed, the very structure of our ethics changes as we draw near to or away from love.

If we draw away from love, the command to love, in which all other commands are fulfilled, disintegrates into a multiplicity of individual commandments that function separately according to the situation in which we find ourselves. But because these individual commandments can be observed only in sequence, since each of them is applicable to only a part of our lives, their emergence from collective unity creates a kind of ethical time. Between their individual demands there are lacunae in which nothing of moral significance seems to be occurring. Hence, when a situation arises that makes some demand upon us, we are obliged to recollect ourselves and to ask: What is now (so soon again!) being required of me? The farther we have erred from the center of love into ethical time, the more onerous the law seems to become. Then, perhaps, it will happen that an individual command will admonish us, will remind us again of the wholeness that exists at the center. And perhaps we will ask ourselves: What must I do if I am not to be wholly separated from love (for that would be death)? Where is the boundary I must not transgress under pain of death? Even in this instance, however, we would be thinking minimalistically; the "choice" of love would have become the "obligation" of law. When we are swimming far from shore and scarcely able to keep ourselves above water, love must be content to hold out to us only the broadest and least exacting of precepts. For the time being, we are incapable of appreciating its nobler secrets; what is pleasant and satisfying to those who love seems to us oppressive and over-burdensome.

But all this is changed if we draw near to love, if we strive to make its law the law of our lives. Then the plurality of the commandments yields once more to unity; the parts become integrated; the horizon of eternity shimmers through ethical time. The more we come to regard the action of love as definitive and as an end in itself, the less likely we are to lapse into the indifference of a time that is punctuated by individual directives. The commandments resolve themselves into unity, thus rendering superfluous the distinction we have drawn between "obligation" and "choice". If we were or are sinners, this distinction is not forgotten; we keep it in memory as something into which we can fall again if we do not hold fast to what is timeless—to love. But if we look forward and upward, love's wish will seem to us not less important than its command; we will free ourselves of our tendency to regard this wish as "merely a wish" and will discover that more urgent matters can lie hidden in precisely those wishes and requests of love that are not clothed in the form of commands than in the directives we have always with us.

In biblical history, which is the history of God's love in search of fallen mankind, man makes visible progress, under the tutelage of love, along the path that leads from the multiplicity of individual commandments under the Old Testament to the formulation of the commandment of love, which is at the center of all history, and thence to the promise that a new and eternal covenant will make possible the keeping and fulfilling of the commandment of love in hearts henceforth united. It is the path from slavery under many commandments to the freedom of "sons of the house", which they enjoy who have received the Holy Spirit of love poured into their hearts by the loving action of God and the Incarnation and Cross of his Son. Since it was the absolute love of God that manifested itself to us acting and suffering in the actions and sufferings of Christ, we can learn from it what it means to overcome the dichotomy between the Father's wish and his law, between counsel and command, between choice and obligation. Since the Son has no other wish than to fulfill every wish and will of the Father, he has bridged the gap between ethical time and loving eternity.

Christ's entire redemptive work is encompassed by his loving obedience, of which we are unable to say whether by it he fulfilled the wish or the will of his Father—or better, of which we must say that the wish of the Father, which in human terms contained neither command nor compulsion, could not be interpreted otherwise by Christ, who loved unto the end, than as a command. "For I have not spoken on my own authority, but he who sent me, the Father, has commanded me what I should say, and what I should declare. And I know that his commandment is everlasting life. The things, therefore, that I speak, I speak as the Father has bidden me" (Jn 12:49–50). ". . . That the world may know that I love the Father, and that I do as the Father has commanded me" (Jn 14:31). "For this reason the Father loves me, because I lay down my life that I may take it up again. No one takes it from me, but I lay it down of myself. I have the power to lay it down, and I have the power to take it up again. Such is the command I have received from my Father" (Jn 10:17–18). The Son, in other words, does freely and spontaneously whatever the Father commands him to do: "Thus human nature gave to God in that man [Christ], spontaneously and not as though it were a debt, what was its own . . . [doing so] by its free choice alone . . . and not by the compulsion of obedience."[2]

"In [Christ's] voluntary obedience you have, then, the fulfillment of the will of the Father, which, the Son says, is for him a command. For since, as the Word, he knows the counsels of the Father . . . he pursues [the Father's] will in respect to the work [he has come to accomplish], holding it in place of a command" (Cyril of Alexandria on Jn 15:9–10, PG 74, col. 373). In consequence, Christ's loving obedience is not just the dutiful carrying out of a command, since the Father leaves him free— ". . . He permitted the Son to suffer" (Cyril of Alexandria on Ps 68, PG 69, col. 1173); "For if he had so willed, Christ could not have died" (Ambrose, "De Excessu Fratris Sui Satyri Libri Duo", lib. II, sec. 46, PL 16, col. 1385). Neither is it the fulfillment of a nonbinding wish, for

[2] S. Anselmi, *Opera Omnia* I, "Liber Meditationum et Orationum" in J. P. Migne, ed., *Patrologiae Cursus Completus*, Series Latina, 221 vols. (Paris, 1844–1866), vol. 158, col. 766. Further references to this series (henceforth PL) will be given in parentheses in the text.

Christ regards the will of the Father as a command. Rather, its unity and necessity lie not in the realm of command or counsel, but in the unity of the love that unites Father and Son within the divine nature. Franzelin is correct, therefore, in saying: "These commands are eternal counsels that the Father communicates to the Son by way, not of precept, but of generation."[3]

It is precisely this obedience, however, this form of loving self-surrender that springs, not from the differentiation of duty and counsel, of strict command and nonbinding wish, but from the innermost source of God's love, that is henceforth to be the model and type of Christian love and self-surrender. It is a love that knows itself to be so absolutely bound by the will and wish of God that not only is no escape possible for it—"If he had not suffered out of obedience, his suffering would not have been so commendable"[4]— but its free choice can actually be experienced, in the Garden of Olives, as an obligation (which would be impossible if we were to speak here, as many contemporary theologians do speak, of a "broad commandment"). Nevertheless, it is a love that binds itself to the utmost degree out of love alone and for the sake of love: "I do always the things that are pleasing to him" (Jn 8:29); "But this is the most perfect and free obedience of human nature, that it submits its free will spontaneously to the will of God,"[5] so that it is possible to say with equal accuracy either that the Father delivered him (Rom 8:32) or that he delivered himself (Eph 5:2) to death on the Cross.

At this point, we begin to see how closely related to Christ's loving obedience is the form of obedience under vow, which, out of pure love, gives its freedom the form of unfreedom and, like the Redeemer in his relationship to the Father, lets its choice become an obligation. "Supererogation is the air it breathes." This obe-

---

[3] Joannes Baptist Cardinal Franzelin, *Tractatus de Verbo Incarnato*, 3rd ed. (Rome: S. C. de Propaganda Fide, 1881), 445.

[4] Thomas Aquinas, *Opera Omnia*, vol. 21, *Commentarii in Epistolam ad Corinthios I [et] in caeteras omnes Epistolas S. Pauli*, ed. Stanislaus Eduard Fretté (Paris: Ludovicus Vivès, 1876), "Epistola ad Philippenses", lectio II, 357. [For an English translation, see Thomas Aquinas, *Commentary on Saint Paul's First Letter to the Thessalonians and the Letter to the Philippians*, trans. F. R. Larcher and Michael Duffy, in *Aquinas Scripture Series*, vol. 3 (Albany: Magi Books, 1969), 83. (Tr)]

[5] Laurentio Janssens, *Summa Theologica ad modum commentarii in Aquinatis Summam*, vol. V, "Tractatus de Deo-Homine sive De Verbo Incarnato", (Freiburg: Herder, 1902), pt. II, 737.

dience of the incarnate Son of God reminds us—and herein lies the downfall of the polemic that is (often so foolishly) waged against Anselm today—of the unsearchable mystery of the Trinity: how from all eternity, before time was made, the Son freely accepted the trinitarian decree that he should underwrite the risk of creation by his death on the Cross; and how the Father embraced this free offering of love with as much love as that with which the Son embraced it in and after the Incarnation when, by the Father's acceptance of it, it had become a "command". From this, we understand how the Holy Spirit is the epitome of the most free, and yet the most demanding, love.

And if the Son did not disdain for our sakes to become acquainted even with temptation, to let himself be put into the position that Adam had taken for himself, a position from which both God and the devil were visible to him, he did so for one purpose only—so that in this position he might cling to the will of God in perfect love, so that in ethical time he might hold fast to ethical eternity. This action of Jesus, whereby he let himself be placed in a position of *choosing*, belongs to the mystery of his assuming the likeness "of sinful flesh" (Rom 8:3), which likeness reached its fullness in the Garden of Olives and on the Cross. But even if, to redeem us, the Son was willing to assume the burden and experience the anxiety of mere "duty" and, for this purpose, to conceal the love he knew and felt, he did so only because we were in a state of sin and alienation from God and because, for love of us, he chose to give his eternal love this visible form of perfect obedience.

We can see, however, that the obedience made manifest in this action of love had always lain hidden in the nature of love. The person who loves renounces, in ever greater measure, every autonomous determination or ordering of his own deeds and omissions, his own thoughts and feelings, so that everything he has may be left more freely and more completely at the disposal of the beloved. Because he thus equates the one law of love more and more closely with the law of his own being, he becomes increasingly free of the external compulsion of law. Paradoxically, however, he is at the same time raised to a new and more binding obedience since every act of love commits him more deeply to love. For this reason, the disobedience of one who loves to even the least wishes of love is much more serious than that of one who is far from love, who hardly suspects the existence of love or of the laws of love. Both the internal and external actions of one who loves are weighed in a different balance; such a one calls in vain upon the larger distinctions that are valid for others. A wish that God whispers in his ear because there is a possibility that it may be heard, but which he rejects, can wound God's eternal love more deeply than the transgression of a major commandment by one who is as yet unaware of the rules that govern the etiquette of love.

Nevertheless, we should not give too much emphasis (as dialectical theology is inclined to do) to the demonic aspects of this shifting of ethical norms in response to man's changing relationship to the center of love, as though man's approach to love were somehow counterbalanced by an increased potency for sin; as though heathens who do not know love were innocent in comparison with Christians who do know it but reject its advances; as though growth in love were ipso facto to be identified with growth in sin. Such an interpretation does not correspond to the laws of love. For it does not generally happen that one who makes progress in love thereby falls into the temptation of absolutely rejecting love. What he rejects is, as we have seen, the genuinely demonic situation into which the serpent tried to lure Adam: the situation that would have him choose with indifference between good and bad. It is more true to say that he commends himself and all his freedom to the protection of love; that he surrenders his freedom to the beloved in order to receive in return the law of love. There is no progress in love without at least a modicum of this *attitude of self-surrender*. Love can never be content with an act of love performed for the present moment only. It wants to abandon itself, to surrender itself, to entrust itself, to commit itself to love. As a pledge of love, it wants to lay its freedom once and for all at the feet of love. As soon as love is truly awakened, *the moment of time is transformed for it into a form of eternity*. Even erotic egoism cannot forebear swearing "eternal fidelity" and, for a fleeting moment, finding pleasure in actually believing in this eternity. How much more, then, does true love want to outlast time and, for this purpose, to rid itself of its most dangerous enemy, its own freedom of choice. Hence, every true love has *the inner form of a vow*: It binds itself to the beloved— and does so out of motives and in the spirit of love. Every participation in the love of God partakes of the nature of a vow: The entrance into Christian life through baptism, for instance, explicitly requires the taking of the baptismal vow by the one being baptized as an answer to the gift of divine love. Indeed, the more intimately one is involved in love, the more his love comes to bear the inner form of a vow in which he exchanges his freedom from bonds for the bond of love.[6] Thus the bond that seemed to him, in the beginning, to be exactly the opposite of the freedom of love, to be a burden and a duty, appears now to be ever more clearly identical with the freedom of love. And if, to the first stage of ethics, which is farther removed from love, the power of binding and loosing, as it was conferred on Peter, seemed to be a twofold power composed of antithetical functions (wherein the positive power of loosing was conjoined with the negative power of binding only because the freedom to loose could not otherwise be guaranteed), the power to bind is seen now also in a positive light, as the power, namely, of being able to bind so effectively those who want to bind themselves freely in love that their will to love is recognized and ratified in heaven.

---

[6] ". . . Some vows made to God are common to all men, as for instance those without which there is no salvation, such as baptismal vows and the like. . . . Other vows, such as chastity, virginity and the like, are proper to individuals. To these, we are invited. . . . Thus some vows are matters of precept, others of counsel", Thomas Aquinas, "De Perfectione Vitae Spiritualis", chap. 12, in S. Thomae Aquinatis, *Opuscula Selecta* I (Paris: Lethielleux, 1881). [Further references to this treatise (henceforth cited as *De perf*) will be given in parentheses in the text. For an English translation, see Saint Thomas Aquinas, *The Religious State, the Episcopate, and the Priestly Office*, ed. John Procter, S.T.M. (Westminster, Md: Newman, 1950). (Tr)]

But only love can claim the sovereign right of binding every-thing to itself in order to free it. If it is truly the absolute, it has no choice but to bind everything in order to loose it and redeem it.

What is astonishing about the great commandment of love is that it demands perfect love of God and neighbor, not in the form of a simple invitation, of a suggestion that we are free to follow or not to follow as we choose, but expressly in the form of a commandment (*mandatum*), and that it does so with such stringency that it contains in itself all that the other command-ments require under pain of severest sanctions. In no way can it be said to command a certain degree of love and to leave the rest, the perfection of love, to the free judgment and noble rivalry of those who love. The commandment includes everything, the whole way and the goal: complete and perfect love.[7] Hence it includes also what we are accustomed to distinguish from the point of view of imperfect love as the spheres of "duty" and "counsel". This distinction is not required for perfect love; absolute love has no need of a commandment. If it can be said that ". . . love is strong as death, jealousy as hard as hell: the lamps thereof are fire and flames" (Song 8:6), then death and hell are but the sediments, the dregs of a power that love has already transcended: "Light grows all that I conceive,/ Ashes everything I leave;/ Flame I am assuredly."[8] Or perhaps: "It is not death that kills, but the more lively life."

---

[7] In the case of the great commandment, the saying "The goal of the law does not fall under the law" is no longer applicable. Here, as Cathrein has pointed out, we must "distinguish the commandment to love God from the other commandments. For the commandment to love God, the goal is union with God through love, but this goal is, at the same time, its object. Thus it is impossible, in speaking of this commandment, to distinguish between the goal and the object" (Victor Cathrein, S.J., "Unvollkommenheit und lässliche Sünde", *Zeitschrift für Aszese und Mystik* [now *Geist und Leben*] III [1928], 135).

[8] Friedrich Nietzsche, "Ecce Homo", in *The Gay Science*, trans. Walter Kauf-mann (New York: Random House, 1974), 67.

3. LOVE AND COUNSEL (THOMAS / IGNATIUS)

Even though perfect love is a commandment and, as such, includes in itself the "counsel" of love (since, for those who love, love is not a "duty", but the very wish of the beloved is a command), there are, nevertheless, within the Church two forms or "states" of life that are distinguished from one another as "the way of the commandments" and "the way of the counsels" (*Sp Ex*, 135). (The priesthood will be discussed in a later chapter.) The way of the counsels was institutionalized at an early date as "the way of perfection". There can be no doubt that "the evangelical counsels of chaste self-dedication to God, of poverty and obedience" were founded on the "teaching and example of Christ",[9] but, as Paul tells us (1 Cor 7:25), Christ did not prescribe this way for all the faithful even though it is apparent from Luke that what some are chosen to observe to the letter others are required to observe in a broader sense.

This differentiation of the states of life raises a difficult question: How can the "counsel", which was formerly but a constitutive part of the unconditional "commandment" to love, now divorce itself from this commandment and become a separate entity in its own right? Is it permissible to distinguish, within the perfect love to which every Christian is called, degrees of love that range from the lower one of duty to the higher one of a free acceptance of the counsels?

This is the direction in which Thomas Aquinas seeks a solution to the problem, and it will be helpful for us to review his thought here. In the treatise on "The Perfection of the Spiritual Life", Thomas speaks first of the most perfect form of love, which can be realized only in God. Only God himself knows how worthy he is of love, and only he can love himself as he merits to be loved.

[9] *Lumen Gentium*, 43, *Vatican Council II. The Conciliar and Post Conciliar Documents*, gen. ed. Austin Flannery, O.P. (Northport, N.Y.: Costello Publishing Co., 1975), 402.

In second place, Thomas puts the love of God as it is exercised by the blessed in heaven, who fulfill the great commandment as perfectly as it can be fulfilled by created beings, and who as subjects (that is, as those who love) are at the same time filled to capacity with love, although even in heaven God, who is the eternal object of their love, will always surpass their ability to love.

In third place, he discusses the perfection of love as it is prescribed in the great commandment of love and insofar as it can be achieved in this life: "There is another way in which we love God with our whole heart, soul and mind, namely, if nothing in us is withdrawn from divine love, but everything, whether in action or in disposition of mind, is referred to God. And this perfection of divine love is given us by way of precept. Its first requirement is that we refer everything to God as to our last end according to the words of the apostle: '. . . Whether you eat or drink, or do anything else, do all for the glory of God' (1 Cor 10:31). We fulfill this precept when we order our lives to the service of God and when, in consequence, we virtually order to God all that we do except those actions, such as sin, that can lead us away from God. In this way, we love God with our whole heart. The second requirement is that we subject our intellect to God, believing those things that have been divinely transmitted to us, as the apostle admonishes us, '. . . bringing every mind into captivity to the obedience of Christ' (2 Cor 10:5). In this way, we love God with our whole mind. The third requirement is that we love all that we love in God and refer all our affections to the love of God, as the apostle says, 'If we were out of our mind, it was for God; if we are sane, it is for you. For the love of Christ impels us . . .' (2 Cor 5:13–14). In this way, we love God with our whole soul. The fourth requirement is that we let all our exterior words and works be strengthened by divine love according to the words of the apostle: 'Let all that you do be done in charity' (1 Cor 16:14). In this way, we love God with all our strength. This, then, is the third degree of the perfection of divine love, to which we are all obliged by precept" (*De perf*, chap. 5).

In other words, Thomas interprets the universally binding

content of the great commandment as it relates to the love of God, first, as the ordering of our lives to God with the consequent exclusion of every form of disorder; and secondly, as the readiness to regulate everything from the perspective of the service of God, which Thomas more precisely defines as that fundamental obedience of the intellect by which it receives the law of its life, not from itself, but from God. To live by this law means—and these are the third and fourth requirements—that we love all creatures in God and let every expression of our own lives proceed from love of God. If we realize this interpretation of the great commandment in our lives, we will, beyond all doubt, bear in ourselves the fullness of love of God insofar as it can be achieved in this life.

Thus it becomes even more important for us to inquire into the relationship of the evangelical counsels to Thomas' interpretation of the great commandment. Can the love it commands and that we have just described be achieved without the counsels? Or are the counsels the sine qua non without which love cannot attain this fullness? Thomas responds in these words: "After the apostle had said, 'Not that I have already attained this, or already have been made perfect,' he added, 'but I press on hoping that I may lay hold of [it]', and concluded, 'Let us then, as many as are perfect, be of this mind' (Phil 3:12, 15). It is abundantly clear from these words that even if the perfection of those who have attained heaven is not possible for us in this life, we should nonetheless strive to imitate that perfection as much as we are able. It is in this that the perfection of that life consists to which we are invited by the counsels. For it is obvious that the more the human heart withdraws from a multiplicity of objects, the more intensely it is drawn to one. In like manner, the more man's soul is withdrawn from concern for temporal things, the more perfectly it will be drawn to love God. Hence St. Augustine says that the hope of gaining or keeping material things is poison for love; that cupidity decreases when love increases; and that it is annihilated when love grows perfect.[10] All

[10] Sancti Aurelii Augustini, *De Diversis Quaestionibus Octoginta Tribus*, liber

the counsels by which we are called to perfection have as their goal to emancipate our spirit from dependence on earthly things so that we may more freely strive toward God: contemplating him, loving him, and fulfilling his will" (*De perf*, chap. 6).

From this perspective, the three counsels represented by the vows of poverty, chastity and obedience are seen primarily as means to an end that is the same for all: perfect love. For ". . . the love of God and neighbor does not fall under a commandment just by way of limitation (*secundum aliquam mensuram*), so that the higher stages are reserved for the counsels. That is clear from the very wording of the commandment, which treats of perfection. . . ."[11] In relation to the common goal, then, the counsels appear to function secondarily and nonessentially (*accidentaliter*) as a means of disposing us to remove not only the things that are incompatible with love, but also the impediments that, without being incompatible, render the exercise of love difficult (cf. ST 2a 2ae 184, 3 responsio; 186, 2 responsio). Thus, even though we have the Lord's word that it is a difficult and rare achievement for a rich man to attain to perfection—so rare, indeed, that ". . . it is easier for a camel to pass through the eye of a needle than for a rich man to enter the kingdom of heaven" (Mt 19:24), we know that the renunciation of earthly goods does not pertain to the essence of perfection if only because we have the example of a man like Abraham, who, despite his riches, walked in perfection before God. In other words, it cannot be assumed that what rarely happens never happens. The same point of view predominates in Thomas' discussion of virginity, although he takes care to note that all forms of physical dependence, especially

unus, in *Corpus Christianorum*, ed. Almut Mutzenbecher, Series Latina, 44 A (Turnhout: Brepols, 1975), xciv–ci.

[11] St. Thomas Aquinas, *Summa Theologiae*, 60 vols. (New York: McGraw-Hill, 1964–1975), vol. 47, *The Pastoral and Religious Lives*, 2a 2ae 184, 3 responsio. [All further references to the *Summa Theologiae* (henceforth ST) will be given in parentheses in the text and will refer to this edition, which contains both the Latin text and an English translation. (Tr)]

sexual love, "destroy the keenness of the spirit and darken its clarity" (*De perf*, chap. 8).

In the discussion of obedience, the perspective seems to have shifted somewhat. Thomas begins with the affirmation: "For the perfection of love it is required not only that a man renounce earthly goods, but that, in a certain sense, he also renounce himself. Dionysius says . . . that divine love causes ecstasy, that is, that it takes a man out of himself by not allowing him to belong to himself, but to him whom he loves" (*De perf*, chap. 10). To strengthen his thesis, Thomas quotes first from St. Paul: "It is now no longer I that live, but Christ lives in me" (Gal 2:20); "For you have died and your life is hidden with Christ in God" (Col 3:3); ". . . Christ died for all, in order that they who are alive may live no longer for themselves . . ." (2 Cor 5:15); and finally from the words of the Lord: "If anyone comes to me and does not hate his father and mother, and wife and children, and brothers and sisters, yea, and even his own life, he cannot be my disciple" (Lk 14:26). He adds: "On the one hand, the practice of this salutary self-renunciation and this loving hatred is necessary for salvation and common to all who are saved; on the other hand, it is the complement of perfection (*perfectionis complementum*). . . . This self-renunciation and this hatred must be measured, then, according to the degree of divine love (*divini amoris gradum*). It is necessary for salvation that man love God to such a degree that he makes God the goal of his striving and admits nothing that he regards as contrary to the love of God. . . . But it belongs to perfection that, for the love of God, man renounces even what he might lawfully use in order thus to be freer for God. . . . It is obvious from the way in which the Lord speaks that what he is proposing pertains to perfection. For just as he said, 'If thou wilt be perfect, go sell what thou hast and give to the poor' (Mt 19:21) without intending thereby to place an obligation upon us, but to leave us free, so he says here, 'If anyone wishes to come after me, let him deny himself, and take up his cross, and follow me' (Mt 16:24)" (*De perf*, chap. 10). Our model for this self-abnegation is Christ our Lord, who renounced every activity of his own will in order to do in all things the will of him who sent him. From here, it is only a step—which Thomas takes in the next chapter (*De perf*, chap. 11)—to regarding all three vows from the standpoint of sacrifices by which, under the impulse of love, we place at God's disposal all that we possess of external, corporal and spiritual goods.

Thus the evaluation of the counsels as "the way of perfection" (*De perf*, chap. 7), as merely a means of attaining a goal toward which all must strive, shifts noticeably to an evaluation of them as a "degree of love" (ibid., chap. 10), as the higher level of a love that itself seems to be greater because it proceeds from greater self-renunciation. In a later chapter (13), where he discusses love of neighbor as both a commandment and a counsel, this ambiguity causes Thomas some embarrassment. He begins by stating that "there are many degrees of perfection as it relates to love of neighbor", and continues, "There is a certain perfection that is necessary for salvation and that falls, of necessity, under a commandment. But there is also a broader, supererogatory perfection that falls under the counsels." Thomas treats the command to love our neighbor with as little minimalism as he treats the command to love God. He makes four demands upon it. First, it must be sincere. We must not love our neighbor, whom we are to love as we love ourselves, simply to satisfy our own ego or to secure our own advantage. Charity "is not self-seeking" (1 Cor 13:15). Secondly, our love of neighbor must be proper and well-ordered inasmuch as we selflessly desire and are more eager to procure his spiritual well-being than his temporal well-being. Thirdly, it must be holy. It is not enough that we love our neighbor because he is related to us or belongs to the same nation or is a fellow member of the human race. If our love of neighbor rests on these natural bonds, we must take pains to order it expressly to God. We must love and cherish our neighbor for God's sake and because we share the same divine origin and the same heavenly heritage. Thomas quotes here from St. John: "This commandment we have from him, that he who loves God should love his brother also" (1 Jn 4:21). Fourthly, it must be active and efficacious.

The love of neighbor that is necessary for salvation is transcended by the love that is not commanded, but counseled (*De perf*, chap. 14). According to Thomas, this second love is superior to the first in three ways. First, it is superior in its comprehensiveness. It expressly includes love of enemies, which the Lord designated as pertaining to perfection when he said: "You therefore are to be perfect, even as your heavenly Father is perfect" (Mt 5:48). "St. Augustine makes it clear in the *Enchiridion* that this perfection transcends ordinary perfection when he says that it is proper only to the perfect children of God although all the faithful should strive to attain it and to conform their human sentiments to it by prayer to God and by conquest of self. And yet, he adds, most men do not achieve this great good even though we believe that God hears them when they pray, 'Forgive us our trespasses as we forgive those who trespass against us.' " Thomas finds a solution to the dilemma in the fact that whereas Christ did not expressly *ex*clude love of enemies from the general commandment of love of neighbor, it belongs to the perfection of the counsel expressly to *in*clude it. This latter form of love (of enemies) proceeds directly from divine love; it has no natural basis in human sympathy however narrowly or broadly conceived.

Secondly, the love of neighbor that derives from the counsels is superior in its degree of intensity: The more intense the love, the more easily will one who loves renounce his own well-being for the sake of his neighbor. He is able to sacrifice his external goods—his body and even his life—in the service of his neighbor. St. John describes the last stage for us: "In this we have come to know [the love of God], that he laid down his life for us; and we likewise ought to lay down our life for the brethren" (1 Jn 15:13). Thus it comes about that this highest degree of love falls under the commandment when there exists no other way of achieving the salvation of one's neighbor, but it belongs to the perfection of the counsel willingly to sacrifice one's life for the sake of the brethren.

Thirdly, this love is superior in its efficacy. We can procure material goods for our neighbor; we can bestow spiritual benefits upon him; we can enrich him with supernatural gifts by instructing him in divine truth and communicating to him the grace of the sacraments. Thomas, it should be noted, is no longer speaking in this last instance of the perfection of love as a counsel. The dispensation of these benefits belongs primarily, not to the evangelical state, but to the priesthood and especially to the episcopate.

Closely examined, this train of thought reveals an even more obvious shift in viewpoint than did our meditation on the love of God. More and more prominence is given to the question: "To what does the commandment of love oblige us and what can we freely accomplish beyond what is required?" This distinction will guide us in discussing the differences between the two states of life (i.e., the state of those who have embraced the counsels and the state of those who have not). As we have already noted, this is not a question that love would pose. For love does not inquire how far it *must* go, but how far it *may* go. We do not have to urge love to action, but rather to restrain it. Judged solely from the perspective of self-giving love, then, the state of life that is characterized by the absence of an obligation to observe the counsels would have to be called the state of imperfect love. Originally, Thomas wanted to avoid such a designation: ". . . The love of God and neighbor does not fall under a commandment just by way of limitation, so that the higher stages are reserved for the counsels" (2a 2ae 184, 3 responsio). Yet he was obliged to admit in the same article: "One does not transgress a commandment simply by not fulfilling it to perfection. It is enough if he fulfills it in some way. . . . The lowest degree of love of God consists in not loving anything more than God, contrary to God, or as much as God. Whoever falls below this degree of perfection does not fulfill the commandment at all. But there is another degree of perfect love that cannot be reached on this earth. If one does not attain this degree, he obviously does not transgress the commandment. In like manner, one does not transgress the commandment by not attaining the middle degree of perfection provided only that he attains the lowest degree" (ibid., responsio ad 2).

When we state the problem in this way, it becomes clear that we have not shown sufficient cause for differentiating the two states (i.e., of commandment and of counsel) when we have defined love as a movement of self-giving. For in speaking of love it is meaningless to distinguish between commandment and counsel. If there is any way at all in which the counsels can admit of *more* love, then one who does not embrace them must have *less* love and the two states of life must be designated respectively as the state of perfect love and the state of imperfect love. Since there is nothing, however, in the structure of the Church to indicate that the differentiation of the two states is explainable in terms of man's love for God, we must seek to explain it from other points of view.

1. First, there is the elementary fact that men as they are do not strive to fulfill the commandment of love, do not think of finding in its fulfillment the sole meaning of their existence. It is precisely because they no longer possess love, because they have fallen away from the glowing center of love, that love has to be presented to them in the form of a command. Who now observes the great commandment on which depend the whole law and the prophets? Who would be able to say that he loves God, not just with half, but with all his heart if, out of pity for sinners, this wholeness had not subsequently been interpreted in such a way that by struggling he is at least able to attain its "lowest degree"? Even then, does he really attain to this lowest degree as Thomas has described it above: as the ordering of his whole life to God, as the subjection of his intellect to God, as the love of all earthly things for the sake of God, as the renunciation of all that he is out of love for God? Sin reigns so powerfully in the hearts of men that they regard as not quite of this world a person who directs his life to the attainment of this lower degree, even though it is strictly commanded us. Only by reflecting on the reality of sin do we

come to understand why so much emphasis has been placed on the counsels as a means of removing the obstacles to love. Only thus can we fully explain their secondary character as a means, not as an end in themselves—as a means of making straight the path of love that, in St. Augustine's words, is all too cluttered with egotistical greed. Only thus, finally, can we understand why they are called "counsels", not commandments; why the course of man's life, as a journey from nonlove to love, seems to proceed in this way through all the stages of imperfect love.

2. But we must again turn our discussion to fundamentals. The at once flexible and dynamic form in which man receives the commandment of love is determined not only by the fact that he is on his way from sin to love, but also by the more significant fact that he is a creature who, by his nature, stands initially before God in a very precise relationship of obedience and law, but who is drawn by grace into a "participation of the divine nature", into a loving communion with the Father and the Son in the Holy Spirit, whereby his relationship to love undergoes another dynamic change. Because he is a sinner, man is always in danger of regarding the commandments of love minimalistically, of opposing to the eternally insatiable demand of love the cool inquiry, which can have its source only in nonlove: "What is the utmost degree of self-giving to which I am obliged?" On the other hand, mere creature that he is, he stands before his eternal Creator in a primary relationship of reverence, of *religio*, of submission, which Thomas quite properly classifies under the virtue of justice (ST 2a 2ae 81, 5 responsio ad 3). On the basis of man's creaturehood, religion offers guidelines regarding the proper relationship of creature to Creator—guidelines that of necessity encompass the limitations that are equally inherent in the distance between God and creature and in the intrinsic finiteness of the creature. And indeed we must ask ourselves at this point whether the concept of love of God above all else, of a love that must be ready for and capable of every self-giving, has any proper place in the purely natural relationship of Creator and creature. As we know, Thomas, in speaking about this "natural" love (*amor Dei naturalis*), does not distinguish between an order of "created" nature (*ordo naturae "creatae"*) and an order of "elevated" nature (*ordo naturae "elevatae"*). But, in point of fact, the completely selfless love that he considers natural to the creature owes its form and intensity to supernatural *caritas*, which

was first proclaimed to us by revelation. Just as Thomas does not distinguish plainly here between the natural and the supernatural, but mixes elements of the supernatural with his description of the natural, so he later allows elements of the natural to enter into his description of the supernatural relationship of love. Thus he introduces the concept of "justice" and hence of obligation—in the sense of a requirement that must be fulfilled—even into the structure of perfect love, where it interacts with the concepts that had to be included in his discussion of the commandment of love because of man's fallen and sinful nature.

Our discussion takes a singular turn with this twofold application to the laws of natural love of factors (justice and obligation) that have neither meaning nor validity with respect to love. Insofar as its logic and necessity are comprehensible only to those who love, there is something esoteric about love. When John says, for instance: Because the Lord gave his life for us, "we likewise *ought* to lay down our life for the brethren" (1 Jn 3:16; italics added), the necessity of doing so is comprehensible only to one who loves and only from the standpoint of love; to one who views it from the standpoint of justice, that is, of natural "rightness" and *religio*, it remains incomprehensible. One who takes this standpoint, who speaks of love as an outsider, has no recourse but to distinguish between "commandment" and "counsel". Precisely because he moves outside the life and laws of genuine love, he will distinguish between what he is "obliged" to do *ex iustitia* and what he is "obliged" to do *ex caritate*. The concept of duty that thus enters our discussion has nothing to do with that order in which the Lord fulfills the absolute and loving will of the Father and transmits it unmitigated as a norm for his disciples (Jn 15:9–14); it belongs rather to the order that is under the "law of nature", or even the "law of sin", insofar as this order has not yet been permeated by perfect love. It is from this point outside love, which is admittedly a reality, and for most men an all-too-importunate reality, that there arise distinctions between duty (or commandment) and non-binding counsel that are legitimate for those who do not love. And precisely because there exist on the road to love, on which most men find themselves, not only this "point outside love", but also the less easily defined position "between" nonlove and love, it is fitting that the laws that are valid for perfect love, for love per se, should be stated for those who have not yet achieved the perfection of love in a form that is necessarily flexible and, in consequence, somewhat distorted. Viewed in this light and at this level, the truth of the statement that Thomas and other theologians uphold is incontestable: Man is not bound always to do what is most perfect; if he were, the distinction between precept and counsel would be eradicated.[12] At this level, too, we can appreciate the validity of those other distinctions that Thomas applies to the very essence of the great commandment and that enable him not only to say that "the perfection of love . . . falls under the precept in such a way that even the perfection of heaven is not excluded from the precept" (ST 2a 2ae 184, 3 responsio ad 2)—and to say it, indeed, to everyone, "whether religious, or secular, or priest, or even a lay person joined in matrimony" (*Quodlib*, 3 q. 6 a. 3), but also to distinguish even within the "perfection of love" those degrees and levels of which the lowest, the avoidance of serious sin, is an acceptable fulfillment of the commandment of love (ST 2a 2ae 44, 4 responsio ad 2). Since the commandment of love is an affirmative commandment and, as such, does not bind continuously, Thomas further contends, the unwavering choice of a habitual turning to God is sufficient for its fulfillment (ST 1a 2ae 88, 1 responsio ad 2). The limitations that he recognizes in regard to the commandment of love can be reduced to three:

a) the limitation imposed by man's creatureliness as such, by reason of which it is impossible for God to be loved by any creature to the extent that he is lovable (ST 2a 2ae 184, 2);[13] to which must be added Thomas' understanding of vows as a form of *religio* (ST 2a 2ae 81)—his measuring of the highest form of self-giving possible for a Christian by something that is, in the last analysis, an expression of the creature's *analogia entis*;

b) the many limitations imposed by the circumstances of man's life on earth, by reason of which he is unable to attain to the perfection of love that God intended as a goal (ST 2a 2ae 44, 6): ". . . Religious are not bound except to those things that they are

---

[12] See Thomas Aquinas, "De Veritate", 17, 3 ad 2 in *Quaestiones Disputatae*, vol. I (Rome: Marietti, 1949). [Further references to "De Veritate" (henceforth *De ver*) and to *Quaestiones Disputatae* (henceforth *Quaes Disp*) will be given in the text. For an English translation of the "De Veritate", see St. Thomas Aquinas, *Truth*, trans. Robert W. Mulligan, S.J., 3 vols. (Chicago: Regnery, 1952–1954). See also Thomas Aquinas, *Quaestiones Quodlibetales* (Rome: Marietti, 1949), 3 q. 5 a. 4. Further references to this work (henceforth *Quodlib*) will be given in the text. (Tr)]

[13] Cf. Thomas Aquinas, *Scriptum super Sententias Magistri Petri Lombardi*, vol. III, ed. R. P. Maria Fabianus Moos, O.P. (Paris: Lethielleux, 1933), "Scriptum super III lib. Sententiarum", dist. XXIX, quaes. 1, art. VIII, solutio 2 ad 4.

obliged to do by the vows of their profession; otherwise, their obligation would be limitless, even though nature and ability and every law have certain limitations" (*Quodlib*, 1 q. 7 a. 2);

c) the limitations imposed by man's fallen state, by reason of which he is prone, as long as he lives, to become hardened in certain weaknesses and imperfections.

And yet, Thomas is not entirely comfortable with this static account of the limitations that exist within the limitlessness of love. For one thing, he is aware that the love demanded of us in the New Testament finds its measure, not in the limitations of our nature, but in the gift of divine love that is bestowed upon us and poured into our hearts by the grace of God, and that this love opens the creature, despite his limitations, to a participation in the limitlessness of divine life: ". . . For love has the power to transform, . . . whence Dionysius the Areopagite says: '. . . Divine love causes ecstasy, not allowing those [who experience it] to be lovers of themselves, but of those whom they love'[14]. . . . One who is totally transformed into God by love has perfect charity" (*Quodlib*, 3 q. 6 a. 3). But because the commandment of love thereby itself acquires an irresistible dynamic in which—since the dynamic has its source in the commandment—the distinction between commandment and counsel at last disappears, it follows properly that ". . . when it is written, 'Thou shalt love the Lord thy God with thy whole heart', this is understood to be a *precept* according to which the totality excludes everything that prevents a perfect adherence to God, *but this [perfect adherence] is not a precept* but the goal of a precept. For it is not what we must do, but whither we must tend that is thereby indicated to us" ("De caritate", 10 ad 1 in *Quaes Disp* II; italics added). Since it is precisely this exclusion of everything that hinders the full union with God that is the object of the counsels, we are reminded again of that precise and simple statement in the "De perfectione vitae spiritualis": "All the counsels by which we are called to perfection have as their goal to emancipate our spirit from dependence on earthly things so that we may more freely strive toward God: contemplating him, loving him, and fulfilling his will" (chap. 6). Nevertheless, Thomas is unable to avoid a certain tension in his description of the counsels themselves, depicting them now as a means to a goal that transcends them, now as participation and repose in that goal, now again as a representation and exemplification of the goal: "The religious state can

[14] See Dionysius the Areopagite, *The Divine Names and the Mystical Theology*, trans. C. E. Rolt (London: S. P. C. K., 1940), chap. 4, 105.

be considered in three ways: first, as a certain exercise for tending to the perfection of charity; secondly, as a freeing of the human spirit from external cares . . . ; thirdly, as a kind of holocaust by which one offers to God oneself and all that one possesses" (ST 2a 2ae 186, 7).

We are now in a better position to understand how the positing of a certain dynamic, but variable, differentiation between commandment and counsel, between what is required and what is of supererogation, can be justified not only by the fact of man's sinful nature, but also by the more significant fact of the dualism of nature and supernature, of the order of "justice" and the order of "love". And yet, our initial question remains unanswered: Why do we not regard as unambiguously inferior to the state of evangelical perfection that state of life in which man fails to follow the counsels (at least literally), in which he does not embrace this essential means of achieving love? Why is this state not regarded as a state of imperfect love?

3. By way of answer, we must introduce a second, very different, mode of contemplation—one that gained prominence in the *Spiritual Exercises* of St. Ignatius Loyola and has shed a new evangelical light on the forms of life within the Church. Thus far, we have described love as though it concerned ourselves alone. But even when we love God, it is still God himself who is love and, consequently, also the measure of our love for him. God is never merely an object that we are permitted to love. He is the infinite subject who, even before we existed, freely chose to love us and continued to love us "when as yet we were sinners" (Rom 5:8), when as yet we were turned aside from him in hate. From whatever standpoint it is viewed, his love surpasses human love, for every human love is but an answer to his love. It is only because God's love for us is so infinite and undivided that we are commanded to love eternal love in return with all the powers of our being. But love does not urge itself or its self-giving upon the beloved. It inquires into the wish and will of the beloved and regulates the degree of its self-giving accordingly. To love with

all our strength does not mean indiscriminately to drag into the house and cast at the feet of the beloved all the outward and inward gifts we possess. To do so might prove embarrassing to the beloved. At the very least, it would be indiscreet and might well result in the rejection and return of these untimely gifts. This does not mean that love cannot from time to time offer a gift of friendship, perhaps as a surprise. But, for the most part, the gift proper to it is to place itself and all it possesses at the disposal of the beloved, allowing him to decide, to choose, what will be given him. This presumes, on the part of the one who loves, a disposition of self-giving that is no less perfect than that required for a literal and voluntary renunciation of all one's possessions. True love is radically and fundamentally disposed to renounce everything so that everything may be held in readiness for the first sign of the will of the beloved. It is ready to follow any path, whether rough or smooth. It is as ready to follow the way of the commandments as the way of the counsels. Such a love is perfect even when the ultimate gift is not required of it. It is perfect as the servants in the Gospel are perfect who, whether their Lord comes or not, stand throughout the night with girded loins and burning torches. Those who love in this way listen for the voice of the beloved whether the call comes to them or not. They are content even if more is not demanded of them as it is of other, more privileged, souls. They accept it as a sacrifice not to have been called upon to sacrifice all they were willing to sacrifice.

If the state of the commandments were characterized by this disposition, it would suffer no disadvantage when compared with the state of the counsels. But this would presume that it manifested in itself the disposition that is properly contained only in the counsels, that is, perfect indifference in choosing one state in preference to the other according to the will of God. Something of this disposition was evident in Thomas' description of the love of God *qua* commandment: If a person, having fully subjected his understanding to the rule of faith, does in fact order his life to the service of God; if he truly loves no creature except in God; if he measures all that he does or says by the intensity of his love for God (*De perf*, chap. 5), he inevitably possesses also the complete indifference that will enable him to offer no resistance to the will of God when it is made known to him, whether God calls him to one state of life or another.

In this context, the first point of view from which we sought to explain the differentiation of the two states of life (pp. 41–54) acquires renewed relevance insofar as it reminds us that man's sinfulness is an impediment to his entering upon the way of perfection. St. Ignatius Loyola bases his whole Spiritual Exercises as a matter of course on the disposition of indifference, which he examines in ever greater depth as the Exercises proceed (*Sp Ex*, 98, 155, 166). At the end of the First Week,[15] however, he excludes from further participation in the Exercises—which have as their sole purpose to assist the exercitant in his choice of a way of life and, to this end, to help him evaluate the possibility that he is being called to the "way of evangelical perfection"—all those whom he deems incapable of achieving the necessary degree of indifference, which extends also to the increasing challenge to follow Christ in love even to the Cross. Anyone, he says, who lacks the spiritual breadth and intellectual stamina to want and expect more than "a certain degree of peace of soul" (*Sp Ex*, 18) should not be introduced to the Exercises pertaining to the "choice". In any event, such a one will already have failed to hear in the Exercise on the "First Principle and Foundation" (*Sp Ex*, 23) what Ignatius undoubtedly considered of most importance there and what is, in fact, its express object: namely, the laws of "counsel" and "supererogation", which are as much a "duty" for one who wants to love as are the "commandments". This does not mean that Ignatius intended the Spiritual Exercises forcefully to remove the tension that exists between the two states of life—that of the commandments and that of the counsels—as well as between the two worlds of duty under pain of sin and voluntary performance beyond the call of duty. Even though he

---

[15] For an explanation of the division of the Exercises into weeks, see *Sp Ex*, 4. [Tr]

attempts to build bridges and to facilitate the transition from the first of these worlds to the second; even though, living as he does by love and by the laws of love, he regards such a transition as a matter of course and has no greater desire than to communicate to everyone the (for him) evident necessity of a generosity that gives all for love and to assume that it is, in fact, possessed by everyone, Ignatius is, nevertheless, well aware of the difficulties this entails. On the one hand, not everyone has access to this inner world and logic of love (and it is well to exclude betimes those who do not in order to avoid harming or confusing them, to avoid forcing them to an explicit hardening of heart); on the other hand, not everyone who has access to this world is actually called to it.

Thus our second mode of inquiry ends also in inconclusive opacity. From one point of view, the way of the counsels seems unambiguously better than the way of the commandments (*Sp Ex*, 14–15, 356–57); from another, the perfection of love seems to be grounded so thoroughly in that disposition of indifference that is lovingly ready for all that can be asked of it that it is no longer possible to understand why the way of the counsels should be considered "more perfect" than the way of the commandments. And it is no clearer now than it was when we were speaking of sin why the way of love should be split into two paths so fundamentally different that they actually constitute two different "states of life". Just as we can conceive of innumerable variations in man's passage from sin to love, so we can conceive here of innumerable calls from God and corresponding Christian vocations that would all issue from the identical point of human readiness. But neither in the naked will of God as such nor in his loving will can we find any explanation for the existence of these sharply distinguished states of life within the Church.

It would seem, then, that our study is thus far without results. We can understand, certainly, that beyond the sphere of "duty" there is another sphere in which one binds oneself freely out of love—and that from the standpoint of duty this sphere must be regarded as one of "counsel". But, since all men are called to perfect love, we are unable to account, either on the basis of man's love for God or of God's elective love for man, for the existence of those states of life within the Church that are the object of our study. In that case, we must approach the subject from yet another standpoint.

4. LOVE AND THE VOWS

First, however, what we have just said must be compared to and brought into harmony with what was said earlier concerning the vowlike character of all pure love. As we have seen, there existed within the Church prior to the differentiation of the various states of life an indisputable relationship between the nature of perfect love and that which might be designated—in a most general sense and quite apart from the Church's later concept of "vows" as a distinctive mark of the "state" of the counsels—as a vow. This is so true that the distinction between love itself and the vows as the formative principle of a state of life that is thereby distinguishable from all other states can exist only where love itself, though still in the process of developing, has not yet reached perfection: that is, in man's pilgrim state on earth, where he seeks in various ways and degrees to return to the homeland of divine love from which he takes his origin. Only in this state can the vows be regarded as an external form distinguishable from love itself and conceived as a training ground for the exercise of perfect love—like a vessel shaped from the beginning to the measure of love it is to contain and destined to fill itself more and more until it has reached its capacity. As a distinct state of life within the Church, the so-called "state of perfection" presumes the general imperfection of love on earth since its formative principle, being but one among many others, is not coextensive with its content, which is love. Thus Thomas can speak the oft-quoted words: "It is one thing to be perfect, another to be in the state of perfection. For there are many in the state of perfection who are not yet perfect, but are still sinners. And there are even some who are perfect, but who are not in the state of perfection" (*Quodlib*, 3 q. 6 a. 3). Viewed thus, the state of the counsels and of perfect love is best described in the first of the three ways noted earlier by Thomas: as the means to an end that is superior to the means and that, under certain circumstances, can be achieved without them—that is, "as a certain exercise for tending to the perfection of charity" (ST 2a 2ae 186, 7 responsio).

But as soon as we contemplate love in its perfection, the relationship changes; the outer relationship of means and end undergoes a twofold transformation of both form and content.

1. Perfect love consists in the unconditional *surrender of self*, in the *donum Dei*. ". . . Love consists in a mutual sharing of goods; for example, the lover gives and shares with the beloved what he possesses, or something of what he has or is able to give; and vice versa, the beloved shares with the lover" (*Sp Ex*, 231). So true is this that in the perfect love of God for the creature the whole existence of the world—whether of nature, of grace, or of the uniquely personal predestination of each of us—is but a demonstration and proof of God's all-surpassing love for his creatures, of ". . . how much God our Lord has given me of what he possesses and . . . how much, so far as he can, the same Lord desires to give himself to me according to his divine decrees" (*Sp Ex*, 234). The corresponding attitude of the creature, which proceeds of necessity and "according to all reason and justice" from God's gift of himself, is expressed in the *Suscipe*, the prayer of total self-giving that Ignatius places here in the *Spiritual Exercises*: "Take, Lord, and receive all my liberty, my memory, my understanding, and my entire will, all that I have and possess. Thou hast given all to me. To thee, Lord, I return it. All is thine, dispose of it wholly according to thy will. Give me thy love and thy grace, for this is sufficient for me" (*Sp Ex*, 234). The content of every genuine love is expressed in this act of self-surrender that places at God's disposal and surrenders to him all one possesses as a votive offering in the inner form of a vow. Ultimately, every external, formal vow derives its

authenticity *from just such a vow that has its origin in love and its motivation in the total gift of self*.[16] We see this even more clearly when we consider that the will to give oneself, if it is perfect, is unconditional and irrevocable. The *Suscipe* in which Ignatius summarized the fruit of the Spiritual Exercises is not a provisional act that is intended to be temporary, but the expression of a choice intended to be both absolute and definitive. Just as God's love is exclusive yet, in a certain sense, also inclusive, so that it neither knows nor wants to know anything that lies outside the mystery of its own self-containment, so the answering love of the creature takes its place once and for all in the closed circle of God's will, locking the door behind it to all that lies outside love. In the act of self-surrender to God it offers him its freedom in respect to all else, thus voluntarily depriving itself of the freedom to seek or decide anything outside the freedom that now belongs to God. Once and for all, it chooses what God chooses; once and for all, it rejects any freedom of choice that would choose anything but what God chooses for it. Henceforth its freedom will consist in choosing not what is pleasing to itself, but what is pleasing to God. Only one who stands outside love, who identifies freedom with egocentric self-determination, can regard this loving surrender of freedom as a deprivation of freedom. But "just as the inability to commit sin does not lessen freedom, so the necessity that impels a will firmly fixed upon good does not lessen it, as we can see in the case of God and the saints. Such also is the necessity imposed by the vow, which resembles the

---

[16] Thomas, as we have already noted, classifies vows under the virtue of religion or reverence for God, which he classifies in turn under the virtue of justice (ST 2a 2ae 88, 5). This conforms to the general plan of his treatises on ethics, which consistently proceed from "natural ethics" to the supernatural form that perfects them. Thus he begins his discussion with the known form of the external vows in order thereby to reveal their religious meaning. Our discussion proceeds in reverse order. We seek to make the meaning and form of the external vows clear by relating them to the totality of Christian love, which, in an eminent way, contains the form of the vow.

confirmation of the saints in good" (ST 2a 2ae 88, 4 responsio ad 1). Definitiveness is inherent in self-surrender. A self-surrender that is temporary is not a genuine self-surrender; at best it is but a preliminary, tentative, experimental stage—a prelude to genuine self-surrender.

The moment of solemn promise inherent in love itself is expressed in the Lord's words: "He who loses his life for my sake will find it" (Mt 10:39); ". . . He who would save his life will lose it; but he who loses his life for my sake will find it" (Mt 16:25); "He who loves his life loses it; and he who hates his life in this world, keeps it unto life everlasting" (Jn 12:25). The "losing" that is spoken of here is the total and definitive surrender of oneself in love. It decreases in fullness and strength with every egotistical attempt to retrieve something from it for oneself by somehow limiting either its content or its duration. This vow, let us remember, is something inherent in love itself and antecedent to every differentiation of individual Christian states and forms of life. Precisely because it is an essential characteristic of perfect love, and because all states within the Church are called to this love, every objective differentiation of the individual states of life will be based on the extent to which the totality of this vow to love is realized in each of them and the extent to which the very form of a given state of life pledges the Christian, not just to a gradual "losing" of self, but to a state in which the self has actually been totally "lost" for God's sake. All small, repeated, and limited sacrifices are efficacious and pleasing to God only insofar as they express and confirm the undivided sacrifice of a love that is ready to give all and to let God take all that it pleases him to take.

2. Corresponding to the inner, formal, vowlike character of perfect love, there is also a *material* totality that is hardly in need of differentiation or detail: "All is thine, dispose of it according to thy will." Since the twelfth century, this *material* totality has been divided into three areas which together represent the totality of

what perfect love has to offer: all the goods of this world that one has at one's disposal; all one's corporal goods; and all one's spiritual goods, namely, memory, understanding and will insofar as one is free to dispose of them. Corresponding to these three areas, finally, are the three vows of poverty, chastity and obedience, which are identified with the three basic evangelical counsels.

We call these counsels "basic" because, especially in recent times, attempts have been made to diminish the significance of the three vows by presenting them as just three among other and—so we are given to understand—equivalent counsels to be found in the Gospel.[17] Such a view is doubly refuted by Thomas Aquinas, who names these three vows the *tria principalia vota* to which all other good works and practices are directed: First, because from a material point of view they include all that man is capable of giving in love (ST 2a 2ae 186, 7 responsio et ad 2); secondly, because in the last analysis poverty and chastity are subsumed under obedience (ibid., 186, 8 responsio), thus making the form of obedience the general form of that self-surrender that makes every individual commandment, every individual counsel, every individual act of self-surrender an expression of the total gift of oneself in love and thereby lends to every such act something of the boundlessness of divine love: "For whatever . . . they do is referred to that radical option by which they dedicated their whole life to God. Hence they do not

---

[17] Cf. Désiré Félicien Cardinal Mercier, *La Vie Intérieure* (Paris: Beauchesne, 1919), 177; Wilhelm Stockum, *Priestertum und Aszese* (Freiburg: Herder, 1938): The three religious vows are "neither the only ones nor the absolutely best ones, . . . the Gospels instruct us about many counsels, and if religious orders have selected only three for their purposes out of the riches that are there, this does not mean that the others thereby decrease in value" (87); Edward Schillebeeckx, "Das Ordensleben in der Auseinandersetzung mit dem neuen Menschen- und Gottesbild", in *Ordens-Korrespondenz* 9 (1968): "Holy Scripture contains a large number of evangelical counsels that it would be impossible to reduce to the three so-called classical counsels that, in the Middle Ages, inspired the 'three religious vows' " (118).

ponder what they should do, but rather what they have vowed to do, and thus, in a manner of speaking, they may be compared to those who do some particular good work as the infinite is compared to the finite. Whoever gives himself to another to do all the other may command, gives himself infinitely more than does one who gives himself to do some particular work" (*Quodlib*, q. 3 a. 7 responsio ad 6). The fact that Thomas is referring here to the external vows taken in religious orders does not prevent our applying his commentary to the more general vow that has been described above as the disposition of perfect love or emphasizing the difference between the vow of obedience—and also, in proper measure, the vows of poverty and chastity that are included in it—and whatever other counsels pertain to the striving for perfection.

We shall show later how the *spirit* of poverty, chastity and obedience is incorporated into the individual states of life—the religious state, for instance; or the priestly state, which is made permanent by the sacrament of holy orders; or the married state, which is made equally permanent by the sacrament of matrimony; or, finally, the general, undifferentiated state of the Christian per se. What is essential here is the awareness that perfect love, as a total gift of oneself and of all one possesses to God, and for the sake of God, to one's neighbor, contains an inner relationship not only to the form, but also to the content of a vow. There follows a practical consequence that is of supreme importance for one who is striving toward the goal of love: that he let the concept of total self-surrender be his guide in this pursuit. In the course of such striving, it is neither useful nor advisable to follow every conceivable recommendation, exercise or devotion in order to build from these many small stones a complete mosaic of Christian perfection. This is true even when these practices appear to have a more broadly "positive" and more directly practical character than the seemingly negative one of self-surrender, loss and sacrifice. All these ostensibly "positive" directives about asceticism and a way of life will always bear in themselves a certain character of superficiality and banality, of arbitrariness of choice and perspective, of a clinging to individuality and current taste. The evangelical and traditional guidelines for attaining perfect love, on the contrary, would have everything revolve around the axis of self-surrender, which appears hard and negative only to one who does not love. To one who loves, it is the epitome of all that is worth striving for.

Thus love has a threefold relationship to the three vows. Insofar as the vows, whether spiritual or formal, are useful to a still imperfect love for removing the obstacles on the path to perfect love, they are to be regarded as means to an end that transcends them, namely, love.

But insofar as love is essentially the gift of self, it partakes both formally and materially of the nature of a vow; by its very nature, it contains in itself both the content and the form of the vows, to which it gives a constantly new expression.

Insofar, finally, as love in its total gift of self is, at the same time, indifferent to all that God may ask of it, it is always prepared to let its general character as a vow be actualized in whatever particular way or state of life God's will may make known to it. Thus it contains in itself potentially, even when it is already perfect, the readiness to make vows externally, but without anticipating this action of its own accord. Until it knows the will of God, "it will strive to conduct itself as if every attachment . . . had been broken. It will make efforts . . . to want [nothing in particular], unless the service of God our Lord alone moves it to do so" (*Sp Ex*, 155; paraphrased).

In order to discover a concrete teaching about the states of life, our whole study must advance now from the abstractions that have thus far engaged our attention and that have offered, for the most part, only *an immanent analysis of the nature of love* to a more substantial and concrete consideration of man as God conceived, created and endowed him, not in identity of being with himself, but in an *analogy* of being that extends even to particulars. Only thus can the concept of a *state of life* acquire the visible fullness of a concrete way of life into which man has been placed by God. For man was not created a formless being, distinguished only by his vocation to an endless yet unspecified love. Precisely so that he can fulfill perfectly his vocation to love, he was placed at his creation in that inner and outer state of clear and unambiguous nature that we call his original state (*Ur-Stand*).

CHAPTER TWO

FROM ORIGINAL STATE
TO FINAL STATE

1. CREATION AND SERVICE

In order to learn where man is expected to take his stand and enter upon a state of life, we must ask where God actually placed him: "Let us make mankind in our image and likeness. . . . God created man in his image" (Gen 1:26–27). "Then the Lord God formed man out of the dust of the ground and breathed into his nostrils the breath of life . . ." (Gen 2:7). "The Lord God took man and placed him in the garden of Eden to till it and to keep it" (Gen 2:15).

Thus, though man is created in the image and likeness of God, he is formed from the dust of the earth. Though he is called to be the highest, the nearest to God, he is by origin the most lowly. What lies behind him—the dust of his origin—is a constant reminder that he must not confuse the archetype with the image; the fact that he is an image is a constant reminder that he must conform himself to the archetype on which he is patterned. In other words, *man's first state is to be at a twofold remove [Abstand]*—at a remove from God and from nothingness. Because he comes from nothing, he retains, however great his likeness to the archetype, an even greater and ineradicable unlikeness. Nor can he increase his likeness to God by becoming more and more unmindful of his origin in order thereby to be more like God. On the contrary, it is only in the measure of his striving to be in the image and likeness of God, even though always at a remove from God, that man fulfills the purpose for which he was created. He achieves the highest measure of this likeness when he has the humility neither to forget nor to deny for an instant his condition of not-being-God, the nothingness of his origin. Any effort to establish an identity of archetype with image would bring about

67

man's immediate destruction. For it was only because he was at a remove from God that the grace that called him into being could also bestow upon him the grace of likeness. It is only because he is not God, because he comes to meet God as the unalterably not-God, that he shares in the independence, unity, personality and freedom of his Creator. If a mirror were to be so like what it mirrored that it became identical with it, what was mirrored would cease to exist. If two lovers were to attempt so to possess one another that the two were fused into one, then love—if such a thing were possible—would fall into nothingness. To undertake any movement of love at all, the lover must proceed from the sure state of his own existence.

On the basis of this mystery (that the state of being-at-a-remove from God is precisely the state in which the creature can come closest to God), man's calling to love is seen from a new perspective. Man is indeed called to love, but only in a manner that permits him to live to the full his condition as creature. He not only may, but must, strive for the highest degree of love; but this highest degree must be accompanied by the most complete realization of his true state as creature. In a word, *love must have the inner form* of dependence and submission; it must be identical with the glorification of the Eternal Archetype by means *of reverential service*. Being in the "image and likeness" of God does not mean that the creature must imitate God as its model so exactly that a beholder might easily confuse the image with the archetype. It means emphasizing the distance between creature and Creator so that, from the perspective of this distance, the unmistakable and unique character of the archetype will become ever more apparent. The likeness of the creature to God presumes that the creature will differentiate itself all the more humbly from God in order thus to open itself more widely to the reception of the divine rays. This attitude does not mean the annihilation of the independent self—if it did, it would simply tend to support the identification of creature and Creator, the mystical fusion of archetype and image. On the contrary, it means that the creature accepts its state of image and likeness and renders to God the reverence and service that are his due from one who is at a remove from him. By such an attitude, the creature strives, not for the extinction of its own personal will, but for the assumption of the divine will into its own, with the explicit awareness that the will of the *Lord* is thereby united with and realized by the will of the *servant*.

It is in the form of service, then, that God bestows on his creature the gift of love. When the creature loves God and neighbor as it ought, it fulfills its calling by doing the will of God, not its own will. Whether this love is given gladly or reluctantly, with ease or with difficulty, it is in any case a service—and in that sense a "duty" (*debitum*, ST 2a 2ae 44, 1) that the creature accepts from God with the acceptance of its very existence.

> If we speak here of *"duty"*, it is only in the sense in which duty is the inner form and measure of the love of creatures. Because God is the Lord whose word, whatever it may be, is necessarily a command, the accomplishment of it is, therefore, a duty for the servant to whom it is addressed. The designation "duty" is here intended to express only the relationship between Creator and creature, the *analogia entis* of man's nature. By reason of the infinite distance there is between God and creature, the whole love that the creature must have for the Creator and, for the Creator's sake, for his fellow creatures—that love with one's whole heart, with all one's mind and with all one's strength; that love that is God's greatest gift to his creatures and that can be experienced by the creature only as a privilege [*ein Dürfen*]—acquires the character of a duty [*des Sollens*].
>
> But, as we saw above (pp. 28–31, passim; pp. 32–40) in the distinction between "obligation" as the product of the decomposition of a love that has grown cold and "choice", the necessity that finds expression in love's status as a commandment is not to be confused with the concept of duty as an "obligation" incurred by man's departure from the glowing core of love. If love is alive and vital, we noted, it does not ask what it is obliged to do under pain of sin or what acts and proofs of love it can omit without sanction; it knows only the single movement of a perfect self-giving that engages all the powers of heart and mind in the service of love. Only a love that has been touched and weakened by sin is capable of the loveless notion of distinguishing between what it is required to do (*ex iustitia*) and what it may freely choose to do (*ex caritate*). But if, by reason of the distance from God that is inherent in man's creatureliness, the

concept of "duty" must after all come to be associated with love, it
is only because, for the creature, a love that is whole and undivided
cannot be separated from that *glorification of God in service* that is the
natural concomitant of its creaturehood. Whatever it may be in
itself, the creature has been incorporated into and established in the
service of love. This is the fundamental principle of its original
state.

Apparently, then, man's status, the place assigned to him by
God, is most immediately determinable from his "nature": God
first formed man into a living being, then placed him in the
garden of Eden that had been prepared for him (Gen 2:7–8): "The
Lord God took man and placed him in the garden of Eden to till it
and to keep it" (Gen 2:15). But this first transposition and change
of status, this first distinction between man's (natural) being and
his (graced) calling, is at once superseded, for, simultaneously
with this calling, there is breathed into man a living soul, the final
meaning of his existence. If man wants to understand what he is
in essence, he must not look predominantly backward to his
origin in the dust of the earth, but forward to his calling to be the
image and likeness of God. What he is by nature is related to his
essential calling as the complicated anatomy of the eye is related to
the simple act of seeing. Without consciously adverting to them,
the act of seeing makes use of an infinite variety of physical,
chemical and physiological processes to accomplish the one thing
necessary: the simple, clear and unclouded act of seeing. The
accompanying processes have no other purpose than to make
possible this act of seeing that could not exist without them, but
that in no way derives from them or is the sum of their parts.
The same relationship exists in the creature between its "nature"
as a creature composed of body and soul and its calling, which is
love. Not that the creature itself is love, for only God is love.
The creature is a being in the service of love. Even if, in itself, it
is a miracle of corporal and spiritual organs, connecting tissues,
living sinews and tendons, the complicated maze of which man
contemplates in wonder just as the layman marvels at a tele-
phone exchange whose meaning remains incomprehensible to

him so long as he fails to take into account its purpose, nevertheless the true meaning of the creature, as conferred by God, can be properly understood only if it is explained and interpreted as an instrument of love.

In the case of every other service rendered by the creature in this world, it is always possible to distinguish between what is required for the service of the Lord and what remains in the private sphere of freedom. Service does not fill every moment in the life of a servant, nor does it lay claim to his inmost impulses, emotions and thoughts. Nevertheless, it is obvious even in the case of genuine human service that the value, indeed the meaning, of a life can be measured by the function it fulfills. As a man, the great artist is the instrument of his art; his human nature is like a mine that is evaluated according to the precious material it contains and has value inasmuch as it is capable of delivering what is demanded of it. About what is left when the demand has been fulfilled, about the toil, the sacrifice, the tears, about the whole tragedy of the artist *qua* man, about his inability to adjust to his milieu, no one asks. Something similar occurs in the case of servants in old families who have grown up with the children and like them belong to the permanency of the house; whose nature has gradually identified itself with the function they perform and in the process of doing so has perhaps found its ultimate expression.

But these human examples fail to convey the totality of our meaning, for earthly service can never fill and lay claim to the innermost regions of the soul. To do so is the prerogative of that service to divine love that is required of man by the exigencies of his nature. We do not ask here what man may be above and beyond this function, the fulfillment of which makes him what he is. All beings are, in the last analysis, interpreted according to their goal and calling, which, in man's case, is always love. All else is but means to an end; love alone is the goal. But because man himself is not love, because the calling to love is a grace given him by God to draw his whole nature, like a magnet, above itself to its final goal, for this reason the calling to love has for man the form of service. He *has the privilege* of serving, and there is no other service that ennobles the servant as this one does. He is free to serve, for nothing frees so deeply as love. But he can never regard himself in his human nature as identical with his calling; therefore, his love will always be a service. And herein lies the foundation of the concept of "state of life".

"State" is etymologically related to the verb "stand". It means, in this world, the permanent stationing of an individual in a certain corporal or spiritual position. In civil life, "state" is based on a lasting "obligation of a man's person, as far as he is under his own dominion or another's. . . . Therefore state pertains to freedom or slavery" (ST 2a 2ae 183, 1 responsio).[18] What is expressed in civil life on the basis of a permanent stationing of oneself in one of these two forms of life has its first, deepest and common root in the stationing of man by God in the service of love that both claims and frees him: "But now set free from sin and become slaves to God, you have your fruit unto sanctification, and as your end, life everlasting" (Rom 6:22).

2. GRACE AND MISSION

Rooted in service to the calling originally prescribed for him by God, namely, love of God and neighbor, man's fundamental state of life is none other than "the state of grace" in which God established him and in which he is expected to remain. Corresponding to this state, which is common to all men, is each individual's personal state of life—the unique state that determines his existence, that has been assigned to him by God, and that gives his life its true content, its raison d'être. This state is determined by the *grace of personal mission*.

But the state of life common to all men is likewise a grace from God. Far from being just a gift received passively, albeit an un-

---

[18] Our intention is to broaden the limited Thomistic concept of state by approaching it from the perspective of "Christ's state of life". See below, Pt. II, Ch. 2, sec. 1.

precedented one, it is a commission entrusted to man, a transfer of power from archetype to image, a task man must perform in the freedom of his nonidentity with the archetype, and for which he has been given the necessary powers and means. By relieving man of the feeling of being always a recipient, this active side of his calling justifies in him a corresponding sense of having been called to a "state of life". And in this awareness grace reveals itself in its true character as grace. Were it but the unilateral favor of a king toward a beggar, then only the king and his goodness would stand in the limelight. The beggar would be of importance solely as one who has been exposed to the light; in himself, he would be but an object of indifference. Grace, on the other hand, can be said to have brought its work to completion and to have fulfilled its purpose only when it has touched an individual in his inmost depths; when it has so renewed, exalted and ennobled him that he actually becomes what he has been made by grace—an individual gifted with the characteristics and distinctive qualities of genuine freedom, genuine nobility and a genuine commission in the service of the king; when it has enabled the individual so gifted to fulfill his new function with appropriate dignity and ease and without being constantly inhibited by the remembrance of the chasm that exists between his origin and the task imposed upon him by grace.

From the point of view of him who bestows grace, it is as if grace were to detach itself from him in order to attach itself to the one graced. The one who bestows grace does not deem it necessary to cling to it, making sure that the whole world (to give truth its due) acknowledges at once in the recipient of grace the tokens of his having received that grace freely so that the separation between nature and grace is at once accomplished. On the contrary, he wants the recipient to be as unrestrained in his use of the gift bestowed upon him as he would be if it were his natural inheritance. If he adopts a stranger as his son, he wants him to feel that he is truly a son—to forget and take no cognizance of the difference between himself and the hereditary sons of the house. The recipient will, of course, conduct himself in precisely the opposite manner. Despite all the naturalness that is given and expected of him in his new position, he will never forget that he owes all he is—and truly is—to grace. The higher the position to which he is raised, the less will he confuse himself with the one who has raised him to it. If he were to consider only himself in all this, he might well find himself in a situation that was psychologically untenable, compelled as he would be to vacillate between the naturalness expected of him by the one who has so favored him and the constraint that is rooted in his own nature. The situation could easily be intensified into a kind of split in his consciousness, in the whole structure of his life, with one part of him playing the role of a slave, the other that of a freeman. Under these circumstances, he might soon come to feel a degree of resentment toward the one who had placed him in such an intolerable position.

All this is changed, however, if grace is perceived as the inner form of man's personal mission rather than as a beautiful garment that clothes him without removing the underlying poverty of his nature and origin. Grace brings man a task, opens up for him a field of activity, bestows upon him the joy of accomplishment, so that he can identify himself with his mission and discover in it the true meaning of his existence. Grace gives man a center of gravity that, like a magnet, draws all the forces of his nature into a clear and definite pattern that is neither foreign nor cumbersome to the patterns already formed in his nature, but engages them, like idle laborers, in a task that is both pleasant and rewarding. This is the power of the grace of mission. Whoever understands it will risk all that is in him to place himself in its service. He understands that he has no other center of gravity than that which has been bestowed upon him; that the forces of his nature fall into useless and sterile fragments if they are not held together by the grace of mission; that they can become serviceable only in the light of this grace. For man's mission in life is not something general and impersonal like a ready-made coat; it has been designed specifically for him and given into his possession as the most personal of all gifts. By it he becomes, in the fullest sense of the word, a person.

Man's final goal has always been a supernatural one. He has always been called to achieve his intended development in this "beyond" of his nature. Consequently, it is never possible to arrive at a true definition of human nature on the sole basis of man's natural tendencies and traits. On the one hand, man's obligation under the great commandment to love God and neighbor perfectly is not something that can be inferred or even considered possible of fulfillment on the basis of man's natural gifts alone; on the other hand, the personal will of God, which determines the meaning of human life, cannot be deduced from any configuration of human characteristics. It is quite conceivable, for instance, that two individuals endowed with the same natural characteristics would be chosen for two entirely different missions: one for action in the world, the other for contemplation in the cloister; or one for the development of his natural gifts in the service of God, the other for the sacrifice of these gifts in the same service. What man makes of his natural gifts depends entirely on the mission that God has designed for him and that, in the last analysis, proceeds directly from God. Just as God infused into all men the calling to love and bestowed on them by his grace both the goal and the strength to attain it, so he placed each of them in a particular state of life that represents for the individual the situation and the form in which he is to strive to fulfill his calling. Thus every life contains a center that is eccentric—that is, outside itself. Around this center each person must order and make use of his natural gifts. That is the concrete form in which he will fulfill his calling to love, and this fulfill-ment will be his service.

There is absolutely no point of comparison from which man can shed light on the paradox of his original state. It is never permitted him to interpret his likeness to God as partly identity and partly complete otherness. Although he has been richly endowed by God, he is, nonetheless, totally a creature. He cannot call his "graced" state godlike, and his nature, by contrast, creaturelike. Nor can he regard his mission (which makes him a person) as godlike, but his spiritual submission to it as creature-like. He cannot describe his soul, which was breathed into him by the very breath of God, as godlike, but his body, which was formed from the dust of the earth, as creaturelike. On the contrary, man as a whole, with all the intimate gifts of nature and grace bestowed upon him by God, has been constituted a creature of God who must ultimately fulfill the will of God in his own will. Nor can he comfort himself by saying that he thereby does only the absolute good that every intelligent being must strive to do; that his "heteronomy" is consequently identical with his "autonomy"; that the reverential service by which he praises God is, in the last analysis, but the expression of his own self-determination. To do so would be to identify his own freedom with God's freedom, to proclaim that he has no further need of listening to the word that proceeds from the mouth of God in order to find the path to his own self-realization. For if man equates the love to which he is obliged with his own spontaneity in loving, he will no longer have any object of love but himself.

But if man understands, with St. Augustine, that he must call himself a servant even when God calls him friend (as Mary called herself a handmaiden even when she was addressed with the honor due a queen), then he both may and must acknowledge to himself that the word and promise of God are always right, are truth itself. In the consciousness of the distance that separates him from the divine archetype of which he is but an image, created man, and particularly one who is in the state of grace, has the inalienable and overwhelming knowledge of his nearness to God. But he does not know of himself wherein this nearness lies; it must be explained to him by God. If he is not permitted to seek his perfection in himself, but only in the carrying out of his mission; if, as the image and likeness of God, he must keep his gaze fixed on the archetype in order faithfully to imitate—not in general, but always and in the least detail—every characteristic revealed to him by God, then precisely therein, without suspecting it himself, he shares in the innermost secret of the love of God. Love's character as service, which we have heretofore regarded as belonging distinctively to the love of creatures, reveals itself now as being so essential to love that it is indispensable even to absolute, divine love. The relationship of archetype and created

likeness that we once described as the relationship of master and
servant has unexpectedly revealed itself as the image of a relationship within the Godhead itself—the relationship of Father and
Son.

The Son proceeds from the Father and is sent by him into the
world. Because as a person he is in all things the identical likeness
of the divine archetype, he finds his full expression in being like
the Father in intellect and will. The Son's love is not less divine,
less absolute, than that of the Father, yet it has the inner form
of mission, of service, of "obedience". The Son is not less exalted
than the Father, yet his eternal joy consists in seeing in the Father
one who is greater than he is. He is not less free than the Father,
yet the form of his freedom consists in the exclusion of every
other will but that of the Father. The nature of the Son as the
Second Person in God is identical with his procession and mission
from the Father, yet by accepting this mission and identifying
himself with it, he refers it to the eternal glorification of the
Father. This *divine "obedience" of the Son* is his highest freedom
in love; this *"poverty" of the Son* in respect to every other calling
than that given him by the Father is his eternal riches; this
"purity" of the Son and the exclusiveness of the love by which he
consecrates himself to the Father is his eternal fecundity. His
love is so free, so rich, so fruitful that the mutual love of Father
and Son produces the person of the Holy Spirit—the expression,
the seal, the witness, the infinite climax and communication of
their undivided love.

Every misgiving we may have that our creaturehood may be
prejudicial to our freedom falls silent before the abyss of this
mystery of love. If we find it hard that we must "always serve",
that we must equate the meaning and purpose of our existence
with the mission decreed for us by God, that we may never
have any other will than that which is prescribed for us by our
mission, let us turn our gaze upon the eternal Son of God. Let
us learn from him the name of that ecstasy that can transport us
out of ourselves and into the mission given us by God: the name
of a love that is most free because it is absolute. From him, we
will learn that ecstasy is not a private state bestowed upon us

for our own pleasure and affording us experiences that affect only ourselves. On the contrary, the ecstasy that can take us out of ourselves bears the name of that obedience by which the servant chooses to find his own ultimate pleasure only in fulfilling the will of him who sent him. The Son does not distinguish himself from his mission; he does not remove himself, even for an instant, from the state of life in which the Father has placed him in order thereby to regard himself in an impossible "in-himselfness" [an-Sich] and then to substitute for himself in the state proper to his mission this abstraction and its putative value. The Son finds his raison d'être in cooperating with, approving and giving thanks to the will of the Father by which he has been sent and established in his mission. He knows himself only as that by which he is able to glorify his origin. In his own eyes, he is but a means to this glorification.

The application of the concept of obedience to the divine person is, of course, a figure of speech—an anthropomorphism. But, in the final analysis, all human speech about God is anthropomorphic, and this figure has been made definitive and proper by the Incarnation of the Son (Phil 2:7). In applying it, everything is to be excluded from the concept of obedience that derives from the relationship between God and the creature insofar as the creature is regarded qua creature, that is, as having its origin in nothingness. Everything is to be retained, on the other hand, and translated into the infinite (in the sense of the via eminentiae) that pertains to the analogy between God and the creature as the positive image of God, or more properly, of the Trinity. The obedience of which the Son of God gave us an example in his human nature is by no means merely something that is grounded in his human nature and intended as an example for us insofar as we are creatures. Like all his utterances, it is not only borne by his divine person; it is also a positive revelation of his divine person—and hence of his divine nature—translated into human terms. Precisely this filial attitude, which looks to the Father in everything and wills to be in everything only the representation and brightness (Heb 1:3) of the paternal nature, is the manner in which the Son makes comprehensible to us his identity with the Father, in which he becomes for us the "revelation" (Jn 1:18) of the eternal love of the Father. If the one and undivided love of God takes on a filial, and hence its most obedient, coloring in the person of the Son, the love of the Son is not therefore to be regarded as inferior (subordinated) to the Father's love, but as none other than the eternal "expression" (Heb 1:3) of the perfect selflessness and self-giving of paternal love by which the Father determined, not to keep his divine essence wholly for himself, but to pour it out abundantly on the Son. In other words, the love that is, in the Son, a mission received "by way of . . . generation" (cf. above, p. 36) is the expression of a love that is, in the Father, a mission to generate. In the Third Person of God, the Holy Spirit, this reciprocity of mission becomes the final and fulfilling unity of love whereby the Spirit, in his unique personhood, combines in himself the features of both Father and Son, from whom he proceeds. He is the personification of self-giving, selflessness and mission; of pure and dynamic transparency; of love as service to the love of the Father and Son. When, therefore, the Son reveals to us his love for the Father in the transferred mode of obedience, this revelation is, at the same time, a revelation of the love of the whole Trinity.

On the other hand, it is understandable that the world was created on the model of the Son; that "all things have been created through and unto him"; that he is "before all creatures and that in him all things hold together" (Col 1:16–17), because the filial mode of God's eternal love is the most proper, the most exemplary one for the right relationship between God and creature. ". . . God willed that the *interior communication* of his nature and essence should be projected and continued outside of himself in all its infinity. . . . Thus God extended to man the relationship of natural fatherhood in which he stands to the Son of his bosom, in that he begot his Son not only in the interior of his bosom, but also in the outer world, in a created nature. . . . If there were no interior, infinite communication and glorification in God himself, the sub-structure for the incarnation of a divine person would be lacking, not merely because there would then be only one person in God, but chiefly because there would be no basis, no point of departure, for the idea of an infinite communication and glorification of God within himself." As it is, however, "the Incarnation appears, not as an extraordinary event, but as the flower springing from a root buried in the trinitarian process, as the unfolding of a seed contained therein."[19]

It is only in contemplating the love of the Son that man comes to

[19] Matthias Joseph Scheeben, *The Mysteries of Christianity*, trans. Cyril Vollert, S.J. (St. Louis: Herder, 1946), 358–59. [I quote here from the English translation of a work that von Balthasar quotes in the original German. (Tr)]

understand his own calling: to perceive and understand himself
from no other standpoint than that of mission and, accordingly,
to find in perfect service his perfect self-fulfillment, his eternal
bliss, because there is for him no happiness outside of love, which
has for him the form of service, because there is for him no other
happiness than the accomplishment of the service to which he is
called and which—O wonder of wonders!—consists for him
exclusively in the calling to love.

In this original grace, which was man's portion from the beginning, in which he was created, and in which he shares in the
intimate mystery of the divine love of the Blessed Trinity, he is
also invested with the *twofold gift of action and contemplation*, which
are as inseparable as inhalation and exhalation, as the contraction
and expansion of man's heart. Man's calling is to *action* because
the grace of God always charges him with a mandate or task to be
carried out by his own efforts. In thus charging him, however,
God draws the recipient of his grace into his confidence, reveals
to him a part of the divine plan, and commissions him to realize a
part of it by his own strength and ingenuity. But man's calling to
action is likewise a calling to contemplation because the recipient
of grace can understand and complete the task assigned to him
only by holding all the more closely and exclusively to the
thought of God in gratitude for the trust God has shown him, by
undertaking no deed independently of God or that might run
counter to God's plan, and by seeking, with his gaze fixed
unwaveringly on God, to understand and accomplish the divine
will in all things. Thus the Father has given the Son all power and
judgment, but the Son accepts this power only in order to adhere
more closely to the will of the Father. ". . . The Son can do
nothing of himself, but only what he sees the Father doing. For
whatever he does, this the Son does in like manner. For the Father
loves the Son, and shows him all that he himself does" (Jn
5:19–20). From one point of view, their relationship is an active
one, for both of them work: "My Father works even until now,
and I work" (Jn 5:17). But this action finds its completion in a

mutual relationship of revelation and contemplation, in which the Father eternally reveals himself anew to the Son, and the Son eternally offers himself and opens himself anew to the revelation of the Father. However much this alternation may seem to resemble a rhythm of life, it is not a succession of phases that follow one another in sequence. The Son does not contemplate the Father for a while and then pause in order to imitate in his own activity what he has seen the Father do. Even while he is active, he keeps his gaze fixed steadily upon the Father in order not to lose a moment's direction from him. But he is not inactive while he is contemplating. He understands his contemplation so entirely as service and mission that he translates into action and reality all that the Father shows him.

Man, too, is given a place in this rhythm. In practice, this means that his state is a *state of prayer*. By reason of the original ecstasy by which his nature is transported into the mission decreed by God, he comes to share in that movement that opens the very depths of his being to God. In this act, he acknowledges both his creaturehood, which has the duty of serving and glorifying God, and the infinite dominion of God, which has the right to place him, the creature, in this particular state and to decree this particular calling for him. Thus the act of embracing his calling is a primordial act of adoration and thanksgiving in which man lays at the feet of God all that God has given him as his own possession in order to receive it again in the form most pleasing to God, that is, in the form of the will of God as mission. This act of acknowledging the sovereignty of God lies at the root of action and contemplation and contains in itself the will to embrace both of them. More specifically, to embrace both of them in their indivisibility: to be autonomous because obedience requires it, and not to want to be autonomous except as obedience requires. There can be no doubt that such a decision is meaningful for and can be carried out only by one who loves. But man has, after all, been created out of and for love. If he understands his calling, he will pray always, whether he finds himself in the state of action or of contemplation. If he does not understand his calling, then whatever he does and however much he prays, he will always be outside the world of prayer. For prayer is genuine only when one is fulfilling one's calling. "Not everyone who says to me 'Lord, Lord' shall enter the kingdom of heaven; but he who does the will of my Father shall enter the kingdom of heaven" (Mt 7:21).

All aspects of man's creaturehood meet in the concept of mission: *his mission to love and to serve*, because love fulfills itself in service just as service fulfills itself in love; *his distance from God and his nearness to God*, because his condition as not-God finds its foundation and fulfillment in his condition of being at a remove from love, as the Son also experienced it in his relationship with the Father, whereas his nearness to God reveals itself as a nearness of love and hence also of reverence and of service; *his calling to autonomous action and self-giving contemplation*, because his action can be more autonomous as his contemplation is more self-giving and receptive, whereas his contemplation finds its truest expression when it is translated into action. Thus the concept of mission suffices to express the full measure of what man is; fulfillment of mission encompasses the whole concept of human perfection. It even replaces it, since human perfection is not in itself self-sufficient and purposeful; it stands in the service of the glorification of the love of the Trinity, which is the single ultimate purpose of creation and to which everything else has been ordered, including man's perfection and his eternal happiness.

This seemingly digressive treatment of service and mission was in actuality the quickest way of arriving at a concrete view of what the concept of "state of life" originally entailed. Man's calling to take his place in the will of God is the primal reality that anticipates, conditions and provides the foundation for everything else in his condition as creature, which, apart from this reality, is but an incomprehensible mass of meaningless and formless matter without purpose or stature. If we look at the will of God, which finds its concrete expression in the personal mission of each individual, man's existence becomes meaningful and unified like letters that form a sentence. But if we attempt, apart from the concept of mission, to give ultimate and unified meaning to the corporal and spiritual forces, the fate, and the events that shape the life of an individual, we immediately fall into uncertainty, are enmeshed in a complicated undergrowth that becomes all the more impenetrable as we try to base our interpretation on man and his viewpoint instead of looking, with him, to his divine calling. If men were to interpret their lives a priori in terms of their mission to glorify God, there would be no world problems, no mysteries of existence, no psychic tensions and conflicts, no hopeless situations. For they would not then be concerned with themselves or with a world considered in itself and apart from God and God's will. Rather, they would turn their gaze away from themselves and toward the will of God, who reveals himself to all who seek him and who is the last meaning of all creatures.

3. MAN IN PARADISE

The line of division that will later run through the Church and divide the state of man in the world from the state of the evangelical counsels, thus placing upon the Christian—and this means *every* Christian—the obligation of determining and choosing the state to which God has called him: this line of division was no more foreseen in the original creation of mankind than was the whole visible structure of the Church as a body distinct from the rest of mankind, separated from the "world", and constantly demanding of mankind a decision for or against Christianity; no more foreseen than was the existence of a special order of priests, commissioned to preach the word and administer the sacraments —for neither a circumscribed word of revelation nor the sacraments as we now perceive them were part of God's original plan for mankind. The lines of division that the Christian states of life create in Christianity today are linked to the state of redemption, which presumes the state of sin. In man's original state before his fall into sin, they would have been unnecessary. Since the differentiation of the Christian states of life is the theme of this study, however, it is important that we depict its origin as clearly as possible and, from that vantage point, seek to explain its necessity and present significance. In the last analysis, it is from man's original state, from the state in which God conceived, intended and created him, that every later state of life must take its origin and meaning. That is, the later states must, each in its own way, reflect something of the one idea that God intended from the beginning to realize in the creation of man. It must be somehow possible, therefore, to look back from the states of life as they exist today to Adam's original state and, in doing so, to discover, as it were from the convergence of different points of view, at least an indication of the true state in which man was originally placed by God.

Yet anyone who would venture to express an opinion about man as he was in paradise must first consider how far—not in the temporal order, but in the order of grace—this first man differed from man as he is today. He was, to be sure, the prototype of modern man and hence incorporated in himself *the idea of man*, but it would be presumptuous to believe that we can achieve even an approximate concept of this idea. Many of the characteristics of man in his original state, which revelation shows us almost, as it were, in passing, open such vistas when we try to arrive at their ultimate meaning that we are unable to imagine, to reconstruct for ourselves in any concrete fashion, the inner form of his life, his fate, his awareness of self.

Let us not consider the fact, implicit in the original story of mankind, that Adam had no parents, no tradition in which he grew to maturity; that he named the creatures that God brought before him in solitude, inventing speech in the process, until it became evident that this naming and this speaking required a genuine counterpart and God formed from his side a "thou" and led her to him. Rather, let us consider the fact that both "were naked, but they felt no shame" (Gen 2:25); that neither of them was subject to death, which appeared in the world for the first time as a punishment for the reaching for the tree of knowledge; that neither of them knew the difference between good and evil—was not even supposed to know it. These three characteristics are so different from those of contemporary man that it is difficult for us to realize that man did, in fact, possess them in his original state. *The feeling of shame, the awareness of death and the necessity of distinguishing between good and evil* would appear to be the three foundation stones of our spiritual being, of our ethical and religious conduct.

1. *Shame* is a subtle phenomenon that permeates our entire being, distinguishing us from the animals. It seems to have its source in our double nature as creatures composed of body and soul. Man's most sensitive attitude toward his own body, toward the relationship of the sexes, and, indeed, toward his very condition as man seems to depend on the keenness of his sense of shame. We regard this phenomenon as something purely positive and its absence as something negative—something that brings us closer to the animals. Why did man eventually come to know shame? Certainly not because he had been created without a body, for in paradise God created both male and female; and not because he was more like the animals then than he is now, for it was only later that God clothed man in the skins of animals (Gen 3:21), whereas he had already bestowed on him the seal of divine likeness and established him as sovereign lord over all creatures (Gen 1:27–30). Yet both explanations have had their supporters. Origen and his followers were convinced that the phenomenon of shame had its source in man's body-soul composition; that man was initially a pure spirit and was later confined by way of punishment in the body of which the animal skins were the symbol. But this spiritual interpretation is too obviously in conflict with revelation to be tenable. Its counterpart, the rationalistic interpretation that seeks to explain man's lack of shame in paradise as a kind of animal promiscuity, a stage of man's awareness that was inferior to the stage he has attained today, is equally untenable. In view of the simultaneous existence in man of both sexuality and supernatural spirituality, then, the absence of shame in paradise poses an apparently unsolvable problem. We are com-

pelled to view shame as being in some way a consequence of sin, but one in which, given man's body-soul composition, we can perceive only a positive value.

2. Just as incomprehensible to us is the concept of an *existence without death* and all it entails, above all, the process of aging, which seems to give the curve of man's existence its inimitable meaning and emphasis. In addition to the fact that an organism that does not undergo the process of aging is biologically and physiologically incomprehensible to the natural sciences and to medicine, there are likewise many sociological and ethical problems associated with the absence of death. Are not those philosophers right who envision an indissoluble link between begetting and dying? Would sexual reproduction have any meaning if individuals did not, in a dim awareness that they are doomed to die, seek to perpetuate their species? Does not the act of begetting contain in itself a presentiment of death? Are not begetting and death so complementary that the perpetuation of earlier generations combined with the increased propagation of the race would result in an overpeopling of the earth? And, to pursue the matter even further, are not those theorists right who suggest an inner connection between death and ethical decisions? Could man act morally if he saw before him an indefinite span of life in which he would always have time to repair his past omissions? Is it not, in fact, the pressing finiteness of his earthly position and horizon, the salutary, hidden immanence of death in every moment of his life, that forces him to the heights of genuine decision and thus to genuine morality? From this perspective, death appears as one of the positive, formative forces of man's earthly existence, as a power from which all earthly activity derives its value for eternity. Not to be able to die seems to be the privilege of the lowest elements of creation; the higher a creature is, the more endangered, fragile and mortal it becomes. Death and aging are so inextricably united with the condition of man as we know it that the more exactly we observe this inner bond, the

less we are able to conceive of their being separated. In this world, we cannot picture to ourselves a man who is immortal.[20]

3. We come now to the third characteristic of man before the Fall: *man without knowledge of good and evil*. In other words, man without "ethics"—man without what is for us the epitome of his spiritual dignity: his ability to choose. Without knowledge of good and evil, there is no freedom; without freedom, man cannot be a spiritual being. Even the person who chooses in favor of what is good must have at least a theoretical knowledge of evil if only so that he can turn away from evil and toward the good. Otherwise, he would have no merit; he would have undergone no testing; his goodness would be as natural and unspiritual as that of the animals, which do instinctively what is proper to their nature; or, at least, as that of children who have not yet reached the age of reason and from whom, consequently, we can expect no moral responsibility. It is not surprising, therefore, that the state of Adam and Eve before the Fall has often been compared,

---

[20] In his *Moralphilosophie, eine wissenschaftliche Darlegung der sittlichen einschliesslich der rechtlichen Ordnung*, 5th ed., 2 vols. (Freiburg: Herder, 1911), Victor Cathrein, S.J., emphasizes the wonderful appropriateness of death both in irrational nature and in human life. In the case of man in particular, death is necessary primarily for the common good. "Family life especially depends on the law of death. . . . The family takes death for granted. If death did not constantly thin out the ranks of men, propagation through the family would soon become unnecessary, indeed, harmful." Moreover, death has "teleological meaning for man even as an individual". It makes inescapably clear to him that his earthly life is a time of testing and preparation; it places before his eyes (as Simmel and Scheler have pointed out) the absolute seriousness of the ethical. "How aptly everything is, in fact, ordained for this purpose. This constant being born and dying, coming into being and passing away, this endless change! How well adapted they are to wean the heart from earthly things!" (*Moralphilosophie* vol. I, 150–52). In other words, the teleology of an existence depending on death, which did not exist in original creation! On the philosophical interrelationship of death and sex, cf. the discussion in Hans Urs von Balthasar, *Theodramatik*, vol. II: *Die Personen des Spiels*, pt. I: *Der Mensch in Gott* (Einsiedeln: Johannes Verlag, 1976), pp. 342 ff. Further references to Cathrein's *Moralphilosophie* will be given in parentheses in the text.

even by the Fathers of the Church, to the state of children below the age of reason. But this comparison is fraught with danger. Children are expected to grow; their abilities lie slumbering only to awaken one day. If the comparison were a valid one, the serpent would have been right in advising Adam and Eve to eat the apple so that their eyes would be opened and they would know the difference between good and evil (Gen 3:5), and God would appear to be a father who does not allow his children to grow up. Did he keep them in an artificial state of immature ignorance to prevent their acquiring that knowledge of good and evil that would make them "like unto God"? The serpent says he did and God confirms it: "The man has become like one of us" (Gen 3:22). From the perspective of the serpent, which is directly concerned with the "ethical situation" that embodies the "dignity of man", God's command not to eat of the tree is an apparently meaningless and petty prohibition. Not only is man thereby deprived of something to which he has a right by reason of his dominion over creation, he is also deprived of the very thing that seemed, in the first place, to have made him the lord of irrational creation: his ability to know good from evil. There seems to be an inherent contradiction in this prohibition. God exacts man's obedience, but man is free to make his obedience a spiritual act only if he performs it in full realization of the possibility of disobedience. His obedience will acquire full ethical significance only when he possesses what is withheld from him.

And yet, God created man in his own image and likeness—created him as he would have him. Man ought not, therefore, to assume that he was created in an undeveloped state so that he might have time to grow into something else. The command not to eat of the tree of knowledge of good and evil was not given for a period of time only. It is an absolute command. With its transgression come both the knowledge of one's own nakedness and the punishment of death. It is obvious, then, that we must seek the answer to our problem farther back in man's history if we are to find the point where the threads were still woven together in a harmonious tapestry.

In the beginning, man was placed in a state of nonidentity with God in which he was to rule the earth as the image of the Divine Majesty, subjecting to himself "every creature that crawls on the earth" and taking for his nourishment "every seed-bearing plant on the earth and every tree which has seed-bearing fruit" (Gen 1:28) and "every tree of the garden" (Gen 2:16), while, at the same time, preserving toward God an attitude of perfect service. He was not to presume to touch the tree of knowledge of good and evil that grew, like the tree of life, in the middle of the garden. He had complete freedom over all the earth, provided only that in his God-oriented freedom he persevered in a perfect obedience which has constant reference to the center of all things. Man was not to arrogate to himself this center, which was knowledge and life. He was to receive it from God. Gregory of Nyssa and others comment that, since there could not have been two trees in the center of the garden, there must have been a mysterious identity between the tree of life and the tree of knowledge of good and evil. The tree was forbidden insofar as it gave knowledge of good and evil, for this was the only fruit that man could take for himself. If he were not to die, he would in any case have to receive from God the original life that was opposed to death. And he was to receive it without grasping for it, without seeking it in the knowledge of good and evil. In an obedience that did not seek forbidden knowledge, he was to entrust his life to God and receive from God's hand, and in God's good time, the fruit of life. It is like the unsealing of this mystery that occupies the first pages of Holy Scripture when the Lord of the Covenant promises in the last book: "Him who overcomes I will permit to eat of the tree of life, which is in the paradise of my God" (Rev 2:7), and when we are told that there stands in the heavenly Jerusalem, on both sides of the river of living grace, the tree of life, which bears twelve fruits and whose leaves bring healing to the nations (Rev 22:2). Man was unable to pluck this fruit, this eternal life, for himself because it is the free gift of God's grace. It is, then, not without divine irony, in which mercy is secretly concealed, that God says after the Fall, as a reason for driving man out of the garden: "Indeed! the man has become like one of us, knowing good and evil! And now perhaps he will put forth his hand and take also from the tree of life and eat, and live forever!" (Gen 3:22). For man to do so would, in fact, only have increased his curse, would have made it eternal. It is a grace, therefore, that God drove man out of paradise into earthly mortality in order to lead him back by quite different paths to the tree of life.

1. In paradise, man stood in *obedience* to God and, by reason of this obedience, ruled sovereignly and freely over all the earth. His position was diametrically *opposed* to the serpent's claim that man, who by nature was called to freedom, was intolerably restricted by God's prohibition: "The serpent . . . said to the woman, 'Did God say, "You shall not eat of any tree of the garden"?' " (Gen 3:1). Craftily, the serpent spreads the shadow of God's prohibition over all the trees, turning the freedom of man's obedience into the seeming deprivation of his sovereignty over all creatures. Until that moment, Eve had not found her obedience to God in any way contrary to her freedom. Rather, she had regarded it as the epitome of order: mankind obedient to God, and all creatures, in consequence, obedient to mankind. This order was so transparent, so evident, that she had had no need to reflect on it. Nothing was simpler than an order in which mankind served God and everything else served mankind. It was an obedience against which Adam and Eve had felt no need to struggle because it had never occurred to them to compare their wills to God's will. Consequently, they did not have to renounce their own wills in order to do the will of God. Their wills were simply and unquestioningly identical with this obedience, which was but the instrument by which they accepted the will of God. In the strength of their harmonious relationship with God, they knew and felt themselves to be *sovereignly free* in creation. Their freedom was protected by their obedience, which, in turn, was a

service to God in trust, gratitude and love. In essence, it was *faith*. Faith was the movement by which they accepted their being from God and returned it to him again and again in love. In this faith, they were relieved of the necessity of distinguishing good from evil because they knew only good, while evil remained hidden from them. They lived in the fire of goodness—not yet in the lukewarmness of indifference to good and evil, not yet at the point where the choice between good and evil first becomes possible. They lived not below, but above, this "ethical" situation in a condition of which their already having chosen in favor of good was constitutive. In this state of absolute faith, they were not without knowledge; but their knowledge was so positive that Adam was able to name all creatures, to subject and till the garden and the whole earth—knowledge, therefore, that did not exclude the joy of progress, of discovery, of culture. But all this was, as it were, enveloped by the comprehensive meaning and dependent upon the possibility of an all-embracing obedience in faith. Within this framework, knowledge could thrive and man could fulfill his earthly tasks by the use of reason.[21] But if the framework should be shattered, if man should destroy faith out of curiosity about

---

[21] Above all, the theology of man's original state must not be misled by philosophical assertions about the present state of the world and the present condition of human nature to the point of ascribing such validity to these statements that they come to be regarded as the foundation and starting-point of a doctrine about Adam in his original state. "It is not in himself or in things, but above himself, that the believer seeks for the measure of the known; thus he is not condemned like the mere philosopher to accept the world as it is, but following the teaching of revelation he can ask himself if the world is what it should be to be worthy of God" (Etienne Gilson, *The Philosophy of St. Bonaventure*, trans. Dom Illtyd Trethowan and Frank J. Sheed [London: Sheed and Ward, 1940], 435). According to Bonaventure, who systematizes the common teaching of the Fathers of the Church (cf. von Balthasar, *Kosmische Liturgie, das Weltbild Maximus des Bekenners* [Einsiedeln: Johannes Verlag, 1961], 174–75), Adam, who was created in grace, was able to know the natural in terms of the super-natural, and the material in terms of the spiritual. The normal mode of knowledge of contemporary man—by which the spiritual can only be surmised and inferred by laborious abstraction from the material and which Aristotle regarded as proper

the light—about the naked reason—concealed within it, about a reason without faith, his eyes would indeed be opened and he would indeed know what God knows and what God in his wisdom had kept hidden from him: the difference between good and evil, which, of a sudden, would have no other content than the knowledge of his own nakedness.

2. In this unanticipated revelation of their nakedness at the very moment in which they attained knowledge of good and evil lies

---

to man's "nature"—is for Bonaventure the result of man's fall into sin. In a manner that we shall describe later and certainly without a direct intuition of God's essence, Adam enjoyed both the *cognitio matutina* and the *cognitio vespertina*, that is, a mode of knowledge that proceeded both from the spiritual to the material and from the material to the spiritual. But it was because he possessed the *cognitio matutina* that he was able, by reason of the *cognitio vespertina*, to see all material things directly and clearly in terms of the spiritual. Ramón Lull teaches the same doctrine. Both he and St. Bonaventure were aware that any philosophy that takes only the *status naturae lapsae* [the state of fallen nature] as the starting-point of a valid anthropology is doomed to go astray.

Aristotelianism has so penetrated the thinking of St. Thomas Aquinas that he inserts a philosophical treatise on human nature into the *Summa Theologiae* even *before* he depicts man's original state. This treatise is placed between the theology of the six days of creation and that of man in paradise. It contains the famous *Quaestiones* on the relationship of soul to body, on freedom of will and on (abstract) knowledge. Only *after* he has completely worked out this philosophical anthropology does he depict man's original state—and here we learn, to our astonishment, that Adam, the first man, "had knowledge of all things by divinely infused species" (ST 1a 94, 3 ad 1). In other words, Adam does not resemble the nature just depicted. On the contrary, he belongs to the company of those beings, like the angels, who learn intuitively and abstractly. Did Thomas realize what consequences the construction of such a first man had—and still has—for his whole system? In his teaching about Adam he depends on earlier theology when he speaks, for instance, of the possibility of a twofold knowledge (ST 1a 94, 3) and explicitly labels it *cognitio naturalis* (*De ver* q. 18 a. 4). But whereas theologians regard this original constitution of man's nature as actually intended by God and therefore as foreseen for Adam's descendants, Thomas draws the line of division straight through the center of man's original state by ascribing this nature only to Adam, since he was the origin and source of the whole race, but not to the children who might have been born to him in his original state (*De ver* q. 18 a. 7). With regard to Eve, the theologians are silent.

the key to the second problem to be raised here: *the origin of shame*. Even before they fell into sin, Adam and Eve were man and wife; Adam beheld with joy the woman whom God brought before him and exclaimed: " 'She now is bone of my bone and flesh of my flesh'. . . . For this reason a man leaves his father and mother and clings to his wife, and the two become one flesh. Both the man and his wife were naked, but they felt no shame" (Gen 2:24–25). Even before they fell into sin, they had received from God the mandate: "Be fruitful and multiply; fill the earth and subdue it" (Gen 1:28). And this work and this mandate were among those that God saw and knew they were good. Nevertheless, Adam did not know his wife until they had been driven out of paradise under the curse that made work toilsome and childbearing painful. The first thing reported of them after their exile is, in fact, that Adam "knew Eve his wife" (Gen 4:1). Actually, the solution to the second problem must be sought in a continuation of the solution to the first. We have already seen how the natural powers of man's soul were, so to speak, enveloped and polarized by the all-embracing act of obedience to God in faith. It was only with the destruction of obedience that these powers appeared in their nakedness as "critical intellect" and "freedom of will". They had originally been intended to function as internal organs within faith, which is the form of obedient love. Man's body and its powers stood in the same relationship to his soul as did his natural powers to the supernatural powers of loving faith. It was the soul that enclosed and enveloped the body, as the lesser and serving element is enclosed and enveloped by the dominant one. We are reminded here of Nietzsche's aphorism: "The most chaste utterance I ever heard: In true love, it is the soul that envelops the body." The irradiation of the body by the soul's purity is, in fact, absolute chastity. It is so pure that, with no special effort or forethought, it keeps "within" all that belongs "within" and is tempted neither to give nor to receive a covetous glance, even when it knows it is loved. On the contrary, it is aware that true love has its center in the spirit and that the body is only the sphere of its external expression. Drives existed in man even in paradise,

but only to serve and be helpful to him. Just as intellect and
will exercised their sovereign functions in man only within the
circumference of obedience in faith, so the bodily drives and
functions exercised their role only within the circumference of a
love that was proper to both soul and body. Adam and Eve had,
it is true, received the command to be fruitful and multiply. But
the fecundity of human love would have been quite different in
paradise—if man had persevered there—from what it is since the
Fall. Just as man's spiritual powers were emancipated by sin from
their previous state of loving obedience in faith, so his bodily
potentialities were severed from the fecundity of love, which was
also disturbed by man's disobedience, and appropriated power
to themselves in sexual love. Only then did there come to be a
difference between virginity and fecundity. In paradise, Eve's virginity
would not have been threatened by her motherhood. The love
of man and wife would have been wholly chaste, finding the
impetus for its fecundity in the spirit and admitting the body to
this chaste love only in the role of a servant. We can no more
picture to ourselves the nature of this fecundity of paradise than
we can picture to ourselves most of the other conditions of man's
original state. Only *one* image from our fallen world can be
applied to the lost form of paradisal fecundity: the one that was
presented to Adam and Eve as a ray of hope after their fall into
sin but before they had been driven into exile—the one human
being who, because she knew not man, was able to be at once
virgin and mother.

The virginity of Adam and Eve was so perfect that even concupiscence was unknown to them. But in paradise virginity
meant, not the renunciation, but the fulfilling of love, which was
the form of perfect fecundity. It required painful renunciation for
its accomplishment as little as the accomplishment of obedience
in faith required renunciation of the freedom to choose between
good and evil. This was the original plan of creation. When now,
after they have been broken by sin, the drives of the body issue
naked from the protection of the spiritual, this is the birth of
shame. Neither the drives themselves nor shame is evil. What

is evil is the disorder that the drives cause to appear exteriorly, thus eliciting from the body the response of shame. Before the Fall, shame had existed only in the lovely, unconscious form of innocence; since sin has destroyed the soul's innocence, it has taken the form of personal experience. Thus the immanent relationship of body and soul in man is the exact mirror-image of the transcendental relationship between the soul and God.

All the theologians of the great age proceed on the assumption that in paradise there was and could be no *corruptio* in man's virginity. On the other hand, they are also convinced that man would have "increased and multiplied" even in his paradisal state since God's command to do so preceded the order introduced by sin. As a result, they search for a—philosophically necessary, but inconceivable—synthesis between the married state and the state of virginity. Suárez states the problem as follows: "Whether in the state of innocence true virginity can exist in the same persons simultaneously with a consummated marriage".[22] William of Auxerre gives the clearest response in his *Summa*: For man in paradise, marriage would have been by way of precept (*in praecepto*), hence there would have been no difference between the state of marriage and that of celibacy.[23] The theologians base this conclusion on the argument that "otherwise the state of fallen nature would have been more perfect in virginity than the state of innocence, which seems to be contrary not only to the exceeding excellence of virginity, but also to the fact on which the saints placed so much emphasis: namely, that Adam did not know his wife without deep mystery until after he had been driven out of paradise" (Suárez, 385). They venture to add that even if Christ had become man in a nature that had not fallen, he and his mother would have remained virgins (Suárez, 389)—a concept that points to the absolute, not merely relative, value of virginity.

But when the theologians, not satisfied with simply stating the

---

[22] Francisco Suárez, "Tractatus Primus de Opere Sex Dierum", bk. V, chap. 2, sec. 3, *Opera Omnia*, vol. III (Paris: Ludovicus Vivès, 1856), 385. [Further references to this work will be given in parentheses in the text. (Tr)]

[23] William of Auxerre (Guillermus Altissiodorensis), *Summa Aurea in Quatuor Libros Sententiarum*, reprint, folio ed. (Frankfurt: Minerva, 1964), decimus tractatus, caput 2, quaes. 4. [This work will henceforth be cited as *Summa Aurea*. (Tr)]

fact of this synthesis, attempted also to determine the manner in which marriage and virginity could have been united, they were on difficult terrain. Their views, which are repeated here only in summary, are introduced for the sole purpose of confirming *their unanimous conviction of the unity that must once have existed in the states of life that today are so diverse*.

a) The first solutions have in common their assumption that sexual intercourse would have had the same form before as after the Fall and their attempt to bring virginity into harmony with this view. Thomas Aquinas, for example, in commenting on the *Sentences* of Peter Lombard, had drawn a distinction between corporal and spiritual virginity and had concluded that even before the Fall sexual intercourse would have destroyed the first, but not the second.[24] In the *Summa Theologiae*, however, he later distinguished three elements in virginity: integrity of body, which he defined as incidental to the moral act, "which is considered . . . only in relation to the soul"; inexperience of sensual pleasure, which is "like the material" of the moral act; and an integrity of soul—the form of the moral act—that consists in the decision to withhold oneself from such pleasure and intercourse (ST 2a 2ae 152, 1 responsio). But in view of this precision the hypothesis he had expressed earlier in his commentary on the *Sentences* was no longer tenable (because the third, formal, element of virginity would not have been present in Eve)—hence his adoption elsewhere in the *Summa Theologiae*[25] of the opinion regarding sexual intercourse before the Fall that Augustine, too, had finally come to accept (see below, p. 97).

Theologians also speculated that in the state of innocence Eve's bodily passages would have been opened only for the moments of intercourse and birth, but would have remained closed at all other times; and that this was not necessarily attributable to a special miracle on the part of God, but to a disposition of original nature in which the passages, instead of being ruptured, were dilated. Richard of Mediavilla's thinking takes this direction,[26] as does that

[24] Thomas Aquinas, *Scriptum super Libros Sententiarum Magistri Petri Lombardi*, vol. II, ed. R. P. Mandonnet, O.P. (Paris: Lethielleux, 1929), "Commentum in Lib. II Sententiarum", dist. XX, quaes. 1, art. II, solutio 1.

[25] *De pertinentibus (in statu innocentiae) ad conservationem speciei*, ST 1a 98, 2 ad 4. Cf. also St. Bonaventure, "In Secundum Librum Sententiarum", lib. II, dist. 20, quaes. 4, conclusio, *Opera Omnia*, vol. III (Paris: Ludovicus Vivès, 1865), 82.

[26] Ricardus de Mediavilla, *Commentum super quarto Sententiarum* (Venice:

of Aegidius of Rome.[27] Durandus[28] is so convinced of it that he
tries to apply it also to Mary's virgin birth.[29]

Alexander of Hales adopted a point of view opposite to that first
held by Aquinas.[30] Although he surrendered Eve's virginity, since
she had, after all, willingly consented to marriage, he did so only
to rescue it again by attributing the preservation of her bodily
integrity to a special grace bestowed on her in her original state by
the power of God.

b) With this, something new had been predicated: that the act of
intercourse and, consequently, the birth did not occur in the same
way then as they do today. Durandus' theory had already pointed
in this direction as had, to an even greater extent, that of Alexander
of Hales. St. Augustine's thinking was entirely in this direction
once he had retracted the more extreme position to be discussed below (pp. 101–102). Thomas Aquinas introduces Augustine's revised
theory into the *Summa Theologiae*, where, after stating the problem
as follows: "In the state of innocence there would have been no
corruption. But virginal integrity is corrupted by intercourse.
Hence there would have been no intercourse in the state of
innocence" (ST 1a 98, 1), he resolves it by quoting Augustine:
In that state, ". . . intercourse could have taken place without
prejudice to virginal integrity. . . . The semen could have been
admitted to the womb without injury to the female organs just as
now the menstrual flow is emitted without injury to those same
organs. . . . And just as the stimulus of maturation rather than the
groanings of pain could have brought the child to birth, so sexual
intercourse could have taken place not in the hunger of lust, but by
a voluntary act."[31]

Dionysius Bertochus, 1489), in librum 2 sententiarum, dist. 20, art. 1, quaes. 4.

[27] Aegidii Columnae Romani "In Secundum Librum Sententiarum", dist.
XX, quaes. I, dubitatio 1, lateralis, *In Libros Sententiarum*. [(Venetiis: apud
Zilletum, 1581; facsimile reprint, Frankfurt: Minerva, 1968), 155–56. (Tr)]

[28] D. Durandi a Sancto Porciano *Super Sententias Theologicas Petri Lombardi
Commentariorum Libri Quatuor*. [(Paris: apud Joannem Roigny, 1539), libri quarti
dist. 44, quaes. 7. (Tr)]

[29] Ibid., libri secundi dist. 20, quaes. 2.

[30] Alexander of Hales, *Summa Theologica*, liber II, pars I, inquisitio IV, "De
Homine", tractatus II, sectio II, titulus II, quaes. II, caput IV (Quaracchi: College
of St. Bonaventure, 1928), vol. II 623–26; and ibid., tractatus III, quaes. II,
membrum I, capita I–IV, 698–711. (Tr)

[31] St. Augustine, "De Civitate Dei Libri XXII", bk. XIV, chap. 26. [PL 41,
col. 434; quoted in Thomas Aquinas, ST 1a 98, 2 ad 4. Further references to this

Augustine insisted, however, in a sentence omitted by Thomas, that we can no longer imagine to ourselves such a form of intercourse because we have no experience of it. Earlier he had stated: "Some people today are so ignorant of the happiness that existed in paradise that they can think of no other way of begetting children than that . . . which they themselves have experienced" (*De civ Dei*, bk. XIV, chap. 21). Augustine was, in fact, convinced that the sexual characteristics of the body were essentially the same in paradise as they are today: "To deny it would be folly" (ibid., chap. 22). The only difference lay for him in the fact that in paradise sexual activity was motivated by free will and controlled by reason (ibid., chaps. 23–24). But he was compelled to admit that a form of sexual intercourse that would leave the female organs intact is beyond the ken of modern man. He arrived at this conclusion, however, only because he did not see how his earlier view[32] was compatible with the existence of genuine sexuality in paradise.

c) Perhaps these theologians would have done better to claim only the fact—and omit every graphic description of it—that, in man's original state, virginity and *bodily* (we do not say "sexual") fecundity could have coexisted. What is essential in their arguments can be summarized in two sentences. The first is negative: Since paradise is the realm of virginity, marriage, as we know it, has no place there; it came into being only after man's fall into sin. The second is positive: Men would have multiplied in paradise in a way that the Fathers term "spiritual" and compare with the way in which the angels multiply, but which does not, for that reason, unconditionally exclude the cooperation of the body. This manner of multiplication is no longer comprehensible to fallen man. It is better simply to admit our ignorance of it.

The latter theory is boldly advanced by Gregory of Nyssa:[33] "If

---

work of Augustine (henceforth *De civ Dei*) will be given in parentheses in the text. For an English translation of the complete work, see St. Augustine, *The City of God*, trans. Gerald G. Walsh, S.J., and Mother Grace Monahan, O.S.U., in *The Fathers of the Church*, vols. 13–15, ed. Roy J. Deferrari et al. (New York: Fathers of the Church, Inc., 1952). This series will henceforth be cited with volume and publication date as *Fathers*. (Tr)]

[32] St. Augustine, "De Genesi contra Manichaeos Libri II", bk. I, chap. 19. [PL 34, col. 187. Further references to this work (henceforth *De Gen c Man*) will be given in parentheses in the text. (Tr)]

[33] For evidence that this theory did not originate with Gregory, but had been generally known since the time of Clement of Alexandria, see the latter's

we had not changed for the worse and lost the dignity that made us equal to the angels, we would not have needed marriage in order to multiply. Rather, the same mode of increase that is proper to the angels—a mode that does indeed exist, however unutterable and incomprehensible by human conjectures—would also have enabled those who are 'but a little less than the angels' to increase mankind to the measure determined by the wisdom of the Creator."[34] In providing man even in paradise with the requisite sex organs, God was merely anticipating the coming fall into sin. Gregory of Nyssa thereupon compares man's nature in its original state to those works of art "in which, to the consternation of the beholder, the artist has sketched two faces upon a single head" (ibid., chap. 18) and concludes by arguing that man is free either to subordinate the lower part of his nature to the higher or to sacrifice the higher for the sake of the lower.

St. John Chrysostom is of the same opinion: "Adam knew his wife. And when do you think that happened? Only after they had fallen into sin and had lost paradise did they begin to make use of their sexuality. Before the Fall, they imitated the angels; there was no question of sexual life."[35] "Virginity existed in the beginning, before marriage; marriage became necessary and began later; but it would not have been necessary if Adam had remained obedient. How, then, would so many thousands of human beings have come

---

Stromata, bk. III, chap. 7. [PG 8, cols. 1161–64. For an English translation of the *Stromata* and other works of Clement of Alexandria, see *The Ante-Nicene Fathers*, ed. Alexander Roberts and James Donaldson, vol. II, *Fathers of the Second Century*, arranged by A. Cleveland Coxe (New York: Scribner, 1913), 163–604. This series will henceforth be cited with volume and date of publication as *Ante-Nicene*. It should be noted, however, that in *Ante-Nicene* the translation of *Stromata*, bk. III, is in Latin, not English. For an English translation of this book, see John Oulton and Henry Chadwick, *Alexandrian Christianity*, in *The Library of Christian Classics*, vol. II (Philadelphia: Westminster, 1954), 40–92. (Tr)]

[34] Gregory of Nyssa, "De hominis opificio", chap. 17. [PG 44, cols. 189–90. For an English translation of this work, see Gregory of Nyssa, "On the Making of Man", trans. Henry Austin Wilson, in *A Select Library of the Nicene and Post-Nicene Fathers of the Christian Church*, series 2, vol. V, eds. Philip Schaff and Henry Wace (New York: Scribner, 1917). This series will henceforth be cited with volume and date of publication as *Post-Nicene*. (Tr)]

[35] St. John Chrysostom, "Homiliae in Genesin", hom. XVIII, sec. 4. [PG 53, col. 153. (Tr)]

into existence? If this question troubles you, I pose an answering one: Whence did Adam and Eve derive existence without the intervention of marriage? What, then, you respond: Are all men to be born in this manner? In this or some other manner, I reply; I cannot say more. Only this is certain: that God did not need marriage in order to multiply men on this earth."[36]

Maximus[37] refers explicitly to Gregory of Nyssa, and adds his own comment that it was only after man's fall into sin, when the law of passion had penetrated human nature, that there entered God's plan the method of generation that is associated on the one hand with the concupiscence of the flesh and on the other with death (ibid., quaes. 61). "In fact, it was the original will of God that we should not be born out of the fleeting pleasure of bodily union; it was the transgression of the law that caused marriage to be introduced."[38]

John of Damascus expressed the view that the first human had been created "as male", but since God, "who knew all things, knew also that man would fall into sin and be subject to death, . . . he created out of him a female . . . so that the human race might continue to exist after the Fall by the begetting of offspring. . . . Creation is the manner of man's first formation by God; begetting is the descent of one from another made necessary by the sentence of death resulting from the Fall."[39] "But perhaps someone will ask: What, then, does 'male and female' mean, and 'increase and multiply'? To which we reply that 'increase and multiply' certainly does not mean increasing by marital intercourse. God could have increased the human race by some other means if they had kept the commandment unbroken. But God, who knows all things before they come to pass, saw by his will that they would sin and be condemned to death. He therefore created them from the beginning male and female and commanded them to increase and multiply" (ibid., bk. IV, chap. 24).[40]

[36] Idem., "De Virginitate Liber Unus", sec. XVII. [PG 48, col. 546. (Tr)]

[37] Maximus the Confessor, "Quaestiones ad Thalassium de Scriptura Sacra", quaes. 59, PG 90, col. 613c.

[38] Idem., "Quaestiones et Dubia", interrogatio III, PG 90, col. 788a–b.

[39] St. John of Damascus, *Fons Scientiae*, pt III, "Expositio Accurata Fidei Orthodoxae", bk. II, chap. 30. [PG 94, cols. 969–80. For an English translation of this work, see St. John of Damascus, "The Orthodox Faith" (pt. III of *The Fount of Knowledge*), trans. Frederic H. Chase, Jr., in *Fathers*, vol. 37 (1958). (Tr)]

[40] Cf. also Euthymius Zigabenus, "Commentarius in Psalmos Davidis", Psalmus

St. Jerome says the same thing: "About Adam and Eve it must be said that before the Fall they were virgins in paradise; but after the Fall, when they were no longer in paradise, they were immediately married."[41] "If you object that before they sinned there was a division of sex into male and female, and that they could have come together without sin, it is uncertain what *might* have happened. For we cannot know the judgments of God and freely anticipate his sentence. What *did* happen is clear enough—that they who remained virgins in paradise were joined together when they were expelled from paradise" (ibid., sec. 29; italics added). Jerome insists emphatically that in the new Christian man "there is neither male nor female" (Gal 3:28); that "the image of the Creator does not indulge in sexual intercourse" (ibid., sec. 16). "But since he says 'Be fruitful and multiply and fill the earth,' it was necessary first to plant the forest and let it grow so that it might afterwards be cut down. And at the same time we must consider the meaning of the words 'fill the earth'. Marriage fills the earth, virginity fills paradise" (ibid., sec. 16). In answer to the question as to why, then, the sexual organs were created, Jerome points to the manhood of Christ, which was the most perfect ever created, but which chose not to make use of the sex it assuredly possessed, as witness the circumcision, but rather to sacrifice it for the sake of the kingdom of heaven (ibid., sec. 36).

Sometime in the years 388–390, Augustine had had similar thoughts: " 'Be fruitful and multiply': It is permitted us to interpret these words spiritually in such a way that it is credible that they were converted into carnal fecundity after man's fall" (*De Gen c Man* I, 19). About the year 400, in the *Confessions*,[42] he, like Gregory of Nyssa, distinguished two directions that the act of procreation might take: procreation from below, like that of the animals, and procreation from above, as was intended for mankind, thus opposing a mode of procreation in which the body played a

---

L, PG 128, cols. 550–62; Procopius of Gaza, "Commentarius in Genesin", chap. 4, PG 87, cols. 233–62.

[41] St. Jerome, "Adversus Jovinianum Libri Duo", bk. I, sec. 16. [PL 23, col. 246. Further references to this work will be given in parentheses in the text. For an English translation of this and other works of St. Jerome, see *The Principal Works of St. Jerome*, trans. W. H. Fremantle et al., *Post-Nicene*, vol. VI (1954). (Tr)]

[42] St. Augustine, "Confessionum Libri XIII", bk. XIII, chap. 24. [PL 32, cols. 860–61. For an English translation of this work, see St. Augustine, *Confessions*, trans. Vernon J. Bourke, *Fathers*, vol. 21 (1953). (Tr)]

primary role and the spirit a secondary one to a mode in which the spirit played the primary role and the body a secondary one. In 401, when he attempted, in *De bono coniugali*, to distinguish the value of marriage from that of virginity, he began with the observation: ". . . The first natural bond of human society is man and wife. For God did not create them separately and join them as if they were strangers, but he made the one from the other, indicating also the power of union by the side whence the woman was drawn and formed (Gen 2:21–22). They are joined to each other by their sides who walk together and notice together where they are walking. A consequence is the union of society in the children who are the one worthy fruit, not of sexual intercourse, but of the joining of male and female. For there could have been in both sexes, even without such intercourse, a certain friendly and genuine union in which one ruled and the other obeyed. It is not necessary for us now to examine and express a final opinion on the question as to how the offspring of the first man and woman, whom God had blessed, saying, 'Be fruitful and multiply and fill the earth,' might have come into existence if Adam and Eve had not sinned, since their bodies deserved the condition of death because they did sin, *and there could be no intercourse except of mortal bodies.*"[43] Augustine then proceeded to enumerate three theories regarding the manner of procreation in paradise, the first of which ("they would have had children in some other way" [ibid., chap. 2]) he accepts without criticism, whereas he seems to reject the second, which is purely allegorical, and the third, which is based on the conditional nature of their immortality. He concluded this part of his argument with the comment: "We now say this: According to that condition of birth and death that we know and in which we were created, the marriage of male and female is something good" (ibid., chap. 3).[44]

The teaching of the Fathers of the Church and of the Scholastics can be summarized in this way: They strove to explain in one way or another the union of virginity and procreation in man's original

[43] St. Augustine, "De Bono Conjugali Liber Unus", chap. 1, PL 40, col. 373; italics added. For an English translation of this work, see St. Augustine, "The Good of Marriage", *Treatises on Marriage and Other Subjects*, trans. Charles T. Wilcox, *Fathers*, vol. 27 (1955). [Tr]

[44] Cf. Michael Müller, *Die Lehre des hl. Augustinus von der Paradiesesehe und ihre Auswirkung in der Sexualität des 12. und 13. Jahrhunderts bis Thomas von Aquin* (Regensburg: Pustet, 1954), 19–32.

state, while being more concerned about virginity than about procreation. For us, their various interpretations are significant only insofar as they express their efforts to find an explanation of the one fact that was indisputable to them. If we want to preserve what is of permanent value in their explanations, therefore, we will expressly emphasize that the difference of the sexes belonged beyond the shadow of a doubt to God's original intention in creating man. Consequently, it cannot be regarded as brought about by man's later fall into sin. Rather, the difference is part of the *imago Dei*: "Let us make man in our image and likeness. . . . In the image of God he created them. Male and female he created them" (Gen 1:26–27). If this were not so, Christ could neither have pointed to the relationship of the sexes to describe his mysterious union with the Church, nor have given to the sacrament of marriage the power and the real possibility of symbolizing this perfect relationship in the relationship of the sexes. More will be said on this subject when we speak of the married state.

3. As a creature, man is finite. But because God gave him the power of submitting his spirit to the grace of mission and of letting his body be enveloped by his spirit, his finiteness was open to God. Once he had freed himself from God, however, and had made a goal of what should have been a means, his finiteness appeared openly in all its nakedness. Earthly life, when it is no longer hidden in eternal life, becomes hopelessly immured in its own finiteness. The wall that encloses it is *death*. Through sin death came into the world (Rom 5:12), and through death, anxiety about the flame of life in this world, imperiled as it is from within and without. For death is not just the sudden ending of life. It is also the corroding illness, the aging, the blunting of one's powers, the weariness, the disgust with boredom and barrenness, with the transitoriness and hopelessness of earthly life. Because of man, all nature is affected by this decay (Rom 8:20). The abundance of paradise has been exhausted. Because of Adam, the earth is cursed and will bear henceforth only thorns and thistles. Man will till the ground in the sweat of his brow and will eat his bread in toil until he returns to the earth from which he was taken (Gen 3:17–19). By this curse, which punishes man's concupiscence, Adam and Eve were condemned to what they had

chosen: *to private ownership*. In paradise, they lived in the bountifulness of God's grace from heaven, to which the bountifulness of the garden was, as it were, earth's answer. Because they had an abundance of all they needed, they gave as little thought to procuring anything for themselves as they did to covering their nakedness. They lived in a state that was at once *perfect riches and perfect poverty*. Poverty, because they possessed nothing for themselves that they did not receive from God either directly or indirectly through nature and that they did not willingly and gratefully return to him. Since they felt neither indigence nor want, they needed nothing for themselves that they would have had to conceal or withhold from one another. Only after their eyes had been opened by sin and they saw that they were naked did they begin to make coverings for themselves—each his own, thus marking the beginning of private property. Later, God himself will confirm the concept of private ownership by clothing them with the skins of animals.

Private ownership is, in itself, no more evil than critical intellect, freedom of will or the feeling of shame. Nevertheless, it belongs, like them, to man's existence after the Fall. These realities had been, as it were, suspended for man by the grace of his original state and destined to fulfill their role as inner, unheeded functions of a higher being, to work unseen in grace. Only when the abundance of paradise had yielded to scarcity and man's struggle for existence had begun did the painful necessity of private ownership become unavoidable. Freedom of will, in a love that needs its possessions only to give them away, was replaced by the pressure to divide "justly" the little that man possessed: pressure in the family, where the wife—instead of the unconstrained relationship that had existed between Adam and the helpmate given him by God (Gen 2:18) and with whom he formed one flesh (Gen 2:24)—was placed under the dominion of her husband (Gen 3:16); pressure in procuring the necessities of life, since Adam, by the terms of the curse, had to accumulate, save, worry and plan; pressure, finally, in the political community, where the close association of so many individuals engaged in procuring for themselves the staples of existence inevitably resulted in those conflicts between *mine* and *thine* that can be resolved only by new pressures of authority and power.

It is surprising that the utterances of classical theologians on this subject are so little known to more recent scholars of natural law within the Catholic Church. This fact—which often leads them, for allegedly apologetic reasons, to misconstrue and distort the whole range of patristic and scholastic literature at least to the time of Thomas Aquinas,[45] while such impartial researches as Carlyle[46] and, for the most part, also Troeltsch[47] are able to assess it correctly—has its basis in a concept of natural law that became possible only with the post-Reformation hypothesis of a *status naturae purae* [state of pure nature] that was to be distinguished as a state in its own right from all the concrete states defined above: original state, state of grace and state of redemption. As we shall see, the application of this concept of nature to earlier times led to deep-seated misunderstandings.

If we want to outline the uniformly common teaching of the Christian theology of private ownership up to and even beyond Thomas Aquinas (and this can be done without undue constraint since precisely in this area the various interpretations diverge only

[45] Von Balthasar attributes this observation to Otto Schilling, but without further identification of the source. The most likely source, I think, is Schilling's *Die christlichen Soziallehren* in *Der katholische Gedanke*, vol. XVI (Cologne-Munich: Oratoriums-Verlag, 1926). This book, which is primarily a critique of the first part of Ernst Troeltsch's *Die Soziallehren der christlichen Kirchen und Gruppen* (see below, note 47), attributes the "many errors and misconstructions" in Troeltsch's treatment of the social teachings of the Fathers of the Church to his reliance, not on the patristic texts themselves, but on the "secondary literature" with its many contradictions (Preface, 4–5). Cf. also Schilling's *Die Staats- und Soziallehre des hl. Thomas von Aquin*, Görres-Gesellschaft zur Pflege der Wissenschaft im katholischen Deutschland, Veröffentlichungen der Sektion für Rechts- und Sozialwissenschaft, Heft 41 (Paderborn: Schöningh, 1923), 274. [Tr]

[46] Robert Warrand Carlyle and Alexander James Carlyle, *A History of Medieval Political Theory in the West*, 6 vols. (Edinburgh: Blackwood, 1903–1936). [Further references to this work will be given in parentheses in the text. (Tr)]

[47] Ernst Troeltsch, *Gesammelte Schriften*, vol. I, *Die Soziallehren der christlichen Kirchen und Gruppen*. [(Tübingen: Mohr, 1922). For an English translation of this *work, see Ernst Troeltsch, The Social Teachings of the Christian Churches*, trans. Olive Wyon, 2 vols. (New York: Macmillan, 1931). (Tr)]

slightly and are for the most part complementary to one another),
we can say with Justinian and Isidore of Seville:[48] In *natural law* [*ius
naturale*], and that means in the law that governed man in paradise,
there is no such thing as private ownership. It is a provision of the
law of nations [*ius gentium*], which came to be valid in the state
created by man's sin. It is not significant that the designations *ius
naturale*/*ius gentium* are late borrowings from the language of jurists;
the concept itself has existed from the earliest days of Christian
literature. (We are discussing here only the question of private
ownership. For a discussion of man's freedom and equality, we
would take an analogous approach; for a discussion of political
order as such, a somewhat different one.) From the beginning, the
striking indifference and occasional hostility of the New Testament
to mammon, Jesus' counsel regarding poverty, the common ownership of property in the early Christian community in Jerusalem,
and the praise bestowed on almsgiving caused the first Christian
thinkers to distinguish between an absolute and a relative assessment of riches and private ownership. According to the absolute
assessment, they appeared as that which ought not to exist, as that
which was not originally intended by God; according to the relative
assessment, as that which was partly "permitted", partly "willed"
by God as a lesser evil than sinful avarice. Carlyle, and later
Troeltsch, have shown that the contemporary Stoic philosophy of
law and politics afforded a marked parallel to these assessments
of early Christianity. The Stoics, too, envisioned an ideal primitive condition of mankind founded on an innate law of universal
humanitarianism and selflessness, freedom, equality and community of goods, in contrast to man's present condition, which has
been brought about by lust for power and possessions and by the
self-love that made private ownership, slavery, coercive government and obligatory laws necessary as a protective measure.[49]
Depending on whether they were more intent on the "way of the

---

[48] Cf. *The Institutes of Justinian*, arranged and translated by Thomas Collett
Sandars (Westport: Greenwood, 1970), lib. I, titulus II; *Digesta Iustiniani Augusti*,
ed. Theodor Mommsen, vol. I (Berlin: Weidmann, 1868), lib. I, sec. 1, 3–4, p. 1;
Isidore of Seville, "Etymologiarum Libri XX", bk. V, chap. 4, PL 82, col. 199.
Further references to this work (henceforth *Etym*) will be given in parentheses in
the text. [Tr]
[49] Cf. Ernst Troeltsch, "Naturrecht", in *Die Religion in Geschichte und Gegen-
wart*, 5 vols. (Tübingen: Mohr, 1909–1913), vol. 4, col. 699.

commandments" or the "way of the counsels", Christians could, however, as could the Stoics in their way, reconstruct the original order of law from the existing one, if not perfectly, at least approximately. It is, of course, possible to find in the works of the Fathers of the Church anti-Gnostic and anti-Manichaean statements to the effect that neither the state nor private ownership nor even slavery itself is the expression of an evil principle or of sin; that otherwise Christ and the apostles would not have given the command to subject oneself to political authority, or to be content with one's state in life. Rather, they would have made it a command, not a counsel, to sell all that one possesses.[50] "But", as Carlyle notes, "when we have recognized this fact, we must also observe that this merely means that the Church accepted the institution of property as being in accordance with the actual conditions of life, just as it accepted the institution of slavery or coercive government: It does not mean that the Church considered private property to belong to the natural or primitive condition of human life" (Carlyle and Carlyle I, 136).

Ambrose offers the clearest formulation: "They considered this to be the form of justice: One should hold common, that is public, goods as public, and private goods as private. But this is not according to nature; for nature pours forth all things for all men in common. . . . Nature, therefore, is the source of common right; greed has shaped private right."[51] Cicero had said: "There is, however, no such thing as private ownership established by nature."[52] To quote Ambrose again: "Consider the birds of the air! They rejoice in the abundance of nourishing food available to them without toil only because they know nothing of the presumption that

[50] Cf. among others, St. Augustine, "De Moribus Ecclesiae Catholicae, et De Moribus Manichaeorum Libri II", bk. I, chap. 35, PL 32, cols. 1342–44; ibid., "Contra Adimantum Manichaei Discipulum Liber Unus", bk. I, chap. 20, PL 42, cols. 164–66; St. Hilary, "Commentarius in Evangelium Matthaei", chap. 19, sec. 9, PL 9, cols. 1026–27; St. Ambrose, "Epistolae in Duas Classes Distributae", ep. LXIII, sec. 92, PL 16, col. 1266.

[51] St. Ambrose, "De Officiis Ministrorum Libri Tres", bk. I, chap. 28. [Sec. 131, PL 16, col. 67. Further references to this work (henceforth *De Off*) will be given in parentheses in the text. For an English translation of this and other works of St. Ambrose, see *The Principal Works of St. Ambrose*, trans. H. de Romestin et al., *Post-Nicene*, vol. X (1896). (Tr)]

[52] Cicero, "De Officiis", bk. I, sec. VII. [Trans. Walter Miller, *The Loeb Classical Library* (Cambridge: Harvard University Press, 1947).(Tr)]

would lay claim by a kind of private ownership to what is proffered as the common food of all. We, on the contrary, lose the common gifts because we make certain ones our own."[53] "God our Lord wanted this earth to be the common possession of all men and to offer its fruits to all; but greed has fragmented the right of ownership."[54] The fundamental fact is always this: All earthly goods belong to God. What seems to be ours does not in truth belong to us. It is God's property.[55] On this point, Augustine queries: "Whence does one who possesses derive what he possesses? Is it not by human law? For by divine law the earth and its fullness are the Lord's. . . . But in human law it is said: 'This is my estate; this is my home; this is my servant.' "[56] Zeno of Verona comments: "But, you say, it is right for me to keep what is mine. . . . First of all, O excellent Christian, I desire to know what is yours since all things are common to those who fear the Lord."[57] Gregory the Great expresses the same opinion: "In vain do they consider themselves innocent who claim as their private property the common gift of God."[58] In the state of innocence, that presumption was

---

[53] St. Ambrose, "Expositionis in Evangelium secundum Lucam Libri X", bk. VII, sec. 124. [PL 15, col. 1819. In quoting this text in German, von Balthasar has paraphrased it slightly. I have retained his reading in my translation. Further references to this work (henceforth *In Luc*) will be given in parentheses in the text. (Tr)]

[54] St. Ambrose, "In Psalmam CXVIII Expositio", sermo octavus, sec. 22. [PL 15, col. 1372. (Tr)]

[55] Cf. Tertullian, "De Patientia", chap. VII [PL 1, cols. 1351–52 (Tr)]; Commodian, "Instructiones adversus Gentium Deos pro Christiana Disciplina: per Litteras Versuum Primas", xxix. [PL 5, col. 225. (Tr)]

[56] St. Augustine, "In Joannis Evangelium Tractatus CXXIV". [Tractatus VI, sec. 25, PL 35, col. 1437. For an English translation of this work, see St. Augustine, *Homilies on the Gospel of John*, trans. John Gibb and James Innes, in *A Selected Library of the Nicene and Post-Nicene Fathers of the Christian Church*, series 1, vol. VII, ed. Phillip Schaff (New York: Scribner, 1908). This series will henceforth be cited with volume and date of publication as *Nicene*. (Tr)]

[57] Zeno of Verona, "Tractatus", bk. I, tractatus 3, sec. 6. [PL 11, col. 287. (Tr)]

[58] Gregory the Great, "Liber Regulae Pastoralis", pt. III, chap. 21. [PL 77, col. 87. Further references to this work (henceforth *Reg Past*) will be given in parentheses in the text. For an English translation, see St. Gregory the Great, *Pastoral Care*, trans. Henry Davis, S.J., in *Ancient Christian Writers*, vol. XI, eds.

unknown that would allow man to take for himself something that was held in common. As Chrysostom, the greatest representative of "patristic communism", remarks: ". . . The chilling expression 'mine and thine' " did not exist in those days. "It is the source of contention, the source of trouble."[59] And yet, with equal justification Clement of Alexandria and Lactantius predicate the existence of private property even in the state of innocence since men could take what they needed without experiencing either envy or privation. But they did not take in order to deprive others; on the contrary, they were so generous that they placed all they possessed at the disposal of others. This is the "common life" in which Lactantius sees no antithesis to private ownership;[60] this is the paradisal attitude that Clement recommends and describes as the absence of every distinction, not only between rich and poor, but also between private and common ownership.[61] It would be wrong, however, to set Lactantius and Clement in opposition to the other Fathers of the Church by seeing in their writings even the rudiments of a theory that private ownership is justifiable as a "natural right", for, as a matter of fact, even Chrysostom and Ambrose had no disagreement with their teaching. The *ius naturale* of man's original state was not the absence of possessions as a negative characteristic; as Isidore notes in the *Etymologies*, "natural law is . . . the common possession of all" (bk. V, chap. 4). To understand this sentence correctly despite its ambiguity,[62] we must disregard the dialectic between private property and communism that necessarily arises

---

Johannes Quasten and Joseph Plumpe (Westminster: Newman, 1950). This series will henceforth be cited with volume and date of publication as ACW. (Tr)]

[59] St. John Chrysostom, "Homiliae XVIII in Epistolam primam ad Timotheum", hom. XII, sec. 4, PG 62, col. 564. For an English translation of this and other homilies, see St. John Chrysostom, "Homilies on the Epistles of St. Paul the Apostle to Timothy, Titus and Philemon", Oxford translation revised by Philip Schaff, in *Nicene*, vol. XIII, 399–557 (1914). [Tr]

[60] Lactantius, "Divinarum Institutionum Libri Septem", bk. V, chap. 5. [PL 6, cols. 564–67. For an English translation of this work, see Lactantius, *The Divine Institutes*, bks. I–VII, trans. Sr. Mary Frances McDonald, O.P., in *Fathers*, vol. 49 (1964). (Tr)]

[61] Clement of Alexandria, "Quis dives salvetur?" [In PG 9, cols. 603–52. For an English translation of this and other works of St. Clement, see note 33. (Tr)]

[62] Cf. Carlyle (vol. I, 142–44) [who points out that Isidore's phrase *communis omnium possessio* may mean either "the common possession of all things" (i.e., to

within the *ius gentium* and try to imagine the synthesis—impossible
in this world, but once wholly possible in the world of the *ius
naturale*—of possession and nonpossession, of "riches" and "poverty",
that is clearly predicated in patristic thought as a whole, as witness the fact that the sin of avarice is uniformly depicted there
as the source of (limiting) private ownership in the sense of the
ius gentium. In general, Justinian's *Digest* limits the sphere of the *ius
gentium* as follows: "By this *ius gentium*, wars are declared, nations
are formed, kingdoms are founded, domains are established,
boundaries are set to fields. . . ."[63] Isidore adds: "The *ius gentium*
is [concerned with] the occupation of habitable land, the
erection of buildings and fortifications, wars, captivity, servitude
. . ." (*Etym* V, 6). With Ambrose (*De Off* I, 28), theologians
attribute the transition from the *ius naturale* to the *ius gentium*
to man's "avarice" [*usurpatio*]—or, to use St. Basil's term, to
his "appropriation" [πρόληψις][64] for his own use of goods that
had been given for all. In almost mythic language, St. Gregory
of Nazianzen describes how the equality that had originally existed
between freedom and servitude, riches and poverty, was ruptured
by this means.[65]

The fact that the origin of private ownership coincides so
exactly with man's fall into sin gives rise again and again to
the dangerous query that ranges backwards from one's own
apparently unimpeachable possessions to what has been inherited
from parents and forebears and ultimately to that first ancestor
whose possessions were acquired unlawfully. This thought is
propounded by Irenaeus: "All of us receive a greater or smaller
number of possessions from the mammon of injustice. Whence
comes the house in which we dwell, the clothes we wear, the
vessels we use, and everything else that serves us in our daily

the exclusion of private ownership) or "a form of property common to all men"
(hence not necessarily excluding private ownership) (Tr)].

[63] *Digesta Iustiniani Augusti*, lib. I, sec. 1, 5. [In Mommsen, p. 2. For full
bibliographical information, see note 48. (Tr)]

[64] St. Basil, *Homiliae et Sermones*, "Homilia in illud dictum Lucae: Destruam
horrea mea, et majora aedificabo: itemque de avaritia", sec. 7, PG 31, col. 275–76.

[65] Gregory of Nazianzen, "Orationes", oratio XIV, "De Pauperum Amore",
PG 35, cols. 889–92.

lives if not from that which we gained either through avarice while we were yet pagans or through inheritance of what was unjustly acquired by pagan parents, relatives or friends?"[66] In like manner Chrysostom asks: "Tell me where you got your wealth. You owe it to another. And this other, to whom does he owe it? To his grandfather, you may say, or to his father. Will you be able now, following the tree of genealogy, to give proof that this possession was acquired justly? You cannot. On the contrary, its beginning, its root, must lie in injustice. Why? Because God did not in the beginning create one man rich and another poor . . . but gave to all men the same earth as their possession."[67] So widespread was this view that in the thirteenth century William of Auxerre was still pondering in the *Summa Aurea* "whether he who was the first to appropriate something to himself committed a serious sin". He answers with prudent ambivalence: if he did so out of greed, yes; but not if he did so on the reasonable supposition that the common possession of goods was harmful for man in the present condition of fallen nature.[68] From the distance of time, William no longer understood that for the Fathers of the Church man's fall into sin was coincidental not only with the loss of common owner-ship, but also with the beginning of avarice.

The consequences are manifold. Since the division of goods that became necessary after the Fall took place, according to Augustine, under the *ius imperatorum* [law of emperors], it followed that private ownership, too, was only a relative right under this law: What has been given can, under certain circum-

[66] St. Irenaeus, "Contra Haereses Libri Quinque", bk. IV, chap. 30, sec. 1. [PG 7, col. 1065. For an English translation of this work, see *The Apostolic Fathers with Justin Martyr and Irenaeus*, arranged by A. Cleveland Coxe, in *Ante-Nicene*, vol. I (1913), 315–567. (Tr)]

[67] St. John Chrysostom, "Homiliae XVIII in Epistolam primam ad Timo-theum", hom. XII. [Sec. 4, PG 62, cols. 562–63. For an English translation of this and other homilies of St. John Chrysostom, see note 59. (Tr)]

[68] [William of Auxerre (Guillermus Altissiodorensis), *Summa Aurea*, liber tertius, septimus tractatus, primum capitulum, secunda quaestio; quoted in] Martin Grabmann, *Mittelalterliches Geistesleben*, vol. I, *Von Gratian bis Thomas* (Munich: Hueber,1926), 73.

stances, be taken away, particularly if the individual does not use his right properly: "For that, certainly, is not another's property that is possessed by law. But that is possessed by law that is possessed justly, and that is possessed justly that is possessed rightly. What is possessed wrongly belongs to another."[69] Moreover, it is not just an act of love and of supererogation to strive for the equalization of goods through gifts and the giving of alms; it is also a duty. "It is just, therefore, if you claim as your private property something that has been given to the human race in common, that you distribute at least some of it to the poor."[70] Ambrosiaster comments: "This justice, then, is called mercy. . . . He is just who does not keep for himself alone what he knows has been given to all."[71] Gregory the Great voices this opinion: "For when we administer the necessities of life to the poor, we return to them what is theirs; we do not bestow what is ours, but pay a debt of justice rather than perform a work of mercy" (*Reg Past* III, 21). In a word, Christians will strive to return, insofar as possible, to the *ius naturale* that prevailed in man's original state, modeling themselves on the great example of the early community in Jerusalem, where "not one of them said that anything he possessed was his own" (Acts 4:32). Echoes of this sentence

[69] St. Augustine, "Epistolae", ep. 153, chap. 6, sec. 26, PL 33, col. 665. Cf. also, ep. 31, secs. 5–6, ibid., col. 124; "In Joannis Evangelium Tractatus CXXIV", tractatus VI, secs. 25–26, PL 35, cols. 1436–37; "Sermonum Classes Quatuor", sermo L, chap. 2, PL 38, col. 327. [For an English translation of all the letters, see St. Augustine, *Letters*, trans. Sister Wilfrid Parsons, 5 vols., in *Fathers*, vols. 12 (1951), 18 (1953), 20 (1953), 30 (1955), 32 (1956). (Tr)]

[70] St. Ambrose, "In Psalmum CXVIII Expositio", sermo octavus, sec. 22. [PL 15, col. 1372. (Tr)]

[71] Ambrosiaster, *Ad Opera S. Ambrosii Appendix: Commentaria in Epistolas B. Pauli*, "In Epistolam B. Pauli ad Corinthios Secundam", commentary on 2 Cor 9:9. [PL 17, col. 332. It was Erasmus who gave the name Ambrosiaster to the unknown author of this commentary on the epistles of St. Paul, which had previously been ascribed to St. Ambrose. Cf. Joseph Hugh Crehan, "Ambrosiaster", in the *New Catholic Encyclopedia* (New York: McGraw-Hill, 1967), vol. I, 376–77. (Tr)]

are to be found in the *Didache*,[72] in the *Epistle of Barnabas*,[73] in Justin[74] and in Tertullian,[75] where it leads, not to a demand for the obligatory holding of goods in common, but, as it does in the Acts of the Apostles, to the deeper ethical conviction that "the multitude of believers" must be "of one heart and one soul" so as to have "all things in common" (Acts 4:32). This explains the extreme efforts made by the Fathers of the Church to restore the *ius naturale* on the basis of Christ's restoration of the grace of man's original state. When Chrysostom challenges his congregation in stirring homilies to hold all goods in common and to renounce all private ownership, he is speaking, not as a political economist under the *ius gentium*, but as one who loves and believes, as one who appeals to the generosity of pure, magnanimous love in the hearts of his hearers, as one, in fact, who is himself so deeply imbued with what the Gospel expresses only as a counsel that he believes he can assume the same disposition in all who hear him: "I do not know how I have come to demand such high perfection of those who believe they are doing a great thing if they give from their possessions even a small alms. Let my words, then, be directed only to those who are perfect. But to those who are less perfect, I say: 'Share your goods!' "[76] Actually,

---

[72] *Doctrina [Didache] duodecim Apostolorum, Barnabae Epistula*, ed. Theodor Klauser, Florilegium Patristicum 1 (Bonn: Peter Hanstein, 1940), IV, 8. [For a translation of these two works, see *The Didache, The Epistle of Barnabas, The Epistles and the Martyrdom of St. Polycarp, The Fragments of Papias, The Epistle to Diognetus*, trans. James A. Kleist, S.J., ACW, vol. VI (1948). (Tr)]

[73] See note 72.

[74] Justin, "Apologia Prima pro Christianis", sec. 14, PG 6, col. 347; cf. also sec. 67, cols. 430–31. [For a translation of this and other works of St. Justin, see *The Apostolic Fathers with Justin Martyr and Irenaeus*, arranged by A. Cleveland Coxe, in *Ante-Nicene*, vol. I (1913), 159–306. (Tr)]

[75] Tertullian, "Apologeticus adversus Gentes pro Christianis", series I, chap. 39. [PL 1, col. 535. For an English translation of this and other works of Tertullian, see *Latin Christianity: Its Founder, Tertullian, Ante-Nicene* III (1913). (Tr)]

[76] St. John Chrysostom, "Homiliae XLIV in Epistolam primam ad Corinthios", hom. XV, sec. 6. [PG 61, col. 130. For a translation of this and other homilies of St. John Chrysostom, see St. John Chrysostom, *Homilies on the*

he was aware that "those in monasteries live now as all the faithful once lived."[77] Nor is it entirely contrary to the spirit of the Gospel if considerations of the effects of such generosity and its possible reward are not wholly lacking, for the Gospel itself promises a hundredfold even in this life to those who leave all things, provided they do so for the sake of the kingdom of heaven. Ambrose is right when he says: "Avarice alone is the cause of our poverty" (*In Luc* VII, 124).

By way of summary, we can say that not only the teachings of the Fathers but also their innermost intuitions about life were determined by the distinction of a primary and a secondary level of "natural law". "It was not so from the beginning" (Mt 19:8). If there was never a question of a purely communistic movement in the Church, this only proves how well aware the Church is that it is not charged with leading the "present age" into the "coming" one by external means; how little attraction the qualities that mark sectarian and modern economic communism had for the primitive Church;[78] and how thoroughly this Church was impregnated by the word of the apostle that we must possess as though not possessing (1 Cor 7:30) because the present world is neither the one originally intended by God nor the final one.

This intuitive concern for poverty on the part of the Church Fathers corresponds exactly to their concern for virginity; only their dependence on Roman jurists and Stoic philosophers in the case of poverty prevents a complete parallel (because, in the case of virginity, the union of husband and wife and the procreation of children were regarded as part of the original content of natural law).[79] In the Middle Ages, and even more conspicuously in modern times, this fundamental life-value yielded to the secondary

---

Epistles of Paul to the Corinthians, Oxford translation revised by Talbot W. Chambers, *Nicene* XII (1905). (Tr)]

[77] St. John Chrysostom, "Homiliae LV in Acta Apostolorum", hom. XI, sec. 3, PG 60, col. 97.

[78] Cf. Edgar Salin, *Geschichte der Volkswirtschaftslehre*, 1st ed. (Berlin: Springer, 1923), 37. [Further references to this work will be given in parentheses in the text. (Tr)]

[79] It would be just as unthinkable for the Church to favor the abolition of private ownership as for it to approve the abolition of marriage. (Cf. Ernst Bickel,

level of natural law, and the detachment and pronounced indifference of the first centuries changed more and more into a feeling of responsibility for and mission to a positive Christian involvement in the shaping of today's world. But "a mission to the world" does not remove for the Christian the basic condition of being "not-of-this-world", and even the most joyful affirmation of the world must not be allowed to obscure or supplant for the modern Christian—precisely in what pertains to the question of ownership—the basic values of the New Testament.

A change in the original theory of *ius naturale* was brought about in the time of Thomas Aquinas by the rediscovery of Aristotle. As a result, the concrete and analogous concept of nature (as actually realized only in, not apart from, the three fundamental states of life: original state, state of sin, state of redemption) began to be replaced, slowly and not always with immediately perceptible logic, by the abstract concept of "nature as such"—of a nature that did exist apart from these fundamental states of life. The Stoics' conception of φύσις [nature] and its gradations, which had so profoundly affected the concepts of *ius naturale*, *ius gentium* and *ius civile* in the works of Justinian and Isidore, was not known to Aristotle. Formerly, the *ius naturale* had been regarded as the law proper to man in his original state, the *ius gentium* as the law common to all men after the Fall, and the *ius civile* as the specification of the *ius gentium* in laws proper to each nation. In the new way of thinking, the *ius naturale* came to be defined as the law of human nature as such without regard to human history or the fundamental states of life previously defined; the *ius gentium* and the *ius civile* were thought of as being derived from the *ius naturale* in one of two possible ways: the *ius gentium* from universally applicable conclusions drawn from the basic premises of natural law; the *ius civile* from the specification of certain of these conclusions (ST 1a 2ae 95, 2). From this point of view, the *ius gentium* is merely a connecting link between the *ius naturale* and the *ius civile* inasmuch as "it derives from natural law in the manner of a conclusion that is not far removed from the principles on which it is based" (ibid., 95, 4 ad 1)—a conclusion drawn by right reason itself (ST 2a 2ae 57, 3 ad 3).

"Das asketische Ideal bei Ambrosius, Hieronymus und Augustin", *Neue Jahrbücher für das klassische Altertum, Geschichte und deutsche Literatur* [1916], vol. 7, 465.)

One consequence of this change in the concept of natural law was a new attitude toward private ownership. The rift becomes evident in the works of Alexander of Hales, who strove to adapt the old content unchanged to the new conceptual form. Natural law, he argues in his *Summa Theologiae*, would seem to be changeable since Isidore and Gratian regard common ownership as according to natural law, whereas nowadays it is no longer considered wrong to own private property. By way of refutation, he explains: "By natural law, all things were to be in common. . . . But this was before man's fall into sin; since the Fall, certain things are the property of certain people, and both these ways of ownership are according to natural law."[80] "Depending on the state one is in, [the natural law] dictates that it is good for all things to be held in common and that certain things are one's own property" (ibid.; paraphrased). Pope Innocent IV reflects the same point of view in his Commentary on the Decretals.[81] Despite Alexander of Hales' attempt to retain the old content in the new form, however, it remains true that in his works "the radical undercurrent of remembrance of the absolute law and the truly Christian ideal" has been considerably weakened (Troeltsch). In the works of St. Thomas Aquinas, it has almost completely disappeared. When Thomas, in theorizing about private property, comes to deal with the teachings of Basil, Ambrose, Isidore and Gratian, he makes a distinction of considerable importance: By nature (and this concept is now univocal and no longer analogous according to the states of life), man has the right to *acquire* possessions for himself and to *dispose* of them. The situation changes, however, when there is a question of *using* these goods: "With regard to exterior objects, it is also natural for man to have the use of them. However, he ought not to possess exterior objects [solely] for himself, but for the common good so that he is ready to share them with others as need arises" (ST 2a

---

[80] Alexander of Hales, *Summa Theologiae*, lib. III, pars II, inquisitio II, "De Lege Naturali", quaes. III, caput II. [(Quaracchi: College of St. Bonaventure, 1948, vol. IV, 347–48.) Von Balthasar paraphrases Alexander of Hales' text in Latin. (Tr)]

[81] Pope Innocent IV, *In Quinque Libros Decretalium . . . Commentaria Doctissima* (Venetiis: apud Haeredem Hieronymi Scoti, 1610), super tertio decretalium, rubrica XXXIV, "De Voto et Voti Redemptione", capitulum VIII, 514. Cf. Carlyle, vol. V, 14–20, for further examples of this shifting point of view. For the early Middle Ages, see Carlyle, vol. II, 41–55, 137–42.

2ae 66, 2). Where Isidore taught that the common ownership of
worldly goods is according to natural law (cf. *Etym* V, 4), Thomas
argues that, potentially and of themselves, worldly goods belong
no *more* to one person than to another (ST 2a 2ae 57, 3: "For if this
field is considered in itself, there is no more reason why it should
belong to this person than to that one." Cf. also ST 1a 2ae 94, 5 ad
3); and in this sense, which tacitly presupposes Isidore's concept of
nature, he is able to add: "Therefore, the ownership of possessions
is not contrary to natural law, but is added to natural law as a
conclusion drawn by human reason" (ST 2a 2ae 66, 2 ad 1). In
terminology, this "not contrary to" suggests a last concession of
Aristotelianism to the earlier patristic concept; in content, however, Thomas' demand that private property be possessed in such a
way that it is always in readiness for use for the community and its
needs is very close to the radical concept of the Gospel itself. This
conclusion is strengthened by Thomas' practical application of his
fundamental premise, which firmly removes almsgiving from the
sphere of free choice and brings it closer to justice: ". . . The
division and apportionment of worldly goods that proceeds from
human (!) law must not impede the rendering of help to those in
need. . . ." Free choice is limited strictly to the choice of the
recipient of one's alms: "Hence by natural law those goods that
some possess in superabundance must be used for the maintenance
of the poor. . . . But because there are many who suffer and it
is not possible to help all of them from the same store of goods,
the dispensation of his property is left to the discretion of each
individual" (ST 2a 2ae 66, 7). In case of necessity, a needy person
or a third person acting in his behalf may take from another's
possessions whatever is needed to support the life of the needy
person, for to this the needy person has a right (ibid.). Ownership
is a sin only if the rich person "deprives others unreasonably of the
use of his property" (ibid., 66, 2 ad 2).

But if the evangelical ethic was thus preserved, the rejection of
the patristic analogical concept of nature itself laid the foundation
for the "canonization of private ownership" (Salin, p. 46) that
has taken place in modern times. Albert the Great had already
introduced into the concept of nature a new form of analogy
that later became the basis for considering positive law also as
more or less identical with natural law: Nature can be understood
preponderantly as φύσις [physical nature] or as *ratio* [λόγος:
"reason"] or as a balance of the two (quoted in Grabmann, 92–
93). When we turn to Suárez, we discover that the issue has been

more or less decided in advance by the a priori assumption that the *ius gentium* is completely divorced from natural law as such: "The *ius gentium* is exclusively human and positive."[82] It is distinguished from the *ius civile* only by the fact that it is unwritten and, as such, established by custom in most nations (cf. ibid., sec. 6). With no sense of the falsity of such an observation, Suárez comments: "Isidore seems to have been aware of this." It is not without significance, therefore, that echoes of the earlier teaching on this subject are to be found in the works of certain jurists of this era, whose statements Vásquez[83] has adopted as his own: "The *ius gentium*, as distinguished from natural law, contains in itself not precepts or promises, but simply certain *concessions*—that is, certain authorizations or permissions—to do or not to do a certain act, not merely with impunity, but even justly and properly" (quoted in Suárez, *de Leg.*, chap. 18, sec. 1). That is none other than the original evangelical and Pauline συγγνώμη—the concession of something less good, but not evil in itself, which is the basis of the whole patristic teaching of the "secondary law of nature". But this concept had been so obfuscated by Aristotelianism that Suárez was obliged to admit his honest inability to understand it: "To tell the truth, I do not clearly understand this teaching" (ibid., sec. 2). Nevertheless, Suárez, too, preserved what was essential in the patristic teaching to the extent that he spoke only of the fitness, not of the necessity, of private ownership. He opposed the opinion of Duns Scotus[84] that the common holding of goods was a strict command in man's original state, but had been nullified by the fall into sin. His own opinion was that it is impossible to prove the existence of such a "command" in paradise, "just as, conversely,

---

[82] Francisco Suárez, "Tractatus de Legibus et Legislatore Deo", bk. II, ch. 19, sec. 3, *Opera Omnia*, vol. V (Paris: Ludovicus Vivès, 1856), 167. [Further references to this work (henceforth *de Leg*) will be given in parentheses in the text. For an English translation of some chapters, see Francisco Suárez, "On Laws and God the Lawgiver", trans. Gwladys L. Williams et al., in *The Classics of International Law*, ed. James Brown Scott (Oxford: Clarendon Press, 1944), 21–646 (Tr).]

[83] Gabriele Vázquez, *Commentariorum ac Disputationum in Primam Secundae S. Thomae* (Ingolstadt: Ederiano, 1604), quaes. XCV, disputatio CLVII, capita II–IV, 79–82. Suárez paraphrases this text in Latin and von Balthasar quotes from Suárez. [Tr]

[84] Joannis Duns Scotus, "Quaestiones in Librum Quartum Sententiarum",

the advantages that show that a division of property is better adapted [to man] in his fallen state prove, not that such a division is prescribed by natural law, but only that it is adapted to man's existing state and condition" (Suárez, chap. 14, sec. 13). Lessius[85] and Laymann[86] are of the same opinion: Even in the present state of mankind, private ownership is not necessary, but only more suitable. Nevertheless, Cathrein is right when he argues that, in the last analysis, the reasons adduced to prove the suitability of private ownership also prove its necessity for man in his present state (*Moralphilosophie* vol. II, 326–27). But the essential point is, as Cathrein admits: "In paradise, there would have been no question of private ownership. . . . In view of man's present fallen state, then, we can say that private ownership is the consequence of sin, or better, that sin put man into a situation in which ownership proved to be a necessary ordinance of reason" (ibid., 314).

Man owes both the origin and the indispensability of the concept "mine and thine" to his turning aside from the "riches" of paradise where he could have been completely "poor" without knowing want, where his poverty paralleled the fullness of grace and his calling to love. But love knows only how to give; it keeps nothing for itself. Private ownership, on the contrary, to which man is driven by need, will never cease to present obstacles to his perfect giving of self here below. However generous and poor he may be in intention, he cannot avoid claiming for himself those worldly goods that he has no right to bestow elsewhere because they are necessary for his own subsistence. Nor is it permitted him in this world to renounce the independent use of his intellect and free will. He has, as it were, distilled these faculties for himself out of their unity with the grace of his original state, and

---

distinctio XV, quaes. II. [*Opera Omnia*, vol. XVIII (Paris: Ludovicus Vivès, 1894), 255–65 (Tr).]

[85] Leonardus Lessius, S.J., *De Iustitia et Iure Ceterisque Virtutibus Cardinalibus Libri Quatuor* (Antwerp: Balthasar Moretus, 1621), lib. 2, capitulum 5, dubitatio III, 42–43.

[86] Paul Laymann, *Theologia Moralis in Quinque Libros Distributa* (Venetiis: Georgii Valentini, 1630), lib. III, tractatus primus, caput V, "De Iure Dominii et Rerum Divisione", quaes. 1–3, 274–75.

he possesses them now as an inalienable part of his very nature—not, however, as the invisible organ of faith and love that they once were, but, by reason of the curse, as a part artificially isolated from his wholeness, by whose sole aid he will never again be able to fulfill his first calling. For faith and love, he has substituted the good of self-determination. But this good, which is positive in itself, nevertheless has its origin in man's fall into sin. Without faith and love, it cannot enable him to attain his original calling. This is true also of his newly manifest sexuality. Although in no way evil in itself, it is likewise a consequence of man's deposition, and not even his greatest care to avoid every guilty use of its powers can restore to him his original purity and virginity.

The three consequences of the Fall *are not to be separated. Sexuality* is so closely linked, on the one hand, to death and the signs of death—"I will make great your distress in childbearing; in pain shall you bring forth children" (Gen 3:16)—and, on the other hand, to the will to property and possessions that it, in particular, is destined to be the arena of man's most deadly struggles for power: ". . . Your husband shall be your longing, though he have dominion over you" (Gen 3:16). Moral autonomy, as the *knowledge of good and evil*, is not to be separated from man's freedom to use the specific potencies of his bodily drives or from his right to own property, which are both the guarantee and the exterior manifestations of this autonomy. The *will to ownership*, finally, is basically identical with the will to know good and evil and to be responsible for one's own bodily fecundity. The two sexes differ from one another in this respect only to the extent that the man must strive for external possessions (since the ground has been cursed because of him) and acts more possessively in sexual matters, whereas the mother of all the living (Gen 3:10) has a position that sets her above the man.

Thus the new state of life created by man's displacement from paradise is just as integrated, self-consistent and unified as his original state had been. It is impossible for him to recover by his own efforts even a part of his original calling. For "the Lord God put him out of the garden of Eden to till the ground from which he was taken. He drove out the man; and at the east of the garden of Eden he placed the cherubim and the flaming sword, which turned every way, to guard the way to the tree of life" (Gen 3:23–24).

Looking back now on man's state in paradise, it is possible to gain some understanding of his nature. He was the wholeness of what was later split into opposites: the perfect, seamless and unassailable unity of obedient faith as insight and freedom; of virginal purity as fecundity; and of poverty as fullness and riches without distinction of mine and thine. Because Adam was obedient, he was the sovereign ruler of all creation. Because Eve and he were virgins, they were destined for the highest fecundity, which is the fecundity of purity. Because they were totally poor, they lived in the superabundance of God's gifts and knew neither need nor want. *Man's original state, then, was the perfect synthesis of the Christian state of life whether in the world or in the way of the evangelical counsels, in which the state of the counsels expressed the inner attitude and disposition, the worldly state the outer counterpart and fulfillment.*

Since man's disposition in this state was one of perfect obedience, perfect virginity and perfect poverty, we may conclude that, as an inner disposition, the three counsels express the highest perfection of love to which man can attain by grace. But since, in man's original state, God had not yet expressed a preference for one of the various states of life, the inner disposition that finds expression in the vows was identical with their outer fulfillment. Primitive man was not just inwardly disposed to choose poverty, chastity and obedience *if* God should call him to this state; he had actually been placed in this state, which was the "state of perfection" judged by God to be the best he could design for man.

In man's original state, the three dispositions of love demanded no renunciation; they were rather the expression of a love that possessed in itself all riches, all blessings, all fullness. No one is

more free than one who obeys God; no one is more fruitful than
one who is chaste; no one is richer than one who wants nothing
for his own possession. But he who attempts to harvest these
blessings without the inner dispositions of poverty, chastity and
obedience reaps only the curse that turns his supposed freedom
from obedience to God into a hateful obedience to the laws of this
world, into the bitter drudgery of painful obligation, to whose
yoke he is now harnessed. Just so, the fecundity that fallen
man chooses for himself becomes the fecundity of the curse
placed upon man and is linked by the drives of his lower nature
to his loss of virginity and of the humility of spiritual love. The
ownership that man usurped with the apple becomes the most
visible of the curses laid upon him as creation, unwillingly made
subject to corruption (Rom 8:20), compels him to be solicitous
about the property he cannot acquire without struggle or defend
without struggle and that, in the end, will be wrenched from him
by death if he has not already consumed or lost it.

4. HEAVEN

In banishing man from paradise, God did not condemn him to
despair, but placed at the entrance to the Garden of Eden the
flaming sword that bore the likeness of Mother and Child[87]—the
promise of one to come who would turn Eve's curse into a
blessing. In the full obedience of her assent, she would extinguish
what Eve's greedy disobedience had kindled. In the flawless
purity of her perfect virginity, she would realize—and more
than realize—the fecundity of paradise by bearing God himself,
who would redeem the world from its guilt. In the perfect
poverty that put her whole being, body and soul, at the disposal
of God's design, she would replace with the riches of man's
original self-giving the poverty of need he was compelled to

---

[87] We interpret the Proto-Evangelium (Gen 3:15) here according to an ancient
tradition, which, whatever the exegetes may say against it, is right as regards the
whole economy of salvation.

endure in his fallen state. She would not accomplish this by her own strength and virtue, but as the chosen one, as the one supported by God's grace, more encompassed by this grace than Adam and Eve had ever been, more proof against sin, more immune to every temptation.

Without this promise, man's fall from paradise would have paved the way to certain destruction with no hope of return. With it, there existed from the beginning the prospect—the as yet incomprehensible possibility—that despite all appearances man might still fulfill the calling he had received, together with the fearful capacity of deciding for or against it, at the very moment of his creation. Man was placed on this earth to remain firm in his original state and so to advance toward the final state of union with God in heaven. At the proper time, God would have extended to him the fruit of the tree of life (Rev 2:7) and bestowed upon him that other—heavenly—immortality from which there would have been no falling away. But because he succumbed to temptation, he was obliged to seek by long detours the entrance to the final state that would have been near and easily accessible to him if he had remained in the state of innocence.

Man's journey toward heaven was to have been a way of fulfillment, of expansion, of perpetuation of what had been inaugurated on earth. For *heaven itself is* none other than *the perfect union of what*, in this fallen world, *is now found disunited in the two states of life*. Heaven is the perfection of love, the ultimate initiation into the limitless depth and breadth of the threefold gift of self. It is the perfect union of *obedience* and freedom. In heaven, obedience will be a component of love itself: the simultaneously complete yet ever increasing readiness to be united with the will of God, to recognize this will as the rule and fulfillment of one's own being, as one's great happiness, just as it is the eternal happiness of the eternal Son to do always the will of the Father. When, between visions of life in this world, Revelation grants us glimpses of life in the world to come, there unfolds before us that magnificent scene of adoration in which the angels and all the redeemed fall upon their faces before the throne of God the Father and before the Lamb, cast down their crowns, and, amid the rising incense of the prayers of all the saints, utter every conceivable tribute of praise: "Blessing and glory and wisdom and thanksgiving and honor and power and strength to our God forever and ever. Amen" (Rev 7:12). This is the full assembly of those who love: ". . . The throne of God and of the Lamb shall be in it", in the heavenly Bride, "and his servants shall serve him. And they shall see his face and his name shall be on their foreheads" (Rev 22:3–4). Their happiness consists in taking their place in the vast dwelling place of God, in acknowledging and adoring God as their eternal and sovereign Lord. Thus the prophecy repeated by Christ is fulfilled in eternity: "And they shall all be taught of God" (Jn 6:45). The obedience of heaven is an obedience that knows no fear, since "perfect love casts out fear" (1 Jn 4:18); but it is, for that very reason, all the more filled with a reverence that, together with the knowledge and love of God (Ps 19:10), must increase forever, demanding as it does so the total surrender of man's whole strength, his whole mind and his whole will. It is the freedom of "that Jerusalem which is above" (Gal 4:26). But man will not be admitted to the kingdom of heaven until he has learned in the anteroom of heaven to renounce every will of his own, every desire, all personal autonomy that would oppose itself to the will of God as an independent authority.

The *virginity* of paradise will also find its fulfillment in heaven. But if we can form no concept of the primarily spiritual and only secondarily sexual fecundity of man in paradise, it is even less likely that we can conceive of the fulfillment of this paradisal miracle in heaven. We know only that we shall rise with spiritual bodies and that in these bodies we shall be "equal to the angels and . . . sons of God, being sons of the resurrection" (Lk 20:36). In heaven, there will be no further thought of marriage, for "those who shall be accounted worthy . . . of the resurrection from the dead neither marry nor take wives. *For* neither shall they be able to die any more . . ." (Lk 20:35–36; italics added). The causative "for" of the preceding verse once again emphasizes the fact that man in his original state in paradise, where he was not subject to death, would not have married *in the same way* as "the children of this world marry" (Lk 20:34). A direct transition would have been possible from that mysteriously fruitful virginity, which was not indissolubly linked with humiliation, suffering and death as marriage is today, to the angelic virginity of the new world where "death shall be no more; neither shall there be mourning nor crying nor pain" (Rev 21:4); where that threatening sea (Rev 21:1) will cease to exist from which arises the beast (Rev 13:1) of sensuality; where "there shall be no night" (Rev 21:25) in which man will be exposed to temptation. With body and soul, all will "live to" God (Lk 20:38)—and since there is nothing more fruitful than love, but love is made perfect in the gift of oneself to God, this heavenly love will be a boundless and incomprehensible fecundity. By reason of its bondage to matter, sexual love on earth is something paltry and limited in comparison with the fecundity that will bestow on us the fruits of the tree of life (Rev 22:2) and water from the fountain of life (Rev 21:6). Like all God's graces, these fruits will become in us our fruit, just as the water that the Lord bestows will become in us a fountain of living water springing up unto life everlasting (Jn 4:14; 7:38). In the heavenly kingdom, all the darkness and opacity that cling to man's drives when they are no longer, as they were in paradise, the pure instruments of his spirit will acquire the transparency of glass and crystal. The water on which the virgin Christ walked in safety, on which Peter attempted to walk in faith but began to sink because his faith was weak, will become in heaven a "sea of glass" on which those who have "overcome the beast" will take their stand, singing "the song of the Lamb" (Rev 15:2–3). The spirit will immerse itself only in what is above, in the incomprehensibility of God; but it will stand firm on what is below, on the material world. The streets of the heavenly city will be "pure gold, as it were transparent glass" (Rev 21:21).

In heaven, finally, there will be the perfection of *poverty*. "The chilling expression 'mine and thine' " (Chrysostom) will be heard no more. Men will hold all things in common in a community of ownership that will owe its existence, not to robbery and dispossession, but to voluntary generosity and liberality. Because they will give away all they possess, they will know the *fullness of riches*. They will possess all things save only that which is their own and, for that very reason, will also possess that which is their own, for it will have been bestowed upon them in love by God and neighbor. There will be an end to the calculating exchange of goods in which each one seeks his own enrichment and to all that speaks of trade or commerce. Merchants made their last appearance in Holy Writ at the downfall of the great whore, Babylon. With the kings of the earth, they mourn because "no one will buy their merchandise any more" (Rev 18:11) now that she has been destroyed. Either directly or indirectly, they had grown rich from her wealth, like the shipmasters and mariners who mourn because it is useless for them now to acquire and transport merchandise (Rev 18:17–19). Men will have to divest themselves in the anteroom of heaven of every tendency toward buying and selling, for in heaven they will give and receive all things without recompense (Rev 21:6; 22:17)—just as, in the Old Testament, wisdom dispensed its gifts to those who had no money to buy (Is 55:1) and, in the New Testament, the Lord gave himself freely to all who sought him, admonishing his disciples: "Freely you have received, freely give" (Mt 10:8). The poverty of heaven will exist, not for its own sake, but to serve and bear witness to a love that finds its expression in the eternal sharing of all good things. It will not remove what is proper to each one's nature or the graces and mission assigned to each by God, but it will ensure that what each one possesses, he possesses only for the sake of others: that he not only holds all external goods on loan, as it were, to be used in the service of God and the community, but likewise transforms all that he has and is into a gift. Such poverty is as much a part of the blessedness of heaven as are perfect obedience and perfect purity, for "it is more blessed to give than to receive" (Acts 20:35). Indeed, receiving is itself a form of giving, as witness the example of Paul, who knew how to receive in order to bestow on the Philippians both the joy and the merit of giving (Phil 4:10, 17), and of Mary, who rejoiced at the abundance of gifts bestowed on her by God because all ages would find therein a reason for glorifying God.

In the anteroom of heaven each of us will be purified until he has acquired the disposition of perfect poverty. If every dispute about mine and thine or about the penalty, reprimand, judicial discernment or reversal of judgment that is one's due under law; if every possible distinction between mine and thine and every claim on God or neighbor, on whatever grounds it is based and whether it is raised in one's own name or in that of a neighbor or of some universal world justice—if these ideas and concepts that have flourished in the domain of private ownership have not been relinquished on earth, they will have to be burned away in the fires of purification. But the hardest lesson to be learned there, the lesson that those who have been preoccupied with right and justice in this world will have to struggle to accept, is that there is no distinction of mine and thine even in matters of guilt; that they must see in every sin, by whomsoever it has been committed, an offense against the eternal love of God; that they must be disposed, therefore, to do penance, as long as may be deemed necessary by God, for every sin no matter who is its perpetrator. For it is impossible to enter heaven with a love less perfect than that of St. Paul, who, for the sake of his kinsmen, would gladly have borne their lot of being anathema from Christ (Rom 9:3), thus imitating the disposition of the Lord, who redeemed the world and established Christian love by a suffering that asked, not about the justice of the punishment, but about the grace that allowed him to suffer. This, then, will be the ultimate and absolute poverty of heaven: We will be purified of all thoughts of justice or retribution and "the justice of God" will be "made manifest independently of the law" (Rom 3:21), according to the law of the unfathomable mercy of God, in which all justice is superabundantly fulfilled. For justice will be meted out to us in the same measure in which we exact it (Rom 4:4). But such justice can be only that of judgment: "For with what judgment you judge, you shall be judged; and with what measure you measure, it shall be measured to you." Therefore, "do not judge that you may not be judged" (Mt 7:2, 1). The master of the wicked servant "handed him over to the torturers until he should pay all that was due him" and the Lord added the warning: "So also my heavenly Father will do to you, if you do not forgive your brothers from your hearts" (18:34, 35). But "if you forgive men their offenses, your heavenly Father will also forgive you your offenses" (Mt 6:14). "Forgive, and you shall be forgiven" (Lk 6:37). For this is the utmost poverty: to renounce one's own right and, with it, the whole, deeply rooted concept of a private domain of enforceable rights, claims and justifiable demands. If we relinquish these, we will be "poor in spirit"—and this is the first of the beatitudes (Mt 5:3).

In this way, man's final state in heaven will be the perfection of his original state in paradise. In God's original plan, it would not have been necessary to destroy the unity of the states of life by the differentiation that is known in the Church today. Poverty, chastity and obedience would not have been opposed to riches, fecundity and freedom, but would have been, from the beginning, their first definitive expression and, in the perfection of heaven, their last definitive confirmation. Thus man would have been able to fulfill his first calling—the calling to love. Poverty, chastity and obedience would have been but the three forms in which the full scope of his love would have been revealed. In them, the primary vow of love would have unfolded without need for renunciation; they would have given expression to the basic orientation of man's soul to love, which would have been undifferentiated from his orientation to everlasting bliss. The longing for happiness would have had the form of self-surrender, of an ecstatic outpouring of self, of perfect service to God and neighbor. Man's striving would have been all that was necessary to place him in the role destined for him by God, because nothing in him, no selfish consideration, no darkness of egotistic counter-drives, would have opposed his clear recognition and immediate acceptance of the will of God. This would have been man's unambivalent state: to be at a remove from God by his obligation to serve; to be close to God by his mission to love—because one who loves, though fully aware that he will never be identical with the beloved, nevertheless identifies himself out of love with the will of the beloved.

PART TWO

THE CHRISTIAN STATES OF LIFE

CHAPTER ONE

THE FIRST DIVISION
OF THE STATES OF LIFE

1. THE PROCESS OF DIVISION

The unity that existed in the state of innocence and was intended to continue into the heavenly state was ruptured by man's fall into sin. For the solidarity of those who share human nature is so great that the defection of even one individual cannot be without consequence for all. But one who shares in the corruption of the whole human race cannot raise himself above that race to bring healing to all its members. If God's original plan was to be restored, such a one would have to come, not just from within the race, but also from above it.

The reality of sin could not be transformed into unreality by a purely external decree of God. The Son of God had to take its guilt upon himself and atone for it in the abandonment of the Cross. Yet even this could not be done in a purely external manner. It would have been incommensurate with the dignity of human nature simply to transfer man into another state of life as though he were an inanimate object; it was fitting that the "yes" of his cooperation should not be lacking to the working of God's utterly free gift of grace. For this reason, the Redeemer brought mankind out of the state of sin in which he found himself and into a new state of reconciliation with God, the state of the Cross, in which, by the free gift of the Cross itself, mankind was "en-stated" [in-Stand-gesetzt] in a way of life in which he could cooperate in the redemption that had been accomplished and walk together with his Redeemer along the road that led to his final state in heaven.

Man's "en-statement" [In-Stand-gesetzt-Werden] as cooperator in the work of his redemption was necessary because, in the state of sin into which he had fallen, there was no possibility of his achieving a state of reconciliation with God by his own efforts. In his guilt-laden condition, only two courses were open to him: either to acknowledge the separation from God inherent in his sinfulness and, in despair of reconciliation, to come to terms with his consequent finiteness and transitoriness—"Let us eat and drink for tomorrow we shall die" (1 Cor 15:32); or, with no less despair, to struggle to deliver himself from his finiteness and transitoriness by religious endeavors and techniques that gave promise of loosing his bonds by exalting man into superman, the creature of body and soul into pure spirit, and finite spirit into absolute spirit. The first course is defiant resignation; the second, equally defiant titanism. By either of them, man destroys himself because his calling, which lies beyond his nature and its powers, can be comprehended only if he is reconciled with God, and can be pursued only with the help of God's grace. What Jesus calls "the world", in the negative sense of a realm apart from God and oblivious of its need for God's grace, fluctuates constantly between the two extremes of love of self and alienation from self, thus never escaping its own chaos and darkness. Because sin, inasmuch as it refuses to recognize the original analogy of the creature to God, is basically chaotic, it vacillates in despairing dialectic between the identification of itself with God and the denial of God, only to arrive, in the end, at a chaotic failure to distinguish between the two. Analogy involves the distance-in-nearness of man's relationship to God, in which the clarity of the differentiation creates clarity in the relationship. Chaos, on the other hand, is always darkness, because whether man denies God or makes himself equal to him, without God he can shed no light on the mystery of his own existence.

"God said, 'Let there be light', and there was light. God saw that the light was good. *God separated the light from the darkness*" (Gen 1:3–4). But in the redemption it is not created, but *uncreated light*, God himself—the God who "is light, and in [whom] is no darkness" (1 Jn 1:5)—who has been sent by "the Father of lights" (James 1:17) and who comes as the light that "shines in the darkness" (Jn 1:5) of this world: "I am the light of the world. He who follows me does not walk in the darkness, but will have the light of life" (Jn 8:12). "I have come a light into the world, that whoever believes in me may not remain in the darkness" (Jn 12:46). The light that this Messiah brings is himself—is love; to walk in the light means to walk in his love; means to be "called out of darkness into his marvelous light" (1 Pet 2:9); means to be "made worthy to share the lot of the saints in light" (Col 1:12). To walk in the light means to love as he has loved us, with a love that is "truly perfected" (1 Jn 2:5); to walk in darkness means to reject love—to hate. "Because the darkness has passed away and the true light is now shining. He who says that he is in the light, and hates his brother, is in the darkness still. He who loves his brother abides in the light, and for him there is no stumbling. But he who hates his brother is in the darkness, and walks in the darkness" (1 Jn 2:8–11).

At the beginning of time, before there could have been any union between the two, God separated light from darkness. For it is only when they are diametrically opposed to each other as distinct realities, when they are not blurred by commingling, that a creative order can exist. This is especially true when the light of love opposes itself to the darkness of hatred. For this reason, the Son of God—he who is ultimately to reconcile all things and to break down every intervening wall erected by sin (Eph 2:14); whose Church will be universal and distinguishable from all others by the mark of unity in space and time, in inner structure and attitude; whose followers will be "careful to preserve the unity of the Spirit in the bond of peace: one body and one Spirit, even as you were called in one hope of your calling" (Eph 4:3–4)—makes his appearance as the sign of radical division. Division [διαμερισμός] is the message he brings: "Do you think that I came to give peace upon the earth? No, I tell you, but division. For henceforth in one house five will be divided, three against two and two against three" (Lk 12:51–52). "Do not think that I have come to send peace upon the earth; I have come to bring a sword, not peace" (Mt 10:34). The sword is his distinctive attribute: "And out of his mouth came forth a sharp two-edged sword" (Rev 1:16), because his word—and he *is* this word—cuts and divides the very essence of things: "For the word of God is living and efficient and keener than any two-edged sword, and extending even to the division of soul and spirit, of joints also and of marrow" (Heb 4:12). With the sword of his mouth he threatens to fight against sinners (Rev 2:16) and to "smite the nations" (Rev 19:15); with it he will destroy all who have fought against him (Rev 19:21). With the opening of the second apocalyptical seal, he releases the rider to whom "it was given to take peace from the earth and that men should kill one another, and there was given him a great sword" (Rev 6:4)—the principle of judgment.

Jesus does not hesitate to confront man with the ultimate decision. Indeed, he demands it, thereby creating for himself a multitude of enemies. He recognizes no gray area of neutral theological truths, for "I am the truth" (Jn 14:6). Man's truth and falsehood, light and darkness, salvation and damnation are all judged in terms of his decision for or against Jesus (Mk 8:38). After positing the general statement: "No man can serve two masters; for either he will hate the one and love the other, or else he will stand by the one and despise the other" (Mt 6:24), Jesus draws two conclusions from it: "He who is not with me is against me" (Mt 12:30); and ". . . There is no one who shall work a miracle in my name, and forthwith be able to speak ill of me. For he who is not against you is for you" (Mk 9:38–39). Only lukewarmness is intolerable: "I would that thou wert cold or hot. But because thou art lukewarm, and neither cold nor hot, I am about to vomit thee out of my mouth" (Rev 3:15–16).

Jesus' mission, then, is primarily one of discernment and hence of order. It is only when he has received a clear " 'Yes, yes'; 'No, no' " (Mt 5:37) that he can and will act as love. He knows what will be the result of such a way of acting and persistently makes known to his disciples the fate that lies in store not only for him, but also for them if they want to be his apostles and followers: "No disciple is above his teacher, nor is the servant above his

master. It is enough for the disciple to be like his teacher, and for
the servant to be like his master. If they have called the master of
the house Beelzebub, how much more those of his household"
(Mt 10:24–25). As he will be hated and persecuted and put to
death by the darkness of hate, so will his disciples be hated and
despised and persecuted by all. Whoever is deterred by this fate
from becoming his disciple, whoever hesitates or is uncertain
about following him, is unworthy of him (Mt 10:17–22; Lk
21:8–9). He has given his solemn word that whoever denies him
before men will be denied before God's angels in heaven (Lk
12:9). He is himself the consuming fire (Heb 12:29) that he has
come to cast upon the earth and whose consuming effect upon
himself he awaits with longing (Lk 12:49). Whoever approaches
him, approaches fire.[1] He wants no mass movement that will
envelop the individual in anonymity, but a personal decision that
each individual must make for himself alone: "For wide is the
gate and broad is the way that leads to destruction, and many
there are who enter that way. How narrow the gate and close
the way that leads to life! And few there are who find it" (Mt
7:13–14).

Inflexibly and inexorably, the Son affirms the commandment
of love as *his* command. He it is who summarizes the whole law
and the prophets in words that demand all things for love (Mk
12:29–31) and whose farewell address subordinates all things to
this command. And if, in the beginning, his command that we
love our neighbor as ourselves is couched in the language of the
Old Testament: ". . . All that you wish men to do to you, even so
do you to them" (Mt 7:12; cf. Lk 6:31), he nevertheless exceeds
this measure of love of neighbor, which is still bound to self-love,
by his own conduct—by letting himself be treated in a way no
man would wish for another, by rejecting every standard of love

---

[1] Von Balthasar notes here that he is quoting an *agraphon* but does not indicate
which one. For a discussion of *agrapha* in general and a brief bibliography, see
Conrad Louis' article, "Agrapha", in the *New Catholic Encyclopedia* (New York:
McGraw-Hill, 1967), vol. I. [Tr]

of others that is based on self-love, and by surrendering himself so completely that, by his very abandonment, he rescues all mankind. In his nakedness he opposes sin in order to remove the distance between darkness and light, in order, by his death, abandonment and experience of hell, to let his light shine into the last hiding place of the force that is opposed to God. The intensity of this love (Rom 8:32) that gives its life willingly for its enemies exceeds the Old Testament command of love and justifies its designation as a "new commandment" (Jn 13:34). It is new because the measure of our love of neighbor is no longer our own self and its wishes, but the love of God; because this new commandment of love becomes the criterion for belonging to him: ". . . That as I have loved you, you also love one another. By this will all men know that you are my disciples, if you have love for one another" (Jn 13:34–35). "This is my commandment, that you love one another as I have loved you. Greater love than this no one has, that one lay down his life for his friends. You are my friends if you do the things I command you" (Jn 15:12–14).

The command to love as Jesus loved is represented not as a degree of love that can be achieved only with the utmost effort, as something requiring extreme skill for its achievement, but as something to be taken for granted, something simple, natural, universal in its application, something implicit in the fact of redemption: "Unto this, indeed, you have been called, because Christ also has suffered for you, leaving you an example that you may follow in his steps" (1 Pet 2:21). Nothing is plainer or more compelling than the conclusion drawn by the beloved disciple from the fact of Christ's gift of himself: "He who says that he abides in him, *ought* himself also to walk just as he walked" (1 Jn 2:6). "In this we have come to know his love, that he laid down his life for us; and we likewise *ought* to lay down our life for the brethren" (1 Jn 3:16). "Beloved, if God has so loved us, we also *ought* to love one another" (1 Jn 4:11). "And this commandment we have from him, that he who loves God *should* love his brother also" (1 Jn 4:21). There is no indication that the obligation thus expressed is just a counsel. In the process of dividing light from darkness there is question, not of tentative transitions and twilights, of human effort and failure, but only of black and white. What is commanded is *perfect* love as it was in the beginning: "He who says that he knows him, and does not keep his commandments, is a liar and the truth is not in him. But he who keeps his word, in him the love of God is truly perfected" (1 Jn 2:4–5). "But I say to you, love your enemies . . . be perfect, even as your heavenly Father is perfect" (Mt 5:44, 48). What is required is an unprecedented, apparently totally unrealistic, utopian either-or of God or devil, of absolute love or absolute hate. For ". . . sin is not in him [Christ]. No one who abides in him commits sin; and no one who sins has seen him, or has known him. Dear children, let no one lead you astray. He who does what is just is just, even as *he* is just. He who commits sin is of the devil, because the devil sins from the beginning. . . . Whoever is born of God does not commit sin, because his seed abides in him and he cannot sin, because he is born of God. In this the children of God and the children of the devil are made known. Whoever is not just is not of God, nor is he just who does not love his brother" (1 Jn 3:5–10). Nowhere in the Gospel is the perfection of love depicted as merely a counsel; it is always an explicit command—a command as self-evident as the light that exists only to emit its rays and spend itself unstintingly. For this command is issued by love, and love knows no motive but the motive of love. What belongs to it is necessarily good; what darkens or hinders it is just as necessarily evil and has no place in love. Love does not know it and can have nothing to do with it. Love cannot negotiate and bargain about itself, for it is indivisible. We can only accept or reject, love or hate it.

The process of division leads to the formation of the Church, which is opposed to the "world". As the realm of light, the Church is separated from the realm of darkness that exists outside it. This separation is accomplished by a twofold yet undivided act of God: *election and vocation*. By election, God chooses an individual or a people, thereby distinguishing "the elect" from the "non-elect". By vocation, he makes his choice known to those whom he has chosen, thereby numbering them among those who are called. It is inconceivable that God would choose an individual or a nation without making his election known by divine vocation. Vocation is the revelation of God's choice. Thus Christians, insofar as they form the Church, are ". . . a chosen race, . . . a purchased people, . . . called out of darkness into his marvelous light" (1 Pet 2:9). The two concepts, election and vocation [κλῆσις καὶ ἐκλογή: 2 Pet 1:10], stand together and complement each other to form the basis of the *state of life* of the Christian in the Church. This state of life has its origin simply and solely in the act of God by which the Christian is separated from the world by election and vocation and placed where, by reason of this election and vocation, he both can and must find his state of life. "I have chosen you out of the world" (Jn 15:19). In the New Testament, Christians are known simply as *electi*, "the chosen ones" (Col 3:12; 2 Tim 2:10; Titus 1:1; 1 Pet 1:1; 1 Pet 2:9; Rom 8:33), or as *vocati*, "those who have been called" (Rom 1:6; 1 Cor 1:24; Jude 1:1, and elsewhere). The totality of those so chosen and so called is "that which has been called forth", the ἐκκλησία,[2] the Church.

In its substance, the Church is none other than the objectification of God's choice and the formalization of his call manifested in the world as the state in which man finds himself when election and vocation have touched an individual or community. God's election and vocation are to such an extent that which precedes and sustains, and the role of those elected and called is to such an extent to follow and be sustained thereby, that the Church in its objectification is antecedent to the people who compose it: They live by and through the Church just as they are what they are—namely Christians—by virtue of God's election

---

[2] Etymologically, the word ἐκκλησία is derived from ἔκκλητος, past participle of the verb ἐκκαλέω (call forth), which is formed from ἐκ (out of) and καλέω (call). [Tr]

and vocation. It cannot be doubted that God's election is so constituted that it demands for its accomplishment both the cooperation and the continued effort of the elect; man must, in some manner, both hear and heed the call of God. The evangelists and apostles sought again and again, and by every possible means, to impress this fact upon Christianity. It should not be assumed, however, that the Christian does not take his stand primarily within an act of God that has been accomplished in him, that translates him, by virtue of this election and vocation, into a new state outside the "world" so that he may at last truly comprehend how totally the grace of his calling contains within itself the demand for an answer, for a way of life that befits the state to which he has been elected and called.

Election and vocation have their source in the eternity of God, who "chose us in him [Christ] before the foundation of the world that we should be holy and without blemish in his sight in love" and who made known to us "the mystery of his will" (Eph 1:4, 5) so that we might reach the goal of eternity, since every calling is a calling to an eternal inheritance (Heb 9:15), to eternal glory (1 Th 2:12; 2 Th 1:10), to eternal life (1 Tim 6:12), even though it is initially a calling into the visible Church, the "body" (Col 3:15) with all its members and its means of grace (2 Pet 1:3), and thus into fellowship with the Son of God (1 Cor 1:9). Every calling is an election "unto salvation" and a vocation through the preaching of the Gospel "to gain the glory of our Lord Jesus Christ" (2 Th 2:14), but always "through the sanctification of the Spirit and belief of the truth" (2 Th 2:13), that is, through objective sacramental sanctification and objectively accepted faith, through the objective fact of incorporation by baptism into the death and burial of Jesus Christ, whence arises the—obviously pressing—obligation to respond to this act, this election, and this vocation of God by a life worthy of such a calling (Rom 6:4–14).

From the description in the Epistles of the Church's dependence for its existence on the election and vocation of God, it might seem that the Word of God had thereby completed his work of division. From the great company of the (initially) not-called, from the "world", God has called to himself a "chosen people" in order, by the (for us) paradoxical process of division, to bring about the ultimate union of all. Those so chosen are those whom God has predestined from all eternity to be "called into fellowship with his Son" (1 Cor 1:9) to complete with him the work of redeeming the world, to do battle with the Lamb as "the called, and chosen, and faithful" who remain with him in the great and decisive struggle against the powers of evil and their cohorts (Rev 14:14). By reason of their election and vocation to take their stand within the Church, which is nothing other than the objectification of election and vocation, it would appear that all Christians belong to one common state.

But the Gospel offers a quite different picture. The process of division is not confined to Church and "world". It also becomes immediately operative *within the Church*—and this in a twofold manner that corresponds to the twofold separation of water from dry land and of earth from heaven in the account of creation. In other words, the division is *both horizontal and vertical*—like the form of the Cross: first the division *between the "state of the evangelical counsels" and the secular state*, then the division *between the priestly state and the lay state*. It is not at once apparent in the Gospel that the division is a twofold one. In the first place, the call that divides the elect from the rest of mankind occurs in a primitive community; in the second place, Jesus, who is himself "not even . . . a priest" (Heb 8:4) in the conventional sense of the word, is not primarily concerned with forming a new priesthood, but with winning co-workers to share his life work in the vineyard of the Father. This vineyard is not yet the (post-Easter) Church, but the people of God. Or, more exactly, the lost sheep of this people of God, which represents all mankind. The first division articulated in Jesus' lifetime is the calling of some to share in the divine mission of the Son. Only when this mission becomes identified with Jesus' perfect offering of himself, when he entrusts his sacrifice sacramentally to his followers and gives them power over its effect, the forgiveness of sins, is the second division clearly distinguishable from the first. Only in a later stage of reflection does the difference between the two divisions become so clear for the Church that it can recognize a distinction between different vocations and missions.

During his public life, Jesus encountered two groups of men. The first and most numerous were *the people*. In contrast to them were *the apostles* whom he chose on his own judgment and called apart from the people in a formal ceremony. "And going up a mountain, he called to him men of his own choosing, and they came to him" (Mk 3:13). There is question here of a more selective choice from among the larger number of those who had been called. "He *summoned* his disciples and from these he *chose* twelve (whom he also called apostles)" (Lk 6:13). "And coming down with them, he took his stand on a level stretch, with a crowd [ὄχλος] of his disciples, and a great multitude of people" who had come from far and near "to hear him and to be healed of their diseases. . . . And all the crowd were trying to touch him, for power went forth from him and healed all" (Lk 6:17–19). The force of the symbolism is impressive: The Lord ascends the mountain alone; there calls the Twelve to come to him "that they might be with him" (Mk 3:14); and afterwards descends to the remaining disciples and the people who press upon him.[3]

The difference between the two "states of life" is made clear precisely in this pressing of the people upon him, which is in such sharp contrast to the movement by which the apostles, as those who have been called, step forward to join their Lord. The people

---

[3] In this and the following sections, von Balthasar explicitly defines *the first division of the states of life within the Church* as that created by *the election and vocation of the twelve apostles* to a qualitatively higher state of life. The frequent occurrence of the word "disciples" in the New Testament passages by which he supports his argument should not be allowed to obfuscate his meaning. New Testament authors (especially of the synoptic Gospels, which are the sources most frequently quoted here) commonly employ the more general term "disciples" even when it is clear from the context that they are referring, not to the whole band of disciples per se, but to the smaller group of Jesus' "own choosing" (Mk 3:13) for whom we reserve the title "apostles". [Tr]

follow the Lord with a brash importunity that lets him neither sleep nor eat (Mk 6:13), that almost crushes him (Mk 5:31), that compels him to board a boat in order not to be forced into the sea (Mk 3:9). The people pursue him wherever he goes, find him wherever he hides; they are like sheep without a shepherd (Mt 9:36) and perceive in him leadership, goodness and power. They throng about him, and some individuals—their forerunners, as it were—even offer to follow him although they have not been called to do so (Lk 9:58). But it is not said of those whom the Lord chose for his closest followers that they forced themselves upon him. The first two apostles did, it is true, follow Jesus, but they did so only at the behest of their teacher, John the Baptist. The remainder he seeks out for himself, calling them away from their fishing nets or, like Levi, from their tax-collecting (Mt 9:9); encountering them on his way from one town to another as in the case of Philip (Jn 1:43). Some, like Peter (Jn 1:41–42) and the cautious Nathaniel (Jn 1:45–51), are brought to him by friends and relatives. Some counter his "Follow me!" with excuses (Mt 8:21; Lk 9:59–62), or offer themselves to him only to withdraw at the last moment when they learn what it means to be an apostle (Mt 19:16–22). Nowhere does the election and vocation of the Lord to a closer association with him appear as a continuation or consequence of an impulse to apostleship that has its source in man himself. This fact must be clearly understood, especially when there is question of being an apostle in the special sense: "You have not chosen me, but I have chosen you" (Jn 15:16).

It is confirmed again in the movement of certain individuals from among the people who come into personal contact with the Lord—especially those who have been miraculously healed. With few exceptions—the man at the pool by the Sheep gate, for instance (Jn 5:2–9)—the people themselves bring the sick into the Lord's presence or at least ask his help for them. The Lord does not withdraw from such contact; rather, he allows them to come to him, or even goes himself to those who are sick or to the dead. He bestows on them his graces of body and soul—the first, visible; the second, either explicitly formulated in the forgiveness of sins or implicitly included in the healing of the sick. He reveals himself as their Savior, their Redeemer, their source of comfort and courage, as the true light of the world. But once his grace has been given and they stand in his light, he sends them back among the people. He restores them, transformed into new men, to the ordinary framework of their daily lives. There is scarcely a miraculous healing of the Lord that does not conclude with the constantly repeated "*vade*"—"go now". Thus the lame man is dismissed: "Take up thy pallet, and go to thy house" (Mk 2:11); thus the woman suffering from a hemorrhage: "Go in peace, and be thou healed of thy affliction" (Mk 5:34); thus the Canaanite woman: "Because of this answer, go thy way; the devil is gone out of thy daughter" (Mk 7:29); thus the woman who was a sinner: "Thy faith hath saved thee; go in peace" (Lk 7:50); thus the blind man of Bethsaida: "Go to thy house" (Mk 8:26), and the blind man of Jericho: "Go thy way, thy faith hath saved thee" (Mk 10:52); thus the woman taken in adultery: "Go thy way, and from now on sin no more" (Jn 8:11); thus the centurion: "Go thy way; as thou hast believed, so be it done to thee" (Mt 8:13), and the tenth leper: "Arise, go thy way, for thy faith has saved thee" (Lk 17:19); thus the royal official: "Go thy way, thy son lives" (Jn 4:50). In many instances Jesus returns the person who has been healed or restored to life explicitly to his usual milieu: He commands that the daughter of Jairus be given something to eat (Mk 5:43); he restores the young man of Naim to his mother (Lk 7:15). Even when he raises his friend Lazarus from the dead, he does not draw him to his bosom, but gives the command: "Unbind him, and let him go" (Jn 11:44). Frequently it seems that he cannot accomplish this dismissal quickly enough: He cleanses the leper and "immediately drove him away" (Mk 1:43). And when he has preached or performed a miracle, such as the multiplication of the loaves, before all the people, he concludes his day's work with an explicit dismissal of the crowd (Mk 8:9). The most notable of these dismissals is that of the possessed man of Gerasa, who, after he had been healed, "began to entreat [the Lord] that he might remain with him. And he did not allow him, but said to him, 'Go home to thy relatives, and tell them all that the Lord has done for thee, and how he has had mercy on thee' " (Mk 5:18–19; Lk 8:38–39). The permission to proclaim the miracle is, as it were, a consolation for the refusal of permission to follow Jesus, for Jesus was accustomed strictly to forbid those who had been healed to speak of the miracle accomplished in them. In point of fact, of course, this man had been a plague on the whole region, and the Gerasenes had already come out from the city and had seen all that had taken place. Hence the apostolic mission assigned to him was a relatively limited one and restricted to his own person. It is not to be confused with the mission to preach that was conferred upon the apostles. It is as if Jesus would have among his apostles no one for whom he had performed a miracle—no one with a too distinctively personal background. Rather, at their first calling, he had given those who were to remain with him "power over unclean spirits, to cast them out, and to cure every kind of disease and infirmity" (Mt 10:1), and had charged them: "And as you go, preach the message, 'The kingdom of heaven is at hand!' Cure the sick, raise the dead, cleanse the lepers, cast out devils" (Mt 10:7–8).

Thus the *movements* of the two groups of Jesus' followers are *diametrically opposed*. The apostles come to Jesus because they have been invited to do so, because of a "Come" that is almost as stereotyped as the "Go" with which he dismisses the uninvited. By virtue of Jesus' "Come", his "Come and see", his "Come, follow me", the apostles are henceforth always with him. If he sends them away, it is only that they may return to him to report all they have done and taught (Mk 6:30). The people, on the other hand, approach the Lord from the world, which is their dwelling place. After their encounter with him, they return to that world. The two forms of encounter, the two modes of approach, are in sharp contrast. The people's way to the Lord is to search for him in their necessity; their dismissal is attended with healing and grace for their subsequent existence in the world. The sending of the apostles into the world occurs only by the Lord's commission and for his purposes; their return to him is a return to the place where they belong.

The broad terms in which these opposing movements of one and the same relationship to Christ have been described should not cause us to forget that, in the Church of Christ, both movements will be forms of personal following of the Lord, or that the forms themselves have told us nothing about the perfection of love they may reflect. There are many supplementary aspects that might be explored here, but their significance will be recognized only when we have penetrated more deeply into the relationship between "state of life" and "Christian state", as we shall do below in the section on *Image and Truth* and in our reflections on *The Christian State of Life*. For now, it will suffice to call attention briefly to three points.

a) In referring to Jesus' earthly ministry, the terms "apostle" and "people" do not simply suggest two states of life that will exist in the post-Easter Church. Rather, the state of apostleship and Jesus' call to it also prefigure the [post-Easter] state of believers, while the people—even those who are believers—*also* represent ancient Israel, and even mankind in general, *from which* the Church is called forth.

b) The calling of the Twelve, moreover, not only establishes the apostolic state as such with its nearness to the Lord, but also prefigures the priestly apostolate, the office for which the Twelve are, from the beginning, gifted with "power" (Mk 3:15). After them come the other disciples (Luke mentions seventy-two), who can be chosen and "appointed" (Lk 10:1) for special missions, and in particular the women who follow Jesus (Lk 8:2–3) and whose status—they "used to provide for them [Jesus and his disciples] out of their means", but they also accompany them as they move about—though not immediately clear, will become so when we speak below of Mary's state of life. What we can deduce here from the mere fact of their existence is indicated more formally in those passages in which the active following of Christ is shown by the apostles to be binding on all who believe in him (Lk 9:23–24; 9:37; 12:32–34; and elsewhere). In consequence, we can safely assume that the spirit of radicalness embodied in the calling and "enstatement" of the Twelve is likewise to be the mark of the whole community of believers.

c) The importance that Jesus attaches to this radicalness is apparent in his prediction that all who follow him will unquestionably be exposed to temptation and must remain faithful whatever it may cost them in worldly terms. This is the meaning of the command to "hate . . . mother and father and wife and children" (Lk 14:26), which is a precondition of apostleship as such and which includes a fortiori the relinquishment of all material goods and, ultimately, of one's own freedom ("If anyone . . . does not hate . . . even his own life" [Lk 14:26]). The act of confessing Jesus is no less significant than the act of dying—of hating even one's own life—for him, which, in any event, transports the believer into that "state" of union with Jesus that the apostles enjoyed from the beginning by reason of their call. Thus we see once more how totally the form of the "evangelical state" casts its shadow or its light beyond the actual confines of the state itself and even over the whole Church.

We shall examine the form of this state of life more closely in a later section.

2. THE FOUNDING OF THE STATE OF ELECTION

As described above, the process of division is in no way the separation of a homogeneous mass into two quantitatively dissimilar parts. The call to community with Christ is, from the beginning, analogous, not univocal.

The call to the state of election is a qualitative, special, differentiated call. There is no similarly qualitative call to the secular state, which is characterized by the absence of any such call.

Like the universal call to the Church, *the qualitative call* is unequivocally a calling forth: not only out of the "world" that lies outside the Church, but also out of the world within the Church. The consequence of this call is always the same: "When they had brought their boats to land, they left all and followed him" (Lk 5:11). "And at once they left the nets and followed him" (Mt 4:20). "And immediately they left their nets and their father and followed him" (Mt 4:22). "And they left their father

. . . in the boat with the hired men and followed him" (Mk 1:20). "He . . . said to him, 'Follow me.' And he arose and followed him" (Mt 9:9). "And leaving all things, he arose and followed him" (Lk 5:28). This "leaving all things" is the unequivocal condition for following Jesus. It is implicit in the call itself and is so challenging and clear that no one who hears it can mistake its meaning. This meaning is expressly stated for those who might wish to temper it: "For which of you, wishing to build a tower, does not sit down first and calculate the outlays that are necessary, whether he has the means to complete it? . . . So, therefore, every one of you who does not renounce all he possesses, cannot be my disciple" (Lk 14:28, 33).

There are no degrees to this *all*. It means leaving not only the living, but also the dead (Mt 8:21–22). It is a leaving so basic that it draws man out of every nook and cranny into the total absence of any place on which to lay his head (Mt 8:20); into a place outside [*ein Ausserhalb*] every human comfort this world can offer; a place that cannot be comprehended in any worldly sense because it does not lie within the world of natural ordinances, of calculable possibilities; a place unforeseen in creation; a place that, from the world's point of view, must be reckoned a non-place (οὐκ ἔχει ποῦ). It is par excellence a place outside (ἔξω: Heb 13:12–13). Those who enter it are aware of its indivisibility. They do not compute what they have left; they know they have left everything: "Behold, we have left all and followed thee" (Mt 19:27). The leaving is definitive and absolute and they continue to regard it as such. Even though they must repeat it daily, even though they must work it out in the small renunciations of each day's living, what they leave is, nonetheless, all they possess. And so they take their stand with the world's *all* behind them and before them only the following of him who calls himself the way. From the world, it is impossible to see where he is leading. Hence it is permissible to ask: "What then shall we have?" (Mt 19:27).

If a person is serious about this *all*, it is unthinkable that he should just continue to live in the world as he has been doing. In the world, he will need goods and resources to support his life.

And because these goods are scarce and disputed since the Fall, he will have to give thought to how he is to acquire them. And yet, the place outside, the "not-of-this-world" (Jn 18:36), to which Jesus leads those whom he calls cannot be worldlessness: They must be "in the world" (Jn 17:11) and live in it, even when interiorly they are "not of this world" (Jn 17:14). For the world, then, their state means the incomprehensible and incalculable taking of a stand outside earthly laws and ordinances, from which, however, they are neither exempted nor dispensed. Only with a faith that follows blindly can this "place outside", which is so inconceivable from the world's point of view, be discovered and attained. It *is* the place of faith and apostleship: "If anyone serves me, let him follow me; where I am, there also shall my servant be" (Jn 12:26). The "where" of Jesus, especially on the Cross, is precisely this "place outside" (Heb 13:12), this "nowhere" to lay his head, this "not of this world". For this reason, it is also the place created by his mission. The "where" of the Redeemer *is* his mission from (that is, his "sending" by) the Father. And the "where" of those called by Jesus is their mission from the Son: "As the Father sent me, I also send you" (Jn 20:21).

The privilege of taking one's stand in the place of mission depends primarily on the radicalness of one's renunciation of all things. Every attempt to cling to the world one has renounced threatens not just a part, but the totality of one's apostleship. To secure the hidden treasure or the pearl of great price, a person must sell "all that he has" (Mt 13:44–46). Every looking back, even to bid farewell, is a betrayal of this all: " 'I will follow thee, Lord; but let me first bid farewell to those at home.' Jesus said to him, 'No one, having put his hand to the plow and looking back, is fit for the kingdom of God' " (Lk 9:61–62). The attempt to retain something of what one claims to have relinquished is fatal (Acts 5:1–11). It makes no difference, once the call has been made, whether the seeker after perfection possesses little, like the apostles, or much, like the rich young man; for the rich young man, too, is challenged: "Sell all that thou hast, and give to the poor . . . and come, follow me" (Lk 18:22). There is so obviously a question here of relinquishing all external earthly goods that it would be absurd to seek a symbolical interpretation of the words. Yet the question of internal renunciation, of relinquishing all dependence on the world, is stated with equal clarity: "If anyone comes to me and does not hate his father and mother, and wife and children, and brothers and sisters, yes, and even his own life, he cannot be my disciple" (Lk 14:26). Hatred of self includes also hatred of one's "life in this world" (Jn 12:25)—not, however, with the secret hope of saving this earthly life, but with the certainty of losing it: "Whoever tries to save his life will lose it; and whoever loses it will preserve it" (Lk 17:33).

Integral to this radical requirement, which seems so unrealistic and so impossible of fulfillment because it places man in pure emptiness, is the second command: that in the very process of leaving all things, one is to possess a blind trust, a naive freedom from care. "Do not be anxious." "Fear not." The Lord repeats these admonitions again and again. Everything depends on a right ordering of one's actions. Man must not seek first for earthly security and only then relinquish all things, including himself. Instead, by relinquishing every earthly anxiety and security, every concern about what is or is not possible; by pure dependence on obedience to the Lord's "Follow me"; by forfeiting the very ground under his feet, he must take his stand in that place in which he will henceforth be able to live by faith alone. After insisting that man must not seek to serve two masters, God and mammon, the Lord utters those urgent warnings and promises that are intended to touch and convert the innermost heart of man: "Therefore I say to you, do not be anxious for your life, what you shall eat; nor yet for your body, what you shall put on . . . (for after all these things the Gentiles seek). . . . Your Father knows that you need all these things. But seek first the kingdom of God and his justice, and all these things shall be given you besides. Therefore do not be anxious about tomorrow; for tomorrow will have anxieties of its own" (Mt 6:25; 31–34). "Do not lay up for yourselves treasures on earth" (Mt 6:19). ". . . A man's life does not consist in the abundance of his possessions" (Lk 12:15). Having renounced all earthly possessions, the faithful should be without fear; they are to receive the kingdom from the Father's hands: "Do not be afraid, little flock, for it has pleased your Father to give you the kingdom. Sell what you have and give alms" (Lk 12:32–33).

Of itself, the admonition not to be anxious or afraid is insufficient to induce man to so rash a step. Faith must trust blindly. But the very magnanimity of man's sacrifice demands of the Lord a response a hundred times more generous than any human magnanimity. In the middle of the pure "place outside" to which he has called his faithful following, he must build a foundation on which the apostle can take his stand even as one who is "in the world" but "not of the world". Because he asks the Father ". . . not that thou take them out of the world, but that thou keep them from evil" (Jn 17:15), he must provide a state of life for his own within the created world. Indeed, he must literally create this place and establish it as an authentic sociological possibility, albeit of a supernatural sociology, that will be challenged again and again by every natural sociology, but will afford the faithful themselves a simple, repeatedly tested and proven possibility of actually being able to take their stand in the state to which they have been called. The Lord proclaims the great promise of this new state of life in words that announce its establishment:

"And everyone who has left house, or brothers, or sisters, or father, or mother, or wife, or children, or lands, for my name's sake, shall receive a hundredfold, and shall possess life everlasting" (Mt 19:29).

"Amen I say to you, there is no one who has left house, or brothers, or sisters, or mother, or father, or children, or lands, for my sake and for the Gospel's sake, who shall not receive now in the present time a hundredfold as much, houses, and brothers, and sisters, and mothers, and children, and lands— along with persecutions, and in the age to come life everlasting" (Mk 10:29–30).

"Amen I say to you, there is no one who has left house, or parents, or brothers, or wife, or children, for the sake of the kingdom of God, who shall not receive much more in the present time, and in the age to come life everlasting" (Lk 18:29–30).

The simple statement recorded in Matthew is elaborated in Mark and Luke. Mark not only describes in detail the hundred-fold to be received even in this world: houses and—instead of one mother—"mothers"; he also sets this hundredfold on earth in the framework of persecutions, thus recalling other prophecies of the Lord. Despite the insecurity of having left all things that leads first to the world's hatred and then to persecution, there is ample room for the hundredfold even in this world. Luke adds something new and important: One must leave not only one's brothers, parents and children, but also one's wife. This was, of course, implied in the leaving of house and lands and children, but the explicit statement of it completes a picture that might otherwise have given rise to uncertainty and questions in this significant area.

The solemnity of the texts silences all doubt. The promise is to be understood as literally as the Gospel's command to leave all things. This new state of life, which the world deems impossible, will offer not just a bare existence in the "place outside", but all the security that is offered by the hundredfold of the secular state. It will be the taking of a stand "in the midst of persecutions"—a stand, therefore, that will be a daily reminder of the radicalness of its withdrawal from the world; that will seem to the world more and more like a suspension in nothingness; that is never likely to be stripped of its disguise and revealed as an existence to which has been promised the hundredfold. In the desert, after their departure from Egypt, the people depended solely on God's leadership, on the nourishment they received from heaven, on the drink they obtained from the rock. Or to take an example from the New Testament: At the very moment when the apostle no longer walked in pure faith on the waves of this world, but began to reflect on himself and to lose sight of the Lord, he began to sink. Evangelical poverty is possible only on the basis of evangelical faith. If it is transformed knowingly or unknow-ingly into a merely "moral virtue", into something that must be cleverly adapted to worldly circumstances, it loses its Christian glow and the security of grace. Everything depends on the sincerity of one's total renunciation. Only when this renunciation is undertaken "for my name's sake", "for the sake of the Gospel", "for the sake of the kingdom of God", can it lay claim to the reward of the promise. But this "for the sake of" is absolute not just at the moment of initial renunciation. The renunciation of this world must be determinative for all time. Even when it seems to the believer to be but a march into the desert, there is no return for him to the "flesh pots of Egypt". Receiving the hundredfold is not a turning back from the decision to leave all things; on the contrary, the hundredfold is assured only so long as the apostle continues to follow Christ in poverty, chastity and obedience.

Obviously what we are discussing here is the unity of these three. With a certain comprehensiveness and urgency, *poverty* is always placed first. The demand that one sell one's possessions and give the proceeds in alms is so striking and so impossible to dismiss with subtleties that it is presented as the most visible manifestation of "leaving all things". It would be folly to try to clear a path to evangelical obedience without passing through this entrance gate. Hence the promise itself is attached to this act as explicitly as if the whole structure of the new state to be established were to be determined by poverty; as if virginity and obedience were only consequences or forms of a deeper understanding of this first renunciation.

In Luke, *virginity* is subsumed under the precept of poverty, since the leaving of one's wife is included in the leaving of other relatives and of all earthly possessions. In Matthew, on the other hand, it is presented as being, at least in one respect, parallel to poverty: It is in response to the perplexity and astonishment of the apostles that the Lord comes, on one occasion, to speak of the possibility of poverty; on another, of the possibility of virginity. In reference to poverty, the apostles raise the troubled question after the departure of the rich young man: "Who then can be saved?" (Lk 18:26). In reference to virginity, there is their no less troubled insight: "If the case of a man with his wife is so, it is expedient not to marry" (Mt 19:10). On both occasions, the inexorability of the Christian challenge sets man, as it were, before a stone wall that seems to impede all progress until the miracle of the founding of a new state of life opens a way precisely where there seemed to be no way.

The fact that poverty is assigned so unequivocally to first place while virginity is initially less significant in terms of the promise can be explained as follows: The Lord called his apostles from the Israel of the Old Testament, where marriage was itself a state of promise. He who came to fulfill the law, not to destroy it (Mt 5:17), did not want to build his Church on men who had not lived in the true messianic tradition. In the beginning, therefore, celibacy had to be by way of exception, although it should be noted that, even in the beginning, so much emphasis was placed on this exception—in John the Baptist, in John the Evangelist, in Paul—that through their example it had already become the rule for the generations to be born under the New Testament. Indeed, from the Lord's command to his apostles to be always at the service of the brethren, of which Paul gave the eleven apostles such an illustrious example, it is obvious that renunciation of a wife is no less required than renunciation of house and lands and familial ties. Nevertheless, the New Testament explicitly calls virginity a "counsel": "Let him accept it who can" (Mt 19:12). ". . . It is good for them if they so remain, even as I. . . . Now concerning virgins I have no commandment of the Lord, yet I give an opinion, as one having obtained mercy from the Lord to be trustworthy" (1 Cor 7:8, 25).

If poverty and virginity are the clearly indicated entrance to the new state, *obedience* is its core. The relinquishment of all earthly possessions and dependence is, as the Lord describes it, never more than a means to the end of perfect apostleship, to that outer and inner freedom that enables the apostle to follow the Master wherever he goes, even, by abandoning all things, to that place that is totally the "place outside" (Heb 13:11–13). The two phases are clearly separated: "If thou wilt be perfect, go, sell what thou hast and give to the poor, . . . [then] come, follow me" (Mt 19:21). Thereafter, this following is to be the whole content and rule of the apostle's life. The obedience of the Son who came, not to be served, but to serve, and even to give his life for the redemption of all (Mk 10:45), is the model for the life of the apostle, whose rank will henceforth be determined by the perfection of his service (Mt 20:26–28). The service of the Lord will be the exclusive content of the apostles' lives: They must learn to think as he thinks; they must let themselves be sent out on his business; they must heed his exact, and seemingly almost trivial, instructions about their nourishment, their clothing, their belongings, their food for the journey, their behavior underway and upon entering a strange dwelling; about their wages and their work. They must go out two by two to accomplish the work for which they were sent (Mk 6:7–13; Mt 10:5–14; Lk 9:1–6). Upon their return, they must render an exact account of all they have done or not done (Mk 6:30). There will also be individual commands to be obeyed: to go out and cast their nets (Lk 5:3–4); to have a boat in readiness for the Lord (Mk 3:9); to free an ass and bring it to him, heedless of the difficulties that may ensue (Mt 21:2–6); to prepare the Last Supper according to his precise directions (Lk 22:8–13).

This relationship of the Lord to his apostles typifies not only the later relationship of the teaching to the listening Church, or of the head to the body, but also—and very clearly—the inner life form of those who for his name's sake have left all things in order to follow him: the life form of an obedience that obeys not only in instances of rare *ex cathedra* pronouncements or significant ecclesiastical statements of divine truth, but also in the details of daily living. To appreciate correctly the significance of this obedience, one must understand, above all, that in the years of Jesus' public life the apostles were far from comprehending his divine Sonship, his very Godhood; the most of which they were capable was the acknowledgment of his Messiahship—and even here it is uncertain whether they understood its real implications. God was uniquely visible to them in Jesus, and God's authority in Jesus' commands. But Jesus was for them par excellence a person who made known to them the will of God.

Precisely this concept has been incorporated into the Church: "He who hears you, hears me" (Lk 10:16); the word—in contrast to the office—applies directly to every believer. But how many are there who make of this relationship of obedience not a marginal situation, but a way of life? From this point of view, we can understand that this goal of the evangelical counsels—this obedience—could and had to be concretized with the sanction of the Church itself into a "counsel"—or better, into *the* counsel that contains in itself all others, into a form of apostleship that is the distinctive mark of life in the evangelical state.

In this relationship of the apostles to Jesus, the "leaving of all things" finds its ultimate perfection, and exterior apostleship becomes truly interior, allowing Christ's perfect obedience to the Father (Phil 2:5–8) to become actually incarnate in the relationship of superior and subject within the supernatural sociology of the evangelical state. Far from being a later addition by the Church or even an intrusion of non-Christian elements, obedience as a way of life that, for the Lord's sake, renounces the free control of its own actions, is the closest conceivable following of Christ, who came, "not to do my own will, but the will of him who sent me" (Jn 6:38). Even more than the vows of poverty and chastity, obedience is wholly linked to the existence and example of Christ. Christian obedience, as the definitive renunciation of one's own will and self-determination, is possible only within the obedience of Christ and by his will, which makes it possible to follow in his footsteps (Jn 12:26). If this way had not been traveled by the Lord, if he were not himself this way, it would be, not just meaningless and incomprehensible, but totally impassable. The possibility of surrendering and abandoning one's own self would not exist because there would not be that concept of service that has its source in the perfect love that the Son has for the Father and that he came to bestow upon mankind.

Thus it has become even more evident that the state of election is preeminently the *state of Christ*, which is discussed more fully below. In creating this state out of the secular state by election and vocation, Jesus gave man the possibility of taking a stand where no such possibility had existed before, and made himself the sole foundation of this possibility. It is the possibility of taking one's stand in him, of having one's place in his love for the Father and for men, which is a love of perfect renunciation. Rooted in the call to go to him (πρὸς αὐτόν: Mt 10:1), to be at his side (μετ' αὐτοῦ: Mk 3:14), to be near him (περὶ αὐτόν: Mk 4:10), to be with him (σὺν αὐτῷ: Lk 8:38), it is the possibility of sharing his fate, of drinking his chalice, of knowing his inmost thoughts in order not only to rise with him, but explicitly also (Mt 19:28; 1 Cor 6:2) to judge with him and, having judged with him, to reign with him (Rev 20:4–6).

We can also see now the relationship between this new possibility, which has its foundation in the Redeemer, and *man's original state*. Man's original state was a "state of perfection" in which no distinction between secular state and state of election was either necessary or possible. In it, human nature was so supported by grace and ordered to love that poverty was but the manifestation of the riches of love, virginity but the manifestation of its fecundity, and obedience but the manifestation of its freedom to serve. What the gift of self cost in terms of self-renunciation went unheeded, for it was hidden in the enriching power of mutual love.

For man in his fallen state, the fullness of paradise was turned into the scarcity of earth. As a result, the search for the necessities of life and for private possessions became inevitable; man's drives became the determining factors for the propagation of the race; and the choice between good and evil by an intellect schooled in worldly wisdom became the norm of moral behavior. The program laid down for mankind in the commandment of love did not become invalid, but who could think of making love the rule and principle of his existence when in fact its original wholeness had been destroyed and could not be restored by man? Amid the struggle for existence, who could reflect that love does not seek what is its own? The longing for wholeness could persist, but, as we saw earlier, it was destined, in its attempts to reconstruct the state of innocence by its own efforts, to degenerate from the state of analogy before and in God to titanic forms of mystical identity or of pure humanism that placed man in the place proper to God.

The road between man's original state and his final state had been destroyed. Anyone attempting to pass that way now would plunge into the abyss at the point where the damage had been sustained. So it was with the Son of God. He came down to earth and became man—not a paradisal man, but a man like us. He took ". . . the nature of a slave . . . being made like unto men" (Phil 2:7) and appearing in the nature and form and pattern of a man; he even assumed "the likeness of sinful flesh" (Rom 8:3), "becoming a curse for us" (Gal 3:13); although he was sinless (Jn 8:46; Heb 4:15), God "made him to be sin" (2 Cor 5:21) for our sakes. He put on the body and soul that had not been capable of "original justice", that is, of perfect love, since man's exile from paradise. He assumed the incomprehensible and, for man, impossible task of meeting *from within the fallen world God's original demand for perfect love*. Whoever contemplates the greatness of this marvel will find it less astonishing that this divine-human manifestation of perfect love in weakened nature was able to reconcile the world with the justice of God and to effect the redemption of all nature. But he will understand also that this could have been achieved only by a love that revealed itself in radical *renunciation*, by a sacrifice no longer joined to fulfillment and joy, but accomplished in the night and abandonment of the Cross.

Christ emptied himself so that he might experience the full reality of earthly life as it had been lived since man was driven from the Garden of Eden; yet he lived here below as though he were traveling the undamaged highroad that no longer existed between paradise and heaven. By doing so, he created this road anew. In his own person he reconciled the difference between "below" and "above"; both his way below and his way above are ways of perfect and unmitigated truth. Nor are these two truths unrelated. On the contrary, it is *because* he descended below the heavens that he fulfills all things above them; because he emptied himself and humbled himself beyond all measure, because he became poor and was obedient even unto death on the Cross, "therefore God also has exalted him and has bestowed upon him the name that is above every name" (Phil 2:9). Because he "first descended into the lower parts of the earth", he could also ascend "above all the heavens, that he might fill all things" (Eph 4:9–10).

In the Incarnation, Jesus' descent took the form of poverty, virginity and obedience, and it was these forms that enabled him to live here below as he had lived above. He bore witness that what is impossible for man is possible for God, but likewise that what God makes possible thereby becomes possible for man. By traveling this road himself, he made it possible for others to travel it after him. Once Jesus, who descended from above (Jn 3:13; 8:23), had lived the life of man here below, not in appearance only, but in full reality, doing so divinely and in accordance with God's will, it became possible for man, too, to live in this manner by following in Jesus' footsteps. Man could live on earth as though the laws of paradise were still in effect. "Therefore, brethren, we are debtors, not to the flesh, that we should live according to the flesh" (Rom 8:12). The possibility of bridging the difference between the present world and the promised "new earth" (Rev 21:1) in a life that the world deems utopia, but that is constantly being given anew in the call to be an apostle of Christ, is for the world a genuine sign of promise. Like a sacrament, it "contains" what it signifies.

It is essentially the road of renunciation of which we are speaking, for the difference between the state of innocence and man's present state can be reconciled only by the removal of what was brought into existence by man's sin: greed and a disobedience that has escaped the ordering of love. Poverty, virginity and obedience acquired a negative aspect because of sin. But by the grace of the Lord, renunciation leads the apostle not only to a new and promising fullness of earthly as well as heavenly gifts ("Did you lack anything?" Lk 22:35) and to the freedom of truth (Jn 8:31–32) and of Christ (Gal 5:1), but also to an explicit sharing in the fruitfulness of the Lord's redemptive sacrifice, thus affording proof of the paradisal nature of such renunciation. Only in the eyes of the world are the renunciations of Christendom something negative. Only sinners experience the scepter of Christ as a rod of iron (Rev 12:5). For one who bears his yoke, it is "easy and . . . light" (Mt 11:30) and "his commandments are not burdensome" (1 Jn 5:3). In the meekness and humility of him who "will not wrangle nor cry aloud, neither will anyone hear his voice in the streets" (Mt 12:19; cf. Is 42:2), such a one "will find rest" for his soul (Mt 11:29), and a peace "which surpasses all understanding" (Phil 4:7) because it will be a foretaste of his homeland in heaven (cf. Phil 3:30).

Thus the new state created by the Lord and possible only on the basis of his own way of life, of the unity of the two natures in his divine person, is, in its turn, a synthesis of earthly and paradisal life. It means taking one's stand by the Cross, which is the gateway to paradise, or taking one's stand in the paradise that has been restored to mankind in the form of the Cross. It is fullness despite renunciation, happiness despite suffering. It is heavenly fecundity through renunciation of earthly fecundity, heavenly freedom in the bonds of earthly obedience. In this synthesis, the new state of life is not the final one, in which there will be no more suffering, no further cross to bear, but a principal access by which man can attain to this final state, the mysterious anticipation of heaven in a "first death" and a "first resurrection": "Blessed and holy is he who has part in the first resurrection! Over these the second death has no power, but they will be priests of God and Christ, and will reign with him a thousand years" (Rev 20:6). Those who follow the way of the cross anticipate the death that others must suffer unwillingly in the transition from earthly life to God's paradise: "The rest of the dead did not come to life till the thousand years were finished" (Rev 20:5).

3. ON THE RELATIONSHIP BETWEEN THE STATES OF LIFE

If we look back at this point to our opening discussion of the relationship between perfect love, as that to which all men are called, and the inner form of this love as being essentially a "vow", the connection between the two is even more apparent. Love's character as a vow, we discovered, comes to light in three ways. The vow is, first, that (outer) form that serves as a *means* of attaining (inner) love; next, it is, in form as well as content, the *expression* of love itself since the essence of love is the giving of self; finally, and again in its outer form, it is *potentially* contained in the indifference of perfect love since love does not anticipate God in choosing a state of life but waits for his call.

As we have seen, the difference between the *outer form* and the *inner spirit* of the vows becomes clearer when we apply these general relationships to the concrete state of fallen nature. All love has the inner form of a vow. All imperfect love, if it aspires to be perfect, must realize more and more this form of total and irrevocable self-giving, of surrendering—even of *having surrendered*—one's soul. This does not mean that everyone who strives for love must also aspire to the outer form of actually taking vows. For this, the election and vocation of the Lord are indispensable. He it is who, by his free choice, calls or does not call, invites or does not invite, to the special outward state of the vows. This vocation to a particular life *form* of perfection, which at the same time obliges one to a corresponding perfection of content, is the vocation to a special and distinctive *mission*. Election occurs for the sake of this mission, which, as a summons to leave the things of the world, requires the outer form of the state of life marked by the vows. Depending on whether the Lord's call is to a distinctive mission or to the mission common to all Christians in the world, those whom he calls are placed either in the state of election or in the Christian state as such, in the state marked by the external taking of vows or in the state that has as its goal the spirit of the internal vow of love.

Because of man's fallen nature, the relationship between love and the vows as means of perfection has become closer. In the Gospel, the vows appear almost as the condition of perfection: "If thou wilt be perfect, go sell what thou hast . . . and come, follow me" (Mt 19:21). This kind of perfection is what was wanting to the rich young man who asked about eternal life: "One thing is still lacking to thee" (Lk 18:22). As if to give final confirmation to this hard teaching, the Lord adds, when the rich young man has departed from him: "With what difficulty will they who have riches enter the kingdom of God! For it is easier for a camel to pass through the eye of a needle than for a rich man to enter the kingdom of God" (Lk 18:24–25). The harshness of this "with what difficulty" is mitigated to some extent by the supplementary comment in Mark: ". . . With what difficulty will they who trust in riches enter the kingdom of God!" (Mk 10:24) and by Jesus' mysterious concluding remark: "With men it is impossible, but not with God" (Mk 10:27). With men it is impossible that a rich man not trust in his riches, that he "buy as though not possessing" (1 Cor 7:30). If he were to do so, how could he carry on his business with all the care and intensity it requires? And how can they "who have wives be as if they had none" (1 Cor 7:29), when "he who is unmarried is concerned about the things of the Lord, how he may please God. Whereas he who is married is concerned about the things of the world, how he may please his wife" (1 Cor 7:32–33)?

It would appear, then, that the Lord's call to the state of the vows is practically identical with a call—in the only way in which this call is concretely offered to men in this fallen world—to the perfection of discipleship and, therefore, of divine love. In other words, the calling to a special mission, which is the reason God chooses an individual for the state of election, would appear to be identical with the call to singular holiness, which the state of election *formally* bestows on one who is called to it, and to the content of which such a one is obliged through actualization of this form.

We can understand, then, why historically it has been possible to equate the outer "state of the vows"—the *status religionis* as such—with the state of perfection. "And thus we perceive the identity of the two states."[4] For when the Lord introduces the concept of perfection, he immediately adds—"as the means or necessary way"[5]—the counsel to "leave all things". The necessity of doing so has its source in the evangelical precept that, to be genuine, an internal disposition must reveal itself in external action. The action required is, in this case, none other than the real and actual renunciation of what one possesses in order thereby to be free to give oneself to God. On the other hand, the challenge to accomplish this is a free grace of election and vocation from God—a grace man cannot bestow upon himself since its ultimate foundation is not the abstract perfection of love as such, but the concrete grace and assignment of a special mission. Thus the absolute necessity becomes for man once more a conditioned necessity: "It is possible, however, to distinguish between perfection and the state of perfection, for although it is most useful and even *morally* necessary to abstain from riches in order to acquire perfection, it is, nevertheless, not absolutely necessary. By using his riches well and performing other works of perfection, even a rich man can arrive at a degree of perfection."[6] In other words, the necessity is absolute when it is the consequence of a special call to a distinctive mission. If there *is* such a call, the individual no longer has the option of distinguishing between absolute and relative necessity. All that remains to him is the choice either of renouncing the state of perfection, and in doing so of giving up the special mission and being satisfied with the precepts of the ordinary Christian state, or of accepting both the mission and the life form proper to it.

The second and third relationships between perfect love and (inner) vow also receive a new and more closely defined profile in

[4] Francisco Suárez, "Opus de Religione", pars secunda, "De Statu Perfectionis et Religionis", bk. II, chap. 1, sec. 4, *Opera Omnia*, vol. XV (Paris: Ludovicus Vivès, 1859), 115. Henceforth cited as *De statu perf.*

[5] Ibid., bk. I, chap. 10, sec. 3, p. 49.

[6] Ibid., bk. II, chap. 2, sec. 4, p. 118.

man's fallen and redeemed state. For while the universal vocation to perfect Christian love is extended to all, the calling to an external "state of perfection" is based entirely on the elective will of God. The Lord divides the states of life so completely in accord with his own will that he can even reject and return to the secular state those who offer themselves as his apostles and are ready to believe in him and to follow him wherever he wills. But this nonacceptance into the state of election is certainly not to be identified with a withholding of the perfection of love, which Jesus unquestionably bestowed upon all whom he healed of their infirmities of soul and body and sent away new creatures. The blind man, for example, to whom, in the end, he revealed himself as God and Redeemer and who fell at his feet and worshipped him (Jn 9:37–38); the sinful woman, whose love he praised and whom he forgave because her love was great, thereby endowing her with perfect love (Lk 7:47); Lazarus, his friend, whom he who is "the Resurrection and the life" raised from the dead and restored to life from the fearful shadow of death (Jn 11:25; 33–44); the thief, for whom, from the Cross, he opened the gates of paradise (Lk 23:45)—without sharing in that special mission that is linked to a change of state, these and many others received through their contact with the Lord the gift of perfect love. Because they possessed love, all of them would have been prepared to follow the Lord if he had asked it of them. Since he did not, they were equally prepared to remain in their secular state in the world, to step back into the crowd, to resume the insignificant place assigned to them by the Lord, in order to serve him there with their whole hearts and all their strength. Little more will be heard of them. The Samaritan woman, for example, stepped back into anonymity once she had completed her task of making the Lord known to her countrymen: "We no longer believe because of what thou hast said, for we have heard for ourselves and we know that this is in truth the Savior of the world" (Jn 4:42). Lazarus, who had been raised from the dead, did not go about preaching, but at a later meal simply took his place as head of the household at table with the Lord (Jn 12:2). Although the Lord could have called them to a changed state of life, he did not. But his failure to do so is by no means an indication that he denied them the gift of perfect love.

We find exemplified here the two other forms in which the evangelical counsels are linked to love: the inner readiness of an indifference that is prepared to heed the call of the Lord whatever it may be, and the inner disposition of a love that bears in itself *the spirit of the counsels* and with it the spirit of perfection. As long as the Lord has not made known his will, the best disposition one can have is not the anticipation of God's election by entering uninvited upon the way of the vows, but indifference, in the form of readiness for every indication of the divine will. Until one knows the Lord's will, such indifference is the expression of a love than which no greater love is conceivable. And should the Lord choose not to call one to the external state of the counsels, it follows that this inner disposition of love, which contains in itself the spirit of the counsels, will require one to persist whole-heartedly in the attitude of indifference. This is what it means to possess full love for God and man.

There is, as we have noted above, nothing on the part of the world, of man's nature, or of his striving to realize his calling to love that would justify the dividing of the states of life. Only from the perspective of God and his positive will and vocation is a view of the states of life possible in which both states are shown to be intended by God and, hence, to be two positive forms of Christian life. But this divine will is not without explanation for us; the dividing of the states does not proceed from a naked ultimatum of God's will. On the contrary, God's enactments are always simultaneously the manifestations of the highest wisdom; all ultimate meaningfulness in the world is due, in every instance, to this twofold yet single origin of the divine decrees. To a faith that seeks understanding, it is apparent here, too, that the dividing of the states of life was the most meaning-ful way of establishing within the fallen world an order of redemption.

In such a world, obviously, the integrity of the paradisal state could be preserved and restored only by the renunciation of those goods whose emergence from the grace that had enveloped them in the state of innocence belongs to the essence of man's fallen state: private ownership, sexually motivated fecundity and personal autonomy. But the simple renunciation of these goods is not of itself sufficient to restore the lost unity of the paradisal state. As long as nature is subjected to suffering and death, whether in punishment or as penance, renunciation will continue to be something negative, namely, the loss of the relevant complementary goods: riches, natural fecundity and freedom. *For this reason, the call to such renunciation cannot be a universal one.* If it were, it would endanger, even abrogate, the order of nature as it exists in man's fallen state, since the paradisal demands on man would no longer be fulfilled: "Be fruitful and multiply; fill the earth and subdue it. Have dominion over the fish of the sea, the birds of the air, the cattle and all animals that crawl on the earth" (Gen 1:28). A universal command that, for the sake of the kingdom of God, obliged man to sexual abstinence and the renunciation of earthly goods and free control over nature would be tantamount to a nullification of these initial commands. If he were to command such universal renunciation, the Son, who came to complete the works of the Father and to demonstrate and confirm their goodness, would succeed only in abolishing them and showing them to be superseded and even inwardly imperfect. The universalization of the evangelical state within the Church would lead to Marcionism: to separation of the Old from the New Testament, of the order of creation from that of redemption, of Yahweh from Christ. In its most radical form it would lead, eventually, to the extinction of the human race and the destruction of man's earthly economy. For that reason, the state of election must always exist by way of exception in this fallen world. Those who are called to it will always be in the minority, destined by their exceptional mission to bear witness to the existence of another world, of man's first and last states, rather than to bring these states to pass in the present world. To those not called to the state of election, their relationship must be that of *special to ordinary*, of models to those called to imitate them, of representatives to the wholeness of what they represent. The state of election, then, is not only the universal reminder that man's present state is a fallen one, that paradise and heaven are the common homeland to which all must return, but also the representation of what was once *form-giving* in man's lost state of innocence and will be *form-giving* again in his hoped-for final state: the perfection of love in the gift of all one has—one's possessions as well as one's life and all the goods of one's soul. The state of election is a *representative state*: It brings to mind the idea of man as God conceived him and as he ought to be. It represents this idea within the fallen world in a mirror-reversed negative *form*—the form of a renunciation that has its source and meaning in the Redeemer's love for the world and hence allows the inner fullness of the positive to shine through even here: remembrance of the happiness of paradise and a foretaste of eternal bliss. There are no happier people on earth than those who have completed for love the unique and irrevocable gift of self and who continue to reflect this love in their way of life.

Because it is the prescriptive will of the Church's Founder that those called to the state of election should be a permanent minority in the world in contrast to those forming the general state of believers, it is likewise his prescriptive will that the many who are not called to the special state of life should remain in the general, secular state. By reason of this prescriptive will, we must, therefore, regard the secular state, not as just the negative side of the state of election, but rather as a true state in the realm of redemption and of the Church. Nevertheless, it would be incorrect to designate this will as a second vocation to the Lord's service of equal rank with the first. Being placed in the secular state can be described only as a not-having-been-called to a qualitatively higher state.

On the one hand, the positive aspect of the state of the Christian in the world is that part of the Creator's command that actually remains and must be actualized in the fallen world: the command that rests, not in man's supernaturally raised, paradisal nature, but in created nature as such, and that was, consequently, not abrogated by the fall into sin—the command to subdue the earth, to increase and multiply, to rule the world. This command is recorded in the first account of creation (Gen 1:1–2:4), where man is depicted as the crown of natural creation, but where the supernatural aspect of the paradisal plan is not yet apparent (as it is in the second account of creation: Gen 2:4–3:24). This command, which resides in man's nature, persists even in his fallen state although the integrity of the state of innocence cannot be restored. Consequently, the Christian in the world is also obligated by this cultural command rooted in his nature; he has to fulfill it in the same way as persons living outside the Church.

On the other hand, and this is the second positive aspect of this state, the Christian is, in a general, ecclesiastical sense, one who has been called out of the world; one who has been touched by grace and translated into the company of the Redeemer; one who has been placed on the road to perfect love of God and neighbor and commissioned with the general, but still charismatically personal, task of bearing witness to Christ. Nevertheless, he is and has all this without having received the qualitatively higher calling to follow Christ in total renunciation. His position is, consequently, more complex and more difficult than that of one who has actually been called. He is bound by the cultural command of his nature, which persists, but his nature is no longer perfectly ordered to its fulfillment. Instead, he has only those "goods" that came into being with the fallen state of nature: private property, coercive law, reproduction on the basis of sexual appetite, freedom to make one's own decisions. He cannot escape these modalities of nature by acting as though they did not affect him or were not binding on him—as though he were still in the original state of paradise. He cannot claim to represent the integrity of the paradisal state by virtue of the Creator's cultural command as fully as the elect represent it by virtue of their renunciation. Nor can he join with the elect to represent its totality as though elect and non-elect each possessed half of the lost unity and could supplement each other within the

Church to form a whole. The cultural command inherent in man's nature and the calling to the evangelical state are far from being two equal halves of one whole.

The Christian in the secular state must not only carry out the Creator's cultural command, but must also follow the universal calling to Christian love, which summons him out of the fallen world and into the order of redemption. He is bound by a double precept, and the tension grows greater as he becomes increasingly aware of his situation. "He is divided" (1 Cor 7:33). He, too, knows the separation from the world that is the hallmark of the Cross and has been the state of the elect from the beginning. But he experiences and suffers it as the separation of nature and supernature. The elect live in the wholeness of a renunciation established by the call of the Lord, which allows them to share in the unity of Christ, who comes "from above", but dwells below. They take their stand in the Cross and, in doing so, regain something of the wholeness of paradise. The Christian in the world, on the other hand, is left within the order of fallen nature, but in such a way that the shadow and form of the Cross fall upon him; in such a way, therefore, that, although he obeys the law of this world, he is nevertheless not of this world. Thus he, too, lives an "as if": "It remains that those who have wives be *as if* they had none; . . . those who buy *as though* not possessing; and those who use this world, *as though* not using it, for this world as we see it is passing away" (1 Cor 7:29–31).

Inevitably, then, *the secular state is governed by the same law as the state of election*. The cultural mission that it shares with the world outside the Church is not a specifically Christian one although the Christian must try to carry it out in the spirit of Christian love. The specifically Christian mission, on the contrary, is no different for one in the secular state than for one in the state of election: renunciation and sacrifice on the way of redemption to a hoped-for final state. Thus, while the state of election, by reason of God's special call, allows one to anticipate the world to come even in this world, but always on the foundation of the Cross, the secular state embodies life in transition from this world to the world to come. The "division" inherent in it is bearable only in the movement of transition. It is not possible to establish a peaceful balance between affirmation of this world and rejection of it, between earth and heaven or between family and state on the one side and ecclesiastical life on the other. Every synthesis that strives for a final solution in this direction will be ruptured again and again by the ceaseless movement that is the only medium in which Christian life can be lived in this world: ". . . For this world as we see it is passing away" (1 Cor 7:31). "Mind the things that are above, not the things that are on earth. For you have died and your life is hidden with Christ in God" (Col 3:2–3). ". . . Our citizenship is in heaven" (Phil 3:20). In consequence, the Christian, when he seeks to fulfill the cultural task assigned him by God, performs works of longing rather than of fulfillment, or, at most, those works of fulfillment that he achieves are designed to awaken in the receiver a longing for the heavenly abode of all beauty, goodness and truth.

In the transitoriness of the Christian's life in the world is to be found a kind of surrogate for the special vocation not accorded him. By reason of his baptism and with or without his awareness, *the spirit of the vows* pervades his life with increasing clarity and, in a mysterious manner, enables him to participate interiorly in the essence of the other state of life, in the spirit of undivided love in the forms of poverty, virginity and obedience. As long as the Christian does not withdraw himself from God's guidance, he is assured that these forms will be realized in his life without an explicit severance from the world. If the elect live a priori in the Cross, the Christian in the world lives always toward the Cross, and a part of the burden he must bear lies in the fact that he will remain to the end in a state of tension—a stranger in this world, but not yet a citizen of heaven. In this in-between existence, he, too, "has nowhere to lay his head" (Mt 8:20) and is required, often more unwillingly than willingly, to carry the cross after the Lord. Both states of life find themselves, then, on the same sacrificial course: "For everyone shall be salted with fire, and every victim shall be salted" (Mk 9:48).

In the last analysis, the common denominator of the two states consists in their readiness for the renunciation that makes one free for love. It is readiness *as* sacrifice—because Christian perfection consists in placing oneself at the disposal of God's entire will and renouncing one's own choice of a way of life. This readiness is the indifference that allows God to choose *the* state that he has decreed—or, to phrase it otherwise, it is the indifference that is fundamentally satisfied with either state. But it is also a readiness *for* sacrifice—a readiness that must persist even after one has chosen a state of life, whether that state is the state of sacrifice through renunciation or the secular state that acquires its Christian form solely from the sacrifice that the Lord can at any time require of it and inflict upon it anew.

4. IMAGE AND TRUTH

By the Lord's election and vocation, the Twelve were separated from the multitude for a qualitatively higher mission. They were not to return home, like the healed man of Gerasa, and announce what great things the Lord had done to *them*. They were no longer to think of themselves, but were to proclaim the nearness of the kingdom of heaven (Mt 10:7). They were to renounce themselves in order thereby to identify themselves with the mind and mission of him who sent them, just as Jesus identified himself with the mission given him by the Father: "He who receives you, receives me; and he who receives me, receives him who sent me" (Mt 10:40).

This mission, which was a participation in the mission of the Son, presumed that those who had been elected and called to it understood the essential message of the Gospel. Just as the Lord assumed full personal responsibility for announcing the Father's message to the world and received from the Father (Jn 5:22) full authority for exercising this responsibility in the pasturing of his flock (Jn 10:11, 18), so those whom he called were not to be "hirelings", but true "shepherds", with all the duties, knowledge and responsibilities therein entailed (Jn 21:15–17).

On the other hand, this insight into the truth of the Gospel could be experienced only by those who lived the truth they received, by those who shared the life form of the Redeemer who gave his life for his sheep. For with God truth and life are so intimately united that "he who does not love does not know God" (1 Jn 4:8).

Not least of the reasons why the Lord calls some to take their stand apart from the multitude in the way of election is that this way of life is the necessary precondition for their understanding the Gospel to the full extent possible to man and making it comprehensible to others by their life and preaching. The light that is the Lord and that shines probingly into the darkness of this world (Jn 1:4–5) does more than shine upon the elect: It causes them to be, in their turn, sources of light. In contrast to the singular: "I am the light of the world" (Jn 8:12) stands the plural: "You are the light of the world" (Mt 5:14), a light that must be completely consumed in the mission of lighting—but of lighting the world, not self. It follows that the state of qualitatively higher vocation is related to the general Christian state as the generator of light is related to what is lighted, as truth is related to image. The state of election, then, is *forma sui et totius*, the definitive form of Christian life, which as "form" must also inform the "matter" of the Christian secular state.

To the multitudes, Jesus spoke only in images: "All these things Jesus spoke to the crowds in parables [according as they were able to understand . . .], and without parables he did not speak to them" (Mt 13:34 [Mk 4:33]).

The apostles wondered at this: " 'Why dost thou speak to them in parables?' And he answered and said, 'To you it is given to know the mysteries of the kingdom of heaven, but to them it is not given' " (Mt 13:10–11). " 'To you it is given to know the mystery of the kingdom; but to those outside, all things are treated in parables' " (Mk 4:11). This explains why the Lord sometimes waited until the crowds had dispersed and then "privately . . . explained all things to his disciples" (Mk 4:34). Because of this distinction between parable and truth, the apostles were permitted to ask about the meaning of the word of God: "But Peter spoke to him, saying, 'Explain to us this parable' " (Mt 15:15). "And when he had entered the house away from the crowd, his disciples began to ask him about the parable" (Mk 7:17). But Jesus required more than their mechanical acceptance of the interpretation he provided for them. He wanted them to find for themselves the key to the parable. If their eyes and ears were blessed because they had seen and heard what "many prophets and just men have longed to see . . . and . . . have not seen" (Mt 13:17), this blessedness also entailed the obligation of seeing and hearing in such a way that the divine meaning became visible in the earthly parable. That is why Jesus reproved the apostles when they failed to penetrate the true meaning of his words (Mk 8:15–21). They were to be capable— ultimately it was only the descent of the Holy Spirit that made them so—of changing the letter into the living spirit whose glow would ceaselessly illuminate the true meaning of the parables (2 Cor 3:6, 10).

Jesus spoke to the people in parables that he did not interpret —a method that befitted their ability to understand. They were to be touched by the power of his word, were to be astonished at his wisdom, were to praise God for it. They were to be attracted by the greatness of its content, which was beyond their comprehension. The glory and brightness of the divine sun was to shine upon their lives in the world: "The people who sat in darkness have seen a great light" (Mt 4:16); they were to have the possibility of believing in the light, of walking in the light (Jn 12:35–36) while it was still day, while the light still shone upon them. It was enough if their lives moved within the circum-ference of this light, if the secular activities they must perform were illumined and given new value by the rays of light shining upon them. In this way, they could fulfill their daily earthly task, which was to become images of eternal life and eternal truth. They might not know this truth as it was in itself, but they knew that what constituted life for them was not the ultimate and final truth of existence; they recognized in its transparently symbolical meaning a reference to another, definitive world, and they looked forward with patience and faith to the time when this world would be revealed to them. In this way, they gained perspective on their lives and realized, though often not knowing that they did so, the warning of the apostle: to live in marriage as though not married; to weep as though not weeping; to rejoice as though not rejoicing; to buy as though possessing nothing; to use this world as though not using it (1 Cor 7:29–31). In the parable of the Lord's word, they learned that the world itself is but a parable and that "it is passing away" (1 Cor 7:31); that "the world with its lust is passing away, but he who does the will of God abides forever" (1 Jn 2:17).

Whatever the Lord taught the people in parables, he also interpreted for his apostles. Thus the same word was addressed to both people and apostles, but always "according to their ability to understand" (Mk 4:33): to the former, in the darkness of a symbol that made its human meaning comprehensible, but left its divine meaning incomprehensible; to the latter, in the revelation that let the divine appear, but made the word harder to bear. *There is no question here of* the Lord's presenting *an esoteric teaching to the apostles, but a popular, exoteric, attenuated and shallow one to the people.* God's word is always the same, as is the message the Son has to transmit from the Father to the world. He is himself that word, and his witness is identical with his life: Thus there can be no division in him. But just as the voice of the Father, which spoke to him before his passion and confirmed before all the people the redemptive will of heaven in his regard ("I have glorified [my name] and will glorify it again")—just as this voice was received by the Son in all its fullness, but was heard by men in so weakened a manner that some thought they heard the voice of an angel while others believed they heard only the roll of thunder (Jn 12:28–29), so the same word of the Son is received from different degrees of proximity and with different intensity by apostles and multitude. Every word of the Gospel has meaning for the whole Church, even those words that were spoken to particular individuals in particular situations. In the canon of

Holy Scripture there is no word of the Lord in which a Christian cannot find meaning. Even those words that were addressed to the apostles and were intended primarily for the elect are directed to the whole Church and to every Christian in the secular state of life—not only so that the people may know what the Lord expects of his apostles and how he has taught and trained them, but, equally or even more importantly, so that the people may understand the full significance of the one indivisible word of God to the world and may live their lives accordingly. For this reason, Jesus often spoke directly to his apostles even in the presence of the multitude: "Now when immense crowds had gathered together, so that they were treading on one another, he began to say to his disciples, '. . . What you have said in darkness will be said in light' " (Lk 12:1, 3). Indeed, he continued to address them on this occasion until Peter interrupted with the query: " 'Lord, dost thou speak this parable [of the watchful servants] for us or for all alike?' " (Lk 12:41). Jesus' reply is couched in mysterious words that offer a precise analogy to his preaching of the word of God in a manner corresponding to each one's ability to understand it: "But that servant who knew his master's will, and did not make ready for him and did not act according to this will, will be beaten with many stripes. Whereas he who did not know it, but did things deserving of stripes, will be beaten with few. But of everyone to whom much has been given, much will be required; and of him to whom they have entrusted much, they will demand the more" (Lk 12:47–48). This response of the Lord is a clear indication that the parable is offered as an analogy to the word of God: The apostles, who know the meaning of the word in all its divine clarity, have a greater responsibility for acting according to it than does the multitude, for "hearing they do not hear, neither do they understand" (Mt 13:13).

There can be no better confirmation of this analogy than the fact that *words which in one Gospel seem to apply only to the apostles are, in another, nearly always addressed also—or even primarily—to the people*. Nothing seems more exclusively characteristic of the state

of election than the great address in Matthew in which the Lord
sends the apostles out on mission, in which he explains to them
their apostolate, and in the course of which he speaks the words:
"He who loves father or mother more than me is not worthy of
me. . . . And he who does not take up his cross and follow me, is
not worthy of me" (Mt 10:37–38). Yet in Luke these same words
are addressed specifically to the great multitude of people (Lk
14:26–27). In Matthew, the words about losing one's life are
spoken to the apostles alone (Mt 16:25); in John, to a larger group
(Jn 12:25); in Mark, explicitly to "the crowd together with his
disciples" (Mk 8:34). Most impressive of these dual addresses is
the Sermon on the Mount, which is spoken with both the larger
and the smaller group simultaneously in mind: "And seeing the
crowds, he went up the mountain. And when he was seated, his
disciples came to him. And opening his mouth he taught them,
saying, 'Blessed are the poor in spirit' " (Mt 5:1–3), or, as Luke
describes the scene: ". . . He lifted up his eyes to his disciples,
and said, 'Blessed are you poor' " (Lk 6:20; cf. 12:22–32). The
smaller group of apostles surrounded the Lord most closely. Yet
even while looking upon them and teaching them, he addressed
his word at the same time to the great multitude of listeners
who stood below them on the mountainside. From this fact,
the whole Sermon on the Mount acquires a unique double base
and *perspective* by reason of which it is always susceptible to a
twofold interpretation—either as strict and literal truth or as
parable, as a "tendency" of Christian life in the world. The
admonition, for instance, not to be anxious about the morrow
—not to ask, "What shall we eat; what shall we drink"—will
be obeyed by those who have left all things and placed their
entire hope exclusively in the Lord in a way radically different
from that of the housewife or father of a family who must
understand it rather as a recommended attitude toward the usual
daily anxieties. Both groups are immeasurably enriched by the
same word, but must interpret it in their own way. Both interpretations are true, but not interchangeable since they apply to
two entirely different states of life.

When individuals are observed in their concrete situations, it may well be that no exact lines of division can be drawn between the understanding of the apostles and that of the multitude, that the gradations between them are infinitely interchangeable. We have already called attention to the larger group of disciples—the seventy-two, the women who followed Jesus, those who were his friends, those who were well-disposed toward him. But even these personal gradations do not remove the original polarity between the two states of life or the polarization that is inevitably consequent upon the Christian's final choice of a state of life. In its turn, this state of life operates to differentiate the manner in which the individual receives the word of God. The state of election is the state of those called to a qualitatively higher mission. Hence grace will be accorded them to hear the word of God in a way that actively includes the acceptance and furtherance of Christ's mission. Later, they will be called to be "a pattern to the flock" (1 Pet 5:3), a model to which the community can look when it seeks to put into practice the Christian life: "Brethren, be imitators of me, and mark those who walk after the pattern you have in us" (Phil 3:17).

Nevertheless, the relationship between the two states is *more than just* that of pattern and copy, *truth and image*. The common calling to perfect love is a fact that continually permeates this relationship and is superior to it. The picture of Christian life that both the Lord and his apostles described for the community is far from being a pale image, a compromise with the world. On the contrary, it contains the undiminished challenge of the whole deposit of faith, hope, love and every other Christian virtue. Because all Christians are called to walk according to the grace of Christ, all are obliged to strive for the goal of perfect love. For Paul (Rom 6:1–14) as for Peter (1 Pet 2:13–17) and John (1 Jn 3:16), the progression from the mere fact of being a Christian to the requirement of perfect love is absolutely binding in the logic of grace. So compelling is this logic that it retains its validity even when it seems to have no basis in reality, even when the ideal picture of the community seems to be a utopia painted on empty air. Even though the state of Christians in the world does not cease to be structurally "a state formed by division", those called to it cannot escape the demand that they be "a pattern to all believers" (1 Th 1:7). The state of election, on the other hand, is established so entirely for the service of the community, for the purpose of patterning what is communicated to those for whom it is communicated (that is, for the community), that this service becomes its whole raison d'être, to which it is ordained as the secondary is ordained to the primary,[7] because, in the last analysis, one can be greater in the Christian order only to the extent that one is, by calling as well as by voluntary inclination, the servant of those who are lesser (Lk 22:24–26). "But God has so [fashioned] the body . . . as to give more abundant honor where it is lacking; that there may be no disunion in the body, but that the members may care for one another" (1 Cor 12:24–25)—that those in the secular state (the state of those not chosen) may acknowledge as such the state of those who are chosen and may model themselves on the pattern of their lives, but that those in the state of election may acknowledge that they are entirely at the service of those in the secular state since the greater one's grace and insight, the greater also is one's obligation to give and expend oneself in the service of the brethren.

Instead of a one-directional subordination of the secular state to the state of election within the truth of love, then, there exists between the two states a totally different relationship in which now one, now the other, assumes the ascendancy. Like the two

[7] Von Balthasar's argument rests on ST 2a 2ae 184, 3, which reads in part as follows: "Perfection can consist in something in two ways, in itself and essentially or secondarily and accidentally. In itself and essentially the perfection of the Christian life consists in charity. . . . Secondarily and instrumentally, however, perfection consists in the counsels, all of which, like the precepts, are ordained to charity, but in different ways. For the precepts are aimed at the removal of those things contrary to charity, i.e., those things incompatible with charity. But the counsels are aimed at the removal of those impediments to the exercise of charity which are not incompatible with charity, such as marriage, secular occupations, etc." [Tr]

complementary halves of a whole, the two states *move toward each other* in such evident articulation that, in the supernatural order of the Church, their relationship acquires a meaning *analogous to that of the relationship of the sexes* in the natural order. The subordination of wife to husband that is described in the account of creation and confirmed in the New Testament does not preclude the equal status of both before God: "For man was not created for woman, but woman for man. . . . [But] as the woman is from the man, so also is the man through the woman, but all things are from God" (1 Cor 11:9, 12). And if wives are to "be subject to their husbands as to the Lord", husbands are to give themselves in love for their wives "just as Christ also loved the Church, and delivered himself up for her" (Eph 5:22, 25). The ascendancy of the husband is relative and functional, obliging him to greater love and service on the model of Christ, who "did not consider being equal to God a thing to cling to, but emptied himself, taking the nature of a slave" (Phil 2:6–7). An analogous gradation exists between the states of life within the Church, but only for the purpose of reciprocal subordination in love. The disintegration of the paradisal state in consequence of sin was transformed by God's redeeming grace into a means of greater love, just as Plato's *androgyne* divided into both sexes and, by this "fall" from original unity, made possible the wonder of *eros*.

It would be premature to attempt to delineate here all the consequences for the Church of this relationship between the states of life, because Church order with its offices and charisms cannot be considered apart from the second division of states within the Church—that between priesthood and lay state. Far from exceeding the first division in importance, however, the second one is unthinkable without it—and this for two reasons: First, the state of election must be a priori the state of those who serve if the priestly state is to be ordered to service; secondly, as qualitatively higher states both the priestly state and the state of election must enter together into the service of the non-elect according to the admonition of the Lord: "Let him who is the greatest among you become as the youngest, and him who is the chief as the servant." And then, to dispose of the "as" of his admonition, he adds: "For which is greater, he who reclines at table, or he who serves? Is it not he who reclines? But I am in your midst as he who serves" (Lk 22:26–28). In reference to the Lord, the "as" is *obligatory*; it is not even permissible in reference to man's serving man.

CHAPTER TWO

THE CHRISTIAN STATE OF LIFE

1. CHRIST'S STATE OF LIFE

We have not yet sufficiently penetrated the mystery of the division of the states of life, for it can be understood in a Christian sense only from the perspective of Jesus Christ. What the Christian recognizes as the state of election will be regarded from every extra-Christian—as it were, sociological—perspective as just a form of *flight from the world* on the pretext that withdrawal from the Many and Relative enables one to draw closer to the One and Absolute, to find in him one's state of life. Such a way out of the world to God has been sought so assiduously and in such a variety of ways by the religions of the world that it might seem to have its roots deep in human nature. Nevertheless, we have seen that, left to itself, it leads only to betrayal of the original analogy between God and creature and to the destruction of mankind, whose proper place is at a remove from God.

From the beginning, however, we have transcended this natural, sociological perspective by taking as our point of departure man's original state in paradise—by assuming a priori that man was created in a proper relationship to God (in "righteousness", according to Anselm; in "original justice", according to all theologians), and that this relationship could on no account be regarded as alienation, rootlessness or abandonment in the world. The alienation man experiences can have come about only as a result of guilt—hence our need of the lesson to be learned from man's original state, which was "very good". With this lesson, we are no longer in the realm of sociological criticism: *The state of election* no longer *refers* to a God outside the world but *to the originally created synthesis* between man and world of which this lesson is the formal sign and which will be regained at the end of time.

183

It is significant that we were unable to reconstruct the relationship between the state of election and the state of innocence without raising the question of Jesus Christ and his state of life and that, in doing so, we were obliged to inquire also into the relationship between his state and man's original state. But we pursued the question only to the point of learning that it was Jesus who forged the link between the way of love "above" and the way of renunciation "below". Coming down from above and living the "life of the evangelical counsels" even to the full renunciation of the Cross, he made it possible for man to experience, even in his fragile earthly state, the characteristic wholeness of his first and last states. But have we said enough when we have said this? What we seem to be saying is that Christ created a synthesis of fallen and unfallen nature. But does Christ not come to us *from higher than* Adam's *paradise*? Does he not come from the Father? And does he not, therefore, aim at a higher synthesis than that which we have depicted here as paradisal? Does not Holy Scripture, in its final utterances about him, hint at something of this kind when it says that he is "the firstborn of every creature. For in him were created all things in the heavens and on the earth. . . . All things have been created through and unto him" (Col 1:15–16)—including, then, also Adam and his paradisal state. As Holy Scripture explicitly comments: " 'The first man, Adam, became a living soul'; the last Adam became a life-giving spirit. But it is not the spiritual that comes first, but the physical and then the spiritual. The first man was of the earth, earthy; the second man was from heaven, heavenly" (1 Cor 15:45–47). We must, then, abandon any point of view that would interpret Christ's state of life as a mere overcoming of the difference between the state of innocence and the state of fallen nature and *adopt one that explains even the state of innocence in terms of his state*.

In doing so, we shed entirely new light not only on the Christian state of election, which is always a placing of oneself in Christ's state of life, but in consequence also on every other Christian state.

In essence, Christ's state of life is the taking of a stand eternally "with the Father" as the original Word in whom the Father creates and sustains all things (Jn 1:1; Heb 1:3). No movement or mission can abolish his place with the Father. But if he is the Word of God through whom everything is created, then he is himself (as the Fathers of the Church have pointed out) the original idea of all that is created; when he comes into the world, he comes ultimately "unto his own" (Jn 1:11) even though the world, alienated by sin, does not receive him but makes itself a stranger to him. Yet whether the world knows it or not, whether it chooses it or not, it has in him its beginning, middle and end. In him it is most intimate to itself.

These statements based on Holy Scripture are confirmed by the anti-Arian and anti-Monophysite teachings of the ancient Church: If Christ is the Word in whom God created and, through the redemption, completed the world, then this Word cannot be below God, cannot achieve the synthesis of God and world from a state that is proper to neither God nor creature. He cannot lure out of its genuine creaturehood and into an imaginary in-between world the creature he has come to save, but must set it in its proper state before and in God—a state that, in the last analysis, is made possible and is determined by his own state as Son of God. This, then, is the description of the Christian state of life. It is taking a stand "in the faith" (1 Cor 16:13), in "grace" (Rom 5:2), and, therefore, also "in all things perfect" (Eph 6:13). It is taking a stand that has been made possible by the decree and ordering of the Lord, for "where I am, there also shall my servant be" (Jn 12:26). But the Christian does not take his stand in some external—as it were, geographical—location, but in the personal divine-human reality that is Christ. "To take one's stand in Christ" means so to take one's stand in this reality that one is thereby fashioned and marked as what one will henceforth be by nature. For in Christ, in the Word, is to be found the very idea of the Christian. It is important, then, that we consider more fully what we know by faith about Christ's state of life.

The "where" of the Son is the Father. "Dost thou not believe that I am in the Father and the Father in me?" (Jn 14:10). The Son is "in the bosom of the Father" (Jn 1:18). This being in the Father is also true of the time the Son spends on earth, during which he fulfills the mission he has received from the Father. This work, this mission, requires both a going forth from and a return to the Father: "I came forth from the Father and have come into the world. Again I leave the world and go to the Father" (Jn 16:28). Both statements are true and are intended to be taken literally: "I am in the Father" and "I came forth from the Father." *His going forth is not just a simulation* while he himself remains actually unchanged in the Father. *Nor is his remaining with the Father just a fiction*—a remembrance, as it were, from afar—while he himself is actually in the world. On the contrary, he is, at one and the same time, both in the Father and gone forth from the Father. The incomprehensibility of this "where" that is the Son's state of life has its source in his divine nature itself. For he is that one who "is God" because he is "with God" (Jn 1:1), because he is "the brightness of his glory and the image of his substance" (Heb 1:3). His being and remaining eternally in the Father and with the Father take their form from his hypostatic difference from the Father—from his procession from and return to the Father. In his divinity, the Son is the mission of the Father: His person is the revelation of the Father. In his own person, he reveals the nature of another Person; his knowledge, his love, his activity have no other raison d'être than to serve this revelation. He is not an "autonomous" person who subsequently undertook, as a service to the Father, to transmit the Father's message to the world. He is a person in God only to the extent that he is "service" to the Father—a "service" that is wholly identified with love because the Father generates the Son in love and the Son knows that his own essence consists in returning this love in the same infinite perfection in which he has received both it and himself from the Father. The Son, then, is the first mission within the Godhead. He expresses in himself the being and will of the Father. He cannot possess the Father more perfectly in himself than by letting himself be "missioned" [sent forth] by the Father. He cannot be more perfectly with the Father than by proceeding from the Father in order to return to him in love.

When the Father sends the Son into the world, the Son reveals simultaneously in his going forth from God both the Father and himself. And if, in a sense, he distances himself from the Father, since the world is not the Father, he just as truly remains in the Father because he has the Father's mission in himself—in fact, he is this mission. To be with the Son, then, the Father does not have to perform all the actions of the Son with the Son; he is in the Son because, even in the world, the Son is the perfect "brightness of his glory and the image of his substance". When the Son utters the message the Father has given him, he speaks, it is true, as the one sent by the Father, but the Father also speaks in him because he is the very Word of the Father: "I am not alone, but with me is he who sent me, the Father. . . . And he who sent me, the Father, bears witness to me" (Jn 8:16, 18). Nor does the unity of their message owe its existence to an accidental coincidence of the views of Father and Son. It comes, rather, from the fact that the Son is, from the beginning, the Word of the Father, that he uses his whole being—memory, understanding, will—for no other purpose than to express the Father's will. ". . . The Son can do nothing of himself, but only what he sees the Father doing. For whatever he does, this the Son also does in like manner." And to exclude the possibility that this inability of the Son might seem to limit or constrain him, he adds: "For the Father loves the Son, and shows him all he does" (Jn 5:19–20). The perfect gift of self for the glorification of the Father, which is the root of the Son's being, blossoms into complete divine fullness—the Father has given "all judgment . . . to the Son, that all men may honor the Son even as they honor the Father" (Jn 5:22–23)—but in such a way that the root from which it springs is neither abandoned nor forgotten: ". . . My judgment is just because I seek not my own will, but the will of him who sent me" (Jn 5:30).

The Father looks upon the Son and is infinitely well pleased because he sees in him the entire perfection of his fatherly love returned to him in a filial manner. Three times during the Son's earthly life the Father allowed his voice to be heard in order to bear witness to his love for the Son: at Jesus' baptism, as vocation and mission: "This is my beloved Son, in whom I am well pleased" (Mt 3:17); at the transfiguration on Mt. Tabor, as endorsement: "This is my beloved Son, in whom I am well pleased: Hear him" (Mt 17:5); before the Passion, as consent to Jesus' suffering: "I have both glorified [my name], and will glorify it again" (Jn 12:28). The Father sees himself so perfectly expressed in the Son that he has only to point to the Son to bring men to himself, even to know that he is himself perfectly glorified in the Son's decision to undergo the Passion. Thus the mystery of the Son's earthly mission is a purely trinitarian one, and the going forth (the mission) from the Father that will lead to his abandonment cannot be separated from this mystery. For whether the Son is in the bosom of the Father or treading the paths of earth, there can be no doubt that the "where" that determines his state of life is the mission, the work, the will of the Father. In this "where", the Son can always be found, for he is himself the epitome of the paternal mission.

As the substantive mission of the Father, the Son is, humanly speaking, the person predestined in God from all eternity to accomplish the task of reconciling the world with God. Hence his coming into the world was no more a distancing of himself from the Father than it was a distancing of himself from himself. For him there was, from the beginning, no dichotomy between distancing himself (being sent forth) from the Father and being with the Father. Even though he became the eternal worshipper of the Father in praise, reverence and service by reason of his distancing himself from the Father, who is "greater than I" (Jn 14:28) because he is the eternal source and goal of all things, yet the distance between them is bridged from all eternity by their unsurpassed nearness, by their unity of love in the Holy Spirit: "I and the Father are one" (Jn 10:30), and by their sharing of the one divine nature. Since the world is not God, the "emptying" (Phil 2:7) that the Son accepted when he came into the world necessarily entailed for him a new relationship to God in the midst of creation. But this emptying was not something unfamiliar to him; it was foreshadowed and made possible by the *eternal self-renunciation* of the Son in relation to the Father, in which the Son desires nothing but to be the adoring mirror-image of his source. The potentiality that he realized in the Incarnation even to the total renunciation of obedience unto death on the Cross had its foundation in the pure actuality of the eternal life of the Blessed Trinity. There could be no going forth that was not subsumed in and surpassed by the eternal procession of the Son from the Father, and no return that could be accomplished apart from the eternal return of the Son to the Father. Hence the action of going forth into the world and of returning from the world to God does not interrupt the eternal procession of the Son from the Father and his return to the Father. The mystery of the economy [οἰκονομία] of salvation has its foundation and, indeed, the locus of its final accomplishment in the mystery of life in the Trinity [Θεολογία]. Whether, during the Son's earthly sojourn, the divine Father draws him so close that his Godhead shines through as it did on Tabor, or whether he delivers him over to the utter abandonment and desolation of the Passion, the perfect unity of Father and Son is in no way diminished thereby; the Son's state remains unaltered; his distance from and nearness to the Father in the Holy Spirit are always the same. So great is the inner richness of the eternal life of the Trinity that every aspect of Christ's Incarnation—the joyful union with the Father and the desolate abandonment by him—are but outward expressions of the inner possibilities of divine love. Just as all the words Christ spoke on earth are but facets and aspects of the one eternal Word that he is, so all the states that he experienced in the course of his life, death and Resurrection are outward manifestations of his unique eternal state in the Father. And if his life in the world is a restless activity whose "where" and "whither" are incomprehensible to the world because such activity seems to transform all that is static into the dynamic of his coming from the Father and his returning to the Father, yet this ceaseless movement is generated and guided from a single point: his state of being always in the Father. Precisely because this state is infinite and therefore unchangeable, it is eternal and never-ending life and the fulfillment of every potentiality. The Son's state is so securely in God that he can, at the same time, perform actions outside the Godhead; for every distancing of himself from the center has no other purpose than to show how immovably he has taken his stand in this center. The identity that persists despite the mighty swing of the pendulum of his earthly life is the identity of his going forth from and his return to the Father—the identity of his mission, which, as Word of the Father, he not only *has*, but *is*. The *ex-centro* orientation of the Son in his earthly state does not derogate from the *ad-centrum* orientation of his state in the Father. Both his eternal and his temporal missions are accomplished in the Father. "In the midst of the throne", which is the Father's throne, stands "a Lamb . . . , as if slain" (Rev 5:6). The Lord himself affirms, precisely with regard to his life on earth, the genuineness of his stand in the Father: "Dost thou not believe that I am in the Father and the Father in me?" (Jn 14:10). But the changed relationship of Father and Son as a result of the Incarnation is comprehensible only in terms of the new role of the Holy Spirit in the economy [οἰκονομία] of the Incarnation. The Spirit sent by the Father is active in the Incarnation: *He* bears the Son—who *allows* himself to become man—into the womb of the Virgin. At Jesus' baptism, *he* is sent down upon the Son as the abiding mission that both resides in the Son and comes to him from above and that he looks upon as an objective norm for being always obedient to the Father. The Spirit rests in fullness upon the Son (Jn 3:34), who acts in the Spirit (Mt 12:28), but does not bestow the Spirit (Jn 7:39) until he breathes him forth to the Father on the Cross (Jn 19:30). There can be no doubt that Jesus obeys the Spirit, not as one alien to or outside himself (any more than a religious does when he obeys his rule), but as the bearer of God's will. Nevertheless, by the self-emptying of the Incarnation, he has placed himself in a position where, *even within the Godhead*, he must first *receive* from the Father the possibility of breathing out the Spirit together with him—that is, *in the position proper to created man*, who has no other way of receiving the Spirit (or of bestowing him on others) than by obeying him as the missioning Spirit (that is, as the Spirit who conveys God's will).

This "inversion" of the roles of the Second and Third Persons of the Blessed Trinity in the Incarnation explains, above all, how the Son, without changing his personal essence, can become obedient to the Father even to death on the Cross and thus become the model of the obedience—not servile, but filial—of every creature. The obedience of the Passion is possible only because the Father externalizes his will to such an extent in the Holy Spirit that he is able to disappear as a person behind this externalization. The Spirit vouchsafes for the perfect identity of the Father-Son relationship even during the time of personal darkness (for the Son) and apparent absence (of the Father). Thus, the not only creaturely but also sinful orientation of the world away from God, for which the Cross is the atonement, can be drawn into the trinitarian intimacy that remains unchanged even in the Son's abandonment by God; and, when the Son's obedience to his mission has been fulfilled to the utmost, the Spirit can be breathed into Church and world, since the Son, whom "God has made both Lord and Christ" (Acts 2:36), can henceforward send (Jn 14:26), pour (Rom 5:5) and breathe (Jn 21:22) him forth both from and with the Father.

In the last analysis, the created world can turn *away* from the Father only because, in the embrace of the incarnate Word of God, it is incorporated into his orientation *toward* the Father. Revelation tells us of no other plan of God for the world than that by which, from all eternity and "before the foundation of the world, . . . he predestined us to be adopted through Jesus Christ as his sons"—through Jesus Christ in whom "we have redemption through his blood, the remission of sins" and in whom he purposed "to reestablish all things . . . both those in the heavens and those on earth" (Eph 1:3–10). The cosmos and those who dwell in it have no autonomous history, no ultimate meaning, beyond that bestowed upon them by the fulfilling mission of the Son, by which those predestined in the Son also receive their mission and with it the idea and purpose of their existence. Granted that "in the beginning . . . all things were made through him [the Word], and without him was made nothing that has been made. In him was life, and the life was the light of men" (Jn 1:1, 3–4). Yet this statement is but a prelude to that which follows—that the light came into the darkness, where it illumined every man, and eventually became flesh in order to bring to all men the fullness of grace and truth. This action is the primitive history, the turning point, in which are subsumed all the events and happenings of world history.

As a logical consequence of the Incarnation, the Son of God is at the same creaturely remove from God as we are—at the remove proper to the "servant of God". Without changing his state, he can now be laden with the full alienation of sin. He does not shun the anonymity that befalls him as but one among countless possessors of human nature; he looks up to the Father with human eyes and speaks to him with a human mouth. He does not except himself from the analogy of God and creature. He does not want to be separated from his fellow humans by a wall of glass, but chooses to be "tried as we are in all things except sin" (Heb 4:15) and to learn obedience (Heb 5:8) even in the all-embracing experience of being "made . . . to be sin" (2 Cor 5:21), of bearing the "curse" (Gal 3:13) of all flesh.

Yet in all this he is, in his own person, the realization of the comprehensive and unified idea of the world that the triune God had in the beginning. He is this idea, not in some unspecified place outside the real world and its history, but by his very coming into that world and its history "to reestablish all things" (Eph 1:10) from within in himself as head. Because he is himself the measure of the analogy between the world and God without thereby creating a dichotomy between his state in the world and his state in the Father, he becomes the model for the analogy of all creatures; *he becomes the concrete analogy* of being. Whoever seeks to take his place at a proper distance from and in proper nearness to God must pattern himself on Jesus. For "he is before all creatures, and in him all things hold together" (Col 1:17). He is "the First and the Last" (Rev 1:17; 2:8), the model for creation even in its most innerworldly aspects. So true is this that it is pointless to object that he came into the world only in the fullness of time, for the process of creating the world would never have been begun if this moment in the fullness of time had not been foreseen. Indeed, this realization of the idea of the world in the Incarnation was possible only because it already existed as a concept among the free possibilities of the eternal reality of trinitarian life. For this reason, the Son's historical movement from the Father to the world and from the world to the Father—this movement that overcomes all distance—is the immovable axis around which all world history turns. Even man's *primitive state* is no exception. In God's plan for the world, the primitive state is *not an absolute state*, but a beginning and a transition. It does not embrace all dimensions; its boundary is the temptation in the Garden of Eden, which Jesus absorbed into his own single, all-embracing state. Thus it contains, within the perfect identity of ideality and reality in Christ, a one-sided ideality (and a corresponding unreality).

This means that for creation *there is ultimately no other relationship to God than that established in Christ the Lord*. For man, it means even more concretely that he does not have to discover for himself the true relationship between creation and God, between natural order and supernatural grace; that he does not have to determine the measure and proportion of the relationship between the two since their unity has been concretely established in Christ and bestowed on mankind as the greatest of gifts. Nor can man take his place midway *between* the natural world and Christ in order thereby to establish a proper balance between them. For if Christ, in order to mediate between God and world, took his stand neither outside the Father in an imaginary (and, in practice, Arian) center equidistant from both, nor on both sides in order to find a just settlement between them as one might between partners having equal rights, neither can the Christian take his place between Christ and the world or between the Church as the body of Christ and the natural order in order thereby to derive from this imaginary, but untenable, vantage point a norm for the relationship of one to the other. Because Christ, as a divine person with both a divine and a human nature, established for all creation by the unity of his person the true relationship between God and man, it follows that the Christian can enter upon no state that does not transfer him in faith into the reality of Christ and that only in Christ can he judge the relationship between grace and nature, faith and reason. Just as the Son adopted no neutral position between God and the world, but pursued his way to and in the world with an eternal orientation to God, so there can be for the Christian no neutral position between Christ and the world. For "I am the way, and the truth, and the life" (Jn 14:6). Man finds himself on this way, which is the only way that leads to truth and life, only if he makes it his definitive choice. "He who is not with me is against me, and he who does not gather with me scatters" (Mt 12:30).

By making it impossible for man to take a double stand both in God and in the world so that all stands must be united in his own single and all-embracing state, *Jesus becomes not only Lord of the states of life, but also*, and even paradoxically, *the cause of their division*. To divide them in such a way that both states continue to be Christian, he himself must be above both in the unity of a state of life in which both can participate. But if their duality is not to be separated from his unity, it is not enough to regard his state of life as transcendent to the two states; there must also be explicit evidence that it is likewise immanent in each of them. It must be possible to make the source of their division within and from the unity of his state visible in a manner that does not separate them from him. The one way of Christ from the Father, through the world, and back to the Father must be so understood that he can be the *source of both possible states of life* without himself having to take a double stand.

In the first thirty years of his journey through the world, the Lord exemplified the secular state. During this time he was a member of a human family, born and educated like everyone else and, above all, obedient to his parents in the relationship that is characteristic of the secular state. Jesus' state during this time is the model for the secular state, not the secular state itself. For he was not bound to this state by nature, as other men are, but submitted to it voluntarily. He was not the offspring of an ordinary marriage, nor did he himself contract marriage as those in the secular state are wont to do. The stand he took in the world disguised, as it were, his permanent (that is, his primary) stand in the Father, but we ought not, for that reason, to describe it as being itself the state of election. For the state of election is characterized, above all, by the loosing of those natural family ties that actually characterized Jesus' first years in this world. These years remain, then, the genuine—not merely the ostensible —model of the worldly state because, within a genuine human framework and in genuine obedience to the laws of the natural family and society, the Son exemplified the possibility of taking one's stand as child, youth and adult in the Father and in his will and mission. Later, at the beginning of his public mission, when he left this framework to enter upon a new way of life and, with his disciples, formed a new community, he did not simply continue, in this second stage of his life, what he had begun in the first, but emphatically underscored the distance that lay between them. By the distinctiveness of his second state, he showed beyond a doubt the distinctiveness of the first. The confrontation between the two occurred when he denied his earthly relationship to his mother and brethren in order to put primary emphasis on his supernatural relationship to those who do the will of the Father (Mk 3:31–35; Mt 12:46–50; Lk 8:19–21).

In the antithesis between the two states, we have a para-digmatic demonstration of the unity of Jesus' own state, which persists throughout his two earthly states. Just as he fulfills the will of the Father by being born into the first state, so he fulfills it in the second state, which is opposed to the first, by freeing himself from the ties of the first state in order to assume those of the second. The identity of the two states lies in his identical fulfilling of the will of the Father; the consequent transfer of obedience takes the form of an emancipation from his earthly ties. Jesus does not hesitate to use even his mother to demonstrate the greatness of the abyss that separates the two states. From the fact that she comes with his brethren in search of him, she must be seen to belong still to the secular state, whereas Jesus himself has already advanced into the state of election. This use of his mother to illustrate the other—opposite—state of life does not (as some Fathers of the Church have erroneously assumed) indicate any imperfection on the part of his mother, for Jesus himself had only recently left that same state. He permits an interval of time to elapse between his own passage from the first to the second state of life and his mother's passage only so that he can use this interval to show the articulation of the two states. The new community is not hostile to the first state. Even though the Lord begins, at Cana, by indicating the distance that now separates him from his mother's state of life (Jn 2:4), he has, nevertheless, brought her with him to the wedding feast and he fulfills her request, even while intimating to her the point of convergence that lies ahead of them in the Cross where their states of life will again be identical. Thus the new community, which is so distinct from the first, does not mean for the Son a break with his first state—even in his secular state he had already given the sign of the twelve-year-old that seems to bind the two states together (insofar as it was a withdrawal out of the "world" and into the sphere of the Father) —but it does reveal the unity of the Son's state of life in the unchangeable will of the Father. *Only* because the Father binds him to the secular state is he obedient to his parents in the first stage of his life on earth, and *only* because the Father calls him out of the world does he free himself from this state to found a supernatural order.

It is clear, from this, that *the secular state is by no means an enslavement* to the laws of this world (Gal 4:3–7), but rather a voluntary surrender of oneself to God in obedience. While the natural man is bound to the things of this world by his very nature, the Christian, who is "buried with [Christ] by means of baptism into death, in order that . . . [he] also may walk in newness of life" (Rom 6:4), is freed, even in the secular state, from slavery to "the elements of the world" (Gal 4:3). So free is he in his detachment from the things of earth that he is not a debtor "to the flesh, that [he] should live according to the flesh" (Rom 8:12), but is "called to liberty" (Gal 5:13), "no longer a slave, but a son" (Gal 4:7), bound only by the law of love by which all the laws of this world are fulfilled insofar as they have their source in God (Gal 5:14). But in this freedom from the world that is proper to every Christian by reason of Jesus' all-embracing state, it is again clear that the secular state receives its ultimate substance and form from the state of election. The Lord makes it abundantly clear in the painful scene in which he turns his relatives away that, in the will of God, Christian freedom within the ordinances of this world does not represent man's ultimate freedom; that beyond this there is the agonizing call to follow the Father to the point at which he chooses to loose these earthly bonds—even, if necessary, to break them by force. Thus, while the freedom of the Christian in the world allows a certain leeway in that one who has been redeemed from the destructive bonds of sin finds in the ordinances of the world both the material and the occasion for leading and demonstrating a Christian life and receives from God the grace and privilege of acting as a child of God in all spheres of secular activity, there nevertheless also exists, by reason of the unsearchable decree of the Father, the possibility that one who wants to be obedient to the utmost degree may be loosed from his worldly ties and led to a place "outside" [*ein Ausserhalb*] that is beyond our ken. We have already designated this "outside" not only as the taking of one's stand in the pure mission of the Father, but also as the cross, that is, as the renunciation that allows the Father to strip one of all one possesses. Now that we have contemplated the states of life in their birth from the single state of Christ, it becomes clearer that, while the state of election may be called the radicalization of the secular state, it is so not primarily because man, on his own initiative, seeks or has found a better or more perfect means of attaining the goal of love, but rather because the Father, in his incomprehensible wisdom, can so ordain the taking of a stand in his will that it leads to the renunciation and rejection of all that is not this will itself.

"Led by the Spirit" (Lk 4:1), that is, in obedience to the Father, the Son took his course *out of the world*. It is the Father who draws him, as it were, out of the world—out of the world not only of his family, his relatives, his country (Mk 6:4), but also out of the world of his human nature and its laws, out of the world of his memory, his understanding, his will. In the dark night of his redemptive Passion, the Father demands of the Son and the Son freely offers the Father all the inner resources of his humanity. The Father can dispose of these inner resources as he will, can withhold from the Son the knowledge "of that day and hour" (Mk 13:32), can take from him the knowledge of the Father's paternal nearness and essence (Mt 27:46), can subject him to human wilfulness in order to make him totally submissive to the divine will even to the suffering and death of the Cross. As exemplified by the Son, then, this placing of oneself at God's exclusive disposal, which is the basic prerequisite of the state of election, means surrendering to God all that one has and is in such a way that he becomes the sole arbiter of one's whole being as of something totally subjected to him. To endure the Cross, which was the only reason for his coming down to earth, the Son had first to enter upon the second phase of his earthly life, the state of election, for the Cross is but the high point and last consequence of the Son's total vow (that is, his total surrender of himself to the Father's will). In the Cross, the Father takes and receives what is offered him. In the Cross, the full ecstasy (that is, the total self-abandonment) of the Son is oriented toward and consummated in the Father, for everything in him that seemed, however justifiably, to claim independence from the Father is surrendered without reserve in the mystery of the Cross so that the pure act of the Father's will can be accomplished in the pure suffering of the Son. The world cannot comprehend such a surrender of one's own being to the pure will of the Father. It is not within the sphere of the analogy of being. For the actualization of this state of life is dependent on the effort and good intention, not of him who wishes so to bind himself, but solely of him who both bestows and accepts the bond in an act that lies beyond all human expectation. From the disposition of sacrifice per se it is not possible to know whether he to whom the sacrifice is offered will actually accept and take possession of it. Consequently, the innermost essence of the state of election, as it takes its origin in the state of the Son on the Cross, is by no means something that can be envisioned and calculated from the world's point of view or from that of the Christian in the world. The radicalization of the secular state is not in itself sufficient to give form to the state of election; for that, there is needed a new and qualitative act of God who, in an ecstatic transcendence of all secular possibilities, establishes a new state of life through his acceptance of the Son's sacrifice on the Cross.

In this highest act of service and self-surrender "to the end" (Jn 13:1), the Son, it is true, does no more than reveal where, from all eternity, he has always taken his stand: at the very center of the Father's will. And if, to furnish proof of this stand in the Father, he lets himself be divested and stripped with inconceivable violence of all his natural and human powers, even the extremity of such treatment does not alter his state of life, for as God his place with the Father has been from the beginning a going-out from himself in order to return to the Father. Where previously he offered positive proof in the world that " my food is to do the will of him who sent me" (Jn 4:34) and that "I live because of the Father" (Jn 6:58), so now he offers negative proof by dying from the withdrawal of this food. Nevertheless, when he commends his spirit into the Father's hands, even this death, which is willed by the Father and which the Son willingly accepts and offers to redeem the world, is transformed into the most positive proof that he has taken his stand in the Father.

By thus fulfilling the plan of the triune God for the world, Jesus does not flee the world and go to God; he goes, rather, to the very foundation of the world—or, more precisely, he reveals himself as the innermost foundation of this world. For this reason, the state of election, which has the Cross as its point of reference, can be designated as the deepest and innermost secular state—as the taking of one's place in the ideal-real foundation of the world. Those in the state of election know this—or ought to know it.

Both the secular state and the state of election, then, are rooted in the one state of Christ. In both, he fulfills the one will of the Father: in the first state, by submitting himself to natural ties; in the second, by submitting himself to supernatural ties that find their justification only in the act of redemption. Interiorly, his first state is a single-minded adherence to the will of the Father, but in such a way that this interior state is hidden from without: "Is not this the carpenter, the son of Mary, the brother of James, Joseph, Jude and Simon? And are not also his sisters here with us?" (Mk 6:3). This hiddenness is normative for the secular state, because the ordinances of this world are themselves the veil behind which the reality of the Christian life lies hidden: "For you have died and your life is hidden with Christ in God" (Col 3:3). For this very reason, however, the sudden revelation that accompanied Jesus' second state was of necessity both a stumbling block for those not closely associated with him: "And they took offense at him" (Mk 6:3), and a source of incomprehension even for those of "his own house" (Mk 6:4)—not excluding Mary and Joseph (Lk 2:50). For the world in general and even for the Church, Jesus' entry into the second state of his life on earth will always retain something of the scandal it had during his lifetime because, ultimately, this state relies for its justification, not on human reasons (however exalted they may be), but solely on the will of the Father. Because he represents the nakedness of that place "outside" the world, he can appear to the world both within and without the Church only as an impossible possibility unless the Spirit of God, who is likewise the God of the Cross and of sacrifice, stirs the hearts of those who are in the world and enables them to share in the spirit of those who leave it. This unity of spirit is not impossible since both states of life are one in the unity of Christ's state of life.

2. MARY'S STATE OF LIFE

Christ did not choose to stand alone in his all-embracing state of life, which not only encompassed the two states that would exist in the Church he was to found, but even made possible their division within its unity. He chose to share this state with his mother, who was to be his Bride as the Church, so that, *transcending both states in a manner analogous to his transcendence*, she might also be cofoundress of both. Because Mary is at once virgin and mother, both states can claim her as their model and patroness. Yet she belongs to neither; even though she passes successively through both states, she stands, like her Son, above both and, by her transcendence, participates with him in the actual founding of both.

Even more by her spirit than by her body Mary is the source of the Redeemer's human nature. For God does not use force against his creatures. He wanted man's consent to the Incarnation, and the "yes" that Mary gave as representative of the whole human race was the necessary condition for her overshadowing by the Holy Spirit. But such an unqualified "yes" can be spoken only out of the utmost purity of soul. Hence the Immaculate Conception was the ultimate prerequisite for the Incarnation. Because she was preserved from the sinfulness of the human race by a special grace conferred upon her by the triune God through the merits of the Cross, Mary stands outside the fallen world in an innocence like that of Adam and Eve before the Fall. For this reason, the division of the states of life does not affect her. She will help to found the two states, will even, in her own way, live them both, but without thereby losing the incomparable unity of her whole existence. As virgin and mother, she, more clearly even than her Son, will let the glory of God's plan to engrace mankind irradiate the world.

As the Immaculate Conception, her spirit has always been oriented toward God and subject to his will. Consequently, her interior state is identical with that of her Son: She takes her stand in the will and at the disposal of God. Yet, because she is a created woman, the "how" of her state differs in two ways from that of her Son. The Son, who is God, takes his place from all eternity in his "yes" to the Father's will. The mother, who is human, grows toward this will in the course of time and out of the unawareness of youth, but in such a way that even the unawareness that thus yields to awareness in her was never anything but a "yes" to God. Moreover, the Son, as a man, assumes active responsibility for carrying out the will of the Father, while she, as a woman, must wait until she has been touched and taken possession of by him. Until her meeting with the angel, she was indeed at God's disposal, but only in the mode of a waiting that did not yet know its true mission.

Mary's waiting for the will of God to be made known to her is anterior to every Christian choice of a state of life. Because the Old Testament did not know the alternative of marriage or virginity, marriage was the normal way for a believer to direct his life according to God's promises. Hence the absoluteness of her self-surrender was not limited by her engagement to Joseph. She did not even have to detach herself from it interiorly in order to preserve her complete indifference as to what God might ask of her. Externally, her waiting was like that of any young woman who waits in indifference for God to indicate which of the two states he has destined for her. Yet the quality that distinguished her from all other members of the human race was already in evidence. Mary was innocent not only in the sense of inexperience in sexual matters, as young women well may be who before marriage consider in all naiveté the two possibilities of "convent" and "marriage", but without forming a clear concept of what is involved in either. Mary was innocent in the sense of the Immaculate Conception—of a grace that preserved her from contact with the realm of fallen nature, including sexuality as it has been since the Fall. Whether consciously or unconsciously, her indifference, her readiness, for all that God might demand of her excluded those potentialities for evil to which human nature is heir. She was, therefore, not less, but more open to God. From the perspective of God and his original ideal for mankind, her indifference was only seemingly a limitation. Its effect was broadening, not narrowing. Without being aware of it, she was open to God for possibilities known only to him and reserved by him for the wonderment of those wholly dedicated to him. Mary's indifference was the indifference of the most perfect love, of a love that opened itself only to divine love and excluded the possibilities of imperfection inherent in life in the world. The very fact that she was able to offer this love of indifference to God is a sign that God had already bestowed on her the unique grace to which he proposed to respond with the superabundant grace of the Incarnation. Even before she uttered her "yes" to the angel, the form of her indifference had already placed her above the states of life as they would appear in the Church, and the interior structure of her waiting in indifference was totally different from that of the most perfect indifference of every other Christian. By reason of his baptism, the ordinary Christian is called out of the world of sin and, before making his choice of a state of life, stands in obedient expectation before God to learn the state to which he has been called. Only two possibilities open themselves to him and he awaits the moment when either a special call will summon him to the state of election or the absence of such a call will indicate that he is to remain in the secular state. Although Mary was already engaged, her indifference was directed to no such limited possibilities. The readiness of her waiting love was unbounded. She had no preference for any known state of life, but was open to whatever possibilities God might devise for her or were already known to him. She had taken her stand so firmly in God that only he could choose and determine the state that was to be hers.

In her perfect expectation, she received from God the perfect answer: the Word that was the basis of her expectation and that was, therefore, fulfilled by coming into the world. And yet her "yes" was not something extrinsic to the Incarnation, but by grace was made one of its intrinsic conditions. Henceforth, Mary possessed in herself a new center, the eternal Word of God himself. As a mother she was the sheath that surrounded and encompassed this center that was not herself, that was infinitely superior to her, but that yet had been given to her as her Son. Even more, she was pure readiness to expend herself and to be expended in the service of this center. The stand she had always taken in God found its fulfillment at the moment when the divine center of her being made his abode within her. In this she resembled, as much as a creature can resemble, the model of her Son, who, at the center of his being, possessed the will of the Father. In her it was visibly demonstrated that such an ecstatic surrender of one's whole being to the will of God is by no means an absurdity that destroys man's inner harmony; on the contrary, all man's fulfillment, all his fecundity, all his happiness lie in the identification of his own center with the divine will. Never was a life more fulfilled even in a human sense than Mary's life, on which, for the gift of her perfect "yes", God bestowed all the gifts of heaven.

Although Mary's single state, in which she is at once virgin and mother, transcends man's two states of life within the Church, it nevertheless reflects the exact ordering of these states. *Her spiritual "yes" is the cause of her bodily fecundity.* Her virginity, by which she places herself entirely at God's disposal, stands at the point of origin of her motherhood, which is a consequence of it—not, certainly, a natural consequence, but a supernatural one bestowed on her by grace. In the "yes" by which she responds to God through the angel she expresses her whole being, offering it in the all-embracing vow: "Behold the handmaid of the Lord; be it done to me according to thy word" (Lk 1:28); and within this boundless readiness there occurs the miracle of her motherhood. What she has in common with the secular state, her bodily fecundity, is itself the fruit of what she has in common with the state of election—the spiritual fecundity of her grace-filled "yes". Thus there is repeated in her what we have already seen in reference to the Son: In the Incarnation her stand in the will of the Father reveals itself on the primary level as the state of election even though, on the secondary level, this state is hidden for the time being behind the "secular state". In general, then, it is true to say that in Jesus and Mary the proposition is affirmed that the state of election is *forma sui et totius*. It was so in the paradisal state, in which all fecundity came into the world through the primacy of spirit and love; and it is so in the order of redemption, for, in the Incarnation of the Son, it is revealed how deeply this order has its roots in God.

Mary, then, is not virgin and mother by equal title. She becomes a mother because she is and remains a virgin, because she is the one totally consecrated to God. In her, the preeminence of the state of election over the secular state is fully evidenced. On the other hand, the purpose of her whole existence lies in her motherhood. *She is a virgin so that she may become a mother.* In the eternal design of the Incarnation, God created this spotless being to become spiritually and physically in time, by the total gift of herself to him, the perfect vessel of his divine will. Consequently, there is also affirmed in her that other proposition—that the second state of life within the Church is not an end in itself, but is ordered to the first just as everything higher in the Church is higher only because it renders or may render and is ready to render greater service. In fact, the readiness to humble oneself— to take the form of a servant—*is* itself this "higher", for the only value that can truly claim such a qualification is love. But love is ever ready to serve and to give itself in service.

The service rendered by the second state to the first is a real one, not just the setting of an example in some inaccessible and self-contained sphere. In the Incarnation, as we have seen, the Son, without leaving his stand in the Father's will, nevertheless enters into the full reality of being man and experiences in their totality all the heights and depths of human life and consciousness. Precisely because he is in God, his stand in God is not closed upon itself, but offers the world the greatest possible access: the access ordained by the Creator himself. In like manner, Mary is not removed by the uniqueness of her Immaculate Conception to a sphere that is inaccessible to the real and realistic world. Her innocence is not ignorance or lack of inner concern. On the contrary, nothing makes one more concerned for one's neighbor than selfless love, whereas the experience of egoism and greed shuts men off from one another. In Mary is proof that one does not have to experience all the ways of the world in order to know them. She, the Seat of Wisdom, knows the whole truth about the fallen world, for she sees in the torn body and spiritual anguish of her Son what this world actually does and is. In God's view, no further knowledge about sin is either valid or useful. Mary does not have to leave the contemplation of her Son to dispense her love, her assistance and her mediation on all the paths of earth. She does so because her Son has done so before her in eucharistic prodigality, and it is no more necessary for her than for him to alter her stand in God's will in order to bend pityingly and efficaciously over all the world's suffering and guilt. She is so pure and loving that she *needs no cloister* to remain undefiled by the world. Wherever she goes, she brings purity, love and heaven with her; her love is its own cloister: Every dividing wall between world and cloister, earth and heaven, falls as she approaches it. She teaches Christians to be fearless in their following of Christ, who does not hesitate to send his own among wolves and to expose them unprotected to the hostility of the world. Where a cloister does exist, it is not an invention of fear; like the whole state of election, it has a representative value as the manifest symbol of withdrawal from the world and the taking of a stand in God.

From this we see also that Mary does not simply echo the paradisal synthesis, but has her own indisputable place in the all-embracing christological synthesis. The test to which her freedom was subjected when she had to consent to the total abandonment of her Son and by her Son is greater than any that can have been imposed upon man in paradise. From the beginning, the freedom of her love found its support in the Cross.

Taking one's stand exclusively in God and being open to the world are, as Mary has shown, complementary concepts.

Whether this openness reveals itself in a visible mission like that of the apostles and members of active religious orders or in the invisibly effective intercessions of contemplatives, the law is always the same. Sometimes, as in the case of St. Thérèse of Lisieux, the radiant inner strength of contemplation may become manifest to the world—she, for instance, was named patroness of all missionary activities; but in most cases its strength remains hidden or, at most, only minimally suspected by the faithful. The unity of Mary's mission as mother, which combines the taking of a stand in God with the fruitfulness of this stand for the world, is a guarantee for the entire Church that the fruitfulness of the internal and external apostolates is to be equated, not with being "conformed to [the spirit of] this world" (Rom 12:2), but only with the radicalism of one's stand in God. All methods of attracting the world in order to win it for Christ remain subject to this first principle.

Like Jesus, Mary also *lived first in one state of life, then in the other*. By the law of the Old Testament, she entered first into the natural community of her life with Joseph; by the mystery of her crucified Son, she took her place with John in the supernatural community of the elect. But just as Jesus entered into the secular state not only in spirit, but also in the truth of his commitment to the Father, thus prefiguring the later state of election, so Mary, though married, lived not only as though she were not married (1 Cor 7:29), but also in the full truth of poverty, virginity and obedience. Yet Mary's life, both with Joseph and in her widowhood from the death of Joseph to the crucifixion, was still genuinely a life in the world. It was a life bound by the prescriptions and rules of family, household, education of children and the thousand other anxieties of life in a poor family. The Holy Family practiced poverty, for the Lord's call summoned them again and again to abandon their possessions and establish themselves elsewhere; they practiced virginity, for the tender love that united Mary and Joseph demanded of him this genuine sacrifice within a marriage that was not merely ostensible, but real; they practiced obedience, for Mary accepted God's message to Joseph as unquestioningly as she accepted the message delivered to her personally by the angel. For the Holy Family, the counsels were not merely of equal importance with family life; they were its heart and center. Mary sought to fulfill them only in the accomplishment of the tasks and duties required of her within the framework of the family.

The extent to which Mary laid the foundation of the secular state in this first phase of her life is apparent in Jesus' disavowal of her in the scene discussed earlier. Because he has already moved into the second state of life, he detaches himself from her who here signifies the "flesh and blood" that must be abandoned by those who will come after him. The Son seems to leave her behind on this stage of his journey through life. He explicitly repudiates her; he refuses to receive her; he renounces her in her role as (natural) mother and points to his disciples and faithful followers as his spiritual mothers and brethren. Yet, precisely in this most bitter experience of abandonment, she is mysteriously drawn by her Son into the new state into which he has already entered. By abandoning her, he forces her to be detached from him even though she understands neither the meaning of nor the reason for this abandonment. What is begun here has its culmination on the Cross, where the Son, in his complete abandonment by the Father, finds no other way of giving his mother a share in his mystery than by completely abandoning *her* and transferring her motherhood to a new son, John. Just as the Son, in his Passion, enters into the passivity of being-sacrificed, since the Father hides himself from him and thus deprives him of his inmost life so that he has no choice but to sink into the abyss of death, so, in that same Passion, the Son deprives his mother of the place in which she has taken her stand, that is, himself, so that she may share with him this death that is the birth of the new world. Perhaps there is nothing more incomprehensible and supernatural in Mary's life than this—that she does not die with her Son; for, in fact, she lives by the Son no less than he lives by the Father. The Father and the Holy Spirit encompass her and keep her supernaturally erect while she is deprived for three days of the center of her soul, her Son. And in this interim John, and with him all the friends of the Lord and the whole community of believers, begin to fill the place thus prepared for them. Where previously her God had been in the form of man, there is now the friend of her God and, through him, everyone in whom she recognizes the love of her Son. Thus the mystery of the identity of interior and exterior consecration to God, of giving oneself exclusively to God yet being open to the world, is perfected on the Cross—not, however, in such a way that total surrender to God is rewarded there with earthly fecundity. Rather, in the place previously reserved for himself, God substitutes the world, which, because it has become his place, is now to be loved for his sake. But this exchange is no facilely accomplished synthesis of love of God and love of the world. On the contrary, it takes place at the foot of the Cross, at the pinnacle of the state of election, where, in the passivity of suffering, Jesus' mother too is deprived of all she has and is—not only of herself, but also of that in her that is more than herself, her inmost center, her Son. Only by embracing the extremity of this suffering does Mary become the mother of all Christendom. For the mystery of her virginity and exclusive dedication of herself to God must extend to that final emptying of herself of all things that is possible only in God if it is to attain beyond all worldly fecundity to the new fecundity that is likewise possible only in God. The state of life in which Mary is placed by her complete readiness for whatever sacrifice may be required of her, the state that was already latent in her married state, but that becomes ever more nakedly revealed in her increasing separation from the Lord—in the disappearance of the twelve-year-old and the departure of the thirty-year-old, in the revelation at Cana of the difference between her mission and that of her Son, in Jesus' disavowal of mother and brethren, in his withdrawal on the Cross—this state is henceforth Mary's final and irreversible state. Her life with John, then, will be lived wholly on the supernatural level. At the explicit bidding of the Lord and brought together by him under the law of love, these two, who were closest to him during his earthly life and who are exclusively dedicated to him, are to form a community of virgins. In them is to be portrayed visibly and in a manner appropriate to their state of life the transformation of the visible presence of Christ on earth into his invisible presence wherever two or three are gathered together in his name. They are to prove to all ages that Christianity is possible: that man can truly find God whom he loves in the neighbor whom he loves without thereby jeopardizing the absoluteness of his love for God by the love he is to have for his fellow man. For this turning to the neighbor is more than just a command of God. The divine Son and Friend lives so truly in the neighbor that it is henceforth possible to seek and find him wholly in one's neighbor.

Mary's state of life, which is not only superior to the two states of life within the Church, but also the foundation of their unity and their difference, confirms what was said earlier about the Church's anteriority to the faithful who comprise it. For it is apparent that in speaking of Mary's anteriority we are not speaking of the anteriority of an "institution" to the way of life it embodies, but rather of the anteriority of a life freely subjected to grace and able, of its fullness, to establish institutional patterns for those who would imitate it.

The Church began, not at Caesarea Philippi or with the calling of the Twelve, but essentially in a chamber at Nazareth: with the consent of the virgin to become the mother of the Son of God and of his "brethren", the "rest of her offspring" (Rev 12:17).

3. THE CHRISTIAN'S STATE OF LIFE: "IN CHRIST"

Our first, general description of the Christian state of life showed it to be based on the Christian's election and vocation by God to leave the fallen world—a process of division that continued to operate within the Church in the division into the state of election, which has its origin in God's calling to a qualitatively higher state of life, and the secular state, which is the state of those called to live a Christian life within the ordinary round of daily duties. The state of election was described as the state of those privileged to take their stand in the place and in the state of Christ, a state higher than that of paradise and partaking of both heaven and the Cross. The call to perfect love, we noted, is equally binding on one in the secular state, but his task is more difficult since he must attain the same goal from a state in which inner-worldly ordinances are inseparably linked to the fallenness of man's nature. In consequence, he is "divided". But the rift that divides him is the form by which ultimately he, too, is drawn under the one law of the Cross. And if the presentation of the twofold concept of the Gospel as truth and image strengthened the impression that the two states are of unequal rank, its sole purpose was, nonetheless, to provide a point of departure for recognizing the reciprocal assistance rendered by the two states and the explicitly stated subsidiarity of the state of election to the secular state. In the pages immediately preceding, we have shown how both states of life participate in the state of Christ and his mother and, consequently, how the unity of the state of life of all Christians continues to endure despite all analogous concepts of states of life within the Church.

The first mark of the Christian state of life was shown to be a formal one—election and vocation by God. Reflection on the state of Jesus and Mary, moreover, added to the concept of a Christian state of life concrete information about its content, thus enabling us to regard the two states of life within the Church in a new way—as the unfolding of the one state of Jesus and his mother, which, although itself analogous, prefigured the two possibilities inasmuch as the one perfect way of Jesus and Mary proceeded (in intertwined phases) from the secular state to the state of election.

But because Christ's one and indivisible state includes in itself his movement from God to the world and from the world to God, what differentiates the two states cannot be the dividing of this indivisible way. It follows, then, that *both states must be able to contain these two movements within themselves in unity*; that both states are called upon to reflect in different ways the totality of

Christ's state of life; that, in both of them, God's election and vocation have no other purpose than to enable the Christian to share in Christ's original state. ". . . Where I am, there also shall my servant be" (Jn 12:26). "Father, I will that where I am, they also whom thou hast given me may be with me" (Jn 17:24). The "where" of the Christian is in Christ himself, just as Christ's "where" is in the Father. This "where" is neither a spatiotemporal one, nor the mere prefiguration of an ideal or life program, nor the external assumption of a task or dignity as would be the case if one were installed in a political or civil office. It is rather a new orientation of the whole existence of those who have been called so that, by their vocation to the state of Christ, they receive a definitive personal orientation by which all else is absorbed and made relative. The taking of his place in the will and essence of the Father in which Christ's state of life coincides with his personhood becomes for the Christian the *form* of his own new stand in Christ. Although he neither becomes God nor is divinized by being called into the Church's membership, Christ's form becomes for him, nevertheless, as truly the form of his being as of his activity. The true source of life lies for him no longer in himself, but—since he has put on the form of Christ (Rom 13:14), the new man created "according to God" (Eph 4:24)—in Christ: "As the living Father has sent me, and as I live because of the Father, so he who eats me, he also shall live because of me" (Jn 6:58).

This means that the Christian, in whatever state he finds himself, must always take his stand in a concentric relationship to Christ. Just as there was no possibility of Christ's taking his stand outside the Father in order to mediate between him and the world, so there is no Christian possibility for the Christian to take his stand outside Christ in order thus to create a bond between Christ and the world. Just as Christ did not leave the Father when he came into the world and just as his transition from the family to the company of his disciples did not signify a return to the Father or even any improvement or advance in his relationship to the Father, so the state of the Christian in the world—and, in the last analysis, Christians of both states are in one way or another in the world—does not mean that he has distanced himself however slightly from Christ. The Christian in the world is not "divided" because he must live under natural ordinances, for Christ, too, led this kind of life without distancing himself in the least from the Father and his will; he is divided only because he is tempted to be "concerned [not] about the things of the Lord, how he may please God . . . [but] about the things of the world, how he may please his wife" (1 Cor 7:32–33). In what this temptation consists we can learn by once more contemplating Christ.

The Son lives in the world, but is not of the world. The statement has a twofold meaning. As man, Christ shares in the nature created by the eternal Word, but he speaks and acts with an authority that reveals him as being, himself, this eternal Word: "Heaven and earth will pass away, but my words will not pass away" (Mk 13:31). As the source of nature, he is free of its laws, or, more precisely, all things, which have been created not only "*through* him", but also "*for* him", are held together "*in* him" (Col 1:16–17) because they have their origin in the free gift of grace that he brings into the world from God. The natural order has, from the beginning, been ordained to fulfillment in the order of grace. God's plan is not altered by the fact that the fallen world, in its preoccupation with self, is no longer aware of this truth.

When the Son comes into the world as the free Word of God, as the Word that creates and redeems, he becomes the sole norm for the relationship between nature and grace. God, who laid the foundation of the natural order through his "almighty word" (Wis 18:15), will not destroy this order when the Word appears in his creation personally as grace, *but neither will he be interiorly bound by its laws*. Though freely decreed by him, they have no authority over him. If he commanded man in the beginning to multiply and subdue the earth, this does not mean that he will be bound by this decree when he himself, the Lord, appears in the form of man. He is the Father's sovereign and creative Word. His fecundity has no need of the laws of nature; from all eternity, he has himself been absolute fecundity. He does not have to subdue the earth; it has always been completely subject to him (cf. Mk 4:41). By becoming man, he does, it is true, enter the world and subject himself to its laws, but the measure of his subjection rests simply and solely on his own unassailable discretion. No one dares ask him why, if he is truly man, he does not obey the laws of this world like any other man; why he does not marry if it was he himself who gave the command to increase and multiply; why he does not till the earth if it was he himself who ordered man to do so. By using nature for his own ends, which are always divine and supernatural, he enables it to fulfill the purpose for which it was created. It would have been pointless for him to appear personally in the world as the Word of God if his purpose was merely to confirm the laws of nature rather than to reveal a totally new being who surpassed and transcended them. What he came to demonstrate was *God's freedom with respect to his own creation* even when he is within that creation.

The relationship of nature and grace, as Christ depicts it, is a fluctuating interrelationship in which grace willingly submits and binds itself to the laws of nature, while nature finds its fulfillment in being drawn above itself and thus restored to the original idea of its creation. Nature, with all its laws as they have been revealed to us by the natural and cultural sciences, finds its ultimate meaning only in the eternal Word of God, who transcends all created nature. It is the material placed at the disposal of this Word, who is "delighted every day, playing before him [God] at all times; playing in the world" (Prov 8:30–31). His submission to the laws of nature can lead even to death on the Cross, yet it must always reveal the mode of divine freedom. He is Lord of the Sabbath; he foreknows and foretells his Passion; before letting himself be taken prisoner, he throws his enemies to the ground; before paying the tax, he instructs his disciples that the sons are free (Mt 17:27). When he binds himself, he does so freely, out of love; and when he reveals his freedom from bonds, he does so in a way that emphasizes the fact that he has freely chosen all his bonds.

Those who belong to Christ are destined to share his freedom. From slaves, he has made them into sons. He binds them by the law of his own state of life in the Father in order to free them from the laws and elements of this world: "If you abide in my word, you shall be my disciples indeed, and you shall know the truth, and the truth shall make you free" (Jn 8:31–32). In this way, the Christian is removed from his sinful dependence on temporal things and is allowed to take his stand with the Son in eternal life. "The Father loves the Son, and has given all things into his hands. He who believes in the Son has everlasting life" (Jn 3:35–36). If Christians are "predestined to become conformed to the image of his Son, that [they] should be the firstborn among many brethren" (Rom 8:29); if they are already "chosen . . . in him before the foundation of the world . . . [and] predestined . . . to be adopted through Jesus Christ as his sons" (Eph 1:4–5); if, then, God's first concept of them was not in the natural but in the supernatural order in his Son, it is clear that their summons "out of darkness into his marvelous light" (1 Pet 2:9) does them no violence, but simply transfers them to their proper and, in a sense, natural place. If they thereby become "strangers and pilgrims" (1 Pet 2:11) in this world, they nevertheless enter upon the heritage that is theirs; they are made "worthy to share the lot of the saints in light" (Col 1:12); they "have come . . . to the Church of the firstborn who are enrolled in the heavens" (Heb 12:23). This means that participation in Christ's freedom in regard to creation is, for the elect, neither contrary to nature nor presumptuous. For this they have been predestined (Eph 1:4–5), and if the earthly precedes the heavenly in time (1 Cor 15:46), it will, nevertheless, eventually and of necessity give place to the heavenly, because "those whom he has predestined, them he has also called; and those whom he has called, them he has also justified; and those whom he has justified, them he has also glorified" (Rom 8:30). "Therefore, even as we have borne the likeness of the earthly, let us bear also the likeness of the heavenly" (1 Cor 15:49). When Christ summons Christians to share in his freedom from the laws and precepts of nature, to leave the narrow byways of earth and travel the broad highways of heaven, they know that they are being transferred not to some acosmic place, but *to that place from which all earthly laws have their source, their direction and the measure of their validity*. When they enter into Christ's state of life, they are at the heart and source of nature. And if the multiplicity of what they see there seems, at first, to be overshadowed by the unity of the central sun "in whom are hidden all the treasures of wisdom and knowledge" (Col 2:3), they nevertheless receive, after this initial moment of blindness, something of God's own power to see, so that with him they can survey the world from its origin. They are initiated into God's plan "to reestablish all things in Christ, both those in the heavens and those on the earth; in him, . . . in whom we also have been called by a special choice, having been predestined in the purpose of him who works all things according to the counsel of his will" (Eph 1:10–11). This call illumines their souls: ". . . It pleased him who from my mother's womb set me apart and called me by his grace, to reveal his Son in me" (Gal 1:15–16). "It is now no longer I that live, but Christ lives in me" (Gal 2:20).

The highest point of this relationship of nature and grace —in which nature is not only perfected and restored to its original purpose by being made the instrument of grace, but also drawn above itself into a new law and thus relieved of its self-centeredness—is achieved *in the Christian relationship of freedom and obedience*. If previously the Christian's state of life was shown to be freedom from the laws of this world, since the Christian is transferred not only partially, but wholly, into Christ's state of life outside the world, this freedom from the world is now shown to be freedom directly for Christ—for being an instrument in his service—just as the members of the body serve not only themselves, but also the head (1 Cor 12:27). From the beginning, our role as instruments has had a twofold basis: first, the subjection of our whole nature and person to the service of Christ inasmuch as we are made for him who is our divine head; second, the simultaneous inner adoption of the mind of Christ, whose divine freedom and personhood are identical with his obedience to the Father. *Under the first aspect, our obedience is that proper to the creature; under the second, it is divine.*

Under the first aspect, obedience is the expression of the instrumentality—and hence of the essence—of the Christian in his engraced state of life; under the second, the compulsion seemingly involved is nullified by the fact that Christ's own state of life consists in the identity of freedom and obedience. Under the first aspect, the Christian state of life appears to be something formal that displaces and, as it were, replaces the essence of the natural person: "It is no longer I that live, but Christ lives in me." Under the second aspect, however, it is immediately clear that the formal element of this state is also its essence, since the nature of the divine person of Christ—to be the image of the Father and, consequently, to be [nothing but] loving obedience to him—is perfectly identified with his state.

From the standpoint of nature as such, obviously, the Christian who has been established in Christ's state of life loses his personal "autonomy". He has no further right to determine his own person or fate, or the conduct and direction of his life. By virtue of his state of life, he is obliged to renounce this right and to receive from Christ and his Church the law of his new life. Even though he is fully responsible for employing all his personal gifts—his memory, his understanding and his free will —in this service, he remains ultimately a servant. He has exchanged the unworthy service of sin for the noble service of "justice unto sanctification" (cf. Rom 6:16–23). As compensation for the emptying of himself that is required by his state of life, the Christian is able to "put on" a correspondingly higher new person. By his state of life, he now shares in the secret of Christ's divine personhood. Hitherto, his person, though deeming itself autonomous, was, nonetheless, "kept imprisoned" under the yoke of abstract and formal laws, was "shut up for the faith that was to be revealed" (Gal 3:23), and, not yet mature, was "enslaved under the elements of the world" (Gal 4:3). Only by submitting his whole person to faith does he come to share in a "law" that is identical with personhood as such, with the infinite person of the Son. Sharing in this "law", the Christian overcomes the dichotomy between the free, concrete person and the binding, abstract law. Thus the one law of the new state of life is the law of love in which the Christian becomes free in service and serves in freedom. He is free "in virtue of the freedom wherewith Christ has made us free. . . . For you have been called to liberty, brethren; only do not use liberty as an occasion for sensuality, but by charity serve one another. For the whole law is fulfilled in one word: Thou shalt love thy neighbor as thyself" (Gal 4:31; 5:13–14). By no means, then, is the Christian's state a formalization of his life. His stand in the obedience of Christ can appear as such only to one outside and lacking in faith. Rather, his state is an incomprehensible quickening of what is still abstract and formal in the natural sphere. For God's "commandment is everlasting" (Jn 12:50) and "he who believes in the Son has everlasting life" (Jn 3:36).

This participation in the free obedience and obedient freedom of divine love is the most superabundant gift man can receive. But if the elevation by which, from being creatures, men come to be "partakers of the divine nature" (2 Pet 1:4) involved no painful renunciation for paradisal man (so long as he remained obedient), it creates for fallen man an agonizing tension between the laws of sinful nature and those of reconciling grace. The obedience of faith means the sacrifice of personal autonomy; the surrender of one's life to Christ means emptying oneself of one's own nature. The state of grace puts the stamp of death on one's innerworldly state. "Do you not know that all we who have been baptized into Christ Jesus have been baptized into his death? For we are buried with him by means of baptism into death, in order that, just as Christ has arisen from the dead through the glory of the Father, so we also may walk in newness of life" (Rom 6:3–4). Though definitive in nature, this death is reflected in man's consciousness as a demand that he "take up his cross daily" (Lk 9:23), that he "die daily" (1 Cor 15:31), that his "inner man [be] renewed day by day" (2 Cor 4:16). In consequence, Christian existence is one of transition and separation (2 Cor 5:1), of longing and sighing because the old man is in the process of disappearing, but the new man is still hidden from view. The Christian is no longer to remember what he was (Eph 4:17–22), but it has not yet appeared what he will be (1 Jn 3:2). The rapture of grace that snatches him from earth and transports him to heaven seems to deprive him of the ground under his feet and the air he needs for his life. In the night of faith, "being rooted and grounded in love" (Eph 3:17) seems to him a pure utopia that is daily belied by brutal reality. For the world and even for himself, his state of continuous transition seems to mean the absence of any state at all, a hanging in emptiness. The expectation of remaining in such a non-place seems the rankest presumption.

From this we see that, in the order of redemption, the Christian state as such is none other than the taking of one's place in the Cross and in reconciliation. To be a Christian means to be sacrificed even before one has consciously associated oneself with the sacrifice of the Cross. For Christianity is the community of those whom God, by his loving choice, has allowed to participate in the redemptive work and suffering of his Son. The company of Christ consists of those who have been redeemed by Christ, but the redeemed are, at the same time, also those who, having been initiated into Christ's redemptive act, become sharers in his work of redemption by the very sacrifice entailed in being Christian.

The formal sharing in Christ's sacrifice on the Cross that is the sine qua non of the Christian state as such is not to be divorced from one's personal sharing of the mind of Christ. The *kenosis* of the Christian who is daily being separated from the "outer man [that] is decaying" (2 Cor 4:16) so that he may become "a new creature" (2 Cor 5:17) in Christ is not something that can find its ultimate explanation either in himself or in his own conversion. It is a sharing of the *kenosis* of Christ himself, who "did not consider being equal to God a thing to be clung to, but emptied himself, taking the nature of a slave and being made like unto men" (Phil 2:6–7). It is not, therefore, a merely psychological or "ethical" sensation of losing the ground under one's feet until one has found new ground in Christ; it is the actual losing of that ground in the company of the dying Christ. ". . . We have come to the conclusion that, since one died for all, therefore all died; and that Christ died for all, in order that they who are alive may live no longer for themselves, but for him who died for them and rose again" (2 Cor 5:14–15).

But this dying together with Christ through baptism and the whole Christian way of life becomes, likewise, a living in Christ or, more specifically, *in the risen Christ* (cf. Rom 6:4); for unless Christ rose from the dead, it would be not only senseless, but even impossible, to die with him. For to die with Christ means also to be "raised . . . up together, and seated . . . together in heaven in Christ Jesus" (Eph 2:6); to share in the same "mighty power, which [God] has wrought in Christ in raising him from the dead, and setting him at his right hand in heaven" (Eph 1:19–20). Thus the Christian's life and state do not simply run parallel to the earthly existence of Christ as though he had to live until his earthly death in imitation of the state in which Jesus lived until the crucifixion. Christian life is not a mere imitation of the Lord's hidden and public life. On the contrary, it is from the beginning and *at every moment a participation not only in the Cross, but also in the Resurrection of the Lord*. The head of the Church, which is the body of Christ, is already a glorified head; the flesh and blood that Christians receive are a glorified and risen flesh and blood. Consequently, the law of love that regulates the life of Christians is in reality the law of "the city of the living God, the heavenly Jesus, and . . . the company . . . of the firstborn who are enrolled in the heavens" (Heb 12:22–23), of the city that already, even on earth, has been found to be "the camp of the saints, and the beloved city" (Rev 20:8). The following of Christ is, then, far more than just a moral acceptance of his commandments and counsels, a mere imitation of his deeds and virtues. It is, here and now, a life based on the reality of his death and Resurrection. In its essence, it is dependent on the strength of the grace won for us by his Cross and Resurrection; in man's consciousness, it is dependent on the faithful reliving—insofar as he calls and enables us to do so—of the way that led him through the world and hell to heaven. In this, the Christian state reveals itself as a true stand in Christ: not, however, as a localized stand, but as a stand in the full revelation of him who "descended into the lower parts . . . [and] ascended also above all the heavens, that he might fill all things" (Eph 4:9–10); in the living reality of him who, in his infinite coming from and going to the Father (cf. Jn 16:28), is "the way" (Jn 14:6), and who has prepared a place for his servants in the "breadth and length and height and depth" (Eph 3:18) of this way.

Nevertheless, the inconceivable fullness and breadth of the Christian state—which is the taking of one's stand with Christ in the Father, with the Redeemer on the Cross, and with the resurrected Christ in heaven—*does not destroy the normal earthly framework of man's existence*. Although the Christian shares in these incomprehensible realities and finds in them his very raison d'être, he is not for that reason any less a member of human society; a loyal servant of the state: "For this is also why you pay tribute" (Rom 13:6); and a custodian of public morals: "[Let] no one transgress and overreach his brother" (1 Th 4:6), of genuine concern about even the material well-being of his neighbor (cf. 1 Jn 3:17; James 2:1–8), and of marital fidelity, familial decorum and the proper relationship between master and servant (Col 3:18–4:1). Christians do not observe these laws exteriorly and ostensibly while engaging interiorly and actually in quite different matters. Because they have taken their stand in Christ, who manifested his divine freedom in service to his brethren, they direct their whole attention to them. The exaltation of the Christian is not antithetical to the humiliation of Christ, but rather its fulfillment in grace. Any tendency, however hidden, that would deny the Incarnation of Christ proceeds, not from the Spirit of God, but from the Antichrist (1 Jn 4:2–3). The genuineness of the Christian state must be preserved in the world as it is here and now.

This means, however, that the grace of the Christian state is never granted except *in the form of mission*, in which is contained all the meaningfulness of this state. But this mission is the love of

God and neighbor as revealed by Christ; it can be accomplished only by taking one's stand where he took his. In it, the Christian is to find his whole work in the world. It is not his task to mediate between Christianity and the world, but to bear witness to, to exemplify and to recall to the world the form of Christ. Even though he continues to be subject to the laws of the world, he has no right to set himself up as a measure of the relationship between nature and grace, world and Church, culture and Christianity. The extent to which he may use the powers of this world depends on the particular Christian situation, whose meaning is to be sought in the here-and-now of the divine call: "Let the word of Christ dwell in you abundantly" (Col 3:16). This word is rich enough to contain the appropriate solution to every worldly situation, although the solution may often be a "doctrine of the Cross" (1 Cor 1:18). Should this occur, the Christian may feel compelled to abandon the state of Christ and to enter into a compromise that seems inevitable to him. Whenever such a compromise is made, however, the unity of Christ has been abandoned through some personal or communal guilt. Nowhere do the Lord or his apostles advise Christians who must live in the world on how to choose "the lesser evil" in perplexing situations. The descriptions of Christian life offered by Holy Scripture always stress the possibility of an unconditional Christianity, of the believer's uncompromising answer to the full gift of the Christian state of grace.

Even in the case of marriage, St. Paul sketches a Christian model based on the absolute ideal of Christ: "But just as the Church is subject to Christ, so also let wives be to their husbands in all things. Husbands, love your wives, just as Christ also loved the Church, and delivered himself up for her" (Eph 5:24–25). He presents this absolute ideal without prejudice to his conviction that "it is good for man not to touch woman" and his desire that all men "were as I am myself" (1 Cor 7:1, 7); without prejudice also to the fact that, by reason of personal and communal guilt, it is only with difficulty that one who is married can preserve the unity of the Christian state as Paul taught it. "He *is* divided", but, from Christ's point of view, he does not *have* to be so. Nor does he have the right to entrench himself in his dividedness as though it were irreversible. He must strive daily to move from his divided condition into the unity that his state demands. What is true of marriage is true also of every other activity of the Christian in the world. Whether in the realm of sociology, economics, politics or culture, it is not permitted him to direct his daily activities by any other law than that inherent in his being a Christian. Since all things have been created in, through and for Christ, and since God has made "all things . . . subject to him" who has overcome the powers of this world, and "has put all things under his feet" (1 Cor 15:27, 26), it would be heresy to act as though the powers of this world obeyed a law that was actually autonomous and emancipated from Christ. Certainly, their subjection, which was "consummated" (Jn 19:30) once and for all upon the Cross where "the prince of this world [was] cast out" (Jn 12:31), is continually in the process of being accomplished since "creation [is] made subject to vanity" (Rom 8:20) and Christ, our life, has not yet appeared (Col 3:4). But this fact gives the Christian no right to gain control of worldly situations by purely worldly judgments and means. Even when compromise seems forced upon him by the finiteness of earthly things and the fallen state of nature, the solution he finds is not the accommodation of his mind to the mind of the world, but whatever response of Christian love is here and now possible. His approach to any given situation—"I became all things to all men, that I might save all" (1 Cor 9:22)—is predicated upon inner freedom, upon pure and uncompromising purpose: "For, free though I was to all, unto all I have made myself a slave that I might gain the more converts. . . . I do all things for the sake of the Gospel, that I may be made partaker thereof" (1 Cor 9:19, 23).

By reason of Christ's mission, the Christian state is ultimately and essentially a communal state. It is social in nature. This may not be immediately apparent if one looks only at the personal urgency of the elective call. For why should God not also call one to serve him in a place apart? But the Christian vocation never has this character. In the first place, it is a call into the Church, which, as we have shown, antedates the vocation of the individual insofar as it is a place of community. In the second place, it is a summons to leave one's selfish and isolated self and to enter a state that is, by definition, the end of all isolation. For it is the state of Christ, whose whole personhood is identified with service and love for the Father and, for the Father's sake, for mankind. The very transition from one's own state to the state of Christ and, in particular, the acceptance of what this transition means make it impossible for the Christian to live henceforth for anything other than God and his neighbor. Because of his new state, he has been drawn from his place apart and into the community of the Church. Because he lives henceforth in Christ, there can be for him no other concept of personhood than that which is expressed in mission, service and the renunciation of self.

4. THE MARRIED STATE

If the Christian state is a communal one, it is so because Christ is par excellence God's gift to the Church and, through the Church, to the world. But his relationship to the Church, which is his Bride and spouse, is not without similarities to the original mystery of the creation of man and woman. "For this cause a man shall leave his father and mother and cleave to his wife; and the two shall become one flesh. This is a great mystery—I mean in reference to Christ and the Church" (Eph 5:31–32). And since the Son did not come to abolish any of the works of the Father, but to enhance and perfect them, it was not enough for him to make the union of husband and wife the model and image of his incarnational relationship of love to the Church; he also rewarded the model thus presented him by explicitly raising it to the dignity of sacramental consecration in his New Covenant.

> By allowing his love to manifest itself in the Incarnation, not in the married state but in the state of virginity, Christ showed clearly that the formal element of the original relationship between man and

woman lay primarily in the spiritual gift of self, and the Church itself watches over the order of the states of life thus established. "If anyone says that the conjugal state is to be preferred to the state of virginity or celibacy, and that it is not better and more blessed to remain in virginity or celibacy than to be joined in matrimony, let him be anathema."[8] By not only not condemning marriage, however, but even sanctioning this primeval relationship between man and woman, confirming its institution by God (Mt 19:6) and sanctifying it by the redemption on the Cross, Christ demonstrated that the form of his love is not irreconcilable with the mystery of man's original state, but capable of making it a true vessel and expression of that love: "Indeed, Christ himself, who instituted and perfected the venerable sacraments, has merited for us by his Passion the grace . . . that makes marriage holy."[9]

In this way, the bonds that join man and woman in marriage on the one hand and Christ and the Church in the redemption on the other hand are so closely related that it is impossible to understand one without reference to the other. The mystery of the original creation comes "first": ". . . It is not the spiritual that comes first, but the physical, and then the spiritual" (1 Cor 15:46); the mystery of redemption finds its form in "being made like unto" this "first". But the assimilation (ὁμοίωμα: Phil 2:17) is so completely a matter of the most absolute obedience that he who accomplishes it becomes himself the absolute model and pattern, indeed the archetype, of all creation, which has no alternative but to model itself on him if it is to attain its ultimate truth. This transforming assimilation to Christ is not only required, but also bestowed—in the sacramental grace that turns the paradisal community of marriage into a Christian community. Just as Christ becomes the absolute meaning of creation by his Incarnation, crucifixion and redemption so that

---

[8] *Concilium Tridentinum: Diariorum, Actorum, Epistularum, Tractatuum*, Nova Collectio, vol. 9, "Concilii Tridentini Actorum", pars sexta, ed. Stephanus Ehses (Freiburg: Herder, 1924), sessio XXIV (11 novembris 1563), "Canones de Sacramento Matrimonii", canon decimus, 968.

[9] *Concilium tridentinum*: "Doctrina et Canones cum Aliis Concernentibus Sacramentum Matrimonii", 967.

outside his sun there is only the darkness of damnation, so there is henceforth in Christian marriage only the either-or of life according to the supernatural meaning and law of sacramental grace or of total failure to discern the true meaning of marriage.

The physical union of man and woman is not something accidental to man: It is so essential and central to his nature that almost the whole account of the ideal man as God created him in paradise is concerned with the distinction between male and female. And although man shares this difference of sex with the animals, there is no reason to doubt that the first division between man and woman—based as it was on the spirituality by which man had dominion over all creation—belonged, no less than his dominion over all creation, to the "likeness to God" that was bestowed on him alone of all creatures: " 'Let us make mankind in our image and likeness; and let him have dominion over the fish of the sea, and the birds of the air, the cattle, over all the wild animals and every creature that crawls on the earth.' God created man in his image. In the image of God he created him. Male and female he created them. Then God blessed them and said to them, 'Be fruitful and multiply; fill the earth and subdue it. Have dominion over the fish of the sea, the birds of the air, the cattle and all the animals that crawl on the earth' " (Gen 1:26–28). Indeed, the fruitfulness of this multiplying that has its source in the union of male and female is the image of that mysterious nature of God that speaks here in an unfathomable plural: "Let us"! God's being in the Trinity is an infinite fecundity that reveals itself externally in creation; whatever is made in his image must, of its very nature, have a share in this fecundity. Since mankind was made male and female and since the first word God spoke to them was "Be fruitful and multiply", it cannot be doubted that human beings were created for fecundity.

This likeness to God is a likeness of both nature and grace, just as creatureliness and engracement were inseparable in man's original state. Man's natural sexuality is bestowed on him in view of the union of natural and supernatural fecundity in him. In no way does the sexual dominate only the physical sphere while the spiritual sphere, which is deemed to be the true seat of his "likeness to God", remains untouched by it. For the division of the sexes touches man's spirit so totally, from its deepest roots to its highest pinnacle, that the physical difference appears insignificant in comparison with this distinction that affects the whole person.

The mystery of the fecundity for which God created man and by which man becomes an image of the eternally fruitful Trinity is even more closely linked to the divine nature than a reading of the first account of creation might lead us to suspect. God did not simply create mankind male and female as he had created the animals male and female. *He not only created them to be one in the duality of sex; he also created their duality out of their own oneness.* He created Eve out of the side of Adam, not by a process of natural generation, but in a preternatural manner through the instrumentality of the sleeping Adam, although he accomplished the rest of the work without him and placed the completed result before him: "And the rib which the Lord God took from man, he made into a woman, and brought her to him" (Gen 2:22). The communal oneness of Adam and Eve was thus the oneness of Adam's flesh, which became by grace the source of the duality of male and female. Adam recognized the gift presented him by God as being, at the same time, himself, his own flesh: "Then the man said, 'She now is bone of my bone, and flesh of my flesh; she shall be called Woman, for from man she has been taken' " (Gen 2:23). Hence God's command to Adam and Eve to be fruitful and multiply was not just a moral command subject to their freedom and through the fulfillment of which they were to reflect something of the archetype according to which they had been created, something of the fruitfulness of the Trinity; it was, at the same time, the result of the physical fecundity that God effected in Adam while he slept and that became, by the formation of Eve from the one living body of Adam, a direct physical image of the origin from the Father's substance of the eternal Son who shares his nature. It would be false to say that Adam and Eve were one only in some abstract "human nature" and achieved concrete and, therefore, fruitful oneness only through their sexual union. On the contrary, the source of their abstract oneness as human beings was the concrete spiritual oneness and fecundity that made them the image of the concrete divine oneness of nature and fecundity within the Trinity. It need hardly be pointed out that man and woman continue to be but an image of God and that their oneness must be accomplished in becoming, movement and ever new actualization, just as the fruitfulness of their union lies always outside their power and must be bestowed upon them by God. Eve said this after she had borne her first son: "I have given birth to a man-child with the help of the Lord" (Gen 4:1). Their communal fecundity is, of course, a natural one, for God granted the blessing of fecundity even to the animals (Gen 1:22) and did not withdraw it from mankind after the Fall. Yet, in the case of man, this natural fecundity is rooted, as it were, in the supernatural source and purpose that his whole nature was designed to serve and must continue to serve. It is precisely *because* Adam recognized in Eve the one who, by grace, "is bone of my bone, and flesh of my flesh" that "a man leaves his father and mother, and clings to his wife, and the two become one flesh" (Gen 2:23–24). Adam's faith, which called him forth from every secret place in himself, his environment and his world that he might find the complement he needed to make his flesh and bones whole again, was no purely natural faith, but faith with a deeper origin and, therefore, with a deeper purpose. The removal of Adam's rib and the division of mankind into male and female was in no way identical with the fall into sin or even a prelude to it. Even the leaving of father and mother to cling to a wife was part of the original plan for man's primitive state. The removal of the rib was for Adam an infinitely ennobling grace: the grace of being allowed to participate in the mystery of the Father's self-giving to the Son, by which the Father empties himself of his own Godhead in order to bestow it on the Son who is eternally of the same nature as he is. It was a wound of love that God inflicted on Adam in order to initiate him into the mystery, the lavish self-prodigality, of divine love.

It is clear, then, not only that a definite natural fecundity continued to exist in marriage after the Fall, but also that, even then, *the origin and purpose of marriage continued to make it more than just a natural community*. What is natural in marriage has a supernatural origin and, therefore, also a supernatural purpose. In the Old Testament, in which marriage was man's normal state of life since the virginity of paradise no longer existed and that of the Cross did not yet exist,[10] the married state filled the whole place between man's paradisal origin—of which he continued to be aware: "Have you not read that the Creator, from the beginning, made them male and female, and said, *'For this reason a man shall leave his father and mother . . .'* " (Mt 19:4–5)—and the messianic future in view of which every marriage was performed and because of which sterility was regarded as shameful and as a punishment from God. Consciously adopted celibacy would have had no meaning under the Old Testament; it would have been regarded as disobedience to the natural and supernatural command to "be fruitful and multiply" given by God in the beginning and as a failure to believe in his promise to Abraham. Thus the angel Raphael said to Tobias: ". . . Thou shalt take the virgin with the fear of the Lord, moved rather for love of children than for lust, that in the seed of Abraham thou mayest obtain a blessing in children" (Tob 6:22); and Tobias himself prayed for three nights before joining in wedlock with Sarah: "Lord God of our fathers, may the heavens and the earth, and the sea, and the fountains and the rivers, and all thy creatures that are in them, bless thee. Thou madest Adam of the slime of the earth, and gavest him Eve for a helper. And now, Lord, thou knowest that not for fleshly lust do I take my sister to wife, but only for the love of posterity, in which thy name may be blessed forever and ever" (Tob 8:7–9). In the Old Testament, sexual union was union in the promise and, consequently, in faith: "For we are the

---

[10] Celibacy was practiced in the Old Testament only by way of exception and as a kind of symbolic taking of one's stand in the purity of the promise. As such, it could not have formed the basis for a state of life.

children of saints, and we must not be joined together like heathens that know not God" (Tob 8:5).

But all this occurred outside the paradisal unity of fruitfulness and virginity. The oneness of the states of life could not be restored; the concept of virginity with its unique spiritual and supernatural fecundity as an essential component of marriage survived only as a distant recollection or an inconceivable hope for the future. Only in the fullness of time would man understand what it meant that "a virgin shall conceive, and bear a son" (Is 7:14). As long as his models were earthly ones, man could not believe that virginity had any meaning or fecundity in the sight of God. He could not comprehend that "the first man, Adam," who became "a living soul", could be redeemed by "the last Adam", who "became a life-giving spirit" (1 Cor 15:45); that the declaration of Jesus son of Sirach that Adam "obtained glory . . . above every soul . . . in the beginning" (Sir 49:19) would eventually be superseded by Paul's proclamation that "at the name of Jesus every knee should bend of those in heaven, on earth and under the earth" (Phil 2:10).

In consequence, fecundity was a limited concept in the Old Testament. The unbounded stream of Catholic fecundity is merely hinted at in the restricted fecundity of marriage under the Old Covenant: "Drink the water from your own cistern, fresh water from your own well. Do not let your fountain flow to waste elsewhere, nor your streams in the public streets. Let them be for yourself alone, not for strangers at the same time. And may your fountain-head be blessed! Find joy with the wife you married in your youth. . . . Let hers be the company you keep" (Prov 5:15–19).[11] Marriage was a mutual protection against the loneliness that harms and threatens mankind: "It is better therefore that two should be together than one. . . . And if two lie together, they shall warm one another. How shall one alone be

[11] This passage from Proverbs, Ecclesiastes, Sirach and Malachi in succeeding paragraphs are quoted from *The Jerusalem Bible* (Garden City, N.Y.: Doubleday and Co., 1966), where the translation more closely approximates the German quoted by von Balthasar than does that of the English text quoted elsewhere in this work. [Tr]

warmed?" (Qo 4:9, 11). "The man who takes a wife has the makings of a fortune, a helper that suits him, and a pillar to lean on. If a property has no fence, it will be plundered. When a man has no wife, he is aimless and querulous. Will anyone trust a man carrying weapons who flits from town to town? So it is with the man who has no nest, and lodges wherever night overtakes him" (Sir 36:24–27; quoted from the Jerusalem Bible). But this securing of one's own existence by means of marriage was not selfish in intent; it was the grace normally bestowed by the Creator on those who observed his law. It was the grace of union and fidelity—of a fidelity that was not to be separated from the believer's fidelity to God. Marriage was contracted in God, who was the source of both its unity and its fecundity. In the Old Testament, marital fidelity and fidelity to the Covenant were inseparable. Fidelity to the Covenant was depicted again and again in terms of marital fidelity (Hos 2:20–24; Jer 2:2; Ezek 16; etc.), and marital fidelity was placed under the aegis of fidelity to the Covenant. Why did God not look more favorably upon the people's sacrifice? "It is because Yahweh stands as witness between you and the wife of your youth, the wife with whom you have broken faith, even though she was your partner and your wife by covenant. Did he not create a single being that has flesh and the breath of life? And what is this single being destined for? God-given offspring. Be careful for your own life, therefore, and do not break faith with the wife of your youth" (Malachi 2:14–15). No marriage could be contracted except in God, from whom stemmed the unity of husband and wife, and who required as well as bestowed the fruitfulness of their union. Only on the spiritual model of the Trinity could the image of God be *one* body. Fidelity was an indivisible characteristic. It was no more permissible to be true to God and untrue to one's wife than to be true to one's wife and untrue to God. Where there was infidelity to God, there was also infidelity in marriage and all fidelity, all trust, all veracity were destroyed. ". . . They are all adulterers, an assembly of transgressors. And they have bent their tongue, as a bow, for lies, and not for truth. They have strengthened themselves upon the earth. . . . Let every man take heed of his neighbor, and let him not trust in any brother of his, for every brother will utterly supplant, and every friend will walk deceitfully. And a man shall mock his brother, and they will not speak the truth . . ." (Jer 9:2–5). Among God's people, truth was indivisible: There was either God's truth or there was a lie. Therefore marriage had to be contracted in God; it had to have God as its witness if it was to take its place within the Covenant of the promise.

This was also true during the period in which the perfection of marriage as it had been foreseen in the beginning had become impossible because of sin; during which the fullness of time in Christ was still distant and God allowed the severed unity to be rent by even deeper gashes: ". . . By reason of the hardness of your heart, [Moses] permitted you to put away your wives; but it was not so from the beginning" (Mt 19:8). "For I hate divorce, says Yahweh the God of Israel" (Malachi 2:16). Every Jewish or pagan practice that deviated from the original unity on the trinitarian model that God had bestowed on mankind as the only true form of fecundity between man and wife must be regarded as a temporary concession brought about by sin and permitted by God's forebearance until the fullness of time in Christ should arrive. God made these concessions to bridge the time between paradise and reconciliation and so that there might continue to exist among men in this in-between time a shadow of what marriage was intended to be from the beginning. Even among Jews, marriage could not be more than a shadow, for the original pattern would not reappear until the virgin conceived and brought forth a son.

For this reason, *Christ could not be the offspring of a union between husband and wife as it existed after the Fall*. This fact is intrinsically related to the σάρξ, the corruption of the flesh: An act that destroys the virginal integrity of the spouses cannot be the origin of him who comes to break the power of sin. But the restoration of man's original state could not be merely mechanical; man's guilt had also to be overcome. Thus the new Adam brought fulfillment from a much higher source than that from which the first Adam had received it. Not content with simply sending his grace upon the earth, he came himself as the grace of God become man, as heaven become earth. He not only embodied in himself marriage as it had been before the Fall; he became himself the prototype of that marriage. And he did so without destroying the old order of creation. By filling all things with his grace (cf. Eph 4:10), *he also filled marriage*, but he filled it *with a grace that had its source more deeply in the mystery of God than did the marriage of paradise*. That is why marriage, as a Christian sacrament, must henceforth issue from this higher source. Having its model and measure in Christ, it must also adopt his mind and spirit if it is to be a Christian marriage.

"But just as the Church is subject to Christ, so also let wives be subject to their husbands in all things. Husbands, love your wives, just as Christ also loved the Church, and delivered himself up for her, that he might sanctify her . . ." (Eph 5:24–26). The measure of married love becomes the love between Christ and his Church. Here, too, there exists a primeval, graced unity of male and female; but the male element is now the new Adam who is God himself and who has for his Bride the whole people of God, the whole Church that is to be redeemed by him. The small and limited fecundity of paradisal marriage has yielded to the universal, eucharistic fecundity of the redeeming love of the Word made flesh and the redeemed love of his Bride and spouse, the Church, which is also his body. The primeval unity lies in the fact that *the Church was fashioned out of Christ just as Eve was fashioned out of Adam*: She flowed from the pierced side of the Lord on the Cross, where he slept the sleep of death inflicted on him by the powers of evil. In this sleep of mortal suffering, he cleansed the Church "that he might present [her] to himself . . . in all her glory, not having spot or wrinkle or any such thing" (Eph 5:27). As man, he allowed himself to fall into the sleep of death so that, as God, he might derive from this death the mystery of fruitfulness by which he would create for himself his Bride, the Church. Thus the Church is, yet is not, Christ himself—his body and his spouse. "He who loves his own wife, loves himself. For no one ever hated his own flesh; on the contrary, he nourishes and cherishes it, as Christ also does the Church (because we are members of his body . . .)" (Eph 5:29–30). We are not speaking here of an individual physical seed introduced into an individual physical body, but rather of the whole fruitfulness of the "seed" (1 Jn 3:9) of God "ingrafted" (James 1:21), in the ecstasy of suffering on the Cross, into the spiritual/physical body of the Church and of all those in the Church who are ready to receive it. We are not speaking, as we did in the case of Adam, of a blessing that flows from the mysterious fecundity of the Blessed Trinity into one who has been created in the image of God, but rather of a direct out-pouring of the divine fecundity itself through the instrumentality of Christ's humanity. This fecundity is, therefore, completely virginal—not only because it restores the virginity of Adam's original state or because it must make expiation for the virginity of that state that was lost through sin, but also and principally because, as a fecundity that is explicitly divine, it cannot be bound to any specific female body, but can have as its body only the universality of the Church of all the redeemed.

We see now to what extent the new virginity of the Cross surpasses both the communal character and the fecundity of paradisal marriage. Were this not the case, it could not, in its new strength, reflect all the perfections of created marriage and, at the same time, cause the sacrament of marriage to issue from the grace of the Cross. If the Cross were antithetical to the com-munality and fecundity of man as God created him, it could not perfect the Father's creation. In fact, however, Christ, who was called by the Lord to transcend the life-form of marriage and participate directly in the virginal life-form of the Cross, was, by the same token, called to participate in a self-surrender to the community and to fecundity for the community that surpasses marriage. Hence virginity, which could have had no positive meaning before Christ (except as a sign of the promise), can have only one meaning since Christ: fecundity for the Church, which springs from a greater self-giving than the married man can achieve. There is no virginity that is meaningful and fruitful *in itself* (it has as little meaning and fruitfulness as the fasting of the hunger artist[12] had for the world around him); it receives its meaning and fruitfulness solely from the totality of self-giving in the Church; from a self-giving that must be more radical, in the sense that the Cross was radical, than the self-giving and self-prodigality of Christian spouses.

The virginity of the Cross excludes the possibility of anyone's choosing celibacy as an *ecclesial* state of life in order thereby to achieve important secular goals or a fortiori to carve out a pleasant life according to his own design. Such a design may well be above reproach from either the ethical or the religious point of view. It may even involve useful philanthropic and social work. But as long as it remains a self-chosen form of life and subject to change without notice, one who chooses it is deceived if he thinks of himself as a Christian, for he has not attained even that degree of self-giving that is demanded by the indissoluble "yes" of Christian marriage. He has not given his soul to God and neighbor in such a way that he cannot demand it back again; and he is even further from giving it as the Son did who, though nailed to the Cross, poured out body and soul for all mankind. Because the grain of wheat did not fall to the ground and die, his virginity remains alone and brings forth no fruit. *Christian virginity stands or falls with the mystery of the Cross*, with the wound in Christ's side and the birth from it of the Church as the "body and Bride of Christ". It stands or falls with the full outpouring

---

[12] The reference is to the short story, *Ein Hungerkünstler*, published by Franz Kafka in 1924. At first, the "hunger artist", who has made a fine art of fasting, arouses the admiration and wonder of the public, who throng to see him. Soon, however, public interest wanes and, in the end, the "hunger artist" dies alone, still fasting and forgotten by a society that has failed to understand either the nature of his fasting or the misdirected idealism that inspired it. A translation of this story by Willa and Edwin Muir can be found, under the title, *A Fasting Showman*, in *German Narrative Prose*, ed. W. E. Yuill, vol. II (London: Oswald Wolff, 1966), 227–54. [Tr]

of spiritual power that takes place, as the Lord has shown us, only *in perfect obedience*. Obedience is poverty of spirit out of love; virginity, which is poverty of the body out of love, is fruitful only where it is based on a preceding spiritual sacrifice. In the course of time, the Church has come to understand this more and more. Whereas in the beginning it was blinded, as it were, by the beauty of this new virginity and regarded it as almost sufficient for the establishment of a state of its own, it soon realized that physical abstention has meaning and fecundity for the Church only when it is combined with a genuine surrender of the spirit: that is, with a form of life that in some way demands true obedience—an obedience that, by action and contemplation, refers its fruit to the Catholic Church and is thus an obedience within the community. Virginity in the Church can never be anything but a partial aspect of the one and only state that exists in the Church along with marriage—the state that Christ on the Cross brought into the world as a new form of divine fecundity through the unity of poverty, virginity and obedience. Only this state can surpass all the perfection of a marriage that is at once natural and supernatural and, at the same time, fulfill and perfect it by a new spirit from above.

This concept can be accepted without difficulty as it refers to members of the male sex. No one would think of setting up, in addition to the married state and the state of election, a separate *third state* for those men who remain single in the world. Because of the multitude of human destinies, particularly after the Fall and its consequences, there will, of course, always be destinies that cannot be subsumed under the usual, more general, forms: There will be those who because of some illness of soul or body are not suited for marriage and thus find themselves compelled to live unmarried in the world; perhaps also those who want to remain true to a love for another person that cannot be realized on this earth; or those who belong in the state of election but for some exterior reason—such as the care of someone close to them— cannot enter it. But no teaching about the states of life can be constructed on the basis of these exceptions, which, given the

limitless variety and contingency of human destinies, cannot fail
to exist. These men, too, have their place within the universal
Christian state of redemption and share in the grace won for this
state upon the Cross. Such men also existed in Old Testament
times, but then, too, they were not thought to belong to a
separate state of life.

What can be taken for granted in the case of men, however,
is less obvious in the case of women, although, from natural
causes, unmarried women are more numerous than unmarried
men. For the man chooses his wife; the woman is chosen for
marriage. Many a woman who would gladly have married was
not given the opportunity of doing so. Here, too, however,
the intervention of chance cannot be the basis for predicating a
separate state for women who remain unmarried. If they are
inwardly receptive to marriage, they may be said, rather, to
belong potentially to the married state, and God will judge their
readiness for self-giving as if it were the deed itself. He will not
overlook the greatness of their renunciation and, in his own
time, will cause their sacrifice to bear fruit if it is borne interiorly
in the spirit of Christ. But to live unmarried for whatever reason
is not to be identified with living in the *state* of virginity—
unless, of course, this physical virginity corresponds to that
which makes the Christian virginity of the Cross what it is: the
voluntary and unconditional renunciation of physical fecundity
for the sake of the greater fecundity that is bestowed by grace
and finds its expression in a community as a bondage of the
spirit in obedience. In this instance, too, exceptions are possible
—borderline cases, as it were, that must not be regarded as
normative: cases in which, because entrance into a community
is impossible for serious reasons, a woman is allowed, within
the context of her life in the world, to make a vow of virginity
under the guidance of the Church—perhaps, or perhaps not, in
combination with the vows of obedience and poverty. Such a
one belongs potentially to the state of election just as the woman
who remains unmarried for reasons beyond her control belongs
potentially to the married state. Nevertheless, care must be exer-

cised that these borderline forms, which are justified and may
even be the only possible ones in particular instances, do not lead
to the belief that *a kind of "third state"* between the married state
and the state of election is something normal and even to be
striven for. If such a "third state" were actually recognized
as valid, it would seriously endanger the Christian radicalism
of both the Christian married state and the Christian state of
election. It would be more difficult for us to understand what it
means to give one's soul in the Church for God and neighbor
so completely and irrevocably that the gift cannot be rescinded.
The "yes" of the marriage vow and the "yes" of the counsels
correspond to what God expects man to be in imitation of Jesus
Christ, who, on the Cross, gave all he possessed, body and soul,
for the Father and the world. In the state of election, the Christian
gives his body and soul to God, and God dispenses the fruit of his
sacrifice to his brethren, conferring on the one who has made the
sacrifice a mission within the Church. In the married state, the
Christian, by his sacramental "yes", gives his body and soul to
his spouse—but always in God, out of belief in God, and with
confidence in God's bountiful fidelity, which will not deny to
this gift of self the promised physical and spiritual fruit. No third
form on which a state of life could be based is conceivable besides
these two forms of genuine self-giving, nor does revelation envisage any such third form.

Once again, then, the theological concept of the states of life
has been justified by reference to virginity.

Within the Church, a state of life is a definite life-form that differentiates the ordinary, generic Christian state by a bond, a *differentia
specifica*, that has Christian (that is, not simply civil or professional)
relevance. Such a life-form binds the Christian irrevocably (*cum
immobilitate, sine facultate resiliendi*) in his inmost being. By this
bond, which establishes him in a state of life, he is enabled to
participate with supernatural fecundity in the mystery of "losing
his soul" and thus in the mystery of the Cross and of redemption.
It is true, of course, that even the generic Christian state confers a
life-form, a bond that is both solemn and radical in comparison
with existence outside the Church. In contrast to the married

state and the way of the counsels (or, for the priest, to the state of election as such), however, this general Christian state signifies no ultimately concrete bond that yokes body and spirit in supernatural servitude. *According to the general tradition of the Church, there are only two such life-forms.* "This truth is derived from the ancient Fathers of the Church, all of whom teach that Christ divided the life and state of the Christian *into two orders*: one, the state of those professing the common life of the commandments, as do those who marry; the other, the state of those professing a higher and angelical life, that is, the religious life."[13] "*Two forms of life* have been instituted within the Church."[14] Because all are not capable of walking the hard road of direct imitation in the way of the counsels, says St. Basil, "our most loving God, out of concern for our salvation, divided man's life into *two states—marriage and virginity*—so that he who is not strong enough to endure the struggle of virginity may take a wife, knowing, however, that he will be required to give an account of his chastity and holiness and of his similarity to those saints who lived in marriage and the rearing of children. Such was Abraham. . . , for he had not heard that it was said: 'Sell what thou hast and give to the poor.' "[15] Many patristic texts juxtapose

[13] Suárez, *De statu perf*, bk. III, chap. 2, sec. 4.

[14] Eusebius Pamphili, "Demonstratio Evangelica", bk. I, chap. VIII, PG 4, col. 76.

[15] St. Basil, "Eiusdem Sermo Asceticus, et Exhortatio de Renunciatione Saeculi, et de Perfectione Spirituali", *Ascetica*, PG 31, cols. 627–28. [For an English translation of this and other works of St. Basil, see Saint Basil, *Ascetical Works*, trans. Sr. M. Monica Wagner, *Fathers*, vol. 9 (1950). For a further discussion of the "two lives" or "two states", both von Balthasar and Suárez refer to St. John Chrysostom, *Homiliae in Genesin*, hom. XVIII, 4, PG 53, cols. 153–54; St. Augustine, ep. 157, "Ad Hilarium" (*not* ep. 79 as Suárez and von Balthasar indicate), chap. 4, PL 33, cols. 686–93; Origen, *Homiliae in Librum Jesu Nave*, hom. IX, PG XII, cols. 870–79. Both authors refer also to St. Basil's epistle 79, addressed to Eustathius. This epistle is, indeed, addressed to Eustathius, but it makes no reference to the "two states". It is possible that the reference should be to letter 223, which, in sec. 2 (PG 32, cols. 823–24), addresses the means of arriving at perfection, but without specific mention of the states of life as such. Finally, both Suárez and von Balthasar refer to the *Chronicle* of Simon (i.e., Simeon) Logothetes (now generally identified with St. Simeon Metaphrastes). Von Balthasar refers in particular to the excerpts from the Fathers of the Church that are contained in the *Chronicle*. For further information about Simeon Logo-

the two states only in the sense of *genus* and *species*: as the general human state (without actually mentioning marriage) and the state of perfection or of the counsels, which is related to the former state "as perfection to that which is to be perfected [that is, to be acquired] or as determinacy to that which is to be determined [that is, to be exercised]" (Suárez, *De statu perf*, bk. I, chap. 2, sec. 9). Thomas Aquinas speaks of no division of the states of life in this sense.[16] Suárez, under the influence of the aforementioned Scholasticism, does not see to what an extent the sacrament of matrimony is the basis not only of a civil, but also of a Christian state, "because, speaking simply and only with respect to eternal life, [matrimony] does not exceed the common state of Christian life" (Suárez, bk. I, chap. 2, sec. 2; cf. also sec. 13).

Nevertheless, it is clear from both the Old and the New Testaments that the person who is unmarried, but not otherwise obligated, is to be regarded, not as the rule, but as the exception. Marriage is so rooted in man's original state, it belongs so intimately to the "image and likeness" in man, it bestows on him so abundantly all the natural means of genuine development in the "thou" and in God, it is so plainly the proper training ground for pure love and selflessness, that the only state of life that can be imagined beyond this one, which has been established by nature and consecrated and ennobled by a sacrament, is a completely supernatural state that excels marriage both in fecundity and in the bond [the *differentia specifica*] that constitutes it. Such a state has its foundation firmly in the marriage of Christ to the Church. Suárez regards the possibility of a third state as so unlikely that he finds it necessary to assign even the secular priest to one or other

---

thetes and the *Chronicle*, see J. Gouillard, "Syméon Logothètes et Magistros, surnommé Le Métaphraste", *Dictionnaire de théologie catholique*, vol. 14, pt. II, cols. 2959–71. (Tr)]

[16] Thomas does, however, speak of a twofold law of life: marriage and the *vita contemplativa* (*Summa Theologiae*, vol. V, *Supplementum Tertiae Partis*, q. XLI, a. II, ad quartum). Although the human race as a whole received a strict command to increase and multiply and hence to marry, the individual can, nevertheless, choose the *vita contemplativa* for higher motives. It is clear that Thomas, in dependence on Aristotle, here substitutes for the Christian concept of the state of election the vaguer concept of contemplation, which, however, as the Greeks understood it, meant the fullest freedom for the highest divine things, the *vacare Deo*. Thomas, too, knows no third state of life. [Further references to this work (henceforth *Suppl*) will be given in parentheses in the text. (Tr)]

of the two states: "From every reasonable point of view, it is certain from what has been said that it [the secular priesthood] belongs to one or the other of these states" (Suárez, sec. 13). Admittedly, there are various ways of realizing the state of election. Properly speaking, a "religious *order*" exists canonically only when the three vows have been made solemnly and publicly to the Church. Wherever this requirement is not completely realized, it is necessary and proper to speak of analogous participation in the state of election. This is also true in the case of a simple vow of chastity, even when it is combined with a vow of obedience or with some other way of living the life of the counsels while still in the world: "Every mode of spiritual life that is ordained to the attainment of the perfection of charity, if it has sufficient permanence and stability to constitute a state, may and ought to be called, in some way, a state of perfection. . . . Therefore [canonically] . . . it must be distinguished into a state that is integral or perfect and one that is imperfect." Of the latter, Suárez says, "It shares in some way in the religious state and, in a wider sense and by a certain analogy, can be called religious" (Suárez, bk. II, chap. 2, secs. 17–18). But in this case, too, the prerequisite of stability (irrevocability) cannot be dispensed with. We may draw two conclusions from these remarks. First, "those who are not married belong, by public law, to the civil state of single persons, but not, by virtue of their unmarried status alone, to the state of virginity. Only one who specifically *chooses* celibacy as such or willingly embraces it for the sake of the kingdom of heaven [and, we may add, through a permanent vow or promise] enters that state. Virginity *of this kind*—that is, the giving of oneself to God and to the service of one's neighbor—is objectively a blessing for the world and comparable to the state of virgins in religious life." Second, if they are to have anything in common with the Christian concept of state, all the secular professions necessarily pursued by unmarried women in the world must offer their members the opportunity of sacrificing the freedom by which they can freely dispose of their own lives for a genuinely Christian "nonfreedom". Only then will women experience the blessing that lies in being unremittingly schooled for Christian maturity by an objective rule of life and be preserved from the threatening fate of desiccation and spinsterhood. Since human society, unlike a beehive or a colony of ants, does not consist of three classes: male, female and sexless, man cannot shape his life and perfect the image of God in himself simply by ignoring his sexuality. It would not be hard to show that truly Catholic countries and times did not know this fundamental affirmation of a "third state" that has become almost an ideal and is regarded even by Catholics as something almost normal in this age of disillusionment with marriage, secularization of religious houses, states like colonies of ants, and a liberalism that values the freedom of self-determination as the highest good. People are inclined to think they have accomplished much if they have dedicated their lives for a while to some humanitarian goal, even when they have done so with the reservation that they can do something else if this "proves unsatisfactory" or if they tire of it.

Our purpose in speaking of analogy in regard to the state of the counsels (because in addition to the total self-surrender of the three solemn vows of religious orders there exist numerous other ways of sharing in this life of self-surrender) was to show that participation in the true state of election becomes more complete as the innermost bond—that is, the spiritual bond of *obedience*—is more intensively understood and lived. Virginity and poverty are Christian goods only when they are the expression of a spiritual surrender and binding of oneself to God. "For by the vow of obedience man offers to God the greatest good, namely, his own will, which is more noble than his external goods, which he offers through the vow of poverty"; indeed, "the vow of obedience contains in itself the other vows, although the reverse is not the case." So true is this that, for Thomas Aquinas, obedience is precisely the distinguishing and formal mark of the state of the counsels: "Even if one who does not have the vow of obedience observes voluntary poverty and consecrated virginity, he does not, for that reason, belong to the religious state, which is preferable even to consecrated virginity" (ST 2a 2ae 186, 8 ad 3). In this formal element is to be found the degree to which the above-mentioned analogy is near to or far from the perfection of the concept of a state of life.

The absolute bond created by sacrament or vow is the fullness of Christianity. Until one chooses a state of life, one must continue in *a state of waiting*, which is far from being imperfect since it corresponds to the will of God. It is here that purely physical virginity has its rightful place. But this virginity of the state of waiting (during which young women properly join together in clubs and associations) is not to be confused with a definitive and absolute state. If the choice of a state of life is not made within the appropriate time, the virginity of this state is not automatically transformed into perfect virginity, for this can be accomplished only by the explicit choice of some form of the state of the counsels. If this does not occur, the life-form continues to be one of pro-longed waiting.

The situation is quite different in regard to the *state of widowhood*. The yoke has been borne; the sacrifice has been offered; one's life has been fulfilled before God. The widow is free now—and this freedom is like a reward from God for the burden she has carried—either to feel herself still bound and so to preserve her marital fidelity to death and beyond, to enter upon a new marital relationship (1 Cor 7:39), or to bind herself spiritually by participation in the state of the counsels. Paul speaks of no third state. He expects widows who have children and grandchildren to "provide for their own household and make some return to their parents, for this is pleasing to God. . . . [For] if anyone does not take care of his own, and especially of his own household, he has denied the faith and is worse than an unbeliever." In the case of younger widows, he desires that they "marry, bear children, rule their households, and give the adversary no occasion for abusing us". For if they take a vow and then ". . . wantonly [turn] away from Christ, they wish to marry, and are to be condemned because they have broken their first troth". He permits only elderly widows to bind themselves in the Church by such a vow (1 Tim 5:4–14). What he hopes to avoid is, above all, the going about from house to house like busybodies (cf. 1 Tim 5:13) that is always a danger for women who belong to no particular state of life. The way has been clearly designated for them: ". . . Women will be saved by childbearing, if they continue in faith and love and holiness with modesty" (1 Tim 2:15) unless they choose to "think about the things of the Lord" rather than about the things of their husbands and to be "holy in body and in spirit" in virginity (1 Cor 7:34). If they choose the latter, they will enter upon a bondage to the Lord that is at least not inferior to the bond of marriage; they will not choose a trial bond or a "supernatural" marriage of companionship, but a form of self-surrender that is a valid response to the Lord's unconditional gift of himself.

Just as the state of election is founded directly on the Cross and receives from the Cross all its potentiality and strength, so *Christian marriage derives its ultimate sanction and perfection indirectly from the Cross*. As a way of life, it does not have its origin wholly in the New Testament—any more than does the priesthood, which we shall discuss in the following section. Its foundation lies in the first order of creation. But even there it was more than just a natural mystery. It sprang initially from a preternatural act of God and was destined to effect, with man's cooperation, the

constantly renewed realization of the more than natural unity
of love. In a single act that is no longer comprehensible to us,
God was eternally prepared to dispense the grace of his creative
fecundity whenever man and woman joined together spiritually
and physically within this grace. In the New Testament, the
general supernaturalness of the grace of marriage became the
concrete, specific supernaturalness of the grace of Christ on the
Cross. Since the Son's appearance in the world, there is for us no
other form of love than the form with which he has loved us.
"In this is the love, not that we have loved God, but that he has
first loved us, and sent his Son a propitiation for our sins" (1 Jn
4:10). "In this we have come to know his love, that he laid down
his life for us; and we likewise ought to lay down our life for the
brethren" (1 Jn 3:16). "This is my commandment, that you love
one another as I have loved you. Greater love than this no one
has, that one lay down his life for his friends. You are my friends
if you do the things I command you" (Jn 15:12–14). This, then,
is the canon for every Christian love, including marital love and
fidelity. Indeed, it is only because Christ bestowed anew from
above upon the mystery of physical fecundity the infinitely
deeper mystery of the *spiritual fecundity of faith, hope and love
and, with it, the spirit of poverty, chastity and obedience* that marriage
can be raised within the Christian Church to the dignity of a
sacrament. It can be so only by sharing in the spirit of Christ on
the Cross. But this is possible only if, through this spirit, it
mysteriously retains something of the spirit of paradise as it was
before the division of the states of life. Hence Christian marriage
cannot be understood if it is regarded primarily as a natural
institution with a particular form of natural love that was later
"raised" by the sacrament into the state of grace. It must be
interpreted a priori from above, in terms of the Christian act that
established it as marriage—the act of living Christian faith that
always includes love and hope and in which marriage vows
are exchanged. This act is oriented directly and immediately
to God—as a promise of fidelity to God because, by his promises
and revelations, he has first revealed himself as the eternally

faithful one in whom man must believe, in whom he must hope, and whom he must love. The promise of fidelity to one's spouse is not to be separated from this promise of fidelity to God. The acts of faith of the two marriage partners meet in God and are accepted, formed and returned to them by God, in whom they find the foundation of their unity, the witness of their union and the pledge of their fidelity. It is God who, in the act of faith, gives the partners to one another in the basic Christian act of self-surrender. Together, they offer themselves to God and receive each other from him in a gift of grace, confidence and Christian expectation. The fidelity that they mutually pledge is so ineradicable because it rests on the fidelity of God; it derives its strength, its inviolability and its eternity from his fidelity, which remains faithful even when man thinks he has exhausted it. Thus the act by which Christian spouses pledge their fidelity to one another is, like the fundamental Christian act of faith itself, one that is absolutely limitless and opened to God: Just as faith believes more than it can understand because God understands and his word suffices, so the marriage vow promises more than human strength alone can accomplish because God is faithful and bestows the strength of his fidelity on those who believe. *This gift of self in life and death is not unlike the ineradicable, eternal vow that is immanent in all love*; it is an act of such finality that it resembles a true "loss of [one's] own soul" (Mt 16:25). Only because the soul has sacrificed the right to dispose of its life as it will can the right so to dispose of the body also be sacrificed: "The wife has not authority over her body, but the husband; the husband likewise has not authority over his body, but the wife" (1 Cor 7:4).

In this gift of self, the spouses learn that they are not two separate entities that later came together and from whom a new entity, a child, was born as if by chance. They learn that they are both "one flesh" and that, without knowing it, they were so even in the beginning because Eve came from Adam; that, in coming together and thereby renouncing the independence they believed they possessed, they but followed a deep-seated law of self-giving, which, through the loss of what seemed to be oneness, finds this oneness with and in the other. But it is a oneness that consists, not just of the two partners, but also of the fruit of their self-giving, which is more than just their seed—which is all that is unsuspected, grace-filled and wonderful in their self-giving: a child. As long as marriage is considered a purely natural institution, the child will always seem to be an accidental, if happy—perhaps even hoped-for—product of their sexual union. In fact, however, this fruit is not the product of their mutual self-giving and cannot be explained in terms of it. Hence it is necessary, in this purely natural consideration of marriage, *to distinguish between the two "purposes" of marriage*: the purpose of procreation of children and the purpose of mutual self-surrender, which can also be distinguished as the "purpose" and the "meaning" of marriage. *But this distinction disappears* (and with it many an embarrassment to which it leads) when marriage is regarded in its sacramental character. For now the spouses are no longer opened only to each other—and hence closed to all others; they stand primarily in openness to God and, from this stand before God, give themselves to him and, at the same time, expect to receive from him the unexpectable: the fruit of his grace. The manner in which they open themselves to God is itself already a grace and, therefore, fruitful because the fruitfulness of grace in them awaits the fruitfulness bestowed by God from above whether as a child sent them by God or as a spiritual fruit if the physical one is denied them. The act of self-giving within the sacrament is as totally different from the act of love in a "purely natural" marriage as the spiritual attitude of a believer is from that of a non-believer. The believer expects every fruit from God without wanting to know in advance what he will receive; he is unrestricted hope, which affirms and accepts in advance every grace of God, whatever form it may take. Hence Christian spouses, when they come together, always expect to receive from God the superabundant response of his grace; it is impossible for them to differentiate between the "meaning" and the "purpose" of marriage.

This is true ultimately because their faith shares in the grace of the Cross, whose fruitfulness is infinite. Their love—exteriorly something that is expended between the two of them—shares in a hidden manner in the unlimited love of the Lord, which is always universal and eucharistic, and whose fruitfulness surmounts every barrier and expends itself infinitely. It can do so because, in the fruitfulness of the Lord's love on the Cross, *the law of trinitarian love is itself revealed*—the love that is not exhausted between Father and Son, but has as its fruit the Third Person, the Holy Spirit, whose prerogative it is to be, in a special way, the love that exists in God himself.

Only by thus sharing in the Cross does the physical self-giving of the spouses achieve its ultimate and redeeming justification, for it no longer appears, as it did in man's original state, as merely a symbol of the invisible grace of faith, hope and charity, but is revealed instead as an *explicit sharing in the Incarnation of divine grace*, which, in the Lord's life and Passion, no longer acts without the *instrumentum coniunctum* of his flesh and blood. It is not correct to regard the married state as exclusively the state of physical love, and the state of election as that of purely spiritual love, for both states of life represent the one spiritual love of Christ for the Church and, in the Church, for mankind. Through the Incarnation of grace, the spiritual love of the state of election became of necessity an incarnate love, and the physical love of the married state became of necessity a love justified even in the body and integrated with spiritual love.

Thus the fruitful and redeeming justification of the Cross has superseded the tragedy of the sexes. After paradise, sexual love had become involved in a dialectic of birth and death from which no human person could rescue it. Inordinate desire and anxiety had been caught up in a circle from which there was no escape because the perfect love that God, in the beginning, had bestowed on husband and wife as the principle of marriage could not be rediscovered in the realm of marital guilt. This tragic circle was not broken until Christ on the Cross, beyond the corruption of inordinate desire and anxiety and in the superabundance of his love, established a new unity by the birth of eternal life in the midst of eternal death: the birth of the Church, his Bride, from his abandonment by the Father and his sinking into the full reality of death. Only in this way could the corruption of the sexes be overcome. Only in this way, although the unity of the original state could not be restored, could marriage find a place among the forms of Christian self-giving—and then only on condition that it be lived henceforth in the disposition of the Cross, in which all desire, insofar as it is disordered and selfish, is vanquished by the selflessness of Christian self-giving.

Thus both states live by the same love: the love of Christ, which is the paradigm of every love. And both states are fruitful by virtue of this love because both bear in themselves the principle of fecundity—namely, love itself, which is poured into our hearts together with faith and hope. For God was not content just to surprise husband and wife by a reward bestowed on them from without; it was also his will that the fruit of grace should issue in them from the love he had bestowed on them as their own: as their fruit and, at the same time, as his fruit for and in them. The more closely human love resembles God's love, the more it forgets and surrenders itself in order to assume the inner form of poverty, chastity and obedience, the more divine will be its fruit: a fruit that surpasses all human fecundity or expectation. This fruit is bestowed in its unity on the state of election, which renounces by vow not only its own physical and spiritual fruit, but also, and more significantly, the privilege of seeing the fruit God may choose to send it. It abandons to God at the same time both its whole self and the outcome of its total self-surrender. For the Lord on the Cross did not see the fruit of his gift of self, but rather placed it in the Father's hands so that, after he had risen from the dead on the third day, the Father might return it to him superabundantly. Christian marriage likewise shares in this fruit, both by the sacramental vow that leaves a priori to God the decision as to what physical and spiritual fruit he may choose to bestow and by being satisfied with whatever decision he may make. If Christian spouses are able genuinely to make this act of perfect self-giving, their limited community is opened to the universality of the Catholic Church, and their love, which seems to be focussed on so narrow a circle, is enabled actively to participate in the realization of the kingdom of God upon earth.

Nevertheless, the Christian remains in all this a "layman". He is not transferred even by this special, christological sacrament into the state of a qualitatively higher vocation. His life-form is not one that was newly instituted by Christ, but rather one that was already valid under the Old Testament and was supernaturally raised by Christ to the dignity of a sacrament. He is still bound to a form of physical self-giving that attains only in exceptional cases to a perfect resolution of all guilt-caused concupiscence. He cannot transfer to his children, who in their turn were born into the corruption of their race, the sacramental grace that has blessed his own marriage. Nor does his state confer on him the right to complete, in poverty, chastity and obedience, the perfect holocaust, not only of the spirit, but also of the body, to which those in the state of election are called. This does not mean that he is a less worthy Christian than they are, for, even when God's gifts vary, his election bestows on each individual only what is best. Both states—the lay state, which achieves its fulfillment in the married state, and the state of election—condition one another and are intimately related to one another; not, however, as two equal and complementary halves are related, but as the special state, which emanates from the general one and returns to it by way of sacrifice and mission, is related to the general state that is what it is—a genuinely Christian state—only because of the special state. This relationship reflects the basic law of the economy of salvation: that the Old Testament is both continued in and surpassed by—both incorporated into and superseded by—the New Testament; that the New Testament complements the Old Testament, yet is itself so new that only God could have seen that it was already present in the Old Testament.

CHAPTER THREE

THE SECOND DIVISION OF THE STATES OF LIFE

I. THE PRIESTLY STATE

We have thus far quite properly spoken only of the first division of the states of life, for which Jesus laid the foundation and which he brought into existence when he called the apostles from their worldly ties to a way of life appropriate to those who would henceforth be with him in his mission. Only in terms of the Cross and Resurrection of Jesus, only with the accomplishment of his sacrificial death on the Cross, in which every new priestly ministry has its origin, is it possible to speak, in the full sense, of the institution of a priesthood of the New Testament. The "fullness of power" that Jesus conferred on his apostles in the beginning was neither Aaronic nor episcopal, but only such as would enable them for the time being to share in spreading the good news, as he did, "with authority" (Mk 1:27). Not until the Last Supper, when he sanctified himself irrevocably for his death on the Cross, did he also sanctify the apostles (Jn 17:17–19). His earlier words to Peter (Mt 16:18) and to the Twelve (Mt 18:18) were an antecedent promise, the fulfillment of which could properly occur only after Easter (Jn 21:15–19). *The state of the counsels existed before the priestly state*, and the apostles were led from the first state to the second. Despite all possible differences that may subsequently have emerged and been realized, the affinity, the inner relationship, of the two life-forms that are especially confirmed in the New Testament is thereby established. To realize the inevitability of this affinity, we have only to contemplate the unity of Christ's state of election, which preceded every division of the states of life, and was also the spring in which both forms of election had their source.

Christ's state of life is characterized by the stand he takes in the loving will of the Father through the perfect gift of all that is his to the Father and, for the Father's sake, to the world. By his Incarnation in the sinful world and by his work of redemption, this surrender acquires the inner form of a sacrifice. In his mission of reconciliation and mediation, Christ invests his gift of himself to the Father and the Father's acceptance of it with the modality that makes it an emptying of all that he is, a deprivation of every light that shines in the darkness. When the Son stands before the Father in readiness to give himself and to renounce what is his—the Godhead that is his by right (and that he can entrust to the Father), the humanity he has assumed (and that he can lose in death), and even the oneness with the Father that is so essential to him; when, in poverty, chastity and obedience, he thus abandons to the Father the disposal of what is his, he becomes potentially a victim to be sacrificed, and the Father can turn this potentiality into actuality whenever he chooses. In the Son's mind, both the positive act of offering himself to be sacrificed and the subsequent passive one of being offered in sacrifice form a unity that is equally perfect under both aspects. His redemptive sacrifice does not commence, then, in the Garden of Olives when the Father begins to withdraw from him, but rather at the first instant of the Incarnation when the Son divests himself of his likeness to God (Phil 2:7) to enter upon the state of one who is both the priest who offers and the victim who is offered. What is truly fruitful and redemptive in his (as in every) sacrifice is the frame of mind that depends on the inner disposition of love. To the extent, then, that *poverty, chastity and obedience are the inner modalities of the Son's perfect love, which becomes, through them, a sacrificial offering*, these modalities cannot fail to signify *the establishment of his priesthood*. For the Lord is priest precisely because, in the very act of offering the sacrificial victim, he becomes himself the victim that is offered passively in sacrifice. What he offers is his own divine–human substance—something so exceedingly precious and perfect that it outweighs all the world's guilt. But because this priestly sacrifice is but a mode of his gift of himself to the Father and because this gift has its source in the very essence of his divine person, it is clear that the priestly character does not accrue to him accidentally and from without, but rather that he is consecrated priest par excellence by his very nature; that he contains in himself the concept of all that is priestly (that he is αὐτο-ἱεροσύνη); and, consequently, that every true priesthood in the world can be no more than an imitation of and participation in his eternal and absolute priesthood.

Two conclusions are to be drawn from all this. *Christ is priest inasmuch as he contains in himself the unity of priestly office and love*; he possesses the office of priest only because he is also the victim. And Christ realizes this unity of office and love only *by being at the same time both priest and victim*, the one who offers and the one who is offered. He performs at one and the same time both the active and the passive roles that are indispensable to sacrifice.

1. If we consider only the first of these syntheses, it might seem that the Lord's priestly character is identical with his love. The whole concept of the priestly *office* seems thus to be absorbed by and submerged in the concept of his loving gift of self. On the Cross, where his priestly function reaches its climax, the office seems no longer visible. From this point of view, he is— according to the central teaching of the letter to the Hebrews—a high priest who supplants the official priesthood [of the Old Covenant] in which function was not identifiable with person, and action was, in consequence, not identifiable with passion. The functional priesthood of the Old Testament was but "a shadow of the good things to come" (Heb 10:1) and, therefore, bound to a particular period of time and able only by constantly repeated sacrifices to recall to men's minds the unique, but unrealizable, meaning of all their sacrifices. By putting in the place of "holocausts and sin-offerings" his own unbounded readiness: "Behold, I come . . . to do thy will, O God" (Heb 10:7), Christ encompasses these sacrifices in himself. ". . . He annuls the first covenant in order to establish the second. It is in this 'will' that we have been sanctified through the offering of the body of Jesus Christ once for all" (Heb 10:9–10). ". . . He entered once for all . . . , by virtue of his own blood, into the Holy of Holies,

having obtained eternal redemption" (Heb 9:11–12). And if the blood of animals was able to effect legal purification under the Old Testament, "how much more will the blood of Christ, who through the Holy Spirit offered himself unblemished unto God, cleanse your conscience from dead works to serve the living God?" (Heb 9:14). This sacrifice is the sacrifice of the "will" of him who comes to do the will of God even to the shedding of his own blood. His is a death of obedience, a death so completely identifiable with obedience that it supersedes all legal and external blood-offerings and marks the end of the Old Testament (Heb 9:15–16). Henceforth, the law must be sought in one's own heart: ". . . I will put my laws upon their hearts, and upon their minds I will write them" (Heb 10:16). Christ's sacrifice is so completely the perfection and end of the earlier legal sacrifices that "if . . . he were [now] on earth, he would not even be a priest" (Heb 8:4). For "the worship they [priests] offer is a mere copy and shadow of things heavenly" (Heb 8:5), whereas the perfect self-offering of the Son—who, "Son though he was, learned obedience from the things he suffered; and when perfected . . . became to all who obey him the cause of eternal salvation" (Heb 5:8–9)—establishes him, "because he continues forever", in an "everlasting priesthood" (Heb 7:24).

The objective office of priest is not, then, something added, but extrinsic, to the subjectivity of the Son's gift of self and its acceptance by the Father. It belongs as essentially to his nature as does his subjective sacrifice. For him, there is no bare *opus operatum*; he must accomplish to the full the whole work of priest and victim, and he does so by loving "his own . . . to the end" (Jn 13:1)—until his work on earth "is consummated" (Jn 19:30). *From this point of view, the state of the counsels—the state of the total offering of oneself (the holocaust)—would seem to be the authentic Christian continuation of the priestly state of the Old Testament.* Whether the one called to it is man or woman, the state of the counsels would be, then, in the fullest sense, the priestly state within the Church, that is, the state of those who offer sacrifice together with Christ. Mary and John, who stood at the foot of the

Cross in poverty and chastity and in a love that was obedient to the end, are the foundation stones of this new state of sacrifice in the Cross. They received and chose as the form of their lives the form of the Redeemer who sacrificed himself for all. For John, the oneness of this life-form is beyond question: "In this we have come to know his love, that he laid down his life for us; and we likewise ought to lay down our life for the brethren" (1 Jn 3:16). The state of the counsels is the grace of entering into this love in such a way that it becomes the form of human life. One who vows himself to this way of life puts it on like a garment and must strive to adapt himself to its dimensions and requirements. He must grow until the garment he wears fits him. This life-form demands the perfect gift of all he has and is—possessions as well as body and soul—so that he can cooperate with the Lord in the work of redemption. Thus, since the Lord redeemed the world by his perfect and loving obedience (Phil 2:7), and since, in the state of the counsels, all that is promised is contained in the vow of obedience (cf. ST 2a 2ae 186, 8 responsio), the vow of total obedience would seem to be the preeminent form of participation in the redemption, in the continuation of the obedience of the Cross.

2. And yet it is in many ways unsatisfactory to speak of the priestly office as being absorbed by love—of the objective act of offering as being absorbed by the subjective passivity of being-offered. Each of the reasons that, even in the New Testament, expressly require the continued existence of the priestly office as well as of the Lord's perfect love is associated, albeit each in a different manner, with the state of guilt and redemption in the world.

a) The most significant of these reasons is that the Redeemer, who, in his Passion, takes upon and into himself the sins of the world, must divest himself so completely, in his sacrifice, of all conscious and sensible love that *his act of sacrifice acquires in the night of the Cross the character of pure objectivity, of an official priesthood*. And the Father himself, who conceals his love in the darkness of that night for the sake of the redemption, appears—as Abraham appeared to Isaac, whom he was about to sacrifice—in the pure objectivity and absolute impartiality of such a priesthood. It is clear that the office bespeaks here no *limitation* of love, but rather the mode in which love itself achieves its ultimate gift—the sacrifice of itself. The greatest sacrifice is not to suffer in love, but rather to renounce the very awareness of love for the sake of love, to lose love for the sake of love, so that everything one does in love seems but the impartial performance of an official act. That is the ultimate suffering that the Redeemer endured for our sake. The formal element of love—the unconditional preference for the will of the beloved above one's own, which under other circumstances would have been the happiness concealed in love as the heart is concealed in the whole organism—appears here, at the zenith of love, in all its naked formality, thus proving that love is truly love and nothing but love. It is for this reason that the infinite love between Father and Son assumes on the Cross the modality of pure obedience, and, hence, of an official priesthood —in this way signifying both the complete obscuring of their mutual love and the complete revelation of its boundlessness. The Son as well as the Father accomplishes the work of love in the pure mode of the priestly office: *the Son*, by submerging all subjectivity (". . . If it is possible, let this cup pass away from me" [Mt 26:39]; "Now my soul is troubled. And what shall I say? Father, save me from this hour" [Jn 12:27]) in his readiness to let the pure will of the Father be accomplished in him even beyond what his human nature is able to endure (". . . Yet not my will but thine be done" [Lk 22:42]; "No, this is why I came to this hour. Father, glorify thy name" [Jn 12:27–28]); *the Father*, by turning upon his Son the face of his severity, and even anger, at the sinfulness of the world ("My God, my God, why hast thou forsaken me?" [Mt 27:46]). This is the mystery of Christ's Passion, in which it becomes evident that the first synthesis achieved in Christ, the priest, does not suffice to explain the nature of the priestly office of the New Testament without the second synthesis: *the synthesis between the activity of offering and the passivity of being offered*. For it is only in the Passion that we are able to discern the last formal element in the gift of self in love—the element that not only is now, but always has been, the most essential component of the love of Father and Son and that must continue to be, in the future, the formal element of the Christian gift of self since the Lord has bequeathed to the Church his own love—namely, *obedience*. To establish at the heart of the New Covenant of love an absolute authority that makes possible an absolute obedience is, then, the highest grace the Redeemer can bestow on the Church he is to found: the grace of being allowed to bring, together with him, the proof of a love so perfect that it is ready to prefer the will of another to its own will even in the dark night of the soul when it no longer comprehends what it does.

By absolute obedience, that is, by fulfilling the Old Testament to the least detail, to the blindest surrender of himself to the will of the Father even when he no longer knows the Father or understands the meaning of his sacrifice, Christ effects the change from the Old to the New Testament. As the central act of his love, this obedience is also the focal point of the Redemption and of the whole New Covenant. For if the apostle's injunction to "have this mind in you which was also in Christ Jesus, who . . . emptied himself, taking the nature of a slave and . . . humbled himself, becoming obedient even to death, even to death on the Cross" (Phil 2:5, 7–8), is to have any meaning, if Christians are actually to achieve this radical and extreme obedience, they must be given *an authority that is or can become* for them as concrete, intimate and inevitable, *as demanding and unrelenting*, as the Father's authority was for Christ on the Cross. A Christianity that would reap only the fruit of the Cross, the "freedom of the Christian man", without wanting to share the mind of the Crucified One himself, would have left the suffering Lord alone on Calvary and so would have separated the mind of the body from that of the head.

By his submission to the law of Moses at the circumcision (Lk 2:21) and the purification (Lk 2:22–24, 27, 39), by his pilgrimage to Jerusalem as a twelve-year-old (Lk 2:42), by his frequent attendance in the temple on Jewish feasts, and by the adaptation

of his whole life to the prophecies by which the Father indicated
the course his life should take (Jn 12:14 and elsewhere), Jesus
proves that the Father's authority is for him a perpetually binding
law incarnate in human law. "For I have come down from heaven,
not to do my own will, but the will of him who sent me" (Jn
6:38). The law of God is in his inmost heart (Ps 39:9) and is the
constant object of his adoring love. As we said earlier, it is the
Holy Spirit above and in him who makes known to him, now
and always, the will of the Father in which the Old Testament,
the law and the prophets are fulfilled and more than fulfilled,
and who, because he is a divine Spirit, does not cease to be for
the incarnate Son the adorable and absolute norm, the ultimate
inspiration for his mission. Consequently, there can be in the
Church, too, only one authority—an authority that nothing, no
human feelings or considerations or opinions, can weaken—to
make comprehensible and even imitable for Christians something of the Son's loving obedience to the Father. For this reason,
the ecclesial office of priest, although still reminiscent of the
Old Testament in its exterior form, belongs intrinsically to the
essence of the New Testament. It makes possible in the Church
the loving obedience that is the hallmark of the New Testament;
it forms the "wall" over which the Christian is expected to
"leap": ". . . In my God I will leap over the wall" (2 Sam 22:30).

By the perfection of his loving obedience, Christ reveals the
absolute authority of the Father, which he demonstrates in his
own person and brings once more to the consciousness of the
world. His obedience is such that the Father can portray his own
authority in the transparency of the Son's love. Even in his
Incarnation, the Son was already the representative of the Father's
authority in the world, for the Father had bestowed on him all
judgment (Jn 5:22), but he becomes so most especially after his
Passion, for it is then that the Father gives him a name that is
above all names "so that at the name of Jesus every knee should
bend of those in heaven, on earth and under the earth, and every
tongue should confess that the Lord Jesus Christ is in the glory of
God the Father" (Phil 2:10–11), for *to him has been given "all power*

in heaven and on earth" (Mt 28:18). Just as he represents the office
and authority of the Father in the whole of creation, so he now
transmits to his Church both his authority and the love that is
inseparable from it. For he cannot confer on the new priesthood
an authority that is less than his own any more than the Father's
authority can be relativized in him: "He who hears you, hears me;
and he who rejects you, rejects me; and he who rejects me, rejects
him who sent me" (Lk 10:16), for ". . . as the Father has sent
me, I also send you" (Jn 20:21). Therefore, ". . . he who receives
anyone I send, receives me; and he who receives me, receives him
who sent me" (Jn 13:20). The parallelism is complete, not because
the one on whom the priestly office is conferred is in any way
comparable to Christ, but because the will of the Son transmits to
the Church the authority he possesses in the Father so that in his
name the Church, too, can make unconditional demands on the
company of believers. Only one who truly humbles himself can
experience genuine love as opposed to the mere imitation of love
that is actually selfishness. The decision to love is not made in a
time of peace, but in a time of severest trial when the apostle's
autonomy is brought "into captivity to the obedience of Christ"
(2 Cor 10:5). But if this obedience is required of the Christian
for the salvation of mankind, then he, in turn, requires of the
Founder of the Church the absolute guarantee that the authority
to which he submits is from God and is exercised in God's name.

b) The other reasons that justify the continuation of a priestly
ministry in the New Testament are derived from and ordered to
this first one. They pertain not only to those who will follow the
Lord in the most perfect love (*ratione caritatis*), but also to those
who will be drawn to perfect love from imperfect love or fear
(*ratione timoris*) only through the ministry and authority of the
priest. Those who, in the "state of perfection", take the vow
of obedience that includes all other vows (ST 2a 2ae 186, 8
responsio) submit themselves voluntarily to the obedience of
Christ on the Cross. Because it is totally voluntary, the obedience
undertaken by vow corresponds more closely to the obedience

of love in the New Testament than to a continuation of the
functional obedience of the Old Testament, for which love was
either not a factor at all or not a major one. But because, on
the one hand, those who take the vow of obedience either do
not all possess perfect love or, at least, are sometimes unfaithful
to it, and because, on the other hand, those not chosen for this
state of life, but nevertheless called to perfect love, are equally
admonished to absolute obedience and can, therefore, rightfully
lay claim to a properly constituted authority, *an authentic priestly
office* must embody for the whole Church what the superior
embodies for a religious community: namely, divine authority.
But religious orders are only a part of the Church whereas the
Lord established the ecclesial office for the whole Church; hence
even religious orders and other forms of the life of the counsels
are subject to ecclesial authority.

This is true primarily because the ecclesial office is more than
just an abstract representation of divine authority; by virtue of
the power vested in it, *it mediates the entire fullness of the concrete
presence of the Lord within the Church and dispenses his grace through
the sacraments*. For, to meet human needs in every state of life,
the Lord did not choose to bestow his grace on fallen nature
invisibly, but rather in the visible signs that are meaningful
for man's corporeal and sense-bound nature, and in which this
constant help from above shines forth actively in the here-and-
now of every time and place. Christ wants not only to remain
present in his Church for all time, but also to let those who are
his own have always before their eyes the evident signs and
pledges of his presence. They are to behold not just more or less
imperfect approximations of the ideal of his perfect priesthood,
but this perfect priesthood itself—veiled in signs, it is true, but
nonetheless visible to a loving faith. They are to find the distance
between this perfection and their own imperfection bridged again
and again by the Lord's grace as he draws them daily into his own
real and enduring sacrifice: as those offering sacrifice with him
at the offertory of the Mass, as those who have been offered in
sacrifice with him at the communion, no longer in an antithesis

of archetype and image, but in a union such as only the love of God can envisage. But the living Christ effects this through his Holy Spirit, who henceforth works and acts effectively and "nourishingly" in the ecclesial ministry with the same objectivity with which he transmitted to the Son on earth the norm of the Father's will: "My food is to do the will of him who sent me" (Jn 4:34). Thus it is not a strange Spirit who makes known the will of God through the ecclesial ministry, but the same Spirit who is poured forth in love upon the souls of those who believe (Rom 5:5).

What is true of the reality of his enduring sacrifice and of the seven sacraments that radiate from the Mass, which is their center, is true also of the Lord's other functions: his perfect representation of the Father's truth because he is the Word of the Father ("For I have not spoken on my own authority, but he who sent me, the Father, has commanded . . . what I should say, and what I should declare" [Jn 12:49]); his perfect representation of the Father's authority because his mission is to represent in the world the Father's complete power over and care for his people ("For neither does the Father judge any man, but all judgment he has given to the Son, that all men may honor the Son even as they honor the Father" [Jn 5:22–23]; "What my Father has given me is greater than all; and no one is able to snatch anything out of the hand of my Father. I and the Father are one" [Jn 10:29–30]). Thus Christ, as priest, is both teacher and shepherd because the Father's love is one with his truth and his power. But Christ could not be truly and believably present in his Church if there were not in the Church, by his gift, a visible representation of his absolute power to teach and to lead. It is inconceivable that a church should possess only the priesthood and word of Christ, but not his guiding power as shepherd, and yet be truly the Lord's Church, for such a church would not represent for men the whole meaning of the Redeemer's presence in the world. That is why Christ expressly conferred on his Church all three ministries: priest, teacher, shepherd (Mt 16:18; 18:18; 28:18–20; Lk 10:16; 22:19; 24:47; Jn 20:23; 21:15–17 and elsewhere).

It is not necessary to prove here that these ministries were actually conferred on the Church. The Gospels state plainly enough that they were. More important for our purpose is the fact that *the Lord bestowed these ministries on a small group whom he himself chose*, his apostles, whom he prepared with infinite patience for their ministries within the Church, installing them in these ministries only by degrees, as though he wanted to accustom them gradually to their new way of life, which was none other than to be his official representatives. As a sign that Peter, the first representative of the ecclesial ministry, was no longer to function as a private individual, but was to submerge his personal identity for the sake of the ministry conferred upon him, he was given a new name at his initial meeting with the Lord. He was shown that he could do all things if he had faith (even walk on water; even truly recognize the Son of God), but nothing by his own strength. When he persisted in voicing opinions that did not stem from grace, he found himself reproved as "Satan" (Mt 16:22–23). When he disregarded all warnings and presumptuously boasted that he would die with Christ (Mt 26:33–35), he ended by denying his Lord three times (Mt 26:69–75). And in his failure, in his subsequent sorrow at being the kind of man he was, he was installed in his unique office as shepherd of the Lord's flock (Jn 21:15–17). Only because he was first among his brethren in the priestly office does the New Testament offer such a minute description of Peter's character and fate; for it was not until they had been jolted out of their pleasant self-complacency by their manifold failures and their shameful abandonment of the Lord in his Passion that the other apostles also learned to perceive the difference between person and office, to distinguish between the significance of their office, of which the Lord was the only true measure, and the insignificance of their persons, and so to become worthy ministers in the Lord's service. Because they had acquired an experimental knowledge of their own insufficiencies, they were given the gift of humility, which is the foundation of the hierarchical order within the Church. Peter's sorrowful "Depart from me, for I am a sinful man, O Lord" was the foundation of the Lord's promise to make him a fisher of men (Lk 5:8–10). His determined "Thou shalt never wash my feet" was the requisite precondition for the Church's realization that without the sacraments one has "no part" with Jesus (Jn 13:6–10). And his burning shame at having to confess his love three times after his threefold denial was the necessary predisposition for a call to the dignity of the hierarchical order. Only because there *was* in the Church this irreconcilable discrepancy between office and person that precluded all identification of the two was the Holy Spirit sent to bestow the certitude (παρρησία) of authority; to render objectively possible the proper discharge of the priestly ministry by guaranteeing the absoluteness of doctrine and leadership; and, at the same time, to make subjectively bearable the awesome burden of a divine office. Preparation for the ministry involved, on the one hand, a constant encouragement to the risk of faith beyond one's human capabilities and, on the other hand, a persistent warning not to ascribe one's successes to oneself or to confuse the furtherance of the work entrusted to one by God with one's own growth in "virtue" and "perfection". To the very end, Peter was ruthlessly humbled; even after he had pledged his love, the Lord's last word to him was an abrupt: "What is it to thee?" (Jn 21:22). These humiliations meant for Peter—and for those who would follow him—the indispensable assistance of grace that they might be truly the servants of all in their ministry (Mt 20:27) and might realize, even in the laborious fulfillment of that ministry, that they were never all that they were called to be. "Does [the Lord] thank that servant for doing what he commanded him? I do not think so. Even so you also, when you have done everything that was commanded you, say, 'We are unprofitable servants; we have done what it was our duty to do' " (Lk 17:9–10).

No human way of life is ever totally adequate to the greatness of the divine mission conferred with the priestly office. For how can any human person be worthy to impart the word of *God*? How can he be permitted to dispense the grace of *God*, to say in the name of God's *Son*: "This is my body" or "Your sins are forgiven you", to bind and loose in such a manner that his action is ratified in heaven? Only the consciousness of an incurable unworthiness that reaches to the very depths of his being can be the halting response to the call to such a ministry. This is true even if the one so called strives in duty and in gratitude to let his whole being be re-formed in accordance with the ministry bestowed on him by God himself. This mark of absolute imparity between person and office is the beginning and end of the Church's authority. It helps him who is charged with the office to bear it and him who must obey it to look beyond the person and even the weakness of the minister to the divine character of what he administers.

For both the minister and him to whom he ministers, the love of the Lord who gave the Church this form of ministerial authority is the content as well as the all-sufficing basis for the existence of the priestly office; only thus can the presence of the Redeemer's love be guaranteed to the Church in all its fullness as sacrifice, truth and power. *Mutatis mutandis*, the form in which this love is made present in the Church is, of necessity, *a continuation of the form of obedience in the Old Testament*. Even though perfect love is both the content and goal of man's obedience to authority, he cannot discard the external form of authority as long as he remains a sinner. It is impossible to think of ecclesial authority without thinking also of fear, for with the authority to issue commands the Lord also imposed sanctions on those who failed to obey them: "He who rejects you, rejects me" (Lk 10:16). On the other hand, the concept of authority belongs intrinsically to the New Testament, not only because the incarnate Lord possessed the Father's authority as judge and arbiter, but also because it was not his task, on an earth where God was despised and rejected, to establish all things in the sweetness of love. Like the Redeemer on the Cross, the Church, too, must assume a form that is appropriate to a sinful world. Certainly, "there is no fear in love; but perfect love casts out fear, because fear brings punishment. And he who fears is not perfected in love" (1 Jn 4:18). But which of us has perfect love?

Which of us does not have a constant need of fear—of that very real fear that so often overshadows Paul's most shining images (Gal 6:12; Heb 6:4–8; Heb 10:26–31) and inspires the visions that grow increasingly more fearful in Revelation until the advent of the new heaven and new earth (Rev 21), thus reiterating at the end of Holy Scripture all that the Old Testament had taught about judgment.

In the last analysis, however, the concept of authority is at the very heart of New Testament love precisely because, as we have seen, the work of redemption finds its completion therein. The original obedience of paradisal love, by which God's commands were fulfilled unquestioningly and as a matter of course, could be restored only in the more stringent form of the obedience of sacrifice. In paradise, obedience to God's authority would have been indistinguishable from a simple attitude of faith and love. If, at that time, God had issued to individuals commands that were to bind the whole community, love would have sufficed to equip those so commanded with the requisite authority and to accredit them among their fellow men. But because the advent of sin had caused the formal element of obedience to be separated from the love that was lived in fullness and happiness, that element had to be revealed once more upon the Cross and incorporated into the official priesthood of the Church. In this way, the priestly office bridges the whole distance between perfect and imperfect love. If it is, in the Church, an expression of the unattainability of perfect love (because the value of the objective *opus operatum* surpasses, in every instance, the value of the subjective gift of self), it is also, on the Cross, a sign that the subjective gift of self has attained the ultimate submission of blind obedience.

There is no clear division in the Church between these two aspects of the priestly office, nor are we speaking here of a "compulsory obedience" for the imperfect and an "obedience of love" for the perfect. On the contrary, the ecclesial office bridges the two forms by its ability to lead the faithful gently, but inexorably, beyond the many stages of constraint to spontaneity, beyond "fear" to fearlessness. Nor is it inconceivable that ecclesial authority should be gentle and kindly toward one who is imperfect while, at the same time, confronting one who is advanced and no longer needs such concessions with the full force of official authority—for this is the only appropriate way of acting toward a follower of the crucified Jesus. Ultimately, then, the obedience of the vows, which is distinguished from the ordinary obedience within the Church as something special, as a pure expression of love rather than a product of fear, can have no other form than that of the obedience every Christian must render to the Church's authority: the submission of his understanding and will in faith and love to a law that will not always be recognized and lived in love even though it has been imposed by love. Because it is itself an effluence and representation of the Lord's pure obedience of love, obedience to ecclesial authority will always seek, in accordance with its natural tendency, to acquire the form of vowed obedience.

2. THE PRIESTLY STATE AND THE STATE OF THE COUNSELS

The call to the priesthood as an objective ministry in the Church and that to the state of the counsels as a subjective way of life in imitation of Christ are both expressions of the ecclesial state of election. Consequently, they must both correspond to the general structure of this state even though each of them is also governed by laws peculiar to itself. In attempting to describe their complex mutual relationships we will do well to avoid all valuation and to content ourselves with showing first the structure that is common to both of them and then that which is proper to each of them individually. The next step will be to test what has been said against the teaching of Holy Scripture, after which it will be useful to review briefly the historical evolution of the state of election, tracing its development from its beginnings to the decisive differentiation of states in the early Middle Ages, then to the teaching of the Scholastics, and finally to the present state of the question. Only by way of conclusion, after the lay state has also been introduced into the comparison, can we conclude our discussion of the relationship between the two states of election. (See the last chapter of this section: "Evangelical State, Priestly State, Lay State".)

a. Way of Life and Ethos

The priesthood is primarily an ecclesial function, an objective ministry, and, on the basis of this ministry, subsequently a way of life. The way of the counsels is primarily a personal way of life that subsequently became an ecclesial way of life—similar, therefore, to the official ministry, but lacking the distinguishing mark of such a ministry. Common to both is the fact that they are forms of special election, rooted in the same disposition of Christ and challenging the elect to total and irrevocable commitment to a more excellent law of life: the priest, through sacramental consecration; one in the state of the counsels, through the taking of vows and the acceptance of a rule that will henceforth govern his whole life. Common to both forms is also a tension, never completely to be resolved, between objective supernatural form—for the priest, his ministry; for one in the state of the counsels, his rule—and the person called to this form, who must adopt it as the norm of his life without ever being able to do so perfectly. This tension is the particular destiny of all those called by God to a special mission, of all those whose subjectivity is placed at the disposal of their objective mission so that, guided by its precepts, demands and requirements, they may come to realize the nature of a faith that lives more in God than in themselves, that is more concerned about the unity of existence in God than about the dualism that exists between their objective ministry [*Sein*] and their subjective commitment [*Sollen*]—between office and person—as they perceive it with the eye of "reason".

Within this framework of structural unity, it is possible now to define more clearly the divisions that have taken place in the state of election. The priesthood is primarily a function and an office. So true is this that its first and lasting characteristic is the imparity between the absoluteness of the function and the relativity of the one who performs it. Even to strive for total parity between the two would be a sign not only of presumption, but also of a complete lack of understanding of the function itself. For it is intrinsic to the function of the priestly office within the Church that it exceed anything a human individual can achieve or represent by his own strength however earnestly he may strive to do so. The official and, therefore, impersonal mark of the minister must always be present in the priesthood so that the personality of Christ may shine through with greater clarity. The more unostentatiously the priest dedicates himself to his ministry in order to live only for it, the better he fulfills it. In such self-surrender, the priest "loses his soul"—his subjectivity—in the act of obedience that is an essential part of every special election and mission. The authority represented and exercised by the ecclesial minister is that of Christ, the Redeemer, who was obedient unto death. It not only demands obedience; obedience is its very nature. Hence it cannot fail to incorporate more deeply into the obedience of Christ those on whom it is conferred. But it is not only authority *as* service; it is also, and explicitly, authority *for* service, for participation in the responsibility of the divine Shepherd who gives his life for his sheep (Jn 10:15) and who, in entrusting to others his pastoral love and responsibility, expects of the recipients that, as "he laid down his life for us", so they, too, will "lay down [their lives] for the brethren" (1 Jn 3:16). Election to the priesthood is equivalent to being made a "libation for the sacrifice and service of . . . faith" (Phil 2:17), to the dedication of one's soul to the Church (cf. 1 Th 2:8), even to becoming "fools for Christ" that the Church may be wise; "without honor" that it may be honored; the "offscouring of all" that it may thereby be purified and made clean (1 Cor 4:10–13).

But this service to his office is, for the priest, not an attempt to identify himself as subject with his office, to bring office and person into congruence by dint of strenuous effort in order thereby "to be equal to" his office. On the contrary, the priestly existence, as we have seen in the example of Peter in the last chapter, is definitively rooted in the gaping discrepancy between office and person and thus in an ethos that stems radically from humility and is kept alive by the constantly renewed humiliations that manifest and actualize the lasting imparity between [official] dignity and [personal] accomplishment. In his effort to be worthy of his office and, in the process, increasingly to sacrifice and submerge his subjectivity, the priest can expect as his only reward the consciousness, not that *he* has become equal to the office, but that the office has been able to succeed in him despite his inadequacies. In the ethos of the priest, the contrast between office and person is dominant to the end—a static dualism that no existential effort can overcome or weaken. His gift of self has primarily the form of humility.

The state of the counsels is not a function; it is an imitation of Christ in the form of life proper to the vows. In poverty, chastity and obedience, one called to this state of life has the privilege of representing the way of the Redeemer in the Church and for the Church; of renouncing everything that Christ renounced in order thereby to bear witness, by the gift of his own existence, to the vitality and permanence of the answer by which the Church accepts the challenge of Christ's word and essence. Just as *in the priesthood the operation of the head of the Church*, in all its integrity and daily renewed actuality, is placed at the disposal of the whole Church through chosen members of the Church, so *in the state of the counsels the personal cooperation of the members of the mystical body* becomes visible by reason of the same grace of the head—insofar as grace can become visible. In the state of the counsels, the subjectivity of the person is molded in a form that is at once objective, because it transcends the measure and potentialities of the one so molded, and anonymous, because it is objectively defined in the rule, and that thus becomes the ideal condition for the withering and extinction of subjectivity. But since the form described here is no longer an official function under the authority of Christ, but rather a personal form of his redemptive gift of himself, the "perfection" of one called to this form must consist in the effort to adapt himself to it more and more perfectly and to reduce to a minimum the distance between himself and it. The goal of his striving is the unconditional self-surrender that the rule presents to him as the form his life must take; and the more perfectly he keeps his vow, the more closely he will be assimilated into the redemptive purpose and thereby into the redemptive work of Christ. Thus he embodies in the Church the subjective, non-official priesthood of love as opposed to the objective, functional priesthood of office. In doing so, he represents the Lord subjectively in his *life* just as the official priest is able by his power to make him objectively present in sermons, Mass, sacraments and pastoral ministry.

> "When I renounce all I possess and take up my cross and follow Jesus, I have 'brought a burnt offering to the altar of God,' . . . or when I give my body to be burned and have love, . . . when I love my brethren so that I give my soul for their sakes, when I 'struggle for justice, for truth, even to death,' then I have 'brought a burnt offering to the altar of God.' When I 'mortify my members' of all concupiscence of the flesh, when 'the world is crucified to me and I to the world,' I have 'brought a burnt offering to the altar of God' and have become the priest of my own sacrificial offering."[17]
> "Those of the tribes [of Israel] offer 'tithes' and 'first fruits' through the levites and priests; but all their possessions are not tithes or first fruits. The levites and priests, on the other hand, who possess only tithes and first fruits, offer tithes to God through the high priests and, I believe, first fruits as well. Most of us, however, who have entered the school of Christ, are nearly always busy about the things of this life and dedicate only a few of our actions to God. . . . But those who are devoted to the divine word and stand solely and properly in the service of God can . . . be called levites and priests."[18]

This interior and subjective priesthood has its center in the always dynamic assimilation of one's whole personal life to the objective

[17] Origen, *Homiliae in Leviticum*, hom. IX, sec. 9, PG 12, cols. 521–22.

[18] Origen, "Johannescommentar", bk. I, sec. II, in *Die griechischen christlichen Schriftsteller der ersten Jahrhunderte*, vol. IV, ed. Edwin Preuschen (Leipzig: Hinrich, 1903), 5. [For an English translation of this and other works of Origen, see his "Commentary on the Gospel of John" and "Commentary on the Gospel of Matthew", trans. Allan Menzies, *Ante-Nicene*, vol. IX (1908), 291–512. (Tr)]

form of self-giving prescribed in the rule, in the daily renewed effort to realize what one has vowed in perpetuity. Of its very nature, moreover, this form of life has no *terminus ad quem*, for the perfection of Christ's gift of self becomes comprehensible to us only in terms of our own unceasing and unconditional striving to attain it. Hence this striving becomes itself the definitive form of the state of the counsels, which is and remains to the end a state of perfection *to be acquired* [*status perfectionis acquirendae*]—of that perfection that the individual has vowed to adopt as the form of his life so that he may never cease striving to attain it.

It belongs to the concept of Christian perfection that it never becomes a goal that has been reached and beyond which there is nothing toward which one can strive, but consists rather in the "perfection of striving for perfection". This is true, not because of the imperfection of man's sinful state on earth, but solely because of a disposition in him that has its source in God and his grace: the striving to become "yet more" and "yet greater" than he can ever hope to become. For this reason, and as befits Christ's participation in the divine nature, the elections and missions of the New Testament are no longer inwardly restricted as were those of the Old Testament and cannot, therefore, be undertaken and brought to completion once and for all. Thus Origen interpreted the "I will hope continually" (Ps 71:14) of the psalmist to mean that man will always find new depths to plumb in his unending search for God.[19] And Irenaeus would have not only charity, but also faith and hope, endure for all eternity because "in all respects God must always be he who is greater . . . and this not only in this world, but also in the world to come so that God is always the one who teaches, and man is always the pupil who learns from God"[20]— even to the equating of "succession" and "fixedness" (*Con haer*, bk. IV, chap. 20, sec. 7). The blessed, too, will "receive the kingdom

[19] Origen, "In Psalmos", Psalmus LXX, 14, *Analecta Sacra Spicilegio Solesmensi*, ed. Joannes Baptista Cardinal Pitra (Veneto: Mechitaristarum Sancti Lazari, 1883), vol. III, 91.

[20] St. Irenaeus, "Contra Haereses Libri Quinque", bk. II, chap. 28, sec. 3. [PG 7 col. 806. Further references to this work (henceforth *Con haer*) will be given in parentheses in the text. For an English translation, see *The Apostolic Fathers with Justin Martyr and Irenaeus*, arranged by A. Cleveland Coxe, in *Ante-Nicene*, vol. I (1913), 315–57. (Tr)]

forever and will forever advance in it" (ibid., bk. IV, chap. 28, sec. 2). By identifying "longing" with "seeing", Gregory of Nyssa described even the eternal happiness of heaven as a ceaseless striving toward God.[21] The same thought occurs in St. Augustine: "When God has been found, he is infinite that he may still be sought."[22] Commenting on the passage (Phil 3:6–16) at the beginning of which St. Paul says that he does not claim to be perfect, but forgets the things that are behind and strives toward those that are ahead, and at the end of which he speaks of himself as perfect, Augustine says: "He called himself first imperfect, and now perfect. Why, if not because man's perfection consists in the discovery that he is not perfect? . . . And if you should, at any stage of your spiritual progress, hold yourselves for perfect, may you learn, from reading the Holy Scripture and from the discovery of what true justice is, that you are guilty; may you condemn the present in longing for the future; and may you live by faith, hope and charity . . . [until] satiety will be insatiable, and there will be no repugnance; we shall be eternally hungry and will be eternally satisfied."[23] Pseudo-Bernard summarizes this teaching and applies it to the evangelical

[21] Gregory of Nyssa, "In Cantica Canticorum", hom. 8, PG 44, cols. 939–41; hom. 6, ibid., col. 889.

[22] St. Augustine, "In Joannis Evangelium Tractatus CXXIV", tractatus LXIII, sec. 1. [PL 35, col. 1803. For an English translation of this and other works of St. Augustine, see St. Augustine, *Homilies on the Gospel of John*, trans. John Gibb and James Innes; *Homilies on the First Epistle of John*, trans. H. Browne; *Soliloquies*, trans. C. C. Starbuck, *Nicene*, vol. VII (1908). (Tr)]

[23] St. Augustine, "Sermonum Classes Quatuor", sermo CLXX, chaps. 8–9, PL 38, col. 931. This is a constant theme with St. Augustine. Cf. also, St. Augustine, "In Epistolam Joannis ad Parthos Tractatus Decem", tractatus IV, chap. 3, PL 35, cols. 2006–7; idem, *Sermones ad Populum, Classis II: De Tempore*, sermo CCXXXIV, PL 38, cols. 1115–17. [For an English translation of this and other sermons of St. Augustine, see *Sermons on the Liturgical Seasons*, trans. Sr. Mary Sarah Muldowney, *Fathers*, vol. 38 (1959). (Tr)] See also *Appendix Tomi Quinti Operum S. Augustini Complectens Sermones Supposititios, Classis Prima: De Veteri et Novo Testamento*, sermo CXIV, "De Verbis Apostoli ad Hebraeos", chap. XII, sec. 1, PL 39, cols. 1971–72; St. Augustine, *De Cantico Novo*, PL 40, cols. 677–88. Cf. also Gregory the Great, "Homiliarum in Ezechielem Prophetam Libri Duo", bk. II, sermo 1, PL 76, cols. 935–48; Cassian, *Collationum XXIV Collectio in Tres Partes Divisa*, pt. I, chap. VII, PL 49, cols. 489–90; ibid., cols. 497–99.

state: "Perfection is required of all of you, but it ought not to be the same for all; for if you are beginning, begin perfectly; if you are already making progress, do this perfectly, too; and if you have attained some perfection, take your own measure and say with the apostle: 'Not that I have already attained this, or already have been made perfect. . . . Let us then, as many as are perfect, be of this mind' (Phil 3:12, 15). In these words the apostle clearly teaches that the perfection of the just man in this life is the perfect forgetfulness of what is behind and the perfect striving for what is ahead."[24] St. Bernard of Clairvaux expresses this even more cogently in one of his letters: "Perfection is said to be a tireless zeal for making progress toward and continual efforts [to attain] perfection."[25]

Beyond this dynamic perfection, there is no higher, static perfection to be sought. And it is this personal dynamic—as opposed to the general tension that exists in both states of election between the form of life one has assumed and one's subjective striving and giving of self—that distinguishes the state of the counsels from the priestly state. Thus, while Peter cannot in his official capacity escape the absoluteness of the antinomy between function and personal adequacy and, at his first encounter with the Lord, is projected forthwith out of the personal ("Thou art Simon, son of John") and into the official dimension ("Thou shalt be called Cephas" [Jn 1:42]), John—who is undoubtedly the anonymous first disciple of the Gospel account—is portrayed with equal immediacy in the dynamic movement of discipleship (". . . They followed Jesus"), of receiving and accepting the invitation to accompany Jesus ("What is it you seek?" ". . . Where dwellest thou?" . . . "Come and see" [Jn 1:37–39]).

From this description, it is clear that both the priestly state and the state of the counsels have their own law within the one form of the state of election. As ecclesial forms, both are pure gifts of God to man, but in the priesthood God, as it were, claims man

---

[24] William of Saint Thierry, "Epistola seu Tractatus ad Fratres de Monte Dei de Vita Solitaria". [Bk. I, chap. IV, sec. 11, PL 184, col. 315. For many years, this work was thought to have been composed by Saint Bernard of Clairvaux, hence von Balthasar's attribution to Pseudo-Bernard. (Tr)]

[25] St. Bernard of Clairvaux, "Epistolae", ep. 254, sec. 3, PL 182, col. 460.

as his instrument and man must surrender himself wordlessly to God's service; in the state of the counsels, on the contrary, the gift assumes more explicitly the form of an answer one is privileged to make to God. In the priesthood, man is so completely a function that God can work in him even when he resists. In the state of the counsels, the gift has rather the complexion of a mutual love in which God will not advance if man does not follow him willingly. If both states reflect a special tension between objective ministry [*Sein*] and subjective commitment [*Sollen*], it may nevertheless be said that objective ministry is dominant in the priesthood and subjective commitment in the state of the counsels.

It is also possible to characterize these two states in their disparity and their congruity in terms of what has been said earlier about the relationship of "Christ's state of life" (pt II, ch. 2, sec. 1) to the Holy Spirit. On the one hand, Jesus' earthly life begins when he consents to become man through the activity of the Holy Spirit and accepts this Spirit, which is both in and over him, as the norm of his life, or—to express it differently—when he enters so deeply into the Father that he receives, in addition to his own property of being Son, the further possibility of breathing forth the Spirit together with the Father. Such an utterly humble openness to the Father and—as the norm of one's life—to the Spirit that proceeds from the Father is the fundamental disposition of one in the state of the counsels: obedience in poverty and purity before the face of the inexhaustibly "greater" Father (Jn 14:28) and, consequently, participation in the eternal movement of the Son to the Father within the Spirit, whether this Spirit sends [missions] the Son from the Father to the world or from the world to the Father. On the other hand, Jesus' earthly life ends in a breathing forth of the missioning Spirit—first on the Cross, then at Easter and at his Ascension to the Father. And it is from this (post-Easter) missioning Spirit that the priesthood draws its life, for it is the primary function of the priesthood officially to mediate this Spirit in a wholeness that the priest can never attain existentially, but that he must never cease striving to attain as fully as possible.

It is clear from the foregoing that the two forms of election *are, as it were, complementary* in their demands. Intrinsic to the priesthood as an objective function in the service of the priesthood of Christ is the demand for a subjective complement, that is, for the priest's unconditional gift of self that includes the vow in which all love has its source—the renunciation of all one possesses. The priest, who by reason of his office is the bearer of Christ's grace, can find no other and no better answer to this grace than to be subjectively the kind of priest Christ wants him to be, that is, as we have seen, a priest who offers his whole life as a holocaust in the service of God and man. No priestly ethic can have any other basic content than the total expropriation of one's own private interests and inclinations so that one may be a pure instrument for the accomplishment of Christ's designs for the Church. Such a gift is intrinsically contained in the decision to become a priest and the grace to make it is conferred on the priest with the gift of sacramental grace and the indelible mark of his priesthood; it is no less demanded and expected of him than of one bound by the irrevocability of the vows. It is in no way correct to say that, of itself, the priestly function demands of the individual a less great and less perfect gift of self than does the grace of election to the state of the counsels. The opposite would be more true: The greatness of the priestly vocation demands of the one called to it the fullest gift of which he is capable. Only when he has given literally all he possesses will he be able to say that he is a useless, but nonetheless usable, servant. Whether or not he takes explicit vows, he must, in any event, respond to the Lord's grace by subjecting all that he has to the Lord's command. Consequently, he will seek his "perfection", that is, the proper conduct of his service, only where one called to the state of the counsels seeks his, namely, in poverty, chastity and obedience, although, in his case, the manner of self-emptying, of renunciation of what has hitherto constituted his life and work, will have points of resemblance to the special anonymity inherent in the functional aspect of his office. The external and internal expropriation of the member of a religious order by the vows is aimed, on the other hand, at fostering in him a general readiness and freedom for every form of imitation of the Lord, however this may be required either by God in contemplation or by the superior for the work of the order. He lives in constant indifference as to the character that may be stamped upon him by the order itself or, within the general structure of the order, by God or by the superior. As all the great rules of religious orders agree, this is the special form his "humility" must take—the attitude of a servant.[26] He must be ready to undertake whatever service may be demanded of him either in prayer or outside it.

Although the basic disposition of sacrificing one's own "individuality" remains the same, the anonymity required of the secular priest is of a different kind; it is the assimilation of the individual to a function that is itself anonymous. Priests are, for the most part, interchangeable in the functions they perform. The more transparent their spiritual substance, the more effectively the Spirit can work through them; the less they dim the presence of the divine that is revealed through them by the colossal proportions of their own so-called "individuality" (or even their "ideal self-image"), the more ideal they will be as priests. Whether they take vows or not, the essence of this pure state of being always prepared, by virtue of their office, for whatever God or the Church may require of them cannot be other than the *spirit* of poverty, chastity and obedience, although it will have the distinctive coloring conferred by their office. Obviously, the anonymity of office that makes the priest an instrument in the hand of God and the Church in no way dispenses him from developing and using the powers of his spirit, for they are the most precious gifts he himself can offer for the service of God, and it would be a lack of gratitude to withhold them. But the measure and manner of their development lies totally in the apostolate of the priest. Even his recreation, even the time he

---

[26] Von Balthasar's play on words: "*Das ist die besondere Form seiner 'Demut'—als Dien-Mut . . .*" (German text, 223), cannot be preserved in English. It is based on the etymology of the German word *Demut*. (Cf. Friedrich Kluge, *An Etymological Dictionary of the German Language*, trans. John Francis Davis [London: Bell, 1891], 54.) [Tr]

may and ought to devote to what he dispassionately regards as beautiful and pleasurable, are not exempt from the higher law of his service: Their only purpose is to enable him to serve better. The content of the priest's service differs in many ways from that of one in the state of the counsels; hence the concrete manner of his work and recreation will, at any given time, also be different. Common to both of them, however, is exclusivity of service and the renunciation of any oases of private existence or interests reserved solely for themselves. No priest can ever say he has done enough; the inevitable comparison between his office and the life of the counsels brings him face to face with the ethos of the evangelical state: The more of his own substance he gives to his service, the more of it will be used for the fruitfulness of that service. In every sermon, in every dispensation of the sacraments, it is his privilege to distribute and bestow not only the Lord and his Holy Spirit, but, within this Spirit, also himself. He is not consumed in vain; each of his hidden sacrifices is absorbed into the divine fruitfulness that he serves. Whether his service is successful or not, he has the certainty that it is completely consumed. To the absoluteness in which he is placed by his office and which he can neither increase nor decrease there is added the relativity of his own readiness. For while it was proper for Augustine to defend this absoluteness against the relativizing of Donatus, it is also necessary, once the absoluteness has been established, to emphasize as well the supernatural fruitfulness of the priest's readiness for sacrifice. Undoubtedly, a good priest transmits more grace than a bad one, not only because a bad priest causes scandal and turns the faithful away from the path of salvation, but also because, in the very nature of things, a priest in the state of grace receives more grace than one who is not.

Both states of election are faced, then, with the task of bringing a subjective attitude into harmony with an objectively given form or function. Both forms, moreover, were explicitly created and intended for the Church by the Lord of the Church. The forms themselves, however, do not strive for congruence, but retain something of the antithesis of the relationship we observed above between the state of the apostles and that of the faithful. Those in the state of the counsels are, after all, "lay persons"; it is not part of their ideal to strive toward the priesthood. Women are banned from doing so; and founders of religious orders like Benedict, Francis of Assisi and others did not wish to do so. As we have already noted, it is the primary function of the priest to represent the head of the Church for the body and he is obliged by this fact to model his life as far as possible on that of the head. It is the primary function of one in the state of the counsels, on the other hand, to represent the body, the Church-Bride; he is the leaven of the people. It is his task to assimilate the "yes" of the whole Church as far as this is possible to the "yes" of Mary, whose model is her Son. The self-emptying of one in the state of the counsels is not, like that of the priest, a service performed *for* the Church, but rather a service performed *by* the Church. To live according to the counsels is far less a means of attaining the personal goal of the individual who strives for "perfection" than an expression of what the Church must be and do in purity if it is to receive as perfectly as possible—and always through the mediation of the priest—what has been promised it.

The two forms of the state of election are not so antithetical, then, that they are not, together, an expression of the Church's life, for even the priest belongs primarily to the Church: He is a "presbyter"—an exponent of the community—before he is chosen and consecrated as its *episkopos*—as both prelate and pattern of the flock; his call to office is secondary to his call "to be with the Lord" and to participate by his whole existence in the Lord's redemptive service to the world. But, in his case, this service means undertaking—even "losing himself" in—the official function in which he is to represent the Lord to his brethren. One in the state of the counsels, on the other hand, "loses himself" in service to the Church's "yes" and is thus included also in the "yes" that the priestly servants have to speak in the Church.

A glance at the Gospels will convince us that this antithesis was intended by the Lord.

b. The Two States of Election in the New Testament

Whatever differences may have developed later between the two states of election, the emphasis in the Gospels is, as we have already noted in our discussion of the vocation and election of the apostles, mainly on the unity of the two forms. For there is, in the Gospels, a personal union between those called to the priesthood and those called to the state of the counsels. It was in one and the same separation from the world and from the "multitude" that the apostles received both the call to a life in imitation of Christ and the bestowal of priestly office. The promises made to them about themselves, their future work, the continued support of the Lord, and their destiny to be exposed and persecuted, yet victorious even in death, applied to them in indivisible unity both in their personal consecration to God and in their call to office. Beyond a doubt, the special fruitfulness promised them as the hundredfold of what they could have accomplished in the lay state in the world had they not left all things and followed the Lord was primarily the reward for their total gift of self, their courage in renouncing all the goods of this world. Indeed, the scene that records the promise is set in direct contrast to the scene of the rich young man who did *not* follow the Lord's call to the state of the counsels (Mt 19:16–30). But that scene also contains another promise: "Amen, I say to you that you who have followed me, in the regeneration when the Son of Man shall sit on the throne of his glory, shall also sit on twelve thrones, judging the twelve tribes of Israel" (Mt 19:28). Luke, we might note, reports this promise as spoken to the twelve apostles during the Last Supper, where it is preceded by the words: "And I appoint to you a kingdom, even as my Father has appointed to me" (Lk 22:29).

> We do not have to wonder what precise significance Jesus attached to the number twelve. The twelve tribes had long since disappeared; hence the number symbolized the original, ideal, qualitatively complete and integral Israel. Jesus had come to restore this qualitative Israel as the perfect people of God, and his chosen

apostles were to form with him its first fruits. Their judgeship was
to consist in fulfilling—in being models of—this ideal. Only when
Jesus' mission began to move more and more inexorably toward
the Cross did the official ecclesial role of the Twelve emerge clearly
from their more general role as Christ's representatives. After
the Lord's Resurrection, the Eleven became fully conscious of
their official status, as witness the words in which Peter proposed
replacing the traitor in the company of the apostles: ". . . He
had been numbered among us and was allotted his share in this
ministry. . . . It is written in the book of Psalms. . . . *His ministry
let another take.*" And they prayed over the candidates for the
ministry, ". . . Lord, . . . show which of these two thou hast
chosen to take [his] place in this ministry and apostleship . . ."
(Acts 1:17, 20, 24–25).

In Revelation, however, where the promised judgeship with
Christ is described as an accomplished reality, John sees how
the thrones that have been erected are bestowed with a kind
of indiscrimination on all who have fought and conquered with
Christ: "He who overcomes, I will permit him to sit with me upon
my throne; as I also have overcome and have sat with my Father on
his throne" (Rev 3:21). "And I saw thrones, and men sat upon them
and judgment was given to them. And I saw the souls of those who
had been beheaded because of the witness to Jesus and because of
the word of God, and who did not worship the beast or his image,
and did not accept his mark upon their foreheads or upon their
hands" (Rev 20:4): the souls of martyrs and confessors. Over them
"the second death has no power" (Rev 20:6), because they have
already died once for all with Christ in this world and have shared in
his Resurrection in heaven. These are the saints who "did not love
their lives even in face of death" (Rev 12:11); these "are virgins.
These follow the Lamb wherever he goes. These were purchased
from among men, first-fruits unto God and unto the Lamb" (Rev
14:4). They are "blessed and holy. . . . They will be priests of God
and Christ, and will reign with him a thousand years" (Rev 20:6),
that is (we may assume) from the founding of the Church to the
last judgment. The priesthood described here is a personal, not an
official, priesthood; it is the participation of virgin souls who have
consecrated themselves unreservedly to God in his redeeming
judgment, in his guidance of the world and the Church. Thus the
"office" of cojudge with Christ that is promised to the apostles in
the Gospels is here extended to all the saints who share, whether by
special election or by a disposition of soul akin to the vows (as in
the case of the martyrs), in the existential priesthood of Christ.

From this perspective, Paul, too, can assign the office of cojudge with Christ to all who are (truly) saints: "Do you not know that the saints will judge the world?" (1 Cor 6:2). His reference is to the community; but only those will be considered "saints" who have separated themselves from the world, have died to it, and are no longer their own (cf. 1 Cor 6:19), who, in fact, live by that same Spirit who, for John, is excellently and perfectly embodied in priestly virginity.

From the beginning, the Lord demanded total surrender of those whom he separated from among the people to be his apostles, requiring them to leave all things and follow him without reserve. He thus based on the totality of their transition from the world to him the totality of the Christian life that would enable his chosen ones to imitate him also in their official ministry by becoming the good shepherds of the "bewildered and dejected" sheep (Mt 19:36). He required this total renunciation not only of his apostles, but also of all those who wanted to give themselves entirely to him, to follow him wherever he went (cf. Mt 8:19)—including then, certainly, those not called to the priesthood. But he required it a fortiori of his priests. Their renunciation of the world is consistently depicted as "leaving all things", that is, as complete poverty, and as "following the Lord wherever he went", that is, as perfect obedience. But the Lord, as we have seen, did not insist on virginity, no doubt because the apostles, whose roots were in the Old Testament, were for the most part already married and "what . . . God has joined together, let no man put asunder" (Mt 19:6). It is here that the first difference between the priesthood and the state of the counsels makes its appearance in the Gospels: The state of the counsels requires virginity in addition to the poverty and obedience required of the priesthood. If Peter, who was married, appears as the representative of the official priesthood, the virgin apostles John and Paul are the designated representatives of that personal and interior priesthood that is the explicit following of the High Priest "who offered himself unblemished unto God" (Heb 9:14).

For *Paul*, who pointed so insistently and with so much emphasis to the model of his own person and mode of life, this needed no explanation. He knew and felt that he was not only a minister of Christ, but very consciously also a "chosen vessel", whose function it was to suffer for the Lord (Acts 9:15–16), to "bear the marks of the Lord Jesus" in his body (Gal 6:17), ("always bearing about in our body the dying of Jesus, so that the life also of Jesus may be made manifest in our bodily frame" [2 Cor 4:10]), and to do so as one representing the Church (1 Cor 4:9–13): ". . . What is lacking of the sufferings of Christ I fill up in my flesh for his body, which is the Church" (Col 1:24). Such a priesthood is thoroughly subjective and clearly based on the counsel—not the precept (1 Cor 7:25)—of virginity. One who, like Paul, is both father (1 Cor 4:15) and mother (1 Th 2:7) of the community will scarcely be able, in addition to the painful bearing of spiritual children, to be also a proper father of a physical family. And how can one who jealously defends the Church's virginity of spirit— ". . . I am jealous of you with a divine jealousy. For I betrothed you to one spouse, that I might present you a chaste virgin to Christ" (2 Cor 11:2)—fail to offer the good example of his own virginity? How can he "most gladly spend and be spent [himself] for . . . souls" (2 Cor 12:15) and rejoice to be "made the libation for the sacrifice and service of . . . faith" (Phil 2:17) if he must be concerned about a wife and children?

Once again, at the end of John's Gospel, the relationship between a predominantly official and a predominantly subjective priesthood—and therefore also, in a broader sense, between the primarily functional (secular) priesthood and the primarily participatory state of the counsels—is demonstrated in a series of increasingly dramatic and increasingly symbolic scenes between *Peter and John* that culminate, at the beginning of the Acts of the Apostles, in a period in which the two apostles are inseparably united (Acts 3:1, 3, 11; 4:13, 19; 8:14). Until his final investiture in office, Peter, who came to the Lord after John did and was called at this first meeting "the son of John" (Jn 1:22), continued to display a certain dependence on John. John, on the other hand, did not have to force himself between the Lord and the official ministry; having been established "in the office of love" by the Lord himself, it was his role to mediate between the Lord and that ministry. Thus, at the Last Supper, Peter turned to him "who was reclining at Jesus' bosom" (Jn 13:23) to learn what he could about the traitor among the Twelve. And the Lord answered openly and clearly, for he would leave unanswered no question put to him by love. On Easter morning, Peter and John ran together to the tomb; love, which is less encumbered than office, arrived more quickly at the goal, but did not use the nearness thus afforded it to take precedence over office. On the contrary, John waited for Peter to come up, let him enter the tomb first, and went in himself only after Peter had concluded his official inspection. "Then the other disciple also went in, who had come first to the tomb. And he saw and believed" (Jn 20:8)—something that is not affirmed of Peter. Again, at the draft of fishes on the sea of Tiberias, love was quicker than office and communicated to office its recognition of the Lord (Jn 21:6–7). Only thereafter did Peter in his official capacity take charge of the situation, throwing himself into the water so as to be the first to reach the Lord and bring him the great catch of fish (Jn 21:11). Until this point, the relationship between the personal and the official following of Christ within the unity of the Church has been demonstrated in a reciprocal super- and subordination. Now, however, the Lord poses to Peter the startling question: "Simon, son of John, dost thou love me more than these do?" (Jn 21:15). What is so incomprehensible in this scene is not the actual questioning of Peter's love as a prelude to his investiture in office, but the addition of the words "more than these". If Peter is to conform to what he is about to receive from the Lord, he must now love the Lord more than John, the beloved disciple, does. When it is a question of learning something from or about the Lord, Peter can no longer rely, as he has hitherto done, on John's greater love. Nor can he justify himself by claiming that the burden of office is already great enough, that he would, therefore, prefer to leave to John, who has been specially chosen for this purpose, the burden of love, which is an office in its own right. He must also become the embodiment of love. As the representative of the *whole* Church, he must incorporate love, too, into himself, for he is, after all, responsible for the whole Church. It is not true that the office is valid only for external matters, whereas nonofficial love governs internal ones. Nor is it true that the office has authority only over certain lower regions of religion whereas the higher regions, those that concern the direct encounter with God, the regions of pure love and mysticism, transcend the office. For one cannot understand anything in the realm of love unless one loves. "He who does not love abides in death" (1 Jn 3:14). "He who does not love does not know God; for God is love" (1 Jn 4:8). That is so universally applicable that the office—especially the office—cannot be an exception to it. By reason of the Lord's question, John's greater love is placed at Peter's disposal. He may use it because the whole office must be his; but he can use it only to the extent that he himself, personally and not just by virtue of his office, makes this greater love his own. *Consequently, an effort is required of both of them: of John, who, in a spirit of renunciation and out of love for the Lord and for the Church, transfers to Peter his primacy of love; and of Peter, who may assume his primacy of office only if he assimilates to himself personally this greater love that is John's.*

The "tension" between love and office was thus overcome. The Lord's sole purpose in bringing about this decisive transfer of power was to achieve unity. Earlier, Peter had been given a function that was to engage and absorb his whole being: "Thou art Simon, son of John; thou shalt be called Cephas (which interpreted is Peter)" (Jn 1:42). Yet at the end of the Gospels he was once again called by his personal name—a name whose hidden symbolism would hardly have escaped the fourth evangelist—and initiated into personal love: "Simon, son of John, dost thou love me?" Whereas John's whole love was poured out and entirely appropriated for the foundation of the Church, the office was filled with the substance of love. It was initiated into love, into the divine and human mystery of friendship and tenderness that existed between Jesus and John, and it had to answer by giving the Lord in exchange its whole self. Peter's "yes" was at least in part due to compunction for his threefold "no". But Jesus was not content with confirming him three times in office; he also presented him with that other gift—the gift of following his Lord even to death. He bestowed on him the withdrawal of his freedom: " '. . . When thou wast young thou didst gird thyself and walk where thou wouldst. But when thou art old thou wilt stretch forth thy hands, and another will gird thee, and lead thee where thou wouldst not.' . . . And having spoken thus, he said to him, 'Follow me' " (Jn 21:18–19). By the manner of his death, in which he would lose both his physical and his spiritual freedom, Peter would glorify God and receive the privilege that is the foundation and heart of the state of the counsels—that of binding himself totally to God. He who can bind and loose must be the first to be wholly bound and loosed from all that is not God.

Nevertheless, Peter did not thereby cease to be Peter rather than John. There was to be no fusion of the two. The state of the counsels was not nullified by Peter's transformation, nor was it combined with the priestly office. Peter still saw following them that other disciple "whom Jesus loved, the one who, at the supper, had leaned back upon his breast and said, 'Lord, who is it that will betray thee?' Peter, therefore, seeing him, said to Jesus, 'Lord, and what of this man?' " (Jn 21:20–21). Love that has sacrificed itself for the official Church remains present even after it has been sacrificed. Even though Peter had received official responsibility for the whole flock and, with it, the grace of a personal following of Christ, the Lord withheld from him the knowledge of John's fate: "If I wish him to remain until I come, what is it to thee? Do thou follow me" (Jn 21:22). *This limitation is imposed upon the office.* It has the right to pose a question to the Lord, but it must be resigned if the Lord chooses not to answer it. The office has received love so that it may know that no office can measure the magnitude of love because love is always more than man can comprehend. In other words, the official Church can— even *must*—demand insight into the consciences of those in the state of the counsels, even of contemplatives and anchorites. But only God knows what graces he bestows on the souls consecrated to him. For there exists an inner kingdom that eye has not seen, that ear has not heard, and that yet belongs so wholly to the Church that without it the Church would be robbed of its most precious life, of its most vital strength. This kingdom "remains" and must remain until the Lord comes again; but only the Lord has dominion over it.

As we have said before, this does not mean that there exists within or alongside the exoteric, official Church one that is esoteric or exclusively spiritual. The genuineness of the hidden kingdom of love is guaranteed only by its inner readiness to reveal and subject itself to the official Church. It is not permitted to withdraw *itself* from Peter's ken; but the *Lord* can reserve it to himself as a region of mystery. John consistently regarded love as an office: an office of service "to the Elect Lady [the Church] and her children" (2 Jn 1:11). He made use of his special prerogative of love only to show Peter what love can accomplish. He who stood beneath the Cross and received as a gift the mother of his dying Friend waited at the grave for the arrival of him who had three times betrayed the Lord and allowed him to be the first to contemplate the Resurrection. John possessed the "mind of the Church" in its totality because he loved what the Lord loved and served those whom the Lord served. On the other hand, he was fully conscious of his office of love. The last word he recorded after subjecting himself and the primacy of his love to Peter's primacy was the Lord's humbling rebuke to Peter: "If I wish him to remain until I come, what is it to thee?" (Jn 21:22). In his Epistles, John developed "the royal Law" [of love] (James 2:8) in truly royal fashion. He did this so absolutely, with a certainty so complete, so self-contained and so full of light that we cannot fail to grasp his meaning: If love obeys office, it follows its own law because it is obedient unto death; the office that commands love does so only that love may be faithful to its own law. Certainly love alone does not suffice for the Church, for love is dependent on the official

Church for the sacraments and for the dispensation of grace; at no "stage of perfection" can it do without the official Church. But the Church has authority over God's graces only for the purpose of dispensing them; its authority is a service to those who love so that they may grow in love.

Moreover, John was himself a priest; as the virgin apostle he represented the "religious priest" as opposed to Peter, the married "secular priest". And as Peter bore John in himself when he was enveloped by greater love, so John bore Peter in himself. But the two were on opposite courses. Peter received an office and love was then bestowed upon him for the sake of the office—that he might accomplish it more perfectly. John was, from the beginning, the epitome of love: It was he who followed the Lord to Golgotha and was there initiated into the ultimate mysteries of sacrifice. He received the office of priest by reason of his personal dedication. There is no contradiction in the fact that all the apostles were ordained priests at the Last Supper (cf. Jn 17:17–19). For John on Jesus' breast, the Eucharist was that love by which the Lord "loved [his own] to the end" (Jn 13:1); it was the "body which is being given for you" and the "blood which shall be shed for you" (Lk 22:19–20), the anticipation of the Cross. For him, it was Love personified that poured itself out in the Lord's farewell words, that expended itself until it became the canon of all love and thus an objective reality that also included the office.

It is of the utmost significance *that John met the Lord's mother at the foot of the Cross and nowhere else*; that he and no one else received her from the Son as his own; that this supernatural community, the original unit of all forms of religious life, was formed in the instant of love's ultimate sacrifice. The office can be conferred before and after the Cross; the protagonist of office does not have to be present under the Cross since his office is not a reward for love. It can be conferred even on one who resists it. In the last analysis, the identity of the person who holds it is a matter of indifference. But the state of the counsels cannot be founded in the absence of those who are called to form it. As a subjective priesthood, it requires its members to suffer together with Christ and to give their consent not only to the Cross, but also to their new loss of freedom in a supernatural community. Members of religious orders meet each other in the Cross, and the Crucified One unites them in love—in a love that can be the sharing of his own abandonment.

Mary had an essential role in the founding of the state of the counsels. It was founded, not just under her patronage, but in such a way that she was explicitly linked to the new community. From this it is clear that she not merely shares in its life of self-surrender, but is also implanted in it as its very soul. She inaugurated the form of this state by allowing her way of life to become its way of life just as the Lord transferred his sacrifice functionally to the priesthood. In doing so, she led *woman as such* into that inner state of the Church that is priestly because it offers sacrifice. By experiencing and accomplishing a living and personal liturgy with the faithful women at the foot of the Cross, Mary earned for herself and for all women a place at the heart of the Church's life. If women are excluded from the functional priesthood and thereby reflect in the Church something of the natural order of creation according to which "man . . . is the image and glory of God, but woman is the glory of man . . . [and] man was not created for woman, but woman for man" (1 Cor 11:7, 9); according to which, as a general rule, what is functional is the prerogative of man, but it is unbecoming for a woman to leave "uncovered" what "is a glory to her" (1 Cor 11: 13–15), this exclusion in no way indicates that woman is inferior to man or that any "degree of perfection" is thereby closed to her. Any theory that attempts to evaluate the states of election in terms of their respective "perfection" is an insult to women in general and to the Lord's mother in particular. The super- and subordination of the sexes that has its roots in creation serves rather for paratactic alignment: "Yet neither is man independent of woman, nor woman independent of man in the Lord. For as the woman is from the man, so also is the man through the woman, but all things are from God" (1 Cor 11: 11–12). This may be applied also to the states of life within the Church. The ranks of the hierarchy, which women are not permitted to enter, are entirely in the service of love, which is not only permitted to women, but, insofar as love is a state of life, was essentially *cofounded* by a woman, while the pure office, represented by Peter, was absent from its own founding. During Peter's absence and without consulting him, the Lord bound the virgin souls at the foot of the Cross into a new unity conferred directly from above, which Peter had later to acknowledge as coming from the Lord. This is also the way in which true religious orders were later established: Apostolates conferred directly by the Holy Spirit filled the founders, as it were, with a new "spirit", a new "spirituality", and, after their genuineness had been properly tested, were acknowledged by the official Church and incorporated into its innermost life.

Mary herself, the cofoundress of the state of the counsels, is only indirectly under the authority of Peter. Her place is above the states of life; together with her Son, she is the principle that makes them possible. But since her final "state" on earth was her relationship to John, and John is under Peter's juris-diction, she participates indirectly in the officially governed life of the Church. *John*, the "religious priest", who unites in his own person both the personal and the official priesthood of the Church, *mediates between Mary and Peter*. Through him are bound together the two points of the Church that transcend the fallen world by the strength of God's grace and promise: the immaculate mother of Christ and the infallible representative of Christ—the bosom of the Church from which the Church proceeds, and the rock on which it rests. Bound to the Church by the state of the counsels, Mary, the mother of the Church (Rev 12:1–2, 17), becomes also a member of this Church. Raised to the state of the counsels, Peter, who holds the external office of the Church, must learn to conform his own life to this way of love.

This entire discussion of the interrelationship of the states of life in terms of the representative and symbolic roles of Mary,

John and Peter must not, of course, be isolated from or considered to be in opposition to the whole process by which the Church was founded. The comment that the religious state was founded from and at the foot of the Cross is to be understood precisely in the way in which we understand the teaching that the Church as a whole originated on the Cross as the new Eve proceeding from the wound in the side of the new Adam. What Christ had done during his public life for the formation of the Church is related to the present state of the Church as the preparation of material—as the formation of the body of Adam out of the dust of the earth—is related to the breathing in of a soul, to the bestowal of an inner and living form. To say that the state of the counsels was founded on the Cross is not, then, to contradict the traditional statement that the Lord founded this state during his public life by choosing his apostles, by imparting to them the evangelical counsels and, above all, by forming together with them a concrete community in which Peter, too, participated in the life of the counsels. The community of the apostles with Jesus represents *in nuce* all the essential ecclesial relationships and structures of the later Church: It is at once the representation of the whole Church (as that which was chosen from among men), of the whole state of election (as opposed to the "people of the Church"), of the priestly state (as opposed to the "laity") and finally of the state of the counsels per se (as opposed to a broader circle of the elect that is perhaps best represented by the seventy-two disciples).

In this sense, the premise that Christ is the immediate founder of the state of the counsels is one of the basic tenets of the Church's tradition. "The state of religion of itself and as regards its substance was delivered and instituted immediately by Christ, the Lord, himself. . . . This is the opinion of all right-thinking Catholics."[27] Suárez adduces a cloud of witnesses to prove his point. He shows further that the Lord instituted the state of the

---

[27] Suárez, *De statu perf*, bk. III, chap. 2, sec. 3. [Further references to this work are given in parentheses in the text. (Tr)]

counsels in such a general form (the state of religion per se) that it could be concretized in the various forms of individual "orders"; but that he likewise formed, with his apostles, a distinctive concrete "order" (*quandam religionem in particulari*) whose form was precisely defined. The apostles, says Thomas Aquinas, would have taken vows at least implicitly: "The apostles are believed *to have vowed* what pertained to the state of perfection when, having left all things, they followed Christ" (ST 2a 2ae 88, 4 ad 3) and would have done so definitively, with no possibility of retraction (ST 2a 2ae 186, 6 ad 1). Suárez goes even further and determines the character of this apostolic "order" as that of the "mixed life" [*vita mixta*] with the special end of cooperating with Christ in the salvation of souls; in other words, as an active ministry rooted (cf. Acts 6:2–4) in the fullness of contemplation (bk. III, chap. 2, sec. 10). This "order" of Christ is based on perfect poverty, chastity and that particular obedience that Christ first made his own and then—since this way of life was to be preserved within the Church—gave to the Church for her imitation (ibid., secs. 12–14).[28] Whether or not we agree with Suárez, it is certain that the state of the counsels did not originate in a later application of some isolated passages of Scripture—those regarding the counsels of poverty and virginity, for instance,

---

[28] Von Balthasar refers the reader also to the following texts: St. Augustine, "De Consensu Evangelistarum Libri IV", bk. II, chap. 17, PL 34, cols. 1094–97; idem, "De Civitate Dei Libri XXII" (henceforth *De civ Dei*), bk. 17, chap. 4, secs. 6–7, PL 41, col. 530 (for an English translation of the *City of God*, see *Fathers*, vol. 8 [1950], trans. Demetrius B. Zema and Gerald G. Walsh; vol. 14 [1952], trans. Gerald G. Walsh and Grace Monahan; vol. 24 [1954], trans. Gerald G. Walsh and Daniel J. Honan); St. Augustine, "Epistolae", classis II, ep. LXXXIX, secs. 4–5, PL 33, cols. 311–12; St. John Chrysostom, "Homiliae XC in Matthaeum", hom. XIV–XV, PG 57, cols. 217–38; and hom. LXIV, PG 58, cols. 603–10 (for an English translation of these and other works of St. John Chrysostom, see *Nicene*, vols. X–XIV [1905–1914]); William of St. Thierry, "Epistola seu Tractatus ad Fratres de Monte Dei de Vita Solitaria", PL 184, cols. 307–64; St. Bernard of Clairvaux, "Apologia ad Guillelmum", PL 182, cols. 895–918. [Tr]

but was willed and instituted as a concrete reality by Jesus and exemplified, just as the priesthood was exemplified and in the closest association with it, in his first community. Heinz Schürmann has confirmed this fact anew in the work mentioned in the Preface.

c. On the Evolution of the Two States of Election

It is not our intent to review here the historical evolution of the priesthood and religious state and their complex relationship throughout the centuries, but only to point to certain fundamental and theologically relevant aspects of that relationship. As in any discussion about the truths of the deposit of faith, we must observe not only the external aspect that can be discovered from a study of secular history, but also the laws of dogmatic development as formulated for earlier times by Vincent of Lérins and for more recent times by Newman. If certain dogmas and truths seem, at first glance, not to have existed in the earliest centuries of the Church's history, they were nevertheless—and the Church knows this from its study of theology—actually, even if only implicitly, present from the beginning, more "lived" than reflected upon.

This is eminently true of the evolution of the two forms of the state of election—the priestly state and the religious state—not only as regards their unity, but also as regards their differences. For we cannot comprehend their evolution properly unless we attempt to keep simultaneously before our minds the two (only apparently irreconcilable) statements that are indispensable for an understanding of the first centuries: 1) There is only one unified state of election and, therefore, only one basic form of Christian "perfection", which must be realized in each of the subdivisions of this state; and 2) each of the individual manifestations of this Christian perfection—whether in the priest, the martyr, the virgin, the anchorite or the cenobite—possesses its own unmistakable and inalienable character. It is precisely because the New Testament so strongly emphasizes the personal and actual *unity* of both official and subjective priesthood that the thought did not immediately occur, despite the many differences in their particular ways of life, of setting up different canons of evangelical perfection. Common to both states was—as shown by the strength and finality of the decision to enter upon a way of life based on the Lord's counsels and directives—the recognition of the evangelical life as a state in its own right. This was the "certain stability" that Thomas Aquinas would later describe as the fundamental characteristic of a state of life (ST 2a 2ae 183, 1 responsio), and that must be, for the Christian, not only an outward stability in time, but also an inward stability based on the intensity of his decision to enter upon such a way of life. Primitive Christianity, with its eschatological orientation, was able to find this intensity perfectly concentrated in the eschatological form of holiness exemplified by the martyr, who beyond the confines of time fully realized in his death the once-and-for-all character of the decision that is the sine qua non of the "state of perfection". Nor is it surprising that later centuries perceived a relationship between the gradually developing forms of the state of the counsels and this form that transcends time: *Virginity and monasticism* are an unbloody, but nonetheless continuous and perpetual, martyrdom. It was, above all, a disposition of mind that the Christians of that time saw in these early attempts to shape life according to the teachings of the Gospel: the will to give oneself totally, the *internal* vow to renounce all things, which soon became also an *external*, ecclesial, vow such as that made by virgins into the hands of the bishop or by monks into the hands of the abbot. Added to this essential disposition were questions of canon law raised by the Church: whether a particular vow was simple or solemn; whether a vow rendered a subsequent marriage invalid. Secondary in nature, these questions seem almost to be anachronisms that an analytical mind has injected retroactively into an age that thought simply and holistically and with scant attention to differences.[29] What was important for that age was the decision to enter a state of life, which, because it was both an internal and an external decision, transferred one immediately into the state of perfection, into the state of belonging to God. ("In Clement, for instance, πρόθεσις [intention], ὁμολογία [confession] and προαίρεσις [choice] appear as synonymous concepts. . . . It is doubtful, however, if he had in mind a proper vow" [Koch, 96]. But what would "a proper vow" be in this context?) It is clear from the extensive literature on the state of virginity that Christians

---

[29] Cf. Hugo Koch, "Virgines Christi: Die Gelübde der gottgeweihten Jungfrauen in den ersten drei Jahrhunderten", in *Texte und Untersuchungen zur Geschichte der altchristlichen Literatur*, eds. Adolf Harnack and Carl Schmid, vol. 31 (Leipzig: J. C. Hinrich, 1907), 59–112, especially 109–12, and his comments on the works of two of his predecessors: Stephan Schiwietz, *Das morgenländische Mönchtum* I (Mainz: Kirchheim, 1904); and Josef Wilpert, *Die gottgeweihten Jungfrauen in den ersten Jahrhunderten der Kirche* (Freiburg: Herder, 1892).

regarded this state as the living out of evangelical perfection, and that they expected of virgins by reason of their virginity not only the absolute disposition of poverty even if they had not explicitly renounced external goods, but also the disposition of self-surrender to the Lord as Bridegroom, which in turn included, at least implicitly, the disposition of obedience in the narrower ecclesial sense. The virgin consecrated herself to God in body as well as in spirit.[30] This is true in an even higher degree of the first forms of monastic life, in which, as a whole, it is especially surprising to note how quickly the implicit presence of the three "vows" changed into a reflective and explicit presence; how quickly, above all, in the *vitae* of the monks, obedience, which had thus far lain in shadow, came not only to be recognized as essential, but also to be practiced and to be given a basis in theology.

The evolution of the *clerical state* likewise followed its own course. The concession allowing priests to marry, which, as we have seen, was made necessary by actual conditions in the first days of the Church, was confirmed in early pastoral letters. There was, at the same time, an equally contingent reluctance to demand total evangelical poverty of the clergy—a fact that probably accounts for the much later explicit division into secular and religious priests. In the beginning, however, the clergy formed, as it were, a special branch of the "state of election", which state one might enter by explicit or implicit "vow" (that is, by intention, by vow per se, or by profession), thus becoming a person "consecrated to God", a *religiosus*. Arguing from a multiplicity of texts, Ludwig von Hertling[31] has shown that certain expressions and concepts were applied indiscriminately to virgins, monks and clergy. The clergy were designated as *religiosi*; they made what was variously called a *religiosa professio*, a *sacra professio*, or a *deifica professio*; they lived "in the profession of religion"; and they "dedicated and gave themselves to God" (*Professio*, 151). He concludes therefrom "that the

---

[30] St. Cyprian, "De Habitu Virginum", chap. IV, in Wilhelm von Hartel, *Corpus Scriptorum Ecclesiasticorum Latinorum*, vol. 3, pt. I (Vienna: apud C. Geroldi Filium Bibliopolam Academiae, 1863), 190. [For an English translation of this and other works of St. Cyprian, see Saint Cyprian, *Treatises*, ed. and trans. Roy J. Deferrari, *Fathers*, vol. 36 (1958). (Tr)]

[31] Ludwig von Hertling, "Die Professio der Kleriker und die Entstehung der drei Gelübde", *Zeitschrift für katholische Theologie* 56 (1932), 148–74. [Further references to this work (henceforth *Professio*) will be given in parentheses in the text. (Tr)]

three ecclesial states—of clergy, of monks and of virgins—were regarded as being in a general way equal; that all three signified the consecration of one's person to God as well as the irrevocable acceptance of sacred obligations; and that all three presumed what theology today designates as vows". In other words, "If we consider that the profession of monks partook of the nature of a vow even though the individual vows were not explicitly and formally pronounced, then the same must also be true of the profession of the clergy; and if we regard the promise of virgins as being from the beginning a vow, then we must place the promises of clergy and monks on the same level" (ibid., 153–54). From the beginning, monks promised, at their profession, "to give themselves wholly to God with all they possessed" (ibid., 155); the promises made by virgins evolved gradually from an explicit vow of chastity to this same gift of self, thus becoming more and more like that of monks (cf. ibid., 157–60).

The promise made by the clergy followed its own independent development principally because the early Church regarded the state of virgins and monks as complementary to the *lay* state. This fact, for which there is ample testimony in the theological reflections of the age (for instance, in Chrysostom, Dionysius the Pseudo-Areopagite, and even Jerome), obscured for a time the original evangelical unity of the state of election. While the basis and starting point of the life of perfection was chastity in the case of virgins and poverty in the case of monks, for the clergy it was obedience to the bishop—a life of external dependence on the Church. Celibacy came gradually to be the rule, "and candidates for orders had to make a formal promise, resolution or profession, undoubtedly also a vow. Later, celibacy was specifically designated as a vow of religion, a vow of chastity" (*Professio*, 161). From the beginning, the profession of the clergy also included the discipline of a holy life, which encompassed at least the spirit of simplicity, generosity and consequently also poverty. Frequent attempts were made to require of the clergy that perfect poverty that the Gospels portray as the condition and entrance gate of perfection. St. Augustine would admit no one to the clerical state who possessed private property. His purpose was to establish as the life form of the clergy the evangelical life of the counsels as practiced by the first apostles and, at the same time, to stress the equality of the various forms under which the one promise, the one profession, existed within the Church. In this he followed the example of Eusebius of Vercelli and St. Ambrose, both of whom had already attempted to introduce common life and ownership

among their clergy. Efforts in this direction were made throughout the Middle Ages. Pope Nicholas II proclaimed in the fourth
canon of the Synod of 1059:[32] "At churches where they were
consecrated, those in the orders of priests, deacons and subdeacons,
who in obedience to our predecessor (Leo IX) observe celibacy,
should, as becomes a pious clergy, have their meals and sleeping
accommodations in common and should hold all ecclesial revenues
in common. We also urge and admonish that they earnestly strive
to achieve an apostolic, that is a common, way of life."[33] The
apostolic way of life means here a life of total poverty in the same
sense and degree that virginity is an "evangelical way of life".
When Augustine said: "The clergy profess two things: sanctity and
the clerical state",[34] he was calling for the original evangelical unity
of function and life, of subjective and objective priesthood.

The form of such holiness is laid down for monks in the rule, for
clergy in the canons. Everything that Holy Scripture, tradition and
the promulgations of Church councils propose as the model of
an ideal clergy according to the mind of Christ and the Church
is contained therein. "The canons were themselves designated as
'rules'. Since the seventh century, these two—the *regula* (rule), and
in particular the *regula* of St. Benedict, for monks and the canons for
clergy—were always placed side by side. A synod in Gaul in the
ninth century stated that both . . . are gifts of the Holy Spirit"
(*Professio*, 163). That throws light on the prehistory of the so-called
regular (i.e., religious) clergy.

Despite the distinctions made between monks and virgins on
the one hand and clergy on the other (who were also indiscriminately called canons and regulars because they lived according
to the canons, that is, according to the ideal and juridical rules
[*regula*tions] of the Gospel and of the Fathers of the Church
(in which connection it should be noted that *regula* is the Latin
equivalent of the Greek κανών [canon]), the first eleven centuries
were basically acquainted with but a single "state of perfection",

[32] See Joannes Dominicus Mansi, *Sacrorum Concilorum Nova et Amplissima
Collectio* (Venetiis: apud Antonium Zatta, 1774), vol. XIX, cols. 898; 908. [Tr]
[33] Quoted in Ludwig von Hertling, "Kanoniker, Augustinerregel und Augus-
tinerorden", *Zeitschrift für katholische Theologie* 54 (1930), 349–50 and footnote 1,
p. 350. Further references to this work (henceforth *Kanoniker*) will be given in
parentheses in the text. [Tr]
[34] St. Augustine, "Sermones", classis IV, sermo CCCLV, "De Vita et Moribus
Clericorum Suorum", I, sec. 6, PL 39, col. 1573.

which as a whole was the complement of the state of lay persons in the world.

From the time of St. Benedict, it was his rule that was increasingly recognized and widely adopted as the canon of monks. The clergy, and those monastic groups that did not follow the rule of St. Benedict, were collectively identified as "regulars" because the conduct of their lives was subject, not to a particular rule, but to the general canons of the Church. "The canons are for the clergy what the rule is for the monk" (*Professio*, 163).

"We should not imagine that the rise of the canons regular in the second half of the eleventh century occurred because secular priests as a group had decided to take vows and become monks. At that time, there were no 'secular' priests, at least not *de jure*. Every member of the clergy was consecrated to God, was a religious and lived a life of holy profession. The purpose of the clerical reform of the eleventh century was not to create something new, but simply to restore to full validity the ancient concept of the clerical state as a holy state, especially through the revitalization of the old canons" (*Professio*, 164–65). "It was not profession under the rule of St. Augustine that brought the *Ordo Canonicorum* into existence and gave it form; on the contrary, the canons regular had existed even before this rule was adopted for the purpose of replacing the canons—which were purely ideal in character and subject to various interpretations—with a single document comparable to the *regula monasteriorum* of St. Benedict" (ibid., 166).

For a description of the Gregorian reform in which, for the first time, the concept of a "secular clergy" appeared alongside that of the "regular" or "religious clergy", we again quote Hertling:

"The reform of the clergy in the eleventh century was a mighty *effort to turn all the clergy into monks*. The treatise of St. Peter Damian, 'Contra Regulares Proprietarios', was directed not at the 'regular clergy' as we understand the term today, but rather at the whole *Ordo Canonicus*, that is, at all the clergy who were not monks, especially those who believed that as regular, canonical clergy they could still possess property. Emulating St. Augustine, Peter Damian addressed these clergy as follows: 'A member of the clergy who possesses money cannot be the property or inheritance of Christ, nor can he possess God as his inheritance.' In another treatise, he says: 'It is certain that the whole Church was founded by monks, not by canons. . . . If you read the New Testament with unprejudiced eyes, you will find that the apostles and their successors lived like monks, not like canons.' It was characteristic of the proponents of the so-called Gregorian reform that they had little concern as to whether their reforms could be executed. This attitude stemmed not so much from unworldly fanaticism as from the deep conviction rooted in their faith and their stark idealism. However unlikely the prospect, right and duty would prevail in the end. There could be no compromise between good and evil even if half the world were destroyed for lack of it. Such was the policy of the reformers. In the matter of celibacy, they eventually achieved full success although the possibility of such success was, if anything, least likely in this regard. . . . The effort to imbue the whole clergy with the monastic spirit was, if not a complete success, at least a very notable one. If we were to say that Pope Gregory VII and St. Peter Damian founded orders of priests concerned with pastoral care, we would be in a certain sense correct, but not if we meant thereby that they had intended to found a new order: What they intended was to lead the whole clergy to the monastic ideal; what they achieved was that part of the clergy became true monks" (*Kanoniker*, 351–52).

"The evolution of the vows proper to the religious state may be summarized as follows. In the beginning, there were three states of life in the Church (that is, in addition to the Christian state in general, which was based on the baptismal promises common to all Christians): clergy, monks and virgins, each with a vow proper to itself, which, however, was generally called a promise or a profession, seldom a vow. The vow proper to virgins was gradually expanded into a monastic vow with the result that the state of virgins was absorbed into the monastic state—a process that was completed in the course of the eleventh century. In the eleventh century, too, the state of the clergy was divided into two parts, with one half taking a vow similar to that taken by monks, although the canons did not actually become monks. At this point, there occurred a complete reorganization of the ecclesial states. The concept of 'monk' came to be identified with the religious state as a whole. Monks, regular (that is, religious) clergy and virgins thus formed a common state (the religious state or the state proper to religious orders), while the remaining clergy—those who did not become monks—came to be known as secular priests. The concept of vow or vows was clarified in religious orders, especially by the introduction of the ascetic trio of poverty, chastity and obedience that was speculatively supported by Scholasticism and particularly by St. Thomas Aquinas. Among secular priests, the concept of vows gradually disappeared, although these priests retained the structure of the obligation of celibacy as a *votum implicitum* and that of obedience, which they no longer understood as a vow, but only as a promise. In essence, however, the division of the states within the Church into the state of religious and the state of secular priests was merely a legal one; in the ascetic sense, secular priests belong now, as they have always done, to the state of perfection. They are consecrated to God not only by sacramental ordination, but also in a subjective and moral sense, and their state obliges them to strive for evangelical perfection through observance of the evangelical counsels—that is, of chastity, ecclesial obedience, and that poverty of spirit that manifests itself as detachment from the things of earth" (*Professio*, 173–74).

We have quoted Hertling thus extensively because he has clearly traced the historical and theological evolution within the state of election. We are now in a position to recognize the danger of any one-sided tendency to place the priest under the special canon of monastic life rather than under the general canon of the state of the counsels, for it limits the analogy that, in the beginning, made the state of the counsels open to so many ways of life. The original analogy and intimate relationship between religious and secular clergy will not appear again until the monastic state has acquired a new analogy through the troubled history of orders, congregations and secular institutes.

d. Scholasticism and the State of Perfection

It was inevitable that the status quo that prevailed in the early Middle Ages would have a decisive influence on Scholastic speculation about the states of life. But because these speculations were based on propositions advanced by the Fathers of the Church and because the patristic texts were carefully incorporated into the philosophical structures of Scholasticism, it was equally inevitable that there would exist a multiplicity of levels and perspectives. It will be well, therefore, before considering the Scholastic "synthesis", to look attentively at its historical context as summarized in the four paragraphs below.

1. The clerical state appeared in a twofold light. On the one hand, it seemed to encompass both the objective and the subjective priesthood, that is, the whole fullness of the state of election as it was known to the first centuries. On the other hand, recent developments within the Church had led to a distinction between pure function (in the case of the "secular" priest) and subjective

"evangelical perfection" (in the case of the "religious" priest) and had produced the strange teaching that the bishop, by reason of his office, was in the "state of perfection" while the clergy under him belonged to the lay state.

2. Through the rapid flourishing of the mendicant orders, the religious state itself had taken an important step beyond the patristic and even beyond the Benedictine era. The concept of "evangelical perfection" had entered upon a stage of reflection and self-knowledge. What had been merely implicit in an earlier age was made explicit in the precise doctrine of the three vows at about the same time that what had been implicit regarding the priestly function of administering the sacraments developed into the explicit doctrine of the seven sacraments. In this way, the distinction between the two forms of the state of election was greatly intensified.

3. Because of its continuing reliance on patristic texts, nevertheless, the concept of the religious state still retained much of its early Christian coloring. Evidence of this may be found in the fact that the religious state was never regarded as anything but a lay state —indeed, the therapeuts,[35] hermits and cenobites, as well as the monks of Saints Basil, Benedict and Francis of Assisi, were all predominantly lay persons. Further evidence may be found in the fact that the contemplative tendency and, with it, the apparently purely personal, almost private, character of monastic perfection was still dominant. The notion that evangelical perfection and ecclesial mission (which does not necessarily have to be functional) belong inseparably together was entirely foreign to Scholastic speculation. This leads to our fourth point.

4. The whole consideration of the states of life was subsumed under the concept of the "state of perfection" with the advantage that the concept of perfection was more clearly defined, but with the considerable disadvantage that the subjective aspect of ecclesial holiness—the individual's own effort and achievement—was given proportionately greater emphasis while the objective aspect, mission and charism, was largely ignored. The monks, moreover, as the

---

[35] In the *Ecclesiastical Hierarchy* (see note 36), Dionysius the Areopagite regularly uses the term "therapeut" (θεραπευτή—"servant", "worshipper", from θεραπεύω —"serve") in referring to monks. [Tr]

ones primarily engaged in this speculation, had a certain advantage over the clergy. In consequence, the development of a doctrine of the states of life took place in an atmosphere of often acrimonious rivalry between the two states.

For Thomas Aquinas, as we have already seen, a state is a stable form of life capable of bestowing on one who lives in it the definite and particular perfection that is proper to it. Thomas immediately refers this perfection, which is proper to every state as such, to the Christian concept of perfection, with the result that the grades of the states of life appear to be also the grades of their perfection: ". . . There is a distinction of diversity among the faithful . . . as regards perfection. And according to this there is a difference of states in that some are more perfect than others" (ST 2a 2ae 183, 3 responsio). Thomas distinguishes this diversity of perfection from the diversity of offices (*officia*) that require certain activities on the part of those who hold them, as well as from the diversity of grades that can exist even within the same state or office without altering its basic nature.

Every Christian state, if it is truly a state, has the perfection proper to it. This teaching is based partly on the philosophical concept of what a state is and partly on the theological insight that a permanent form of life within the Church must be such as to guarantee to those who live in it the attainment of Christian perfection, which consists in love (cf. ST 2a 2ae 184, 3 responsio). In the strictest sense, however, only that state is truly a "state of perfection" whose very form of life—whose stability and immutability—has as its only goal the attainment of perfect love. "Hence one is said to be properly in the state of perfection not because he performs a perfect act of charity, but because he has obligated himself forever, and with some solemnity, to those things that pertain to perfection" (ST 2a 2ae 184, 4 responsio).

To the "state of perfection" Thomas assigns both the members of religious orders and the bishops, but not those members of the clerical state who are below the bishops. Even though their office confers on them a certain dignity, they belong, like the rest of the faithful, to the general Christian state. Members of religious orders, on the other hand, enter the state of perfection by reason of the vows by which they renounce the world in order to live for God alone. "In like manner, bishops oblige themselves to those things that pertain to perfection when they accept the pastoral ministry, as John says (cf. Jn 10:11). Wherefore the apostle says: Thou 'hast made the good confession before many witnesses' (1 Tim 6:12), that is, 'in your ordination', as a gloss adds. Indeed, a certain solemnity of consecration is joined to this profession . . ." (ST 2a 2ae 184, 5 responsio). The bishop, then, takes a "vow" (*professio, confessio*) to place his whole existence finally and forever at the service of the flock entrusted to him. It is significant that Thomas, in this article, quotes Dionysius the Pseudo-Areopagite in order to clarify the reason for and the necessity of this "vow": The bishop "participates integrally in the fullness of hierarchical power"; by his office (and this should be noted!), he is called upon to "enlighten" the whole Church and to transmit to it the divine graces and powers.[36]

For Thomas, neither the orders they receive nor the pastoral ministry (*cura*) entrusted to them by the bishop is sufficient reason for assigning lower priests to the state of perfection. By reason of their orders, he says, "they receive the power to perform certain sacred acts, but they are not thereby obliged to those things that tend to perfection, except that at the reception of sacred orders in the Western Church the vow of continence is taken, which is one of the vows that tend to perfection" (ST 2a 2ae 184, 6 responsio). Without doubt, an interior perfection is required for the exercise of the priestly functions, but since "neither the pastoral office nor the obligation of giving their lives for the sheep pertains primarily to them [priests]" (ibid., responsio ad 3), they are not raised to the state of perfection as the bishop is by his vow. This is true also with regard to their pastoral ministry: "For they are not obliged by the bond of a perpetual vow to continue in the care of souls, but can abandon it either by transferring to a religious order even without the permission of the bishop . . . or by giving up . . . a parish and accepting a simple prebend without the care of souls. But this would in no way be permitted one in the state of perfection: 'No one having put his hand to the plow and looking back, is fit for the kingdom of heaven' (Lk 9:62)" (ibid., responsio).

This teaching of St. Thomas, which seems so strange to us, marks the end of a long development. We can understand it only if we try to think through its various stages. The picture Thomas draws of the bishop is that of the perfect good shepherd, the true image of Christ, who, with Christ, gives his life for his sheep

---

[36] Cf. Dionysius the Pseudo-Areopagite, *Ecclesiastical Hierarchy* (henceforth *Eccl Hier*), chap. V. [Pt. 1, sec. 6, in PG 3, col. 513. For an English translation of this work, see Rev. Thomas L. Campbell, *Dionysius the Pseudo-Areopagite: The Ecclesiastical Hierarchy*, translated and annotated, doctoral dissertation (Washington: The Catholic University of America, 1954). (Tr)]

and solemnly and irrevocably dedicates his whole existence to his mission. Corresponding to the patristic and biblical concept of the unity of the state of election, we find merged in this picture both *Sein* and *Sollen*—both objective ministry and subjective commitment and perfect self-surrender. It is a picture still entirely within the Joannine tradition, like that drawn by Ignatius of Antioch. *It is the picture of the "hierarch" drawn by Dionysius the Pseudo-Areopagite in his "Ecclesiastical Hierarchy".* In Dionysius' mystical and liturgical concept, there is no need for moral deliberation, for personal striving; every rank of the "hierarchy" is described in a purely ideal way in which it appears as the direct image of the heavenly "hierarchy" of the angels. Here each one is what he ought to be; the objective perfection of a given state is the only measure of the subjective perfection that seems to have been drawn into that state. In such a view, the bishop *is* so completely the perfect priest and teacher, his office is seen so completely in terms of pure function into which his whole gift of self and all his personal striving are integrated and, as it were, absorbed, that it would be inappropriate to speak of a *requirement* or admonition that his personal life, too, be conducted in a manner befitting his state. Dionysius describes the structure of the Church as follows:[37]

Teaching states	*Learning states*	*Functions*
1. hierarchs (bishops)	1. monks	1. to perfect
2. priests	2. laity	2. to enlighten
3. deacons[38]	3. penitents and catechumens	3. to purify

From this description we may draw the following conclusions: 1. Since the teaching states are collectively above the learning states, the monastic state must take fourth place after that of the deacons. Thomas reflects this when he says: " 'The agent is always superior to the patient (the one acted upon).' But in the matter of perfection, according to Dionysius, bishops are the perfectors and religious are the perfected; the former pertain to action, the latter to passion (being acted upon). Hence it is manifest that the state of perfection is stronger in bishops than in religious" (ST 2a 2ae 184, 7

---

[37] Cf. *Eccl Hier*, chap. V, pt. 1, secs. 4–7; chap. VI, pt. 1, secs. 1–3. [Tr]

[38] Von Balthasar here uses the German word *Liturgen* to translate the Greek λειτυργοί by which Dionysius refers to "deacons". To avoid confusion with the modern term "liturgists", I have used only the more usual designation "deacons" in this translation. [Tr]

responsio). 2. On the other hand, both the bishop and the monk are at the level of perfection. While deacons are principally concerned with the purifying of penitents and catechumens, and priests with the enlightening of the laity, bishops are concerned with the perfecting of monks: "The holy order of monks . . . is subject to the perfecting powers of the hierarchs and . . . by their holy science is raised in appropriate stages to the most excellent perfection" (*Eccl Hier*, chap. 6, pt. 1, sec. 3). In addition to the subordination of the priestly and lay states, to which the monks belong, there is also, then, a juxtaposition of the two states of perfection, as Thomas notes when he says: "And this is why Dionysius [*Eccl Hier*, chap. V, pt. 1, sec. 7] . . . attributes perfection only to bishops as the perfectors and to monks as those perfected; enlightenment to priests as enlighteners through the administration of the sacraments and to the holy people as those to be enlightened; purification to deacons as purifiers and to the order of the uninitiated as those to be purified" (*Quodlib*, bk. III, q. 6, a. 3, responsio).

But that is not all. For Thomas, the Dominican, the monk is not simply a passive recipient of the enlightening and perfecting action of the hierarch; he, too, turns to action. He becomes a "doctor" [teacher] and so advances to the same rank as his episcopal "perfector". "In the spiritual edifice, some are, as it were, manual laborers who pursue the care of souls, for example, by administering the sacraments . . . , but the chief artificers are, one might say, the bishops, who command and arrange how those who have been appointed are to carry out their office; for this reason, they are called *bishops*, that is, *superintendents*; in like manner, doctors of theology are also, as it were, chief artificers who inquire and teach how others are to procure the salvation of souls" (ibid., bk. I, q. 7, a. 2, responsio).

Next to Dionysius, St. John Chrysostom has had the most decisive influence on speculation in this regard. Overwhelmed by the preeminent dignity of the priestly state, he hid himself to avoid being elected bishop. In explaining his action to his friend Basil, he spoke so emphatically of the dignity and responsibility of the priestly state that it is evident he ranked it above that of the monk.[39] Undoubtedly the historical situation described above played an important role in his thinking, namely, that the religious ideal in its beginnings was often (if not exclusively) regarded as a private way

---

[39] St. John Chrysostom, "De Sacerdotio Libri VI". [PG 48, cols. 623–92. For an English translation of this work, see St. John Chrysostom, "Six Books on the Priesthood", trans. W. R. W. Stephens, *Nicene*, vol. 9 (1908). (Tr)]

of life undertaken on one's own initiative and with the primary purpose of ensuring one's own salvation, and was thus seen to be markedly different from the "care for all the churches" to which bishops and priests were obligated. Thomas does not follow Chrysostom in this view. What Chrysostom seems to apply to the priesthood in general, Thomas refers exclusively to the episcopal office (ST 2a 2ae 184, 8 responsio ad 1), which was also the main object of Chrysostom's remarks. More importantly, Thomas rejects as irrelevant all proofs based on the objective *dignity* of the priestly office. "That argument does not pertain to the perfection of [a state of] life, but to a difference in dignity. . . . But it is beside the point whether one having the care of souls is greater in the dignity of prelacy than a religious who does not have the care of souls" (*Quodlib*, bk. III, q. 6, a. 3, responsio ad 4).

It is clear from this statement that in considering the perfection of the episcopal state Thomas was not at all concerned with the *dignity* of that state, but with the existence in it of the ultimate criterion of evangelical perfection: the subjective dedication of all one has and is to the salvation of souls. Neither he nor the Fathers of the Church would seriously have maintained that election to the episcopal state enabled the candidate to achieve, simultaneously and *ex opere operato*, the personal perfection necessary for fulfilling his office in a manner befitting that state. "The giving of one's life for the sheep" is an abiding requirement of the episcopal state. It cannot be satisfied once and for all by means of an initial vow, but must daily be fulfilled anew. Episcopal perfection is, therefore, a twofold inner perfection. It is the perfection of office—the episcopal office is "a place of holiness",[40] a "more divine" order[41]—but it is also a call to the personal holiness appropriate to such an office: "Let there not be sublime honor and a warped life; let there not be deific profession and illicit action."[42] "*Episcopum convenit*. . . ."[43] Far from bestowing this personal holiness, however, the conferring of

[40] Gregory the Great, "Homiliae XL in Evangelia", bk. I, hom. 17, sec. 14, PL 76, col. 1146.

[41] Dionysius, *Eccl Hier*, chap. V, pt. 1, sec. 3.

[42] St. Ambrose, "Libellum de Dignitate Sacerdotali", c. 2.

[43] In these two words, von Balthasar indicates the contents of book III of St. John Chrysostom's *De Sacerdotio Libri Sex* (PG 48, cols. 639–60), which lists the many virtues the priest (and, therefore, a fortiori the bishop) must possess if he is to fulfill his office worthily. For an English translation of this and other works of St. John Chrysostom, see *Nicene*, vol. IX (1908). [Tr]

episcopal dignity rather presumes it, just as the bestowal of a
teaching office does not make the candidate more learned, but
rather presumes his learning: ". . . The office of doctor [teacher]
. . . may be called a state of learning not because it makes a man
learned, but because it *supposes* and requires such perfection. In the
same way, the episcopal state is justly called the state of perfection
or the state of a perfect man" (Suárez, *De statu perf*, bk. I, chap.
15, sec. 11). If the first centuries of the Church, appropriately
enough in view of their general concept of ecclesial life, consciously
perceived *Sein* and *Sollen*—objective ministry and subjective commitment—in this indivisible unity and even dared to regard the fall
from this ideal as that which ought not to be—and actually, from
an eschatological point of view, as that which is not—this does not
mean that they were unaware of the twofold inner aspect of
episcopal holiness. It was, in fact, precisely because of their awareness that they searched so diligently for spiritual men possessed of
personal charism to consecrate as bishops so that, by virtue of such
consecration, they might truly become a "pattern" for the clergy
(1 Pet 5:3), an image of the perfect sacrifice of the Good Shepherd,
which is to be continually offered in the Church.

There is this similarity, then, between episcopal and monastic
perfection. Both the bishop and the monk give themselves totally
to God: the bishop to spend his life wholly in the service of the
Church; the monk to sanctify himself by his personal striving
toward God. Indeed, what is common to the two ways of life so
outweighs their differences that the Fathers of the Church did not
distinguish them as two states of life, but perceived them as the one
state of perfection: ". . . The Fathers did not accurately distinguish
the monastic from the clerical order, but designated them by a
single term as the religious state in general" (ibid., bk. III, chap. 3,
sec. 10).

It soon became apparent, however, that the more the vows
appeared to complement one another, the more fully the state of
virginity was incorporated into the religious state, and the more the
private way of life of the hermits was transformed into the public
and organized way of the cenobites, the more, too, the concept
of analogous Christian perfection that had originally seemed to be
incorporated as much into the clerical as into the monastic state
disappeared and the clergy were faced with a difficult choice.
Should they continue to find the norm of the subjective and
personal perfection proper to their objective office in the canon
of "evangelical perfection" that they had hitherto had in common
with the monks, or should they separate themselves from this ideal

and seek a norm in the different ideal of their own office (which they did not share with the monks)? The great Fathers of the Church had striven to prevent such a split in the state of perfection. Even though there was never a time when all the clergy dependent on the bishop lived explicitly according to the three evangelical counsels, the effort had always been made to enable them to participate in the one evangelical perfection as fully as possible and in a manner appropriate to their office. Historically speaking, then, Suárez was correct—and Hertling's research supports his findings —when he insisted that Augustine had introduced nothing new with his clerical reform (ibid. III, chap. 3, sec. 8), but had merely bolstered a discipline that had begun to relax, and had thus become the connecting link between the primitive clergy of the Christian Church and the regular and canonical clergy of the Middle Ages.

The ultimate identification of evangelical perfection with the monastic way of life resulted in a growing division of the clergy into two groups—those who, like the members of religious orders, lived according to the canon of evangelical perfection, and those who did not—and in a consequent deepening of the rift (that had not originally existed) between the bishop, in whom resides the fullness of the priestly ideal, and the lower secular clergy, whom Thomas excluded from the state of perfection. This is, in itself, a surprising development. Since the bishop is bound not least by virtue of his *office* to the ideal of laying down his life for the sheep, it is strange that the distinction between the episcopal and the priestly office should have become so absolute that they were consigned to two different states of life. What is involved here is undoubtedly a degradation of the priestly ideal that can be understood only in terms of the bitter experiences of the eleventh century when it finally became clear that it was not possible to win all the regular (canonical) clergy to the ideal of the evangelical life. The result was an even greater insistence that the bishop, who, as the true and perfect type of Christ, the priest, was obliged to give his life for the sheep, must represent the fullness of evangelical perfection in some form. A significant reflection of this situation is to be found in the decision of the Eastern Church at about this time that the lower clergy belonged to the lay state and ought to marry, while the bishop not only ought not to do so, but, as had been the custom, should be chosen from the monastic life. This decision of the Russian synod of 1274 was also adopted by the Greek Uniate Church.

But the change did not end here. Through Saints Benedict, Francis and Dominic, the state of perfection had received such a distinctive form that the question now arose whether even the bishop should not adapt to this way of life that part of his priestly perfection that lay, not in official ministry [*Sein*], but in personal commitment [*Sollen*]. Thomas, indeed, had spoken unconditionally of bishops and religious as belonging to the state of perfection. But as bishops were not obliged to take the vows of religion and, in fact, only few of them did so, the difference between the episcopal and the religious states became more and more pronounced. Relying on the teaching of Dionysius the Areopagite, Gerson[44] and Dionysius the Carthusian[45] began to distinguish between a "state of perfection to be acquired" in the case of religious and a "state of perfection to be exercised" in the case of bishops. Indeed, there developed an almost categorical antithesis between a state of perfection to be acquired and a state of perfection acquired or attained;[46] the ideal of the bishop was thus greatly exaggerated, for, according to this concept, the bishop already possessed what the religious was striving to attain. Explaining the antithesis from a different point of view, Cajetan gave it its true interpretation by distinguishing the state of perfection for oneself [*status perfectionis propriae*] from the state of perfection for others [*status perfectionis alienae*].[47] The religious strives for his own perfection; the bishop, as the perfector of the Church, has by reason of his office the obligation of requiring and inducing the perfection of others. But to do this, he must himself be perfect. For it is not permissible to speak of the state of perfection as applied to bishops in so attenuated a fashion that it comes to signify only the "grace of state" that is conferred on them by their consecration or with the bestowal of office. But it is even less permissible to say that the

[44] Jean Gerson, *Oeuvres complètes*, ed. Palémon Glorieux, vol. III, *L'Oeuvre magistrale* (Paris: Desclée, 1962), no. 88, "De Consiliis Evangelicis et Statu Perfectionis", 10–26.

[45] Doctoris Ecstatici D. Dionysii Cartusiani, *Opera Omnia* (Tornaci: S. M. de Pratis, 1910), vol. 7: *Opera Minora*, "De Doctrina et Regulis Vitae Christianorum Libri Duo", bk. II, art. 1, p. 526.

[46] St. Robert Bellarmine, *De Membris Ecclesiae Militantis*, bk. II, "De Monachis", chap. II. [In *Disputationum Roberti Bellarmini . . . de Controversiis Christianae Fidei . . . Tomus Secundus* (Naples: apud Josephum Giuliano, 1857), 218. (Tr)]

[47] Thomas Aquinas, *Secunda Secundae Partis Summae Totius Theologiae*, Reverendissimi Domini Thomae a Vio, Caietani, . . . illustrata (Lyons: apud Ioannam Iacobi Iuntae F., 1581), commentary on 2a 2ae 184, 8, pp. 633–35.

grace dispensed by the bishop is effective *ex opere operato*. Granted, "one can exercise oneself in the works of perfection without being perfect oneself; one can induce others to chastity without being chaste oneself or to poverty without being poor oneself. The reason for this is that one's own perfection is not the adequate principle of perfect actions, especially when they are directed to the perfecting of others. Hence one can be a perfector of others without being perfect oneself. To be in the state of perfection it suffices that one be in the state 'of those who perfect others', even when one is not perfect oneself. But because such a way of doing what is perfect is very imperfect and ineffective, and it is, one might say, impossible that any fruit should come of it—for the Lord says, 'If the salt loses its strength, what shall it be salted with?' (Mt 5:13)—it must be admitted that this state of perfection to be exercised, if it is to be rightly undertaken, requires a personal perfection in him who will live in it. It will be best if such perfection is already present (*ut perfectio antecedat*) as a proper and very necessary disposition for entering upon this state, just as the Lord, before appointing Peter as his vicar, asked him, 'Do you love me?' It is not necessary, however, that this perfection be acquired in a state of perfection; it can also be acquired outside any such state. But if this state requires personal perfection as the proper disposition for entering upon it, it is, nevertheless, not a state of perfection to be acquired and does not of itself bestow this perfection, *but rather requires that it have been acquired elsewhere*" (Suárez, *De statu perf*, bk. I, chap. 14, sec. 8; italics added).

By now, speculation about the two elements in the concept of the state of episcopal perfection had progressed to such a point that personal perfection seemed to be the indispensable prerequisite for the perfection the bishop was to communicate and transmit to others through his office. The source from which the bearer of the office was to receive the perfection proper to it was not stated; all that was certain was that it was not conferred on him by his office, but must be sought elsewhere.[48]

---

[48] To the contention that all those in the state of perfection who are not personally perfect are liars and hypocrites, Billuart answers that this may well be true if they do not strive for perfection since men embrace the state of perfection not as professing to be already perfect, but as professing to strive for perfection. Later, he speaks of an "episcopal state of acquired perfection", but fails to show how this sentence relates to the previous one (cf. Charles René Billuart, O.P.,

Such a view, which weakened and undermined the concept of the state of perfection, did not prevail overnight. There must previously have been—in conjunction with the more precise concept of personal perfection presented by the new orders —an intense effort to preserve the former ideal of episcopal perfection. Evidence of this is to be found in the quasi-sacramental interpretation of the *votum episcopale* as the perfect, indelible and holy marriage bond between the high priest and his congregation (whether this was understood as the individual diocese or the whole Church)—a marriage bond that was regarded as just as demanding, just as exacting, as the bond of natural marriage. As marriage partners no longer live for themselves, but find, in the form of the married state, the means of giving themselves wholly to one another, according to the word of the Lord that one must "lose one's soul to save it", so, in this spiritual marriage, the bishop gives his life for his Church, his diocese, his sheep. Such a total gift of self in the exclusivity and finality demanded by the Gospel is truly an act sufficient for establishing a state of life and is thus comparable to the vow taken by monks. Pope Innocent III presented this concept of the episcopal vow, which was already current in the Church, in his *decretals*, thus paving the way for its further acceptance. Even those authors who did not make use of the image of spiritual marriage adopted the opinion that only such a vow suffices to establish a state because "they hold that the state of perfection cannot exist without a solemn vow" (*De statu perf*, bk. I, chap. 16, sec. 24).

By reason of its artificiality and almost rigid character, however, this opinion, which Thomas shared with many others, was not proof against ultimate collapse. On the one hand, there was the historical reality that gave evidence of no such definitive bond between bishops and their dioceses or even

---

Summa Sancti Thomae Hodiernis Academiarum Moribus Accommodata [Paris: Victor Palmé, n.d.], vol. 5, "Tractatus de Statu Religioso", dissertatio I, art. 1, pp. 309–10).

Passerini expresses the view that perfection that is only *presumed* can in no way suffice for the concept of a state (cf. Peter Maria Passerini, O.P., *De Hominum Statibus et Officiis*, vol. I [Lucae: Typis Leonardi Venturini, 1732], quaes. CLXXXIV, art. VI, pp. 80–83). He likewise contends that a "state of acquired perfection" cannot exist at all in the Church (cf. ibid., art. V, 9, p. 71). Many recent scholars have also adopted this view.

between bishops and their office, but did reveal a far greater
leniency in the granting of dispensations to bishops than was
customary in the case of married persons. On the other hand,
there was considerable doubt as to the existence of a vow con-
nected with the assumption of episcopal dignity, and Suárez,
finally, had no difficulty in proving that such a vow either
had never existed at all or no longer existed. Once the vows
related to the evangelical life had been specified in the Middle
Ages as poverty, chastity and obedience, and the implicit, general vow of total surrender was not only eliminated from among
them, but was no longer even recognized as a vow, it was
not difficult to show that the bishop did not take a vow, but
merely concluded with his diocese "a kind of pact" (*pactum
quoddam*) that could be dissolved by either side (ibid., chap.
16). Cajetan, who in principle espoused the view of Thomas
Aquinas, nevertheless so weakened it that he interpreted those
passages in which Thomas had used the word "vow" as referring to "a vow in the broad sense", which is precisely the
"pact" mentioned by Suárez. It is not surprising, then, that
the secular priests among the Scholastics—Henry of Ghent,[49]
for instance, and Gerson—should have attacked the very foundation of the Thomistic definition of states of life by attempting to exclude from it the concept of immutability. Just as
an individual can be in the state of grace but lose it again,
and just as a member of the lower clergy can be in the clerical
state and lose it through marriage, they said, so the concept
of states of life can exist within the Church without this further
specification. As a result, the whole concept of states of life as it
appeared in the New Testament was called into question as soon
as it seemed to demand permanence in any of the forms and grades
of Christian self-giving.

By the end of the Scholastic era, when the concept of *vow*
in relation to the ideal priestly gift of self as it was thought
to be manifested in the bishop had been thus secularized, it
was necessary to find a new norm for personal priestly perfection. Since the "state of perfection to be exercised" had been
transformed into "a state of perfection for others", it no longer

---

[49] Henricus Gandavensis, "Utrum status prelatorum melior sit et perfectior
quam status religiosorum", *Aurea Quodlibeta*, commentariis illustrata M. Vi-
talis Zuccolii (Venetiis: I. de Franciscis, 1613), 2 vols., *Quodlib.*, 12, quaes. 29
ad 1. [Tr]

afforded such a norm. Nor was there, surprisingly enough, any attempt to find one in the priesthood itself, for even Suárez repeated the old adage that ordination to the priesthood does not constitute a state of perfection "because it does not oblige to any works of perfection, but only bestows a certain capacity and power . . . , nor does it in itself have joined to it a vow of chastity . . . but at most, on account of a certain dignity of the person, such a person will be bound to give a greater example of virtue and propriety within the sphere of the precepts, which obligation is common, in proper measure, to all persons in any positions of dignity" (Suárez, *De statu perf*, bk. I, chap. 15, sec. 3). Here, then, the norm for the secular clergy is sought in a certain general "virtue and propriety", in which, it is true, they excel others by reason of their dignity, but which has no further relationship to the absolute norm of the life of the evangelical counsels. Moreover, since Cajetan and Suárez, by denying the existence of a vow, had reduced the concept of "perfection to be exercised" to the status of an exterior title with no interior foundation, the entire clergy, insofar as they were not also members of a religious order, were thus relegated to the state of *general* Christian perfection, and the original priestly mission and challenge to a total following of Christ, as Christ had established it in the state of election, appeared now as a personal union of subjective and objective perfection that was to be understood in a purely historical sense and that had no further relevance for the secular clergy.

A last symptom of the deterioration of the Christian concept of states of life should not go unmentioned. A state of life entered upon by reason of a particular election was regarded earlier as a *form* of life, which, in contrast to the general Christian state and the general baptismal vow proper to it (ibid., chap. 2, sec. 8), incorporated the individual into a definitive moral order in which he could exercise in a particular way his gift of self to God and neighbor. Augustine of Ancona,[50] for instance, distinguished four states of life—of married persons, of clergy, of religious and of bishops—and assigned to each a specific task that laid claim to and engaged the whole life of the elect. While the first of these four states comprised a special bond for lay persons within the general Christian

[50] Agostino Trionfo (Augustine of Ancona), *Summa de Potestate Ecclesiae* (Romae: In domo de Cinquinis, 1479), quaestio septuagesimasexta ad 1.

state of life, the other three combined to form, as it were, the state of those who had chosen God in a special way. As a result, there arose within the Church two great states, two classes of Christians. Once the concept of state had lost its *ratio formalis* and had become only a means of *material* classification, however, the thought inevitably occurred that this division was not adequate, that the unmarried laity ought, in fact, to be classified in a fifth state (if one used the categories of Augustine of Ancona) or a third state (if one thought in terms of the two great states of Christian life): the state of the unencumbered, that is, the state of those whose special state consisted in having no special binding form of life and who thus represented, as it were, in the body of Christ nothing more than the "freedom of the Christian individual". Suárez says in this connection: "Since there exists a state not only of obligation and servitude, but also of freedom . . . , not only those who are subjected to some obligation or responsibility, but also those who are free from such obligations, whom we called the unencumbered, ought to be assigned to their own special state" (ibid., sec. 11). With this call for a "state of those who have no state" in the sense of the old concept of state, the Scholasticism of the Baroque era may be said to have approximated—in a not inconsiderable degree, although assuredly unknowingly— the absence of states that is characteristic of Protestantism.

It was inevitable, therefore, that discerning priests, who regarded their priestly state as something far more than the mere faculty for certain cultic acts and a degree of pastoral responsibility given, or more accurately lent, them by the bishops, and saw shining forth from the ancient picture of the priest as drawn by the primitive Church and the Fathers an ideal that not only was worth, but even demanded, the highest and most perfect gift of self—it was inevitable that such priests should discover anew the unity of the life of evangelical mission. The move in this direction was fostered not only by the historical development of the parish, which laid more and more clearly on the pastor the independent responsibility that had seemed earlier to be reserved to the bishop, but also by the deterioration of the former theology of the episcopal state.[51] Who

---

[51] It was understandable, therefore, that secular priests should, from the beginning, have opposed any division that would place the bishop in a state different from that of the clergy under him. Thomas himself was aware that "priests . . . are more like bishops than religious are" (*Quodlib*, bk. III, q. 6, a. 3,

but the priest was obligated to give the example of an evangelical perfection, not based on the canons of a merely natural morality, but discoverable only in the actions of Jesus? He who celebrated the objective sacrifice could conform himself to this office only by the subjective offering of himself. "It was ordained", says Gregory of Nazianzen in his second oration, "that only the perfect should offer perfect sacrifices. . . . Since I knew these things and this besides, that no one is worthy of the great God and sacrifice and High Priest unless he has first presented himself to God as a living and holy sacrifice, which is the only sacrifice that God, who has given us all things, requires of us, how could I have dared to offer him that objective sacrifice [τὴν ἔξωθεν (θυσίαν)] . . . or to assume the dignity and name of a priest . . . before all my members had been made instruments of justice?"[52] Ambrose, too, teaches that the priest who will offer sacrifice worthily must first offer himself wholly as a sacrifice to God.[53] Indeed, Christ himself has clearly

---

point 3), from which Godfrey of Fontaines ("Les Quodlibets cinq, six et sept de Godefroid de Fontaines" [texte inédit], *Les Philosophes Belges* III, Maurice de Wulf and Jean Hoffmann [Louvain: Institut Supérieure de Philosophie de l'Université, 1914], 71–86) concluded that the state of the secular priesthood excels the religious state because, by reason of its eminence, it demands persons who are already perfect, not those who want to become so by joining a religious order (quoted in Martin Grabmann, "Katholisches Priestertum und christliches Vollkommenheitsideal nach der Lehre des hl. Thomas von Aquin", *Zeitschrift für Aszese und Mystik* II/3 [1927], 202–4). If this argument seems to reveal the drawbacks of a too instrumental interpretation of the counsels, we must nevertheless admit with Gerson that religious have no monopoly on the "state of perfection" and that the secular clergy can practice poverty and obedience as well as religious can (cf. Jean Gerson, *Oeuvres complètes*, vol. IX, *L'Oeuvre doctrinale* [Paris: Desclée, 1973], no. 424, "De Statu Papae et Minorum Praelatorum", 25–35; vol. III, *L'Oeuvre magistrale* [Paris: Desclée, 1962], no. 88, "De Consiliis Evangelicis et Statu Perfectionis", 10–26). Such an argument presumes, of course, that the immanent vow-character of the commitment of priestly ordination will receive greater emphasis. Gerson, however, carries the concept of perfection into the objectively sacramental when he refuses to acknowledge anything but a "perfection to be exercised" (vol. VIII, *L'Oeuvre spirituelle et pastorale* [Paris: Desclée, 1971], no. 413, "De Perfectione Cordis", 120; 122).

[52] St. Gregory Nazianzen (the theologian), "Orationes", oratio II, secs. 94–95, PG 35, cols. 495–99.

[53] Cf. St. Ambrose, "De Caïn et Abel Libri Duo", bk. II, chap. 6, sec. 19, PL 14, col. 369.

described the subjective sacrifice by which we are conformed to his sacrifice. It means leaving all things—family, possessions, and even oneself—in order to take up one's cross and follow him. How one is to take this step wholly and unconditionally—whether by vow, by promise or by oath, and whether in this or that form recognized by the Church—is of secondary importance; all that matters is that one actually take it. One who does so formally enters the state of the counsels; one who has and keeps the readiness to follow every call of God, but does not receive a special call, belongs to the state of Christians in the world. "You will object: The clerical state is neither a state of perfection nor a state of the common life, therefore the proposed division is not adequate. I answer . . . there is indeed controversy among scholars as to whether the clerical state in the strict sense, that is, as distinguished from the episcopate, is a state of perfection. But whatever opinion is preferred in this matter, it is certain that this state is included in the traditional division of states of life. For if it cannot be called a state of perfection, it must be placed among the states of the common life, because the meaning is the same whether we say that a state of Christian life is not a state of perfection or that it is a state of the common life."[54] Suárez had already said this: "About the clerical state . . . there is disagreement. From every reasonable point of view, however, it is certain from what has been said that it belongs to one or other of these states" (*De statu perf*, bk. I, chap. 2, sec. 13). But it is small comfort to the priest that Suárez includes him "in a manner and at least inchoatively in the state of perfection" (ibid., chap. 17, sec. 4).[55] He will not be satisfied until he has rediscovered the primitive evangelical correspondence between objective mission and the subjective gift of self to the extent that such a gift is possible for man.

e. More Recent Pronouncements

In their encyclicals on the priesthood, recent popes have cut a determined path through this dense thicket of concepts by pointing mainly to the necessity of a direct correspondence between the objective function of the priest and his mode of life. They base their comments on St. Thomas Aquinas who, despite the fact that the lower clergy were generally relegated to the lay state, was obliged

[54] Dominique Bouix, *Tractatus de Jure Regularium*, vol. I (Paris: Jacobus Lecoffre, 1857), 24.
[55] Cf. also St. Antoninus, *Tertius Tomus Summae Summarum* (Lyons: Vincentius, 1542), Prologus, IV–VI.

to admit: ". . . Through holy orders, one is committed to those most worthy ministries by which Christ himself is served in the sacrament of the altar, and this requires greater interior sanctity than does the religious state" (ST 2a 2ae 184, 8 responsio).

Pius X admonished the Catholic clergy to what he himself practiced so perfectly: union with Christ in prayer, meditation and spiritual reading that they might become mirrors to which the people could look for models.[56] St. Charles Borromeo and St. John Vianney, he said, were such models, for their lives exemplified with great luminosity what the priestly function can and ought to be for the Church.

Pius XI spoke even more clearly in his encyclical *Ad Catholici Sacerdotii*,[57] which describes the characteristics of priestly holiness. Despite the *opus operatum*, the Pope notes, that is, despite the fact that "the unworthiness of the minister does not make void the sacraments he administers . . . it is [nevertheless] quite true that so holy an office demands holiness in him who holds it. A priest should have a loftiness of spirit, a purity of heart and a sanctity of life befitting the solemnity and holiness of the office he holds" (21). "For this reason even in the Old Testament God commanded his priests and levites: 'Let them therefore be holy because I also am Holy: the Lord who sanctify them' (Lev 21:8)" (22).

". . . For as the Angelic Doctor teaches: 'To fulfil the duties of holy orders, common goodness does not suffice; but excelling goodness is required; that they who receive orders and are thereby higher in rank than the people, may also be higher in holiness.' . . . 'Realize what you are doing, and imitate what you handle', says the Church through the bishop to the deacons as they are about to be consecrated priests" (23). "Hence the Church publicly urges on all her clerics this most grave duty, placing it in the code of her laws: 'Clerics must lead a life, both interior and exterior, more holy than the laity, and be an example to them by excelling in virtue and good works' " (26).

---

[56] Pope Pius X, *Haerent Animo*, Exhortatio ad Clerum Catholicum (August 4, 1908), *Acta Sanctae Sedis* XLI (1908), 555–77. [For an English translation, see "Exhortation to the Catholic Clergy of our Most Holy Lord", *The Catholic Mind* (1908), no. 18, pp. 295–321. (Tr)]

[57] Pope Pius XI, *The Catholic Priesthood (Ad Catholici Sacerdotii)*, encyclical letter (December 20, 1935). [Vatican Press translation (Washington: National Catholic Welfare Conference, 1936). Page references to this translation, from which I quote, are given in parentheses in the text. (Tr)]

This holiness is illustrated by five different virtues. The first is piety—that union with God that is the goal and essence of all holiness; the second, third and fourth are virginity, poverty and obedience. The Pope describes first the constantly increasing practice of the evangelical counsel of virginity in the first centuries of the Church: "All this had almost inevitable consequences: The priests of the New Law felt the heavenly attraction of this chosen virtue; they sought to be of the number of those 'to whom it is given to take this word' [cf. Mt 19:11], and they spontaneously bound themselves to its observance. Soon it came about that the practice, in the Latin Church, received the sanction of ecclesiastical law. The second Council of Carthage at the end of the fourth century declared: 'What the apostles taught, and the early Church preserved, let us too observe' " (29). "St. Epiphanius at the end of the fourth century tells us that celibacy applied even to the subdiaconate: 'The Church does not on any account admit a man living in the wedded state and having children, even though he have only one wife, to the orders of deacon, priest, bishop or sub-deacon; but only him whose wife be dead or who should abstain from the use of marriage; this is done in those places especially where the ecclesiastical canons are accurately followed' " (30). ". . . How admirable a sight! These young ordinands . . . freely renounce the joys and the pleasures which might rightfully be theirs in another walk of life! We say 'freely', for though, after ordination, they are no longer free to contract earthly marriage, nevertheless they advance to ordination itself unconstrained by any law or person, and of their own spontaneous choice" (32).

The third virtue expected of the priest is poverty—not, however, evangelical poverty, but the spirit that corresponds to it: "Surrounded by the corruptions of a world in which everything can be bought and sold, he must pass through them utterly free of selfishness. He must holily spurn all vile greed of earthly gains, since he is in search of souls, not of money" (33). ". . . Once 'called to the inheritance of the Lord', as his very title 'cleric' declares, a priest must expect no other recompense than that promised by Christ to his apostles: 'Your reward is very great in heaven' (Mt 5:12)" (33). "Judas, as apostle of Christ, 'one of the Twelve', as the evangelists sadly observe, was led down to the abyss of iniquity precisely through the spirit of greed for earthly things. Remembering him, it is easy to grasp how this same spirit could have brought such harm upon the Church throughout the centuries . . ." (34). "On the other hand, by sincere disinterestedness the priest can hope to win the hearts of all. For detachment from earthly goods, if inspired by lively faith, is always accompanied by tender compassion towards the unfortunate of every kind. Thus the priest becomes a veritable father of the poor" (34–35). "Like the zeal of Jesus described in Holy Scripture, the zeal of the priest for the glory of God and the salvation of souls ought to consume him. It should make him forget himself and all earthly things. It should power-fully urge him to dedicate himself utterly to his sublime work, and to search out means ever more effective for an apostolate ever wider and ever better" (35).

Whereas the poverty required of the priest is a poverty of the interior spirit rather than an actual poverty, the obedience required of him is hardly distinguishable from the obedience of those in the state of the counsels. The Pope speaks of the "necessity" of such obedience: "Let then obedience bind ever closer together these various members of the hierarchy, one with another, and all with the head. . . . Let it assign to each his place and station. These each should accept without resistance. . . . Let each one see in the arrangements of his hierarchical superiors the arrangements of the only true head, whom all obey: Jesus Christ our Lord, who became for us 'obedient unto death, even to the death of the Cross' (Phil 2:8). The divine High Priest wished us to have abundant witness to his own most perfect obedience to the Eternal Father; for this reason both the prophecies and the Gospels often testify to the entire submission of the Son of God to the will of the Father. . . . On his very Cross he consecrated obedience. He did not wish to commit his soul into the hands of his Father before having declared that all was fulfilled in him that the Sacred Scriptures had foretold; he had accomplished the entire charge entrusted to him by the Father, even to the last deeply mysterious 'I thirst', which he pronounced 'that the Scripture might be fulfilled' (Jn 19:28). By these words he wished to show that zeal, even the most ardent, ought always to be completely subjected to the will of the Father; that our zeal should always be controlled by obedience to those who, for us, have the place of the Father, and convey to us his will, in other words our lawful superiors in the hierarchy" (37–38).

As the fifth virtue that must characterize the priest, the Pope names and recommends dedication to learning. Even more than the monk, as Dionysius has pointed out, the priest, whose duty it is to purify, enlighten and perfect, has the professional obligation of being "graced by no less knowledge and culture than is usual among well-bred and well-educated people of his day" (40). In the apostolic exhortation *Menti Nostrae*,[58] *Pius XII*, who frequently addressed himself to this topic, used as his point of departure his encyclicals on the mystical body and the Redeemer. The priesthood, he said in *Menti Nostrae*, is established in the place where the Church is drawn into the sacrifice of its head. This fact demands of the priest who offers the Eucharist for and with the people that he be "a living image of our Saviour" (5). Like Pius XI, this Pope, too, stresses the importance of obedience in the Church: "Christ himself established in the society he founded a legitimate authority which is a continuation of his own. Hence he who obeys the authorities of the Church is obeying the Redeemer himself" (8). In like manner, he urges priests to practice "daily a detachment of your hearts from riches and from the things of earth" (10). Even those who have not taken a vow of poverty "must always be guided by the love of this virtue" (10). Only thus can they attain what the Pope earnestly desires for them: that they put on the mind of the head of the Church, who offered himself in sacrifice for all.

John XXIII, in his first encyclical *Sacerdotii Nostri Primordia*[59] strongly supported the teaching of his predecessor, Pius XII, that those in the clerical state are not bound by divine law to practice the evangelical counsels of poverty, chastity and obedience: "Yet the man who should presume to infer from this that clerics are less bound than the members of religious communities by the obligation of tending to perfection is certainly misrepresenting the true meaning of this same Sovereign Pontiff, who was so concerned with the holiness of the clergy, and is contradicting the constant teaching of the Church on this subject. The truth is completely opposed to this unwise inference. For the proper performance of the priestly duties 'there is required a greater inward holiness than even the state of religion requires' (ST 2a 2ae 184,

[58] Pope Pius XII, *On the Development of Holiness in Priestly Life* (*Menti Nostrae*), apostolic exhortation (September 23, 1950). [Trans. by National Catholic Welfare Conference News Service, ed. Very Rev. John P. McCormick (Washington: National Catholic Welfare Conference, 1950). Page references to this translation, from which I quote, are given in parentheses in the text. (Tr)]

[59] Pope John XXIII, *On the Priesthood* (*Sacerdotii Nostri Primordia*), encyclical letter (August 1, 1959, for the centenary of the death of St. John Vianney). [Trans. Rt. Rev. Joseph C. Fenton (Washington: National Catholic Welfare Conference, 1959). Page references to this translation, from which I quote, are given in parentheses in the text. (Tr)]

8 responsio). Even though the evangelical counsels are not made mandatory by the force of the clerical state itself for ecclesiastics so that they may be able really to attain this sanctity of life, nevertheless for ecclesiastics as for all the faithful these same counsels constitute the surest way to attain the desired goal of Christian perfection. Furthermore, and this is a great comfort to us, there are many priests today, endowed with genuine virtue, who, although belonging to the diocesan clergy, seek aid and support from pious associations approved by the authority of the Church in order that they may be able more easily and more readily to enter upon the way of perfection" (6–7). Thereupon the Pope draws a striking picture of St. John Vianney's extreme poverty, of the "angelic chastity" (11) that shone from his face, and of his perfect obedience to the Church. Toward the end of the encyclical, John XXIII quotes what the saint once said to his bishop: "If you want the entire diocese to be converted to God, then all the parish priests must become saints" (35).

It is significant that *Vatican Council II* also adopts this view in the *Decree on the Ministry and Life of Priests*.[60] Whether the special function of the priest is regarded as derived from the general priesthood of "all the faithful" within the Church (PO 2) or from above as a "sharing in the unique office of Christ the Mediator",[61] the result is the same: Through holy orders the priest is summoned to be "configured to Christ" (PO 12), for only thus can he effectively represent Christ among men. "The very holiness of priests is of the greatest benefit for the fruitful fulfillment of their ministry" (PO 12). In the description of the special spiritual requirements in the life of the priest, this holiness is again depicted in terms of evangelical counsels: as "that disposition of mind by which they are always prepared to seek, not their own will, but the will of him who sent them" (PO 15) and to "accept and carry out in the spirit of faith the commands and suggestions of the pope and of their bishop and other superiors" (PO 15); as celibacy, which "has always been highly esteemed in a special way . . . as a feature of priestly life" (PO 16); and as poverty, above all of spirit, although priests are also "invited to embrace voluntary poverty. By it they become more

[60] *Decree on the Ministry and Life of Priests (Presbyterorum Ordinis)*. [Vatican Council II, *The Conciliar and Post Conciliar Documents*, gen. ed. Austin Flannery, O.P. (Northport, N.Y.: Costello Publishing Co., 1975), 863–902. Quotations from this document (henceforth PO) are identified by section number within the text. (Tr)]

[61] *Dogmatic Constitution on the Church (Lumen Gentium)*, sec. 28.

closely conformed to Christ and more ready to devote themselves to their sacred ministry. . . . Even some kind of use of property in common . . . provides an excellent opening for pastoral charity" (PO 17).

In his encyclical *On Priestly Celibacy*,[62] *Paul VI* emphasizes not only the point at which the role of the priest and the life of the evangelical counsels are most visibly united and the difference between function and counsel (15; 42), but also the oneness of the original call of Jesus to both the priestly office and the religious life in imitation of Christ (22–23) and the inner necessity of "assimilation to the form of charity and sacrifice proper to Christ our Saviour" (24), especially "in the ministry of the Eucharist" (29).

In *1971*, the *Synod of Bishops* also turned its attention to the priestly office. Its most important accomplishment in this regard was a theological definition of the indelible "seal" imprinted by priestly ordination. "The lifelong permanence of this reality which imprints a sign—and this is a doctrine of faith referred to in Church tradition—expresses the fact that Christ irrevocably associated the Church with himself for the salvation of the world, and that the Church herself is consecrated to Christ in a definitive way for the fulfillment of his work. The minister, whose life bears the seal of the gift received through the sacrament of orders, reminds the Church that God's gift is irrevocable."[63] Standing thus with his whole existence at the precise point where these two "irrevocables" meet, the priest symbolizes both of them—a fact that again underscores his specific obligation to advance from *Sein* [objective ministry] to *Sollen* [subjective commitment] and action. The priest's life is understood in the Gospels as a call to be near the Lord (Mt 3:14) and a summons to sanctify himself (Jn 17:19). The bishops also defended at length the retention of celibacy in the Roman Church and emphasized its voluntary acceptance by the ordinands. By speaking not only of the "full harmony" [*plena concordantia*], but also of the "intimate . . . coherence" [*intima . . . cohaerentia*] between the priestly office and celibacy, they made it impossible for anyone to see in priestly virginity a special, limited "charism" that is offered to but a few and is, therefore, easily detachable from the priestly vocation (371–73).

---

[62] Pope Paul VI, *On Priestly Celibacy (Sacerdotalis Caelibatus)*, encyclical letter (June 24, 1967). [(Washington: United States Catholic Conference, n.d.) Quotations from this encyclical will be identified by section number within the text. (Tr)]

[63] Synod of Bishops, 1971, *Das Priestertum*, with an introduction by Joseph Cardinal Höffner and a short commentary by Hans Urs von Balthasar

f. The Present State of the Question

Dissenting from Thomas Aquinas' teaching about the states of
life, *Cardinal Mercier*, philosopher and primate of Belgium, ranked
the secular priesthood unambiguously above the religious state.[64]
Among his followers, there arose a new "theology of the secular
priest", represented especially by the clergy of Belgium and north-
ern France. Deploring the "persistent prejudice" (185) that placed
the religious ideal above that of the secular priesthood, Mercier
blamed it also for the malaise (211; cf. also 161) he detected
particularly among zealous secular priests who had become dis-
satisfied with their state and were choosing to direct their striving
for perfection according to the monastic ideal. Since the more
gifted younger men in institutions conducted by religious orders
preferred to enter these orders, the Cardinal noted, the secular
clergy were acquiring the reputation of being an inferior, even
an imperfect, institution. For this reason, he sought to eradicate
the "objectionable" term "secular clergy" (161), proposing as
a substitute "diocesan clergy" (198)—a proposal that met with
marked enthusiasm.

Mercier then proceeded, as Thomas Aquinas had done, to make a
precise distinction between the state of perfection and perfection
itself. The state of perfection, he said, is an external, social state
established by canon law; perfection itself is the internal disposition
of an individual before God (165–67). Bishops and religious are in
the state of perfection, but with this distinction, that the bishop is
presumed to be perfect at his consecration whereas religious are
bound only to strive for perfection. "The bishop is presumed to
be perfect" (167). "The difference between the two is this: It
suffices that perfection be for the religious a way of life, a hope,
while it must be for the bishop an accomplished reality" (192),[65]

(Einsiedeln: Johannes Verlag, 1972). [Page references to this work are given in
parentheses in the text. For an English translation, see "The Ministerial Priesthood", text approved by the 1971 Synod of Bishops, in *The Pope Speaks* 16, 4
(1972). (Tr)]

[64] See Désiré Félicien Cardinal Mercier, *La Vie Intérieure* (Paris: Beauchesne,
1919). [Page references to this work will be given in parentheses in the
text. (Tr)]

[65] Eugène Masure has found the ultimate formula: "To put it simply, one
might say that the bishop does not need to practice asceticism in order to be

since the bishop, as the *sponsus Ecclesiae*, offers his life solemnly and irrevocably for his sheep (Mercier, 195). But, Mercier continued, the diocesan clergy, although they are not in the external state of perfection, participate closely in the episcopal office, forming, as it were, an extension of that office. He concluded that they must, therefore, participate just as closely in the episcopal perfection, and that they do so by virtue of their office, their function, which in itself *requires* holiness—even, according to Aquinas, a greater holiness than that required of religious. Although Mercier never quotes the texts of the *Summa* that oppose his view, he refers repeatedly to one text in particular—the article entitled: "Whether parish priests and archdeacons are more perfect than religious" (ST 2a 2ae 184, 8). One might object that "presume" and "require" are not synonymous. But Mercier was only at the beginning of his argument. His first concern was to fix the requirement of greater holiness as firmly as possible precisely in the office of the priest (Mercier, 169): "By virtue of your priesthood, you are obligated to a greater perfection than religious are!" (198). Even a priest who chose to enter a religious order "would still be obliged both before and after his entrance to seek in his priesthood the most profound basis, the decisive basis, of his vocation to *religio* and to holiness" (199–200). "In fact, if the religious consecrates himself irrevocably to God, the priest, through the sacrament of holy orders, is already consecrated to God by a better title" (216). But if there exists for the priest this intrinsic and inalienable obligation to holiness, then the means necessary for attaining it must be bestowed by his priestly ordination (174)—and must be bestowed explicitly as the means of attaining evangelical perfection: "You are called no less than the monk—and, indeed, more strictly—to evangelical perfection" (184). Thomas assigned three advantages to the evangelical counsels: deliverance from dependence on the world, rest in God and the holocaust of love. Mercier, on the other hand, argued that there are other ways of being delivered from dependence on the world; that contemplative love is not man's noblest pursuit, for according to Thomas renunciation of contemplation for the salvation of souls is even more noble; and, finally, that the holocaust of love consists in love itself, which achieves its fullest perfection only when it gives itself wholly in selfless service for the salvation of souls. "What gives the religious state its superiority over the lay state is not,

---

perfect" (*De l'Eminente dignité du sacerdoce diocésain* [Paris: Bloud et Gay, 1938], 25).

properly speaking, the counsels of chastity, poverty and obedience, as practiced by religious, but the more selfless love that dictates them and makes them a purer sacrifice to the majesty of God. For there are other sacrifices of pure love, some of them—like the service of souls—even higher than those inherent in the religious vocation" (Mercier, 180). Indeed, the counsels add to the theological virtue of charity only the merit of the moral virtue of religion (177). "Whoever truly has charity, possesses therein the essential virtues of the religious, and has no need of slavishly imitating his way of life. The letter kills, but the spirit quickens!" (183; paraphrased). The external observance of the counsels undoubtedly presumes a "special calling" to that way of life, but it offers only certain "means", a "point of departure" for striving for perfect love (176). These "means" may be appropriate for some, but they are not so for all (177). They are neither the only means, since the Gospel names many counsels, all of which can be realized in a variety of ways (177), nor are they the best: "Proof of this is in the fact that the bishop, who has vowed neither the poverty nor the obedience of the religious, is in a state of perfection before the Church that is higher than that of the religious, and possesses means of perfection that are higher than those of the religious" (178). "Whatever a superficial public may think, it is nevertheless true that the state of the bishop, who lives in a palace, who perhaps has a fortune of his own, who administers properties, is involved in business matters, and commands his subordinates, is higher than that of the religious who has bound himself by vow to observe the three evangelical counsels of poverty, chastity and obedience" (200). For Thomas teaches that detachment from material goods in the sense of being indifferent to them is all that is required, as the apostle also says (Phil 4:12): "I know how . . . to be filled and yet to be hungry" (Mercier, 202–3). Finally, the Cardinal called attention to the limitations of the religious state. Often, he said, the urge to enter the cloister is an egotistical flight from poverty and responsibility (213–14). More importantly, the religious is concerned with his own personal—even "private"—salvation (157) while the priest almost forgets this as he consecrates himself wholly, in the perfect love of the Lord and his apostles, to the salvation of others (181; 206). Basically, the religious does no more by his three vows than the ordinary Christian does by his baptismal vow: Both commitments are "essentially of the same nature" (187). The clerical state forms the real dividing line between the states of life. It alone is a true "calling" to leave the general Christian state to which lay persons and religious belong, and this calling can occur only through the bishop (187–88). Since the priest is obliged to higher perfection by reason of his ordination than the religious is by his vows, it follows that "the priest who becomes a religious mounts no higher on the ladder of moral and religious obligations" (199). On the contrary, secular priests should be aware that fundamentally they are themselves the true religious (159). "Yes, dear brethren, you belong to the first order that was founded in the Church; your founder is Jesus Christ himself; the first religious of his order were the apostles whose successors are the bishops and, in union with them, the priests, . . . all who make public profession of choosing God alone as their portion and of considering the service of God to be the whole content of their lives" (197). "The clergy, who are the essential organ of religion in the Church, are likewise the official and first religious. The choir of the Church is everywhere reserved for them, and if they are called 'secular clergy', it is only because they do not visibly observe the external way of life of monks who live in community. But this does not mean that they are, in the true meaning of the word, less than religious clergy, who, by comparison with them, are but embellishments and adjuncts" (192). While the other orders have more or less specific goals, the clergy form a truly universal order (207), the foundation of the whole state of election. In their disposition of leaving all to follow Christ, the first members of this order, the apostles, are its models, for they, too, knew no other formula of vows than this promise, this spirit of discipleship (208–9). Thus the priesthood never loses its higher rank: "Religious, whether active or contemplative, . . . must turn their eyes to the bishop that from him they may each according to his particular state learn to know and imitate the most perfect model of love and, consequently, the model of Christian perfection, both religious and priestly" (216). For the same reason, Paul, too, wanted the eyes of all focussed on himself: "Therefore, I beg you, be imitators of me, as I am of Christ" (1 Cor 4:16).

Mercier stated his theory so plainly and clearly that his successors had only to amplify, explain and support his remarks. Masure (*De l'Eminente dignité du sacerdoce diocésain*) called attention in particular to the fullness of ecclesial perfection that resides in the bishop and in which the "diocesan clergy" directly participate. Gustave Thils[66] stressed the apostolicity of this "first order"—that is, of the clergy —and sought the norm of priestly perfection in the concept of

---

[66] Gustave Thils, *Le Clergé diocésain* (Bruges: Desclée, 1942), enlarged and documented in *Nature et spiritualité du clergé diocésain* (Bruges: Desclée, 1946). [Page references to the latter edition are given in parentheses in the text. (Tr)]

service (*ministerium*), which is at once *magisterium* and *regimen* (35). Entrance into this service represents "the fullness of a universal and unconditional commitment" (57) to a way of life that is both contemplative and active (270) in the universal "order" that existed before the foundation of all individual orders and that still preserves as its "spirituality" the universal character of Christ's redemptive work (295–328). Thils repeated and developed Mercier's statements about the relative meaning and value of the vows (371–82). Nevertheless, he added, all who want to follow the Lord to the end must accept at least the spirit of the vows. Christ's words, "Let him accept it who can" (Mt 19:12), "are not directed to religious alone; the clergy and the faithful have also understood and accepted the full Gospel message" (374). The situation and with it the state of the secular clergy have changed since Thomas' time. In practice, what Thomas applied to bishops alone—the total dedication of themselves to the flock entrusted to them—has become the disposition of every secular priest. His life requires the same gift of self as that by which the bishop is established in the state of perfection (393–96).

The whole movement, which was under the leadership of Monsignor Guerrys, Archbishop of Cambrai, engendered a lively debate.[67] Its primary goal was to remove from the diocesan clergy the allegedly restrictive spirituality proper to each religious order so that they might take their place at the center of the all-embracing spirituality of Christ and his threefold office. To accomplish this, it demanded, and often with justice, that the bishop should be in closer contact with his priests—in a relationship like that of religious superiors to their subjects, or better, like that of Christ to the apostles and of the first bishops to their communities.

Criticism of the whole theory was not slow to appear.[68] By virtue of his office, it was said, the priest is clearly invited more than

[67] See the various contributions to the anthology *Pour un Clergé diocésain. Une Enquête sur sa spiritualité particulière. Problèmes du clergé diocésain* (Paris, 1947).

[68] Cf. *Revue d'ascétique et de mystique* (now *Revue d'histoire de la spiritualité*) I (1920), 280–88; *La Vie spirituelle*, no. 16 (January 1921), 313–17; René Carpentier, S.J., "La Spiritualité du clergé diocésain", *Nouvelle revue théologique* 68 (1946), 192–217; Marie-Joseph Nicolas, O.P., "Sacerdoce diocésain et vie religieuse", *Revue thomiste* 46 (1946), 169–82; J. A. Robilliard, O.P., "Spiritualité du clergé ou spiritualité sacerdotale?" *La Vie spirituelle* 74 (1946), 186–93. As the final word, we might mention Pius XII's "Allocutio Delegatis Conventui Generali ex Universis Religiosis Ordinibus, Congregationibus ac Societatibus Institutisque Saecularibus, Romae Habita" (December 8, 1950) in *Acta Apostolicae Sedis* 43 (1951), 26–36.

others are to make use of the best means Jesus has given for the achievement of perfect love. But these means are, above all, the counsels, which should be observed, not out of egoism, but in order better to serve Christ's cause. If there is a "spirituality of the clerical state", it applies equally to secular and religious clergy since both are obliged, for the sake of their ecclesial missions, to hold themselves in readiness for full service (Carpentier). But the priest is able to participate in the pastoral ministry of the bishop only through the bond of obedience that he accepts at his ordination; his readiness for service finds expression in his celibacy. In other words, he is established in his state by signs borrowed from the religious state (Nicolas).

As a whole, however, these criticisms are guilty of *a great oversight*: They ignore the fact that there are also women in the Church; that these women are called to the "state of perfection" no less than the often arrogant clergy; and that, under the patronage of the Lord's own mother, they have a greater claim by reason of their womanhood than men have by reason of their office to represent and cooperate in actualizing the perfect mind of the Church whose function it is to conceive, bring to term and give birth.[69]

Despite these criticisms, however, and they are not the only ones, there will be discovered under the aberrations of the Mercier school a concern that has preoccupied us throughout this book: the need to reclaim the primitive evangelical unity of the ecclesial state of life from the divisions that obscure it. For—with the exception of Mary's preeminence over both the lay state and the state of the counsels (because she was a virgin in order that she might be a mother) and, in the primitive Church, the analogous virginity of those women who, as brides of Christ, sought to realize the perfect mind of the Church—the personal unity between the state of the counsels and the priestly mission as it existed among the apostles under the leadership of Jesus is a unity that Suárez and his sources, as well as Heinz Schürmann in our own time, have not hesitated to call the original "order". Moreover, since the early clergy seriously regarded the *regula* or "canon" of this first evangelical "order" as their way of life, we must assume that (at least until the differentiation of "secular" and "regular" clergy) they, like the virgins and monks, represented a continuous line of development from this first order. Mercier's goal of keeping the diocesan clergy aware of this continuity is always recognizable, even when his polemic

---

[69] Cf. Louis Bouyer, *Mystère et ministères de la femme dans l'église* (Paris: Aubier, 1976). [For an English translation of this work, see *Woman in the Church*, trans. Marilyn Teichert (San Francisco: Ignatius Press, 1979). (Tr)]

attitude toward institutional forms of the state of the counsels[70] and his obsession with a handful of Thomistic texts lead him astray. Nor is his basic perception false when he equates the vow of baptism with the vows of religious life, speaking first of the transition from the "lay state" to the "state of the counsels" as a transition to a radicalization of the lay state, which Church history shows to have been the "fundamental" state, and then making a clear distinction between the two.[71] But, as we have clearly seen in our consideration of Christ's state of life, differentiation and distinction do not necessarily mean division. This is apparent, too, in the way of life proper to active orders and secular institutes.

It would be wrong to regard the various "spiritualities" by which the distinctive charisms of religious orders are made manifest as "limitations" on the basic spirituality of the Gospels as incorporated in the clergy. On the contrary, it is the one Spirit who discloses his fullness and that of Christ in the riches of his gifts (1 Cor 12:4), thereby engendering the inner vitality of the ecclesial organism and, in the process, giving proof that the often paradoxical "monk's answer" to world happenings is essentially the word of the Holy Spirit. Nor is the following of Christ's counsels to be allocated to the realm of the "moral virtues". "The teaching and example of Christ provide the foundation for the evangelical counsels. . . . The apostles and Fathers of the Church commend them as an ideal of life and so do her doctors and pastors. They therefore constitute a gift of God which the Church has received from her Lord . . ." (LG 43). The tradition of the Church has always maintained that the counsels are a meaningful expression of love; that they were understood in this way by Jesus as well as by Paul; and that they are, therefore, incompatible with anxiety about one's own salvation. If they required such anxiety, they would be obstacles rather than helps along Christ's way. If, in the course of history, a certain amount of dross has adhered to the state of the counsels, then, like Mercier's clergy, it too must

[70] Masure reaped the fruit of Mercier's theory when he placed the source of the three vows in the Old Testament: "This is, again, an Old Testament concept that has been replaced in the New Testament by a much more dynamic concept of holiness" (*De l'Eminente dignité du sacerdoce diocésain*, 154). On the relationship between *caritas* and *religio*, see Pt. I, Ch. 1, sec. 3 of this work.

[71] Cf. *Dogmatic Constitution on the Church (Lumen Gentium)*, Vatican Council II, *The Conciliar and Post Conciliar Documents*, gen. ed. Austin Flannery, O.P. (Northport, N.Y.: Costello Publishing Co., 1975), secs. 41–43. [Further references to this document (henceforth LG) are given in parentheses in the text. (Tr)]

be reminded of the primitive evangelical state: ". . . Sell whatever thou hast . . . and come follow me" (Mk 10:21). "Have this mind in you which was also in Christ Jesus, who . . . humbled himself, becoming obedient unto death" (Phil 2:5, 8).

The foregoing discussion has served only to reinforce the concept of the two-in-oneness (*Zwei-Einheit*) of the priestly and religious states as it was described earlier in this work. Both states are forms of the one state of election—but the forms differ according to whether the election is primarily to an objective function (and only secondarily to the way of life appropriate to this function) or primarily to personal discipleship (and only secondarily to an objective way of life according to the standard of a rule). Although different, the two forms are, however, much more closely related than is generally believed to be the case. This unity has its foundation not only in the unity of evangelical radicality, which is reflected at best only secondarily in the various states of election, but also, and most deeply, in the unity of Christ's priesthood, which is, at the same time, both official and personal.

3. THE STATE OF LAY PERSONS IN THE WORLD

Members of the Church who are in neither the state of election nor the priestly state belong to the state of lay persons in the world. Although there are priests who are not in the state of the counsels and persons in the state of the counsels who are not priests, it would be false to assume that the opposite of the priestly state is a different state from the opposite of the state of the counsels. The secular state that is not the priestly state and the lay state that is not the state of the counsels are not two different states of life. From this we see again that the state of lay persons in the world is not (theologically speaking) related to the priestly state and the state of the counsels as a third specific state, but rather as a general state to particular states having their own distinguishing characteristics. There is, for instance, no special consecration required for the lay state as there is for the priestly state or the state of the counsels: The consecration of the lay person is that of the Christian in general, namely baptism, which gives access to all the other sacraments and to the whole perfection of love, but is common to all Christians, including priests and those in the state of the counsels. It is true that matrimony is reserved in a special way for those in the lay state and confers on them a new supernatural character that is not accessible to other states. But while matrimony is the basis of the "married state" as a special potential within the lay state, it is not the basis of the lay state itself.

This is not contradicted by the fact that Paul, in teaching about Church ministries, lists far more than the particular ministries appropriate to the special states of life identified above. As gifts of grace (charisms), these "ministries" are certainly more than just temporary occupations; they depend on the dispensation of the Holy Spirit (1 Cor 12:11) and confer on the Christian a genuine function in the total economy of the Mystical Body. But the very differences in the descriptions and classifications of the gifts show that they contain for the most part something transitory that cannot be the foundation of a state of life. The First Epistle to the Corinthians names the gifts of wisdom, knowledge, faith, healing, the working of miracles, prophecy, the distinguishing of spirits, various kinds of tongues, interpretation of these tongues (1 Cor 12:8–10); and a few verses later: "first apostles, secondly prophecy, thirdly teachers; after that miracles, the gift of healing, services of help, power of administration and the speaking of various tongues" (1 Cor 12:28). The Epistle to the Romans distinguishes the gifts of prophecy, ministering, teaching, exhorting, almsgiving, administration and works of mercy (Rom 12:6–8), then proceeds to list general activities within the Church to which a Christian might, under special circumstances, be temporarily inspired by the Holy Spirit—among those already mentioned, exhorting, almsgiving, works of mercy—and to make other recommendations, each of which refers in its own way to the gifts of the Spirit, but none of which would be a sufficient basis for the establishment of a permanent, differentiated function or a fortiori for an office within the Church. On the one hand, Paul admonishes a whole congregation: ". . . Reprove the irregular, comfort the fainthearted, support the weak, be patient towards all men" (1 Th 5:14); on the other hand, he urges Timothy to be diligent "in exhortation and in teaching" (1 Tim 4:13).

Two facts are made abundantly clear by Paul's teaching about these charismatically inspired ministries. The first is this: that the lay state in the Church is far from being an indistinguishable, formless mass whose sole function is to receive God's grace passively through the ministry of the hierarchy; that, on the contrary, this grace always contains also a mission, a well-defined ecclesial task, and imparts a responsibility for the whole body of Christ, which we are, "member for member" (1 Cor 12:27). It is certainly not opposed to Paul's thinking to assign such a charism to each Christian in the Church, for it is in the nature of grace not only to bind one to the Church, but also to confer a personal mission. The personal mission bestowed by the Holy Spirit is linked to the sacrament of confirmation by which the Christian is raised from a life that was predominantly the receptive and irresponsible life of a child to one that has voice and responsibility within the ecclesial community. The Christian is not thereby entitled simply to vote as is one who reaches his majority in the political community. Because grace always differentiates, is always personally oriented, always contains a personal challenge, he also receives an unmistakable and inalienable task within the ecclesial community.

The awareness of this personal function, which the laity do not choose for themselves, but have bestowed on them from above in divine sovereignty, and which they are to fill with the same care and conscientiousness they bring to secular functions, has long been lacking to most lay persons and, even in this age in which the lay movement is strong within the Church, has yet to achieve significant dimensions. Yet Paul's lists show that the difference between the states of life is not emphasized when the ministries are viewed charismatically: Apostleship and ecclesial office (διακονία, Rom 12:7) are mentioned in the same breath with other ministries that are open to or reserved for the laity.

Indeed, Paul reproves the congregation because through their own fault they have been slow—or have neglected—to make the transition from a way of life in which they passively receive to one in which they actively give; that they have remained fixed in an "infantile Christianity" (ὡς νηπίους ἐν Χριστῷ) that cries for milk and cannot endure solid food (1 Cor 3:1–2). "For whereas by this time you ought to be masters, you need to be taught again the rudiments of the words of God; and you have become such as have need of milk and not solid food. For everyone who is fed on milk is unskilled in the word of justice; he is but a child. But solid food is for the mature, for those who by practice have their faculties trained to discern good and evil" (Rom 5:12–14). Through culpable infantilism, the community forfeited at least three "missions" intended for it by the Holy Spirit: the gift of teaching, knowledge of the divine word, and the distinguishing of spirits, which, though charismatic gifts (1 Cor 12:10), nevertheless presume the cooperation of the spiritually mature and responsible Christian and, therefore, his personal exercise of them.

Secondly, Paul's teaching makes it clear that, while the graces, offices and functions bestowed by the Spirit are not simply private graces, but are intended for the Church and are prerogatives conferred for the good of the community, they are nevertheless of themselves *not sufficient for the establishment of a state of life*. Neither in the Bible itself—as for instance in the description of the community at Corinth with its lively charismatic life, whose personalistic tendencies Paul had to stem by a firm teaching about objective ecclesial ministries and functions—nor in primitive Christianity, nor in Church history as a whole, do these ministries, with few exceptions such as that of "confessors",[72] claim to rival the ecclesial hierarchy or the ecclesial

---

[72] "Confessors" were those witnesses to the faith who suffered torture and imprisonment, but not death, during times of persecution. Since, by virtue of their intention, they were considered equal to the martyrs who had actually given their lives for the faith, and were therefore regarded as persons who shared

state of the counsels. They have perhaps been given too little, rather than too much, attention. In fact, they have, for the most part, disappeared, as witness the fact that the lay community has merited again and again Paul's biting reproof that they are still in need of teaching whereas they ought to have become teachers. It is a long-standing experience of the Church that the laity too often do not *want* to become mature in the Christian sense because Christian maturity does not mean just a serious obligation toward all the ministries inspired by the Holy Spirit and conferred as tasks; it also presumes a supernatural maturity that can be achieved only through much prayer and sacrifice, but that is wanting precisely to many of the laity who most loudly proclaim their own maturity.

If the call to a qualitatively higher state of life does not ensue, this conferral on the laity of special gifts of grace, special instructions and special demands of the Spirit gives rise to the distinctive condition known as the lay state. Earlier, in our consideration of the instrumental character of the ecclesial state and the state of the counsels (cf. ST 2a 2ae 184, 3), we saw that the lay state is to be designated as the primary and, at the same time, *the fundamental state in the Church*. Since this is so, and *since the two other states* are formed by specific differentiations of this first state, they may be regarded as classifications, emphases and *concretizations* of this state, to which they stand in a relationship of service.

This applies to the priestly state, which is essentially a function —that of representing Christ—and is, therefore, ordered to the universal Church. It applies even more strongly to the state of the counsels, whose "highest" ideal is the realization of the general Christian ideal, and which, therefore, must in a special way represent for all Christians the evangelical perfection toward which all must strive. It may be compared to the raising of a number to a higher power, which nevertheless contains the base

---

subjectively in the priesthood of Christ, they were permitted to perform certain priestly functions.

number; to the meeting of a challenge that is made to all; to the
setting up of a model that all are to imitate; to the delineation of
a type with which all are to be identified.

The qualitatively higher states of life are, then, at the service
of the totality of Christians and have no other raison d'être than
this service. It is their task unceasingly and in every possible way
to procure, explain and transmit to the fundamental state in the
Church the fullness of divine grace. The wealth that seems to be
theirs belongs to them only for the sake of the whole Church,
which possesses it when it possesses Christ. They are a treasure
on which the Church of the laity can depend, that it can justly
claim as its possession in Christ. In the name of Christ, the
priesthood shows and gives this Church what belongs to it by
right; by its very nature and example, the state of the counsels
shows it the possibilities of development that are inherent in its
own Christian life and makes them accessible to it. All that
happens to these two states, even their most intimate, most
personal and most God-oriented experiences, happens to them
for the sake of the community. "For whether we are afflicted, it is
for your instruction and salvation; or whether we are comforted,
it is for your comfort. . . . And our hope for you is steadfast,
knowing that as you are partakers of the sufferings, so you will
also be of the comfort" (2 Cor 1:6–7). The whole dramatic chain
of events that made the apostles "a spectacle to the world, and
to angels, and to men" (1 Cor 4:9) did not happen for its own
sake: "For all things are for your sakes, so that the grace which
abounds through the many may cause thanksgiving to abound,
to the glory of God" (2 Cor 4:15). The remarkable gifts of grace
bestowed on those in the qualitatively higher states of life have
no other purpose than that Christians "may have an answer for
them who glory in appearances and not in heart" (2 Cor 5:12);
indeed, the whole special economy that represents the sacrifice of
the Cross either sacramentally or personally is the property of the
whole Christian community: "For all things are yours, whether
Paul, or Apollos, or Cephas; or the world, or life, or death; or

things present, or things to come—all are yours" (1 Cor 3:22). Hence one called to the service of this wealth of the Church bears "all things for the sake of the elect" (2 Tim 2:10); he incorporates himself into the mystery of Christ, who chose poverty and the things that are nought so that his Bride, the Church, might be rich: "For you know the graciousness of our Lord Jesus Christ —how, being rich, he became poor for your sakes, that by his poverty you might become rich" (2 Cor 8:9). The chosen one does likewise: "We are fools for Christ, but you are wise in Christ! We are weak, but you are strong! You are honored, but we are without honor! . . . We have become as the refuse of this world, the offscouring of all, even until now!" (1 Cor 4:10, 13). He humbles himself "that you [may] be exalted" (2 Cor 11:17); he rejoices that he is "weak but you are strong" (2 Cor 13:9). For like the Lord, who was "made to be sin who knew nothing of sin, so that in him we might all become the justice of God" (2 Cor 5:21), so the apostle can say of himself: "Free though I was as to all, unto all I have made myself a slave that I might gain the more converts" (1 Cor 9:19). He places himself and his whole existence at the feet of the community: "What then is Apollos? What indeed is Paul? They are servants" (1 Cor 3:5)—"servants of Christ and stewards of the mysteries of God" (1 Cor 4:1). "For we preach not ourselves, but Jesus Christ as Lord, and ourselves merely as your servants in Jesus" (2 Cor 4:5). "Thus death is at work in us, but life in you" (2 Cor 4:12).

But in pointing out the contrast between himself and the community, the apostle has only one purpose: to strengthen the union that exists between them. For this contrast has for its premise the unity of love and for its goal the increase of love. In pouring out the whole fullness of Christian life upon the community, objectively in the sacraments and in the traditional teaching of the Church and subjectively by their example, by the richness of their Christian experiences in joy and in suffering, in ecstasy and in persecution, those in the state of election want only to give the whole community a share in their riches. By

word and example, they transmit to the community what truly
belongs to it by grace, but what it has never sufficiently realized
or recognized as its own.

By comparison with the priesthood, the lay community may seem, at
first, *to be but a passive recipient*, to be overwhelmed beyond its
power of comprehension by the immense fullness of God as it is
transmitted and represented by those in the state of election. ". . .
We are God's helpers, you are God's tillage, God's building" (1
Cor 3:9). "Are you not my work in the Lord?" (1 Cor 9:1). The
lay community is reminded again and again of its value in the eyes
of God; of how much the Father, Son and Holy Spirit as well as
the elect have done for it; of the extent to which everything it
possesses exceeds its expectation, its comprehension. For what is
promised to and bestowed upon the community by its ministers
is greater than anything its faith can conceive. "Do you not know
yourselves that Christ Jesus is in you?" (2 Cor 13:15). "Christ
in you—your hope of glory!" (Col 1:27). This indwelling of
Christ in the faithful is an actual participation in his death and
Resurrection: ". . . If we have died with Christ, we believe that
we shall also live together with Christ" (Rom 6:8), for God has
"raised us up together, and seated us together in heaven in Christ
Jesus" (Eph 1:6). "If then any man is in Christ, he is a new
creature" (2 Cor 5:7) in Christ, "who has also stamped us with
his seal and has given us the Spirit as a pledge in our hearts" (2
Cor 1:22). The description of Christian election in the opening
chapter of the Epistle to the Ephesians depicts a veritable torrent
of grace—starting with God's original purpose before the foundation of the world, when we were already loved and predestined
in Christ to be holy and to be the children of the Father; continuing into the fullness of time, when we were made coheirs
in Christ "according to the riches of his grace [that] has
abounded beyond measure in us in all wisdom and prudence"
(Eph 1:7–8); and ending with our being stamped with the seal of
the Holy Spirit, the last mystery of the Holy Trinity. Thereupon
the apostle bursts into an almost incoherent paean of praise before

the community: May God enlighten "the eyes of your mind . . . so that you may know what is the hope of his calling, what [are] the riches of the glory of his inheritance in the saints, and what [is] the exceeding greatness of his power towards us who believe . . . his mighty power, which he has wrought in Christ in raising him from the dead, and setting him at his right hand in heaven. . . . And him he gave as head over all the Church, which indeed is his body, the completion of him who fills all with all" (Eph 1:18–20, 22–23).

But the community cannot stand passively by and simply allow itself to be overwhelmed by the mysteries of Christ, to be made a partaker of the divine nature itself, to be unconditionally gifted with all the riches of God—"for the Spirit searches all things, even the deep things of God, . . . the things that are of the Spirit of God. . . . But we have the mind of Christ" (1 Cor 2:10, 14, 16). *One who is merely passive does not really receive*: To possess, one must accept; and the more spiritual the gift, the more gratefully and happily it should be accepted. *Thus the reception of grace becomes automatically an action*—an action that accepts, takes hold of, understands, executes and transmits. For how can one let divine love simply happen to him? How can he receive it without loving in return? The very acceptance of grace demands such a return, and the response to God becomes a spontaneous sharing of what one has received. Indeed, so identified are engracement and mission that this is the touchstone by which one knows that grace has truly been received: ". . . Everyone that loves is born of God, and knows God. He who does not love does not know God; for God is love. . . . In this is the love, not that we have loved God, but that he has first loved us, and sent his Son as a propitiation for our sins. Beloved, if God has so loved us, we also ought to love one another" (1 Jn 4:7–8, 10–11). The life of faith—the life that is designated, in a broader sense, as mission and apostolate—is not a second reality beside the first reality, which is man's engraced state; the challenge of the Christian life is not something derived secondarily from the fact of Christian existence. This is the

Christian paradox: that grace, which of its very nature is bestowed absolutely, includes in itself the absolute challenge to lead a life according to grace, and that God has the mysterious power ultimately to break even man's resistance to grace. God's grace has an "abundance" (cf. Rom 5:15–21) that can be expressed only in the paradoxical formula: ". . . If we disown him, he also will disown us; if we are faithless, he remains faithful, for he cannot disown himself" (2 Tim 2:12–13).

Grace, then, is a challenge to every Christian. And just as grace knows no upper limit, so its challenge knows no upper limit. The mysteries of the priestly and religious states do not form a higher, esoteric level above the modest ground level of "ordinary Christian life". Their purpose is rather to increase and reveal in all Christians "the depth of the riches of the wisdom and of the knowledge of God" (Rom 11:33). *The sacraments* do not have their "truth" outside the Christianity that contains them: What they signify is to be expressed in the life of all Christians. If Christ offers himself for us in the Mass, his sacrifice requires and presumes that "we likewise ought to lay down our life for the brethren" (1 Jn 3:16); that we, too, ought to present our bodies "as a sacrifice, living, holy, pleasing to God" (Rom 12:1) and "offer up a sacrifice of praise always to God" (Heb 13:15). And if Christ remains sacramentally present among us, it is for the sake of the faithful, that they may realize his presence even outside the sacraments: For where two or three are gathered in his name, he is in their midst (Mt 18:20). If there is an official priesthood whose duty it is to administer the grace of God, it exists only that the whole ecclesial community with all the laity may be "a chosen race, *a royal priesthood*" (1 Pet 2:9). If, through the ministry of his priests, the Lord gives himself to all in the Eucharist, it is that "we though many [may be] one body, all of us who partake of the one bread" (1 Cor 11:17), "all [who are] baptized into one body, whether Jews or Gentiles, whether slave or free" (1 Cor 12:13), and may, in our turn, live, care and die for one another. In baptism, we have all truly died to sin and selfishness (cf. Rom

6:2), but this presumes also that we have presented our members to God "as weapons of justice" (Rom 6:13). ". . . Do you not know . . . that you are not your own?" (1 Cor 6:19). ". . . Since one died for all, therefore all died . . . Christ died for all, in order that they who are alive may live no longer for themselves . . ." (2 Cor 5:14–15). "For none of us lives to himself, and none dies to himself; for if we live, we live to the Lord, and if we die, we die to the Lord" (Rom 14:7–8). *To be baptized*, then, means totally to renounce a life lived according to one's own wishes, for "it is no longer I that live, but Christ lives in me" (Gal 2:20). But because "Christ did not please himself, . . . we . . . ought . . . not to please ourselves" (Rom 15:3, 1). The rule that governs what we do and what we do not do will no longer be what is permitted the individual as a private person, what he can allow himself to do on the basis of his own conscience, but only what is most beneficial for the community and can under no circumstances give scandal to its weaker members. "Now we, the strong, ought to bear the infirmities of the weak, and not to please ourselves. . . . Let us, then, follow after the things that make for peace and . . . for mutual edification" (Rom 15:1; 14:19). Let us ". . . bear one another's burden . . ." (Gal 6:2). If, by this means, baptism preserves its immediate truth in the life of the Christian, this is equally true of the sacrament of *confession*. For if the apostles received the power of binding and loosing, that is, of forgiving sins in the name and with the divine authority of Christ, this ministry must, nevertheless, be exercised in the context of the whole Church. This means not only that we must all forgive one another "as also God in Christ has generously forgiven" us (Eph 4:32; cf. ". . . Even as the Lord has forgiven you, so also do you forgive", Col 3:13), but even more expressly that we must open our hearts and minds to one another: ". . . To God we are manifest. And I hope also that in your consciences we are manifest" (2 Cor 5:11). "Confess, therefore, your sins to one another, that you may be saved" (James 5:16)—and this even to the extent of eliciting from a brother the acknowledgment of his sin: "If he listen to thee, thou hast won thy brother" (Mt 18:15). ". . . He who causes a sinner to be brought back from his misguided way, will save his soul from death, and will cover a multitude of sins" (James 5:20). Moreover, the priest's obligation by reason of his office *to admonish* and advise is transferred undiminished also to the laity: "Wherefore, comfort one another and edify one another" (1 Th 5:11); ". . . Do not regard [one who does not obey] as an enemy, but admonish him as a brother" (2 Th 3:15). Finally, the model of Christ is translated so directly into the life of the lay community that the central mystery of his *sacrificial offering* of himself to the Church becomes for the laity a true sacrament, the lay sacrament of matrimony, which the spouses confer on one another in the presence of the priest as representative of the Church (cf. Eph 5:21–33).

Just as the laity receive the sacramental Word of God in order that it may be transformed directly into the truth of their lives and may continue to work independently in them, so also they receive the official preaching of the Gospel *in the homily*, not passively, but always actively, that their lives may proclaim its message. Because the community has "received . . . the word of God . . . not as the word of men, but, as it truly is, the word of God", it therefore "works" in them even to the living out of this word in persecution and martyrdom (1 Th 2:13–14). Indeed, every word of Christ is to be "good for supplying what fits the current necessity, that it may give grace to the hearers" (Eph 4:29). The official homily is the vehicle by which the word of God remains, dwells and operates in the midst of the lay community: "Let the word of Christ dwell in you abundantly: in all wisdom teach and admonish one another . . ." (Col 3:16). The Church expects the mature lay person to be able to use "the sword of the spirit, that is, the word of God" (Eph 6:17) without recourse to the priest. He must know that the transmission of the faith cannot be entrusted to chance, but must proceed constantly from the grace of faith, "as shown in that which is written—*I believed and so I spoke*—we also believed, wherefore we also speak" (2 Cor 4:13). Hence the apostle's words apply to every

Christian: ". . . Woe to me if I do not preach the Gospel!" (1 Cor 9:16). He expects *the congregation* to transmit the word that has been implanted in it; *to become* not only in its clergy, but also in the totality of its laity, *a messenger* of the Gospel. ". . . You became a pattern to all the believers in Macedonia and Achaia. For from you the word of the Lord has been spread abroad, not only in Macedonia and Achaia, but in every place your faith in God has gone forth . . ." (1 Th 1:7–8). It is immaterial whether the Gospel is preached by word or by example, for the two are inseparable; the testimony to Jesus is always a testimony of both word and works (cf. Jn 10:38; 5:36). So true is this that the testimony of the word has no value without works, while the testimony of one's life can speak louder than the testimony of words: "In like manner also let wives be subject to their husbands; so that even if any do not believe the word, they may without word be won through the behavior of their wives, observing reverently your chaste behavior" (1 Pet 3:1–2).

As the lay person must not only allow the priestly ministries— the administration of the sacraments and the word—to become fruitful in him, but must also translate them into the truth of his own state if they are to achieve their purpose in him, so he must translate *the example and ways of the state of the counsels into his life*. It has frequently been noted that all the light that emanates from the state of election is to such an extent oriented away from that state and to the illumination of the entire Church that the lay state itself becomes in the process "the salt of the earth", "the light of the world", "a city set upon a mountain", "a lamp . . . upon the lampstand": "Even so let your light shine before men" (Mt 5:13–16). Paul never wearies of offering his own exemplary life as a "model" for the whole Church: ". . . Be imitators of me" (Phil 3:17); "Therefore, I beg you, be imitators of me" (1 Cor 4:16); "Be imitators of me as I am of Christ" (1 Cor 11:1). "For you yourselves know how you ought to imitate us" (2 Th 3:7). ". . . You became imitators of us and of the Lord" (1 Th 1:6). "But for this reason I obtained mercy, that in me first Christ Jesus might show forth all patience, as an example to those who shall believe in him for the attainment of life everlasting" (1 Tim 1:16). "Hold to the form of sound teaching which thou hast heard from me, in the faith and love which are in Christ Jesus" (2 Tim 1:13). His entire existence is summarized in the words: "But thou hast closely followed my doctrine, my conduct, my purpose, my faith, my long-suffering, my love, my patience, my persecutions, my afflictions" (2 Tim 3:10–11). All that happens to the apostle is nourishment for the community; all that is in him is consumed in order to build up and strengthen the community. He requires the same dedication from them—that they, too, become "a pattern to the flock" (1 Pet 5:3). Paul does not select certain elements of his life and hold them up for imitation. It is not permitted him to do so, for even the sufferings he endures for the community belong to the community and are ultimately the most precious example he can offer for its imitation. Even the special fate that destines those in the state of election to become sacrificial victims is offered to the laity for its imitation. Paul addresses himself first to those who preside over the community: "In all things I have shown you that by so toiling you ought to help the weak and remember the word of the Lord Jesus, that he himself said: 'It is more blessed to give than to receive' " (Acts 20:35). ". . . Enter into my sufferings for the Gospel through the power of God" (2 Tim 1:8); "conduct thyself in work as a good soldier of Christ" (2 Tim 2:3). Then he speaks to the whole community: ". . . All who want to live piously in Christ Jesus will suffer persecution" (2 Tim 3:12). "In this [that is, in persecutions and tribulations] there is a proof of the just judgment of God counting you worthy of the kingdom of God, for which also you suffer" (2 Th 1:5), "for you yourselves know that we are appointed thereto" (1 Th 3:3). "For you have been given the favor on Christ's behalf—not only to believe in him but also to suffer for him" (Phil 1:29). "But if, when you do right and suffer, you take it patiently, this is acceptable with God. Unto this, indeed, you have been called, because Christ also has suffered for you, leaving you an example that you may follow in his steps" (1 Pet 2:20–21).

Thus the community not only shares passively in the fruits of the sufferings of those called to the state of the counsels; it is also allowed to share actively in their sacrificial calling. "I have you in my heart, all of you, alike in my chains and in the defense and confirmation of the Gospels . . ." (Phil 1:7). The two states are united in their efforts—"For you . . . [are] engaged in the same struggle in which you have seen me . . ." (Phil 1:29–30), "striving together for the faith of the Gospel" (Phil 1:27)—which Paul labels comprehensively "our wrestling" (Eph 6:12). Nevertheless, we are all "sanctified . . . and called to be saints" (1 Cor 1:2). The Gospel engages in no casuistry about the extent to which the laity must strive for perfection or to which they may consider themselves dispensed therefrom. Its only concern is with perfection itself: the perfection of what the Christian *is* by reason of his participation in God by grace, and the perfection of what he *ought* to be by reason of that same grace. All Catholics are "God's chosen ones, holy and beloved" (Col 3:12), and the apostle wrestles in prayer for them that they "may remain perfect and completely in accord with all the will of God" (Col 4:12). This perfection is a genuine perfection ("Let us then, as many as are perfect, be of this mind", Phil 3:15), even though it is still a perfection to be acquired, a pilgrim perfection, open to God ("Not that I have already obtained this, or already have been made perfect", Phil 3:12). ". . . Blameless and guileless, children of God without blemish" (Phil 2:15), Christians pursue the way that is an unending "way of perfection", an abounding "more and more" in perfection (Phil 1:9), a striving "after the greater gifts" (1 Cor 12:31). And yet "he who keeps his [Christ's] word, in him the love of God is truly perfected" (1 Jn 2:5).

The result is a reciprocally formative action between the state of election and the lay state: "Become like me, because I also have become like you, brethren, I beseech you" (Gal 4:12). Each state of life is the boast and glory of the other: ". . . I hope you will always understand . . . that we are your boast, as you will also be ours" (2 Cor 1:13–14). The reciprocity is perfected by interceding for one another in prayer. Just as the apostle in his prayer "unceasingly" makes mention of the community (Rom 1:9–10) that is in his heart "to die together and to live together" (2 Cor 7:3), so he confides to the community all his apostolic cares and relies on their prayers to make his mission fruitful: ". . . Pray for us also, that God may give us an opportunity for the word, to announce the mystery of Christ" (Col 4:3). God "delivered us, and will deliver us, from such great perils; and in him we have hope to be delivered once again, through the help of your prayers" (2 Cor 1:10–11). And just as the apostle's prayer becomes more and more universal since his "daily pressing anxiety" is for "the care of all the churches" (2 Cor 11:28), so will the prayer of the churches become correspondingly a universal, Catholic prayer for the whole world: "supplications, prayers, intercessions and thanksgivings . . . for all men; for kings, and for all in high positions" (1 Tim 2:1). Thus the specific universality that is proper to the state of the counsels by reason of the promised hundredfold meets with the specific universality of the Church as a whole, including all the laity, in order that it may grow thereby out of its particularity and into the all-embracing unity of Christ. All the states of life must work together to represent this unity: "one body and one Spirit, even as you were called in one hope of your calling; one Lord, one faith, one baptism, one God and Father of all" (Eph 4:4–6). The "apostles, . . . prophets, . . . evangelists, . . . pastors and teachers" (Eph 4:11), all, then, who are invested with a qualitatively higher ministry, exist "in order to perfect the saints for [their own] work of ministry, for building up the body of Christ, until we all attain to the unity of faith and of the deep knowledge of the Son of God, to perfect manhood, to the mature measure of the fullness of Christ" (Eph 4:12–13).

In this relationship of the states of life to and in one another is perfected to the fullest extent the "general priesthood" of the

Church as a whole, in which the Church, as body and Bride of its crucified head, is drawn into the one unending sacrifice of praise and love to God the Father (cf. St. Augustine, *De civ Dei* X, 6–7). The special functional priesthood of the clerical state and the special existential priesthood of the state of the counsels are henceforth no longer distinguishable from the comprehensive priesthood of all Christians (just as the special priesthood of those in the states of election in no way separates or dispenses them from participation in the general priesthood). If the official priesthood, which represents the head for the body within the unity of the Church, emphasizes the differences between the special and the general priesthood, the state of the counsels is properly associated with the lay state (cf. the references to Dionysius on pp. 302–304 above). By its sacrificial life, it supplies in full measure what is wanting to the sacrifices offered by the general priesthood of the laity.

4. THE STATES OF LIFE AND THE SECULAR ORDERS

Until now, we have been considering the states of life primarily in their reciprocal relationship within the Church of Christ. Yet the Church does not exist for itself alone, but for the ultimate redemption of the world. Its task is to proclaim, embody and establish as effectively as possible among the nations the majesty of God as revealed in Jesus Christ. But it may not identify itself with this majesty that has come, yet is always coming. As an institution, it exists to serve it. As those who have died and are risen again in Christ, the members of the Church are fundamentally incorporated into it, even when, as sinners and those as yet imperfect, they are still *in via* toward it. As the body and Bride of Christ, the Church shares the mind of its head; it seeks not itself, but the perfecting of all things through Christ in God: ". . . God our Savior . . . wishes all men to be saved and to come to the knowledge of the truth. For there is *one* God and *one* mediator between God and man, himself man, Christ Jesus, who gave

himself a ransom for all . . ." (1 Tim 2:3–6). Jesus himself knew
that he had "power over all flesh" (Jn 17:2) in order that, when
he was "lifted up from the earth", he might "draw all things" to
himself (Jn 12:32). By reason of this orientation of the Church to
the redemption of the world, there arises, even for the states of
life within the Church, a new question: How are they called to
share, each in its own way, in the Church's mission to the world?

It is clear in any case that the mission to the world involves the
Church as a whole. It would be erroneous to assume that only
the members of the Church have the obligation of working in the
world, bypassing the Church and functioning as individuals, or
that this task falls exclusively (or nearly so) to a particular state
—for example, to the lay state. At most, it can only be that,
within the mission of the whole Church, certain dispositions and
functions fall to the individual states. The Church as a whole is a
missionary Church because the head, whose body it is, is totally
the *missio* of the Father and because the mission of the "second
Adam" (cf. 1 Cor 15:45) involves, not a chosen few of the
descendants of the first Adam, but rather Adam himself and all
his race: "For as in Adam all die, so in Christ all will be made to
live" (1 Cor 15:22).

Jesus' earthly mission, therefore, the gathering of the lost sheep
of the House of Israel, could be but a temporary one. Only
through his death for all and his Resurrection for all would it
acquire a magnitude compatible with the universal will of God
for the reconciliation of the world (2 Cor 5:19), and only through
the mission of the apostles to the whole world would it be
explicitly extended to all times and all nations (cf. Mt 28:18–20).
In accordance with its obligation to care for "all nations" in their
abandonment and need as the Good Shepherd of the parable (who
is the incarnate image of the Divine Shepherd) cares for the lost
sheep (cf. Lk 15:4–7) and lays down his life for his sheep (Jn
10:11), so the Church must dedicate itself also to the needs of
those sheep who, though outside its fold, nevertheless belong to
the "Good Shepherd" (Jn 10:16). In other words, there will take

place between the realm of the Church and that of the world outside the Church not only an inevitable secular communication and exchange, but also a communication and exchange that have their roots deep within the ordinances of salvation history: an osmosis that operates between the two realms—from the world to the Church and from the Church to the world. This is all the more true because, in a certain inchoative yet real sense, the redemptive work of him who was crucified and rose again is always present in the world outside the Church, whether the world knows it or not, whether it is open to it or not. Nowhere does the Church meet a purely natural world, but always and everywhere one that is polarized for or against God's work of redemption.

The osmosis between the Church and the world takes place in two opposing movements that are, nonetheless, the two sides of a single process: in *systole* and *diastole*. One side is the progressive, transforming assimilation of the world into the realm of the Church; the other is the constantly recurring self-transcendence by which the Church goes to meet the world outside it. This second movement is so essential to the Church as a missionary Church that it may never be completely replaced by the first. What is assimilated from the world into the Church must, as Church, pass immediately into the self-transcendent mission of the inner realm to the outer one.

On the other hand, the Church cannot be defined in theory or lived in practice in terms of its self-transcendence alone; if it were only that, there would be no subject to take the transcending step. More concretely, if the Church were to concern itself only with the needs and necessities of the world outside, it would have nothing to bring to this world—at least, nothing that the world could not acquire, and perhaps better acquire, for itself by its own means. The Church must be truly itself in the first movement and must become even more itself in its assimilation of the world if, in the second movement, it is to proclaim and give itself as it truly is to that world outside. This does not mean that the two movements cannot occur alternately in time; for, in fact, the Church will never discover its true nature without this missionary movement. If the Lord calls his apostles "the light of the world" (Mt 5:14) and if Paul extends this image to the whole Christian community (Phil 2:15), it is nonetheless true that there can be no light unless there is a luminary, for a light without a luminary does not exist even though the luminary always sheds its light away from itself.

This brings us to a most important premise for what remains to be said: The substantive difference that exists between the Church and the world is the prerequisite for and the sine qua non of the permeation of the world by the Church, or, to express it more simply, the broader the crown of the tree, the deeper must be its roots.[73] In practice, this means that the more radical the *systole* was and is, the more efficacious will be the *diastole*. But *systole* does not mean assimilation into the Church of the world as it exists outside the Church, but rather *the Christian transformation of the world* in accordance with the definitive concept that not only is *in* Jesus Christ, but *is* Jesus Christ. This premise must light the way for the whole Church and for each of the states of life within the Church. For, though each state must retain its own particular character, it will already be apparent not only that the Church as a whole must constantly deepen its own spirituality, but also that the individual states of life must do so as well.

This renewal will take on a different aspect according to whether we are referring to the first movement (*systole*), in which the Church becomes aware of its own nature and comes to understand its mission to be the light of the world, or the second movement (*diastole*), in which it actually sends out its rays into the world that is "other" to it. We should note that under the first aspect the crucial active function falls to the religious and priestly states, with the lay state in the secondary role, while under the

[73] Olegario González de Cardenal, *Elogio de la Encina*, 2nd ed. (Salamanca: Sígueme, 1973).

second aspect the primary function is shared by the religious state (which is in itself a nonclerical state) and the lay state, with the priestly state in the secondary role.

1. Under the *first aspect*, the formation of the Church as the luminary of the world, the two complementary *states of election are primarily engaged*. Though they are in the world, they are called out of the world to take their stand by Christ and to represent him who is the alpha and omega of the world as a whole. They take their stand by Jesus Christ in order to complete with him his movement from the Father to the world. For this purpose, they have freed themselves from the "spirit of the world" that they may be totally at the disposal of God's mission to the world in his Son. All the great Christian institutions in the world, in whatever way they have come into being, have been founded by persons who had first dedicated themselves wholly to the cause of Christ. This is true not only of the pioneering cultural activities of the monks in the transition from antiquity to the Middle Ages; it is a basic law even today. The more purely the transcendence, the other-worldliness, of the nature and message of Christ shines forth in the life of the messenger, the more deeply this nature and message will penetrate into the structures of the natural world.

In much the same way as the religious reflects upon his mission in the solitude of the novitiate that he may be able later to carry it out more effectively, so the *concept of separation* from the world was prominent *in the early days of Christianity*. Despite the great missionary command at the end of the Gospel, the New Testament also sounds the alarm against false involvement with the world: "Do not bear the yoke with unbelievers. . . . Come out from among them" (2 Cor 6:14, 17). "Go out from [Babylon], my people, that you may not share in her sins, and that you may not receive of her plagues" (Rev 18:4). ". . . Be not conformed to this world" (Rom 12:2). Before the Church plunged into the action of its apostolate, it allowed itself a long interval during which, like Paul (Gal 1:17) and all great apostles since his time, it let itself be filled contemplatively with the mystery of God.

Before beginning its task of leavening the secular state, it took time to become first a community of saints. Christian culture and art cannot exist until there have been Christian martyrs, virgins, confessors and anchorites; Christian churches cannot be raised until the spirit of the catacombs can be built into their foundations; Christian politics cannot exist until great bishops have denounced every tendency to compromise with the secular powers and have issued the demand for an uninterrupted recognition of the Church. Christian action cannot exist until the original mission has been understood as the "yes" of contemplation and as a sharing in the Passion of Jesus Christ.

If we inquire into the source of the enriching springs of Christian culture that appeared in antiquity and the Middle Ages and continue to appear even today, we are led back again and again *to the sphere of the states of election*, and above all to the state of the counsels. Only when Christians no longer came to drink from these springs, but began to plunge immediately into secular activities, did they draw upon their capital and consume it—as witness the rapidity with which the strength of the "Catholic Action" movement was exhausted. This does not mean that Christians should be engaged today, as they were in the Middle Ages, in the building of cathedrals in the hearts of secular cities or the writing of "Summas" for modern scholarly consumption— the earliest stages of a sacral culture can never be regained; there is question, rather, of an action that has its source in the region of mountains and springs to which the states of election are called, but whose mission is to the region of secularized plains and great rivers.

This "action" must be first and foremost a deepening of the substantive nature of the Church itself if the Church is to be— ever, or after periods of sterility—an effective force for the creating of culture. The existence or nonexistence of a Christian culture is not an unambiguous measure of the Church's inner vitality in any given age. The "holy heart of the nations" may need to retreat at times into its own interior, into the idea of the world as it is found in Christ Jesus, in order to prepare itself there in contemplation and passion (as opposed to action) for an eventual renewal of its cultural activity. The medieval formula *ex plenitudine contemplationis activus* [one whose action proceeds from the fullness of contemplation] is certainly an early one, but the explanation that Thomas Aquinas gives (in summarizing the teaching of Gregory and of ancient monasticism) is still valid: ". . . The contemplative life is prior to the active life because its emphasis is on things that are antecedent and better; hence it moves and directs the active life" (ST 2a 2ae 182, 4 responsio). Only because the Christian teacher "communicates what he has contemplated" is it permitted him to interrupt the act of contemplation for external action. The German mystics expressed this with deep insight. Only because the Christian teacher, in turning to his fellow men, cooperates in accomplishing what he sees God doing in Christ, only because he is therefore attentive in action to what God is doing, will his activity be a further source of his contemplation. The later Jesuit formula *in actione contemplativus* [one who remains a contemplative even in action] does not supplant the Thomistic one, but simply emphasizes the fact that contemplation of Jesus' mission becomes perfect *as* contemplation only for one who shares in the accomplishment of that mission. The Thomistic formula remains as background, as warning, that a "yet more" of action does not guarantee, but rather imperils, a "yet more" of contemplation.

It is time now to ask what is meant by action in a Christian sense. Above all, it does not mean that the Church's activity must always be directed away from itself and into the world even before the Church has established its credibility; it means rather that the deepest effects of the act of self-dedication cannot be measured in secular terms. This meaning is not directly contained in Thomas' formula. From a Christian point of view, the greatest action is Mary's "yes" to the Incarnation of the Word. And the greatest action of this incarnate Word is the Passion by which he destroyed the world's dominion. This analogy of Christian action as that which is interiorly immeasurable and exteriorly measurable embraces all forms of Christian life, especially that of the evangelical state, which, as "the contemplative life", acts for the most part invisibly, while the "mixed contemplative-active life" (there is no such thing as a purely active Christian life!) has effects in the world that are to some extent determinable.

It is true of both forms, however—and this refers especially to the priestly apostolate—that Christian life can be effective in the world only if it has previously contributed to the interior building up and growth of the Church itself. To build up the Christian community as a fellowship of those who love one another in the spirit of Christ is to establish that ecclesial sun that alone can make Christ's message credible to the world. ". . . That they may be perfected in unity, and that the world may know that thou hast sent me, and that thou hast loved them even as thou hast loved me" (Jn 17:23). "By this will all men know that you are my disciples, if you have love for one another" (Jn 13:35). The light of *this* love is a definitive, eschatological love that surpasses all secular activity. Therefore the "eschatological reservation" of the Church regarding every state achieved by secular culture has a critical function, not only on the basis of the Church's better knowledge and more definitive message, but always also on the basis of its brighter illumination of the love that is lived. Otherwise, this reservation could be viewed as arrogance and would vanish without a trace.

All Christian action in the world is to be understood here as an action of the Church. This understanding is central to every work of the evangelical state, for the whole concept of "taking one's stand in the place that is Christ's" is none other than a "putting on of Christ". It explains all that has been thought and realized about religious communities as "models of the Church" (Benedictine monasteries, for example), or as the "heart of vital congregations" (cf. Basil's original conception), or as prayerful intercessors for the Church (cf. Teresa's ideal for Carmelite monasteries). And it is true in an equally central way of every action of the priestly state as well, for the priest, by reason of his participation in the threefold office of Christ, has to work first and foremost for the interior edification of his congregation. In addition to his concern for the congregation or local church confided to his care, he is indubitably also obliged to evangelize the nonbelievers in the world around him; not, however, by leaving his congregation or local church in order to bring his missionary endeavors to others, but by drawing those outside the Church into the congregation for which he has the powers of consecration and absolution. He is the shepherd of the already existing flock entrusted to him by Christ. His primary obligation is, therefore, to preach the Gospel in the place where his congregation is located; any mission to those outside this place is predominantly the task of religious priests and of other men and women in the evangelical state together with lay persons in the world.

In the section on "The State of Lay Persons in the World", we have already spoken to some extent about the *contribution of such lay persons* to the building up of a luminous and apostolic Church. Their task is to demonstrate visibly and practically in the body of the Church how the spiritual and material goods of a fallen world order can be placed at the service of a selfless Christian love. Paul speaks at length of *the liberation of wealth from its antithetical relationship to Christ* (cf. Mt 6:24) by making mammon a visible sign of generous love. He recalls how the churches of Macedonia gave "according to their means, . . . yes, beyond their means, . . . earnestly begging of us the *favor* of sharing in the ministry that is in behalf of the saints" (2 Cor 8:3–4); understanding their service (διακονία) as a kind of "sacrifice", first to God and then to the Church (2 Cor 9:13; cf. Eph 4:12); and performing it not grudgingly, but in "overflowing joy" (2 Cor 8:12). Wealth mediates between love and love: ". . . For the administration of this service not only supplies the wants of the saints, but also overflows in much gratitude to the Lord. The evidence furnished by this service makes them glorify God for your obedient profession of Christ's Gospel and for the sincere generosity of your contributions to them and to all; while they themselves, in their prayers for you, yearn for you, because of the excellent grace God has given you" (2 Cor 9:12–14). Very early in the history of the Church, the apostles consecrated lay persons for the performance of those services that express and quicken love (cf. Acts 6:1–7). From a "mammon" that has been enlisted in the service of love even the apostle can live and, with him, all those who render spiritual service to the churches in the religious or priestly state and who, in a "partnership . . . of giving and receiving" (Phil 4:15) with the laity, are grateful for what they receive, but even more grateful for the concern that prompts it (cf. Phil 4:10).

The second contribution of the laity is the *clarification of the relationship of eros and sex to Christian caritas*. Even though the perfect integration of the sexual order into the paradisal synthesis is no longer possible, there nevertheless is such a thing as a "marriage . . . held in honor by all", a "marriage bed" that is "undefiled" (Heb 13:4). Those who forbid marriage are "deceitful spirits" who proclaim "doctrines of devils" (1 Tim 4:1, 3). The prototype of the Church is the Word that became incarnate, the virgin who became a mother. There can be nothing impure, then, in the ordering of married love to the goal of procreation. In the Old Testament, the Song of Songs described the love between Yahweh and Israel in terms of the potency of eros. Now that the Word of God has himself become flesh with power over all flesh, even, therefore, over the potency of the flesh, and has given his flesh as nourishment for the life of the world, the grace of redemption cannot be unattainable for this flesh even in its fallen and mortal state. But this is true only if the marital union by which man and woman are made to be one flesh becomes not only a sign of the ultimate and indissoluble union of the Lord who gave himself on the Cross with the Church that is his Bride, but also, by reason of its own indissolubility, a sacrament of divine and ecclesial love. A Christian marriage lived in holiness causes the Church to shine forth for the whole world.

The third contribution of the laity is the proof they offer that the Christian can incorporate himself wholly into the Church's all-embracing *obedience* to the Lord, not just by surrendering his freedom of choice, but also *in the lasting autonomy* of retaining his right to choose. The non-Christian and even the non-Catholic world fails, for the most part, to recognize—and even takes scandal at or despises—the luminous sign of the lay person's free obedience to the Church, although it often envies it in secret, especially when it becomes obvious that one who obeys in this manner can move freely within his obedience and even actually achieves thereby his most complete freedom. Yet, even while it is permitted him to determine his way anew day by day, he lives, nevertheless, under the law of the "once for all" of Christ (Heb 7:27; 9:12; and elsewhere) by which he was sealed at his baptism. "Year after year" (Heb 9:25–28), the lay person must offer his freedom again in sacrifice, being always as unable to make the final renunciation of it that the religious makes as he is to make the final renunciation of marriage or possessions.

These contributions of a laity that has been taken out of the secular order and consecrated to the Church are difficult to accomplish and are even harder to persevere in—hence the many warnings associated with them. Prominent among such warnings are Jesus' almost threatening words against those who are rich (Mk 10:23–27) and the Old Testament-like condemnations of them in the Epistle of James (5:1–4); the counsels regarding the proper use of marriage that Paul directs particularly to Christians (1 Cor 7:1–16); and, finally, the admonitions against the misuse of Christian freedom in his two-fronted attack on Jewish legalism and pagan excesses: On the one hand: ". . . Christ has made us free. Stand fast, and do not be caught again under the yoke of slavery" (Gal 4:31–5:1); on the other hand: "For you have been called to liberty, brethren; only do not use liberty as an occasion for sensuality, but by charity serve one another" (Gal 5:13). In all three areas (poverty, chastity, obedience), the lay person must be admonished to overcome his "dividedness" by transcending the fallen secular order that he may find its true idea in Christ: "Draw near to God, and he will draw near to you, . . . you double-minded" (James 4:8).

Thus far we have been speaking of the building up of a Church that will then be prepared to act as the sun of the world, or, more properly, as the sacrament of the redemption of the world. The movement by which the Church draws the world to itself in order to transform it is essentially a universal one, for the Church, because it belongs to Christ and to God, has the power of transforming all things: "For *all things* are yours, . . . and you are Christ's, and Christ is God's" (1 Cor 3:22–23).

2. But this power of assimilation, which makes it possible for the fire of the Church to feed on the flammable material of the world, is only one side of the Church's missionary endeavor; the other side is the action by which the Church *goes out* from itself *into the world orders* to which it has been sent.

It would be one-sided to claim that this permeation of the world is exclusively, or even primarily, the task of the laity in the world. There is, in fact, another aspect to be considered—one that derives from the nature of the mission itself: For all great and qualitatively higher missions in the Church are directly ordered to the *state of the counsels*, which was founded on Christ's state of life that it might share the breadth of his mission to the whole world. It is above all the state of the counsels that is the salt of the earth, the light of the world, the city built on a mountain and thus visible far and wide as a beacon for all. Yet, as we saw in the first point, the Church's mission finds a variety of expressions within the state of the counsels. Nor should we fail to mention the interior fruitfulness that is indispensable to every great mission— a fruitfulness that is just as effective whether it is invisible like the prayers and sacrifices of a Carmelite or visible like the apostolate of a Francis Xavier. For it is a basic law that the "yet more" of the renunciation and of the taking of one's stand at the side of Christ is the sole guarantee of the "yet more" of the effectiveness of every mission, just as the backward pull of the bowstring determines how far the arrow will fly. No fashionable adaptation of the Church to the world on the pretext of thus drawing closer to the world can abrogate this basic law. Any attempt to do so is usually a sign that one is "ashamed of the Gospel" (Rom 1:16), afraid of the scandal of Christianity, for the Christian, in his mission for and with Christ, can become "the fragrance of Christ" and for "those who are saved . . . an odor that leads to life" only if he is not afraid to become for "those who are lost . . . an odor that leads to death" (2 Cor 2:15–16).

Only when this has been said is it possible to speak of *cooperation between the state of the counsels and that of the laity in the world* and *subsequently* of cooperation between the priestly state and that of the laity in the world. (The two pairs will approximate each other more closely to the degree in which the priests themselves are filled with the spirit of the evangelical state.) Only when this has been said is it possible to speak of the impulses that emanate from the state of the counsels or from the state of election as a whole and, in the spirit of the Gospel, demand decisive changes in the world, the implementation of which must be left to the laity because the states themselves have neither the power nor the competence therefor. Unjust social structures and social conditions that cry to heaven are castigated by bishops, religious and priests who have the responsibility of forming the consciences of the laity, but religious and priests must often be warned to give credence only to thorough sociological analyses that can serve as bases for practical changes— and they would do well to leave even these to trained experts, especially where it concerns a judgment as to the most specifically Christian means of carrying out or at least approximating the demands of the Gospel. The diagnoses of dilettantes are insufficient for the purpose; it requires an insight into world economic relations that only an expert can have.

Just as it would have been dilettantism in the Middle Ages for contemplative monks to turn their hands to compass and plumblines when their true mission was to lend inspiration to the master builders of the cathedrals, so it would be dilettantism today for religious and priests to believe themselves capable of solving concrete economic and sociological questions instead of expending their efforts to open the eyes and hearts of capable lay persons and encouraging them to lay the foundations of a Christian social order. Such dilettantism could lead only to a repetition of those medieval fiascoes that occurred when popes and religious called men to secular crusades on the basis of what, today, can be regarded only as mistaken zeal. Obviously the situation is not completely comparable. In the Middle Ages, Christianity as a whole, whether the state of election or the lay state, acknowledged a sacrally symbolic world view; the secularized world of today is more apt to accept a division of spheres and competences. Whereas the spiritual leaders of that time believed they should also engage in secular activities, and the secular leaders believed they should also engage in spiritual ones, many painful experiences since the beginning of modern times have convinced the Church that genuine unity is to be found only in a genuine separation of the competences of the various states of life. In retrospect it is clear that the spiritual authority suffered no loss of respect by renouncing secular power—indeed, the contrary is true; nor did the Christian permeation of the world lose impetus when the Church ceased to brandish the sword of the crusaders. Today, the predominant attitude of the states of election toward the state of the laity in the world is one of confidence—a confidence that presents evangelical truth without insisting on a single interpretation and in the full awareness that there is no timeless formula for applying this truth to the present world situation. The laity, for their part, will demand no ready-made solutions from the "Church" unless they are prepared to forfeit the prerogative of their Christian freedom and maturity. Were they to make such a demand, they would force the "Church" to become a casuistical church—to lay the law as "tutor" upon a laity that would be once more "under guardians and stewards" (Gal 3:24; 4:2). The two goals must be realized together; the coming of age of a competent laity and their acceptance of the full spirit of the Church. Wherever, in genuine contemplation and under the leadership of the states of election, they adapt themselves to the spirit of the Church and are thus able to transfer the fruits of their contemplation to their work, clerical tutelage automatically becomes superfluous. The more the laity are imbued with the spirit of the states of election, the more they will free themselves from their outward dependence on these states. If they were thus to become truly aware of their full Christian responsibility, it might conceivably be no longer necessary for the official Church to issue such detailed statements about the social order, the labor question, marriage and education. Naturally, the official Church has the right to issue statements about any important question, but the fact that, in modern times, it has had to issue such concrete ones is a clear indication that the laity have not been sufficiently aware of their inherent competences and that the Holy See has had, therefore, to surround itself with a staff of clerical sociologists and other experts in order to bring the spiritual word to regions where only the lay person in the world has the necessary knowledge and experience to make valid decisions.

And yet, if we recall what was said at the beginning of this second point, the demand for such a division must not be interpreted to mean that the side the Church turns to the world is the special preserve of the laity, while the states of election are limited to presenting only the side that transcends the world. Every Christian grace is at the same time a mission to the world. But if, as we have said, the great and qualitatively higher missions require that there be a state of the counsels so that the missionary can at all times be free and ready for his only task, this does not mean that *the whole spectrum* of the Church's missionary endeavors, even to a—competent!—dominion over the secular orders, must be undertaken by the state of the counsels alone. Members of *secular institutes* (*instituta saecularia*) strive for a lasting realization of this synthesis, for which an analogous attempt in the priestly state (the experiment of the worker priests) can offer at best only a "sign", a *caveat*—for *while* the priest is working in the factory, he cannot at the same time be exercising his normal priestly functions. In the way of life adopted by the secular institutes, on the contrary, there is no compromise between "Church" and "world" or between "evangelical state" and "lay state"; there is only an attempt to extend the spectrum of mission to its fullest span. That this can be done without compromise has been demonstrated for both the secular institutes and the worker priests by Madeleine Delbrêl, who is without doubt the purest exponent of this way of life.[74]

(Let us pause here to lay to rest a misunderstanding that has caused confusion in many minds. Members of secular institutes insist that they are not to be listed in the ecclesiastical roster as "religious", that is, as members of a religious order or congregation, but as lay persons. We are confronted here with *the manifold ambiguity of the concept "laity"*, of which we have spoken earlier. On the one hand, all Christians, to whatever state of life they may belong, belong to the *laos*, the people of God. Throughout the history of the Church, on the other hand, and this is the relevant concept for the present discussion, the state of the counsels has assumed forms that are historically conditioned and molded, that have been codified in canon law, and to which new forms of the same state can rightly be assimilated if they satisfy the basic requirement of this state, namely, a way of life in accordance with the counsels. This life according to the counsels is fundamental to and binding on the secular institutes. Even while they distinguish themselves from other forms of the evangelical life by defining themselves as lay persons, they must nevertheless be aware that they do not thereby cut themselves off from the evangelical state. If, in order to emphasize their lay character, they speak of the evangelical counsels as being potentially contained in the baptismal vow, this is acceptable only if the emphasis is thereby on the word "potentially"—for every Christian is obligated to the spirit of the counsels; it must not be overlooked, however, that the sine qua non for the foundation of a theologically defined and qualitatively higher state of life is and

[74] In *Ville marxiste: Terre de mission* (Paris: Les Editions du Cerf, 1958), Madeleine Delbrêl, for many years an inhabitant of the communist-dominated town of Ivry in the environs of Paris, describes with the knowledge born of experience the most effective apostolate for such an environment, at the same time offering much insight into the reasons why the experiment of the worker priests had to be abandoned. [Tr]

remains acceptance of the obligation "actually" to live the life of the counsels. How the Christian or non-Christian world regards or ought to regard the members of these secular institutes is theologically irrelevant. —In another vein, the secular institutes have clearly demonstrated that *virginity* is the link between the state of the counsels and the lay state, for it is in their case, as it was in the first centuries of the Church, both *the seed* from which springs the whole life of the counsels and *a way of life* that enables Christians to live in the world without being separated from their families, their communities and their fellow-workers. From a physical and sociological point of view, virginity is a single phenomenon, but it has two faces—one natural; the other, supernatural. Without any hypocrisy, one who lives in virginity can realize the life of the counsels to the full in a secular institute [or in an analogous group that observes the life of the counsels] without leaving his place in the world. Of course, his obedience under vow will have to be "adapted", without weakening or limitation, to his secular condition: Complete readiness and availability must always be required of him as a concrete expression of what the Church never ceases to regard as the fundamental disposition of all the faithful.)

The tensions that must be endured and overcome by this new form of the evangelical state become clearly visible only when there is a question, not just of work among the lower classes of the proletariat, but of work in all secular professions, even—and even especially—those that confer on the one engaged in them various forms of worldly power, whether intellectual or material. For those in the evangelical state who undertake such missions, the demand laid upon all Christians "to possess as though not possessing" will be as *difficult* of fulfillment as it will be *fruitful* if fulfilled. From their stand in Christ, who is the free, personal and transcendent Lord of all things secular and of the powers and forces operative in them, such Christians are able to exert their influence in the secular world that is far from God and antagonistic to him. It may well be, however, that missions of this kind—by which the Christian is called to wield great power for the good of mankind from the Christian powerlessness of the Cross—are just as rare as are genuine missions to pure contemplation.

3. The Church is by nature a mission Church, an apostolic Church. It is and will continue to be a Church "not of this world"—a Church that proceeds from Christ to the world without ever wholly arriving in the world. Nor will it ever wholly arrive. The world's resistance is too great; it may even be said to be always on the increase as it opposes its destructive and contradictory forms of autonomous, "enlightened" freedom to the freedom brought by Christ. Jesus' fate—". . . his own received him not" (Jn 1:11)—must also be the fate of his Church: "It is enough for the disciple to be like his teacher, and for the servant to be like his master" (Mt 10:25); "If they have persecuted me, they will persecute you also . . ." (Jn 15:20). Indeed, this non-acceptance and persecution will play as intrinsic a role in the Church's fate in the world as the Cross did in Jesus' earthly fate. In his failure, he was victorious; in its failure, the Church will remember that its fruitfulness is not determined by earthly successes or by statistics about the number and attitude of the faithful. Like the small remnant in Israel that became the true "Israel of God", so at any given moment will the "little flock" be esteemed in the great ecclesial multitude. Of it alone can be said, as the "Epistle to Diognetus" expresses it, that Christians are the soul of the world.

"The soul dwells in the body, but is not part and parcel of the body; so Christians dwell in the world, but are not part and parcel of the world." The soul's indwelling is not accidental, nor can it be nullified: "The soul is locked up in the body, yet is the very thing that holds the body together; so, too, Christians are shut up in the world as in a prison, yet it is precisely they that hold the world together." That which is superior is held bound by that which is inferior and which is formed by this bond, yet rejects the law that forms it: "The flesh, though suffering no wrong from the soul, yet hates and makes war on it, because it is hindered from indulging its passions; so, too, the world, though suffering no wrong from Christians, hates them because they oppose its pleasures. The soul loves the flesh that hates it, and its members; so, too, Christians love those that hate them. . . . The soul, when stinting itself in food and drink, fares the better for it; so, too, Christians, when penalized, show a daily increase in numbers on that account. Such is the important post to which God has assigned them, and they are not at liberty to desert it."[75] Only when the flesh, which is the world, lets itself be drawn above its own laws and goals by the soul, which is the Church, can it be a living flesh, a meaningful world: Man's social, political and economic orders can be regulated only by the law of Christian love. But instead of seeing in this instinct for self-transcendence the way to its own freedom, the world barricades itself against the freedom to be found in Christ; and the hate with which it persecutes the Church purifies the Church again and again of the danger of secularization, preparing it for its own mission by robbing it of the illusion that it can express itself wholly in secular terms (just as the soul would like to express itself wholly in bodily terms, but cannot) or that eschatological redemption can be transformed into freedom in this world, crucified love into humanity, and God, who will always be a mystery, into a worldliness that will ultimately be fully revealed and in total possession of itself. The more deeply the higher, formative law of the Church impresses itself upon the world, the more the world will strive to overcome this formative power and to extract its whole content by worldly means until the Church becomes but an empty shell—an "institution", an "establishment". This would indeed be proof that body, world and material things are sufficient unto themselves.

For the sake of the Church's mission to the world, then, the

---

[75] For these quotations from the "Epistle to Diognetus", I have used the translation in ACW 6 (1948), 139–40. [Tr]

states of life within the Church have no other recourse than to distinguish themselves more and more consciously from this world/body by a decisive movement toward him who, as the source and head of the Church, is, at the same time, the beginning and end, the alpha and omega, of all creation.

5. EVANGELICAL STATE, PRIESTLY STATE, LAY STATE

At the end of these reflections, let us summarize the manifold relationships that exist among the states of life within the Church. It is not possible to reduce these relationships to a single formula if only because every preference stated in the Gospel is always a preference for those who are not preferred, who are beneficiaries of the strange preference: ". . . Much rather, those that seem the more feeble members of the body are more necessary; and those that we think the less honorable members of the body, we surround with more abundant honor, and our uncomely parts receive a more abundant comeliness, whereas our comely parts have no need of it. But God has so tempered the body together in due portion as to give more abundant honor where it was lacking; that there may be no disunion in the body, but that the members may have care for one another. And if one member suffers anything, all the members suffer with it, or if one member glories, all the members rejoice with it. Now you are the body of Christ, member for member" (1 Cor 12:22–27). This is what distinguishes the hierarchical order of the states of life within the Church from every other hierarchy, whether secular or religious. And the motive for the distinction has its source exclusively in the head of the Church, who found in his deepest humiliation his highest fulfillment: "He who descended, he it is who ascended also above all the heavens, that he might fill all things" (Eph 4:10). "The kings of the Gentiles lord it over them, and they who exercise authority over them are called Benefactors. But not so with you. On the contrary, let him who is the greatest among you become as the youngest, and him who is the chief as the servant. . . . I am in your midst as he who serves" (Lk 22:25–27).

"For I have given you an example, that as I have done to you, so you also should do" (Jn 13:15). This does not mean that the hierarchical order has been totally disrupted. "You call me Master and Lord, and you say well, for so I am" (Jn 13:13); and he is so precisely *because* (Phil 2:9) he humbled himself though he was equal to God. Even in glory, he is not a haughty lord.

Stamped with this image, one who has a place of honor in the Church will never attribute this distinction to the superiority of his own personal qualifications or "perfection" over those of others; he will understand it solely as service with all the responsibility that this entails: ". . . Of everyone to whom much has been given, much will be required" (Lk 12:48). What might at first appear to be a hierarchical ordering of the states of life is, as it were, outshone by the grace common to the whole Church, which all offices and missions exist but to serve: "But do not you be called 'Rabbi'; for one is your Master, and you are all brothers. And call no one on earth your father; for one is your Father, who is in heaven. Neither be called masters; for one only is your Master, the Christ. He who is the greatest among you shall be your servant. And whoever exalts himself shall be humbled, and whoever humbles himself shall be exalted" (Mt 23:8–12). Only in the context of these words is it possible to speak, in what follows, of a higher or lower ranking among the states of life.

1. The first relationship of the states of life stems from the analogy of the call to follow Christ, from their active participation in the reality and effectiveness of the Lord's redemptive mission. It is a relationship of increasing intensity:

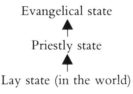

As opposed to the lay state, the priestly and evangelical states represent a special, differentiated vocation; the call to one of these states is the sole means by which a state of life can be established within the Church. Should such a differentiated vocation occur within the lay state, it would automatically lead the one so called to participation in the state of election. The difference between the priestly state and the religious state, on the other hand, lies in the fact that the priestly state requires the closer following of Christ only indirectly by reason of the office it confers, whereas the evangelical state requires it directly by reason of the personal way of life it entails. This difference has been discussed above: Unlike John, who represents the evangelical life, Peter, who represents the official ministry, was not granted the grace of sharing the Cross of Christ; this grace was bestowed on him only secondarily in view of the office to be conferred upon him. Correspondingly, the official ministry established in the New Testament seems, in one respect, to be but a continuation of the order that existed in the Old Testament, whereas the Old Testament depicts only distant images, not the actual foundation, of the evangelical state. This state has its source wholly in the Cross of Christ and is, therefore, solely his foundation. It became possible as a way of life only after Christ, its model, had walked the way of redemption. Even in the Old Testament, moreover, the office seems to spring only partially from the supernatural order of redemption; another part of it is rooted in the order of creation. For it belongs to the social nature of religious man that his service of God be a public one, and that some individuals be therefore designated as its official ministers. The fact that this function was entrusted to and regarded as the heritage of a whole tribe in Israel shows the relationship of its priesthood to that of the nations that surrounded it. In Israel, moreover, God's call to serve in the priesthood was somehow an impersonal one, in sharp contrast to the fully and uniquely personal call of the prophets, who thus became the prototypes of the personal vocations of the New Testament. A trace of this distinction can be found even in the New Testament, not only in the difference between the impersonality of the office and the personal discipleship that is the form of both vocations, but also, as we shall see later, in the dissimilarity that can exist in the form of the call itself.

The position of the priesthood between lay state and evangelical state is evident in the concrete form in which this state exists within the Church and in virtue of which it is able to participate in the other two states of life: in the evangelical state through celibacy and obedience to the bishop, although it is not required to practice poverty; in the lay state through the retention of earthly possessions and the relative personal autonomy required by the pastoral vocation. From the perspective of the lay state, the priestly state seems to share in that separation from the world for pure service to the cause of Christ that characterizes religious life; from the perspective of religious life, on the other hand, it seems to have a kind of organic unity with the lay state because of its relative confinement to the parish and its orientation to family needs and to the formation of the laity— baptism, education, the blessing of marriages, pastoral visits, administration of last rites, burial. This medial position of the priesthood has its advantages, but also its dangers: the advantage of immediate pastoral contact with the lay congregation; the even greater one of sharing with those in the evangelical state the privilege of a personal following of Christ. The priest can, in fact, assimilate his personal life as closely as he chooses to the spirit, and indeed to the reality, of the evangelical life. But there are also dangers attached to his medial position: The priest can fall prey to mediocrity and colorlessness, or even, in human weakness, extract from each way of life all that is pleasant in it while avoiding the radicality of "losing his soul" (in marriage or in the evangelical state). Not that he must inevitably fall prey to these dangers; it was, after all, the Lord who placed the priesthood in this medial position by ordaining the difference between office and personal discipleship. It is for the priest to determine how far he will adapt his life to the office he has accepted and so allow the priesthood to become a genuinely medial state between the evangelical state and the lay state. It is time now to shed light on this medial state.

2. The second relationship of the states of life is, then, an order in which the priestly state ranks above the evangelical and lay

states. This superior ranking has its foundation in the fact that the priestly office represents for the whole Church Jesus Christ in his threefold office of teacher, leader and shepherd and is thus the pledge of the continual presence of Christ in his Church.

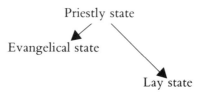

In the strength of this representation and by the explicit command of its Founder, the office as such (and not as a way of life) can and must demand the believing and loving obedience of all Christians. It can and must require this obedience on the basis of the clear distinction between office and person, the clear inviolability of the office whatever the unworthiness of the person. As the situation demands it, Catholic Christianity will bear witness again and again that it lives truly by the Spirit of God by accepting its subjection to the office as unquestioningly as Christ accepted his subjection to the will of the Father for the redemption of the world—to a will revealed to him at the beginning of his life in the legal "formalism" of Old Testament law, to which he rendered silent obedience; to a will revealed to him at the end of his life in the unyielding, and now completely anonymous, will of the Father that he undergo the Passion —a will behind whose fruitful relentlessness the beloved Person of the Father disappeared into the night of invisibility. In the "separation" of Father and Son during the Passion, the Son was deprived of every possibility of finding solace, in the personal relationship that existed between him and the Father, for the purely official and formal obedience required of him as Redeemer: Nothing remained of the Father's "fatherliness" but the unconditionality of the obedience he demanded; nothing remained of the personal attributes of the Son but the unconditional knowledge—in fear, shame and abandonment, in exorbitant demand and inability to do more—that his mission must be accomplished. This central event of Christianity continues to be reflected in the Church in the indisputable ascendancy of the ecclesial office over every personal and charismatic grace, which must, at the very least, prove its genuineness by its obedience to the Church. But because the Son, by his obedience, removed the whole justification of God's anger at sin and thereby brought about a reconciliation between God and man, the Church's very participation in the mystery of official obedience is a sign of God's boundless mercy toward it. It is precisely in the sign of this obedience that salvation arises for the Church in the form of the Eucharist and the other sacraments, for they are pledges that the Word of God is present in the form of the Church's word and in the grace of the Church's binding and loosing, which binds and looses also in heaven—that is, in the absolute grace of redemption.

The priestly office becomes thereby the preeminent *situs* of the presence of Christ in the Church, just as Christ himself became through the official character of his obedience the preeminent *situs* of the presence of the Father in the world. Just as the Father can no longer be approached except through Christ, although Christ has appeared within the boundaries of time and space ("No one comes to the Father but through me" [Jn 14:6]), so salvation can no longer be sought except through the ecclesial office, although Christ "is the Savior of all men" (1 Tim 4:10) and reserves to himself "power over all flesh" (Jn 17:2) and consequently "all judgment" (Jn 5:22). "What is it to thee? Do thou follow me" (Jn 21:22). Just as John, the beloved disciple —not Peter, the official minister—revealed himself by his unquestioning subjection and silent renunciation as the one who knew what it meant to love the Lord, so within the Church one who is more active and dedicated distinguishes himself by his greater respect for the ecclesial office even to the point of "bringing [his] mind into captivity to the obedience of Christ" (2 Cor 10:5). And just as Christ, in the fire of the anonymity of his obedience to mission, placed the fullness of his personal powers at the disposal of the Father, so passage through the fire of obedience to authority becomes, in the Church, a sure guarantee of the salvation of the human person. "For everyone shall be salted with fire, and every victim shall be salted" (Mk 9:48). The apparent forfeiture of personal religious and charismatic powers in Catholicism becomes the precise moment in which these powers are regulated, purified, unfolded and made capable of receiving the kingdom of heaven. The official character of the priesthood is not a foreign body against which the truly Christian virtues of faith, hope and charity are, as it were, to be shattered; the office is, rather, the inner form of these heavenly gifts. Faith, hope and charity as the life of God poured forth in our hearts (Rom 1:1–5) are, indeed, none other than the shifting of the center of gravity of Christian existence from the earthly *self* to the invisible center of God, and hence a dying to one's own self in order to rise invisibly as a new creature in God. One's own plan of life is replaced by the plan of grace, by one's mission, which is henceforth the center of the Christian life. In consequence, everything in the Christian becomes relative to this mission and, to that extent, official and impersonal. Christian life is a "ministration that justifies" (2 Cor 3:9). For this reason, the form of this ministration is stamped upon every Christian life, and the silent subjection of the person to the objective (but not necessarily "experienced") will of God that exists in him as a living mission becomes the mark by which it will be known whether or not he is a Christian. "Not everyone who says to me, 'Lord, Lord,' shall enter the kingdom of heaven, but he who does the will of my Father in heaven . . ." (Mt 7:21).

This conferring of official ministry upon the individual is exemplified in the Catholic priest in a process that is itself official, but in such a way that the grace of the office he receives in the sacrament of holy orders enables him also to make the proper personal response thereby demanded of him. Through the grace of the sacrament his whole person is claimed for the service of Christ's grace that he may be fruitful for the Church together with the Son who was sacrificed. In every absolution he dispenses, in every communion he distributes, in every action he performs in his official capacity, the priest is not merely the passive channel of grace, but also, if he does not close himself to the grace of his office, an active co-worker who gives with the Christ who gives and is given with the Christ who is given. He shares in Christ's giving of himself in the Eucharist because he shares in his loving will to renounce himself even to the point of anonymity. In this sense, the official character of the priest's ministry is both the prototype and the model of every state of life within the Church, but especially of the evangelical state, which, if it is to share ecclesially in Christ's obedience unto death, must borrow from the priesthood the concept of ecclesial office, extending it to include also the office of abbot, provincial or other major superior.

From this perspective, a new ordering of the states of life makes itself visible: The two forms of election are to be, together, "a pattern to the flock" (1 Pet 5:3).

3. As we have shown above, the priestly and evangelical states are permanently united not only historically in the Gospel narrative (since they were initially undifferentiated), but also by their content. They complement each other as the objective and subjective forms of the Christian grace of mission.

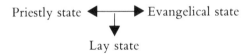

Regarded thus, the priestly and evangelical states appear to be but different aspects of the one call of Christ, which in the last analysis must of necessity be *one* because it is a call to the following of the "one Mediator between God and men" (1 Tim 2:5). The differentiation is solely for the purpose of definitively establishing and ensuring the totality of the one discipleship. If Jesus had made no distinction between official ministry and personal discipleship, there would have been danger that the faithful might come to regard the personal following of Christ as something already guaranteed and conferred along with the official following—that, in view of the absoluteness of the objective ministry [*das Sein*], they might come to forget the equally important absoluteness of the subjective commitment [*das Sollen*]. Yet, if he had treated the call to official ministry and personal discipleship as two separate and entirely unrelated calls, it might have seemed that the desire for personal discipleship was no more than a "moral striving for perfection", not a real participation in the official redemptive act of Christ. But Christ made abundantly clear the reciprocal immanence of *Sein* and *Sollen*. On the one hand, he established a kind of normal personal union between the two forms of discipleship by calling the apostles initially to both forms without distinction, and he kept constantly before them the need for union between the two forms and ways of life. On the other hand, he emphasized the division between the two forms not only by calling some individuals (for instance, the women or the rich young man) to a personal discipleship without offering them the office or bestowing it upon them, but also by drawing a distinction between Peter and John. The absolute guarantee of the official ministry [*das Sein*] does not remove from him on whom it is conferred the duty and necessity of striving for perfection with all his strength, nor does he who thus strives lose the consolation that his striving is supported by the guarantee of the *Sein*. The fact that we *are* redeemed should not be allowed to blunt in us the awareness that we *ought* and indeed must daily be redeemed anew; but this restlessness, in its turn, must not be allowed to darken the "peace that surpasses all understanding" (Phil 4:7) that comes with the certainty that we *are* redeemed.

Those who have received the call of Christ under either aspect strive together, then, toward unity: One called to the priesthood is called primarily to the office, which then requires of him that he assimilate his whole person to that office; one chosen for the life of the counsels is called primarily to a personal following of the Son whose task it is to place his whole person at the disposal of and to submerge it in his official mission, and who requires of his followers that they do the same. Both the one called to the priesthood and the one called to the evangelical state must make his life a ministry—the former through his office; the latter through his person. But since this can happen only through Christ, in Christ and for Christ, one in the evangelical state must depend on the ecclesial office to make Christ present to him here and now in the Church. Since it is, on the other hand, a work of that surpassing love that allows itself to be consumed as a holocaust for the world, the priest must depend on the evangelical state to hold this side of his office constantly before his eyes and in his memory. If Christians were perfect followers of Christ, the difference of emphasis would not be necessary: They would instinctively understand the unity of personal love and impersonal obedience. But since they are still "foolish . . . and slow of heart to believe . . ." (Lk 25:25), the Lord, for their instruction, has placed the two representatives of the one call in contrasting positions so that each may see in the mirror of the other what is lacking in himself.

This tension is not completely absent in the *priest who is also a member of a religious order* even though he seems to combine in himself the prerogatives of both states. For such a one, the vocation to the religious life usually precedes, with the priesthood being conferred later as the highest fulfillment of the privilege of personal discipleship. It is quite possible, in fact, that many persons who feel drawn to the evangelical state have, in the beginning, no inner attraction to or understanding of the priestly function, but acquire them only in the course of their religious life after they have been granted a deep personal insight into the priestly character of Christ's sacrifice. It is also possible that a religious, since he has renounced all autonomy over his own life, will wait in indifference for his superiors to indicate whether they have destined him for the priesthood or the "lay" state and will regard their decision as the will of God. For the religious, then, the priesthood is much more dependent on personal sacrifice than it is for the secular priest. Nevertheless, even though it is permitted the abbot of an exempt monastery to exercise episcopal functions, and the office would thus seem to exist in its entirety within the structure of religious life, it does not follow that the functional aspect of the one state of election has thereby become totally a function of the personal aspect, for the abbot is still dependent on the highest function in the Church, the Holy See.

It should be noted here that the life of the counsels encompasses in itself the full form of Christ's subjective priesthood, which is by no means in a state of tension with his objective priesthood. From this we can understand that, objectively speaking, the religious who has not been ordained priest and the member of a secular institute who remains in the lay state for the sake of his vocation thereby suffer no loss to their Christian life as such, even though, subjectively speaking, they may regard their lay state as a renunciation. To take one example, the ordination to the priesthood of a psychiatrist in a secular institute who can then not only analyze his patients, but also absolve them, shows clearly that ordination to the official priesthood does not take place within the evangelical state for the sake of a higher "perfection", but for the accomplishment of a function. On the same principle, monks in—let us say—a Benedictine monastery do not have to be ordained priests except as the internal and external liturgical services of the abbey may require it.

In this connection, it is obvious, too, that a *woman* called to the religious life suffers no loss because she is not admitted to the priesthood. She shares just as much as, if not more than, men do in the existential priesthood of Christ, in which no one has so deep a share as the Lord's mother at the foot of the Cross. The form of her indifference as a woman to the will of the triune God is so perfect that it completely surpasses the special indifference of a man in the evangelical state as to whether he will or will not be ordained to the priesthood. Even though women continue to be dependent on the ecclesial office, such dependence is an intrinsic part of the existence of every Christian, of every lay person, whether male or female, and even of every priest and every male member of a religious order, who cannot give absolution to themselves (even the pope cannot do so) and who owe obedience in a special way to their ecclesiastical superiors (just as the pope must be obedient in a special way to the whole ecclesial tradition).

Resolution of the tension in the other direction—that of

the official ministry—is just as unlikely, for here the personal aspect can never totally approximate the official ministry. However much he may strive, the priest's subjective commitment [*Sollen*] will never be the equivalent of his official ministry [*Sein*]. Indeed, the secular priest who, to achieve a more perfect gift of himself, adopts in whole or in part the form of life proper to the counsels will never be tempted to believe that, in doing so, he has "done everything" (Lk 17:10). He will always see in the mirror of the "perfect life" of the saints who followed the Lord in poverty, chastity and obedience the unattainable ideal of his own striving. Even if he were himself a saint, he would not know it, but would be all the more aware of the holiness incorporated in his brethren.

Once again, it is the interrelationship of the priestly and religious states that forms a model for the lay state. This does not mean that the laity should imitate the other two states exteriorly, but rather that the spirit of this union of office and person should become the determining factor of their Christian life in the world. Because the union of *Sein* and *Sollen* is thus the exalted challenge of every Christian, the evangelical state, which incorporates the demands of the *Sollen*, once again takes precedence over the other two states.

4. As the state in which the whole person is surrendered to the service of the redemption, the evangelical state seems to be united in a special way with the state of Christ. It acquires thereby a normative function in regard to the priestly and lay states.

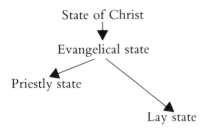

For although Christ (and, with him, Mary) is above all the states of life and is the Founder of all the states, he is so primarily because, even as a youth in the lay state, he already bore within himself, as a seed that would later bear fruit, the hidden form of the evangelical life. Even in the case of the priesthood, he is Founder only because he first united the priestly office of the Old Testament with his own personal role of sacrificial victim so that it might expand from that source into the priestly office of the Church. If even in Christ the personal aspect can never be considered apart from his mission, since from all eternity he is, as person, the Word who comes forth from the Father and places himself at the disposal of the Father's mission to the world, then his redemptive office can have its source only in his personal love for the Father and the world, and the anonymity of his suffering on the Cross is always but the expression of this personal love that loves "to the end" (Jn 13:1). Only in relationship to this love does the whole official priesthood of the Old Testament have meaning, and only by reason of this love does the official priesthood of the New Testament have value as an effective representation of the redemption accomplished once and for all by Christ. The evangelical state becomes, in consequence, the state that gives form to every life lived in imitation of the Lord.[76] For, in the New Testament, the basis of this state—of this way of life rooted in poverty, chastity and obedience—is precisely the explicit intention of sharing the mind of Christ even to the point of becoming a sacrificial victim with him on the Cross. In this sharing and nowhere else is to be found what the New Testament dares to call "holiness": the "sanctification" of oneself for the accomplishment of the will of the Father in sacrifice (cf. Jn 17:19).

The evangelical state is, therefore, not just a "striving for perfection" or "holiness"; it is also a being established in that

---

[76] "Even for those who are not in the religious state, therefore, the religious life can and must be the norm and model of Christian perfection. . . . The more nearly one lives one's life according to the spirit of the counsels and thus more nearly approximates the religious life, the more one approaches perfection . . . or, to express it in another way, the more one resembles those in religious life, the nearer one is to perfection", Ludwig Hertling, *Theologiae Asceticae Cursus Brevior*, 2nd ed. (Rome: Gregorian University, 1944), 37–38.

way of life whose actual realization is the essence of holiness itself. For holiness consists in the content of the three vows and the form in which they are taken. Admittedly, some take vows and fail to keep them; some enter upon this way of life and fail to let it become the law of their lives. But whenever one in the evangelical state does let the content of what he has vowed become existential in his life, such a one has in the vows the pure substance of Christian holiness.[77] There is, in fact, no other form of following Christ, no other way of doing the will of the Father together with Christ, than the love of total surrender. This love, which is the essence of holiness, can reveal itself in the order of the fallen world and of the redemption wrought by Christ only in the renunciation of all one has and is. But no love can give more than possessions, body and soul. This self-renunciation is, therefore, the basic prerequisite for every act of love accomplished in the performance of the spiritual and corporal works of mercy. It is not just the external work that is important, but the inner gift of self; the external work has Christian value before God only insofar as it is an outpouring of the inner "work" of love.

Holiness coincides so closely with that which gives form to the evangelical state that every vocation to holiness is also a vocation to live according to the *spirit* (if not necessarily according to the outward form) of the counsels. This fact is apparent in every example that can be adduced of holiness within the Church. The vast majority of canonized saints have been members of religious orders or persons who shared by vow in the form of that life. Only in exceptional instances (Thomas More, Anna Maria Taigi)[78] have married persons been canonized—unless

---

[77] "The perfection envisioned by ascetic theology cannot be other than that to which the Church invites in the religious state. For if the religious state instituted by the Church did not of itself lead to the highest perfection, the faithful pursuing it would be deceived. . . . Therefore, the most excellent, true and only perfection proposed by the Church [is to be found] in the state of perfection . . . (Since perfection is one, the states of perfection, if they are many, cannot differ essentially either as to their end or their means)", ibid., 24.

[78] Thus perfect holiness and heroic virtue are, it is true, attainable in marriage (cf. the preceding section on marriage, Pt. II, Ch. 2, sec. 4), but only by way

they had entered into a state of total dedication to God after the death of or on the basis of a prior understanding with their spouse. But not only those lay persons have been canonized who left the married state and entered a cloister, as did St. Brigid and St. Jane Frances de Chantal; others, like St. Joan of Arc, broke all natural ties to family and homeland and lived in naked obedience to God, unhesitatingly embracing a life of poverty and chastity. For one who has received a qualitative mission can follow it only by ruthlessly dissolving every other tie in order to dedicate himself exclusively to the task that has been assigned him. What is true of those called to the lay state is no less true of those priests who are called to an extraordinary personal mission. They, too, will have to trample on all conventions and enter the solitude of total poverty and virginity and perfect renunciation of all autonomy over their own lives, modeling themselves on the Curé of Ars, who lived wholly by the spirit of the religious life without ever entering a religious order, although the thought was always present to him as a temptation to lighten his superhuman ministry. It cannot be argued that this orientation of every holiness to the ideal of the evangelical state is in any way conditioned by a particular time or age. The evangelical state is and always will be for the Christian of the other two states that which links both

---

of exception and always in such a way that the spirit of the threefold renunciation [of the counsels] appears fully realized therein. At some point, and especially when they have a great mission to perform in the Church (as did St. Thomas More, for example), these holy people exceed the framework of the family and expand into the area of direct confrontation with the uncompromising missioning will of God. Hertling compares fully achieved holiness and canonization in the lay state to the degree of *doctor honoris causa*. "In the general and more usual course of events, learning is acquired through schooling—through elementary school, high school and university—and is crowned with some degree, some diploma. This is the common procedure. It can happen, however, that an individual without schooling may acquire solely by his own genius and personal effort such genuine culture and learning that he is inferior to none of those who have had formal schooling. . . . Nevertheless, the 'diploma' continues to be the norm by which learning is evaluated" (ibid., 38).

their distinctive and closed state and their ideal of that state with the infinite and unattainable state of Christ. For the evangelical state is most deeply characterized by the inexhaustibleness, the "yet more", of its demand. Marriage and priesthood tend to require a manageable roster of duties and rights with which the Christian is familiar, that are satisfying to him, and by the accomplishment of which he is able to please God. The religious knows no such finiteness. It is his function in the Church to open all closed ideals and pastoral goals to the always limitless demand of Christ. In the parish and the diocese, he is an element of Christian unrest; when all tasks have been neatly assigned, he is there as the uncomfortable "seamless robe", the disturber of the peace, the disrupter of all plans. By his state of life, he shares in a special way in Christ's expulsion and abandonment "outside" the camp, which he, too, experiences; within the Church, his position is analogous to that of the Church as a whole within the world: the position of a stranger who can never be completely at home there. The lay person and the secular priest have this in common, that they are both somehow rooted by their vocation in the order of creation; the religious state, on the contrary, has no foundation in this order. Even from the perspective of the "ecclesial world", it is suspended in mid-air—as the Lord was suspended on the Cross between heaven and earth with no place to call his own. He had no place of his own on earth, for earth had rejected him; he could find no place in heaven, for the Father had concealed himself from him; and he could not yet follow the Spirit, for he himself had, as it were, sent him ahead into the Father's hands. He was suspended in the open place of an ever-increasing glorification of God in the dark night of the Passion; but this open place could not be called a place of his own. There was no one to stand by him in this place that was incomprehensible to the world or to be concerned about him or about those who would come after him—no one to take his part: "He trusted in God; let him deliver him now, if he wants him" (Mt 27:43). God has always done more for the preservation of the religious state than the Church has. New religious communities,

for example, have always been called into existence directly by
God and have frequently been founded against strong opposition
from the Church—have often even had to prove by this very
opposition that they were willed by God. When one of these
orders succeeds in opening the closed mind of the Church—as a
tender seed, a small root, can split a stone—then the Church
recognizes the finger of God ex post facto in this work, lets it
prosper and in the end praises and approves it.

In this fate, the evangelical state as a whole shares the fate
of every qualitative ecclesial mission that must struggle in the
strength of God alone to prove itself, or perhaps to fail; and that,
if it succeeds, will be acknowledged as a "holiness" that, like
the evangelical state as a whole, is a gift bestowed by God for
the good of the Church and of the two "secular states". For
holiness is not the sole privilege of those to whom it is granted.
As a fruitful charism of the whole body of Christ, it has, in the
economy of that body, a function that is just as much an official
ministry as is the official ministry of the priest. "Now there are
varieties of gifts, but the same Spirit; and there are varieties of
ministries, but the same Lord"—not excluding such ministries
as the "gift of healing", the "working of miracles", "prophecy"
and the "distinguishing of spirits" (1 Cor 12:4–10)—in other
words, all those pure "gifts freely given" that so often identify
and confirm the special missions of God and mark the ways of
the "saints". This ordering to the common good of the Church
distinguishes true Catholic mysticism from every other form
of the "supernatural" and can serve as a definitive touchstone
whenever such a phenomenon is to be tested. A mysticism
limited to a mere exchange of "inconsequentialities" between
God and the graced soul without any social or ecclesial dimension
(even if this dimension is not exteriorly observable) is ipso facto
revealed as an illusion. "For whether we are afflicted, it is for
your instruction and salvation; or whether we are comforted, it
is for your comfort . . ." (2 Cor 1:6). "Indeed, the signs of the
apostle were wrought among you in all patience, in miracles
and wonders and deeds of power" (2 Cor 12:12). In the Old

Testament, this kind of charismatic action remained somehow exterior to him who exercised it so that it was not necessarily an expression of inner holiness; in the New Testament, where every mission is conferred in a new and personal way and must, if it is to be carried out at all, become for him on whom it is conferred the whole content of his life, it shares in his inner sacrifice. "But I will spend and be spent myself for your souls . . ." (2 Cor 12:15).

Just as no one is holy for himself alone since this would be a contradiction in terms in reference to a love that "is not self-seeking" (1 Cor 13:5), so no one becomes a monk or a religious or belongs in any other way to the evangelical state for himself alone, but only to become the servant of all in the closer following of Christ who offered not only his body, but even his soul, as an instrument for the sanctification of the Church. "In this we have come to know his love, that he laid down his life for us; and we likewise ought to lay down our life for the brethren" (1 Jn 3:16). The enthusiasm of this kind of self-renunciation can sometimes be as embarrassing to others as was the action of Mary of Bethany to the disciples. "To what purpose this waste? for this might have been sold for much and given to the poor" (Mt 26:8–9). In the normal economy of pastoral care, it is customary to measure sacrifice by its social and charitable impact. Yet the Lord, even though he was a friend of the poor, defended this "unjustifiable" waste whose good odor would spread forever through the whole house of the Church (Jn 12:3). "Amen I say to you, wherever in the whole world this Gospel is preached, this also that she has done shall be told in memory of her" (Mt 26:13). In much the same way, the sacrifice of the evangelical state is and always will be the invisible agent that penetrates all things as "the fragrance of Christ for God" (2 Cor 2:15) and bestows on Christian life in the Church its greatest strength and purest beauty.

5. The relationships are inverted, however, once the functional character and outward orientation of the official ministry and, more especially, of the personal commitment proper to the

evangelical state have been clearly revealed. For it appears then that the two special ways of life are in the service of the principal state in the Church, which is the lay state.

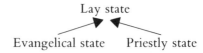

Lay state

Evangelical state   Priestly state

As we have said above, this is not to be understood as an attempt to minimize or vulgarize the significance of the states of election —as though every individual called to a special mission had somehow to be submerged in the mass of those not so called. On the contrary, every special mission bestowed by God for the common good of the Church is bestowed "without repentance" (Rom 11:29); it marks the one called to it not only for time, but also for eternity. In the Church, the principle of a radical "aristocracy" is not merely compatible with the principle of a radical community of goods; it is the prerequisite therefor. Just as God set the sun and moon and stars "in the firmament of the heaven to shed light on the earth" (Gen 1:17), so those "that instruct many to justice [shall shine] as stars for all eternity" (Dan 12:3), and the fact that "there is one glory of the sun, and another glory of the moon, and another of the stars" (1 Cor 15:41) will not prevent all the just from shining forth "like the sun in the kingdom of their Father" (Mt 13:43). Among the elect, then, and this is obvious in the case of Paul, awareness of an obligation to serve the community in no way precludes aware-ness of personal mission; nor does the certainty of personal mission preclude the urge "to spend and be spent" to the end for the brethren. It is not a hypocritical love that leads the apostle to expropriate his whole life and place it at the service of the least likely members of the community, but neither is it a love that spends itself without knowing the value of what it bestows: "I hope you will always understand . . . that we are your boast" (2 Cor 1:13–14); "we hope, as your faith increases, greatly to enlarge through you the province allotted to us" (2 Cor 10:15). Truly the "greatest in the kingdom of heaven" (Paul says this "as it were in foolishness" [2 Cor 11:17]), the greatest "among those born of women" (Lk 7:28), are those who, in following their Lord, "are constantly being handed over to death . . . that the life also of Jesus may be made manifest" (2 Cor 4:11) to the community; those who have allowed themselves to be put in the last place, "like men doomed to death" (1 Cor 4:9), so that the Church may be wise, and honored, and purified. In them, God lays at the feet of the Church, his Bride, his most precious treasure and puts glowing coals upon her head: ". . . I bear all things for the sake of the elect, that they also may obtain salvation" (2 Tim 2:10). "I do not seek what is yours, but you" (2 Cor 12:14). As a result, the whole instrumentality of the priestly and evangelical states together with that of the Son of God is revealed as a means of helping the laity to achieve personal perfection even though, as we have seen, this work can be accomplished only if those who are being perfected by the instruments of God allow themselves to become instruments as well. It should not be forgotten, however, that the lives of the laity will always be directed toward goals proper to themselves and that any attempt to burden them with an ecclesial ministry as well, to force them into a "lay apostolate", a "Catholic Action" in imitation of the apostolate of those in the states of election, will soon prove to be impossible not only because of the practical difficulties involved, but also because of the realistic boundaries that separate the lay state from the states of election. Lay persons are obliged to practice Christian love of God and neighbor as perfectly as possible in their daily lives and so to shed a warm, deep and fruitful light upon their surroundings. But they are not obliged by their general Christian mission to exercise any further special or widely visible apostolate within the Church. Many a young lay person who hopes, in the youthful idealism of his formative years, to be able to combine such an apostolate with his secular profession will soon discover for himself, as he enters his profession and begins to establish a family, that the circle of his mission is of necessity limited to the modest and more homely one of influencing and illuminating the place destined for him in the world. The frequently used expression "lay apostle" should have no more resonance than the no longer used "lay priest". Basically, both terms are intended to convey the same meaning: that within his personal life circle the lay person is obliged, to the best of his ability, to reflect and further in some way the ecclesial ministries of the priestly and evangelical states. Practically, however, this is best done, as we noted above in speaking of liberation theology, when the lay person translates the spiritual impulses emanating from the "Church" (in the narrower sense of the priestly and evangelical states) into the secular sphere and competently furthers them precisely in that place where the competence of the states of election ceases to be operative. In thus adopting the often urgent impulses that proceed from the Church under the inspiration of the Holy Spirit, the lay person is challenged to a degree of personal commitment, and of personal renunciation and purity, that closely resemble those of the states of election.

On the other hand, the lay person, especially the married one, must be constantly aware that he has a very definite responsibility to his place in the world. Just as it is the privilege and boast of priests and apostles that their existence has been made an instrument in the hands of God, so it must be the privilege and boast of the laity that their goal is the building up of their Christian life in the Church. The family, in particular, must understand its "closedness" as a self-contained representation of Christian love in the world. It must not be led by the exaggerated apostolate of its individual members to endanger the greater good of family love itself by an artificial "openness" or a false activity—in Christian organizations, for instance. This is true also of the larger family of the Christian community; whatever the inner vitality of its love, it, too, must not allow itself to be driven by the zeal and over-organization of its members into a false orientation that does not correspond to its nature as a community and can only prove harmful to it. At this point, it is well to remember the principle so emphatically stated by St. Thomas Aquinas: The means, even the best of means such as the evangelical counsels, must not be substituted for the end, which, for every state of life without exception, is the pure love of God and neighbor. For the community, the definitive measure of its instrumentality (in associations and organizations) is always the vitality of its personal love. To the extent that its role as an instrument enriches this love, it is desirable and should be furthered; to the extent that it threatens to stifle the vitality of love by impersonal routine, it is evil and should be destroyed. Everything can be an instrument, even one's own life and self. Love alone is the goal of all goals and the measure of all things. In the Church, this quality of love is reflected in the laity's goal of building up their own Christian life.

6. From the fact of love's superiority over all else is derived a final relativization of the differences that exist among the states of life. Because of love, all forms of the states of life achieve their final meaning only in pure altruism and in a kind of mutual indwelling [*circumincessio*] whereby love becomes the ultimate form of ecclesial life.

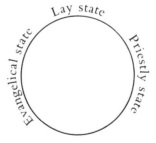

Every state of life is a specific representation of something that is present also in the other states. The priestly state represents the absoluteness of Christ's redemption, the guarantee of his presence and of the sacramental existence of grace in the whole life of the Church. The priest is the guardian of this existence and, by the will of God, the one who continually makes it possible, who cooperates in making every member of Christ a victim to be offered—a co-victim with the head through baptism. The religious state represents the absoluteness of personal commitment on the foundation of the official ministry and the unconditionality of the divine demand that requires of every Christian—of the priest above all, but also of the laity—both personal commitment [*Sollen*] and official ministry [*Sein*]. The lay state is the state of the Church itself, which, removed from the world by the fact of the redemption and chosen by the call of Christ, has been empowered and called by the Holy Spirit to take its place with the Son in the presence of the Father. And if, in this economy, the priestly state is most closely associated with the head and so acts upon the body; if the lay state is most closely associated with the body and so receives the action of the head and lives for the head; if the evangelical state, which belongs primarily to the body, but seeks through obedience to live the life of the head, is thus the mediator between the two, these different orientations of the states of life are, nonetheless, ultimately relative, for even priests and those in the evangelical state belong to the body of Christ, the Church; and Christ, who is the head, is sovereign over all states of life within the Church. Thus, neither the actions of the head upon the body nor those of the body upon the head are directed away from their source and toward some foreign object; on the contrary, they are the immanent actions of the one Christ, who is both head and body: "*One* Christ loving himself" (St. Augustine). In the reciprocity of head and members, this one love, which is not self-love, but a representation of the love of the Blessed Trinity, is able to reflect the fullness that is a priori in the head. It is this love that Christianity is called upon to live and to represent, and it is immaterial whether it represents it through the priestly state as the original love of the head by whom all things were created; through the lay state, which is, as it were, the female complement of the man Christ, as the body's attempt to respond to this love; or through the evangelical state, as the bond of ineradicable love that unites the two. For all states share in the forging of this ultimate bond, which is possible only because "Christ also loved the Church, and delivered himself up for her. . . , in order that he might present to himself the Church in all her glory, not having spot or wrinkle or any such thing, but that she might be holy and without blemish" (Eph 5:25, 27); in order that he might lead her, through the self-renunciation of the Cross, back to the place where that love was originally perfect that was founded in paradise, that appeared once in the fullness of time in the virgin motherhood of Mary, and that is predestined for all in the world to come where the wholeness of the covenant will be identified once again with the fullness of all riches, all fecundity, all freedom.

But until that time—until renunciation will no longer be necessary, until there will be "neither . . . mourning, nor crying, nor pain any more" (Rev 21:4), until "they will neither marry nor be given in marriage" (Mt 22:30), until there will be no more "buying and selling" (Lk 17:28), the Church, and with it the states of life, must be, in the midst of the secular world, a *sacrament* that not only reflects this true and absolute love in an outward sign, but also possesses it interiorly and pours it out upon the world, so that, in loving, it is, in its totality, both an end and a means to that end.

PART THREE

THE CALL

CHAPTER ONE

THE NATURE OF THE CALL

The call of which we are speaking is not just something required for the establishment of a state of life; it is the very essence of the Christian state of life and even of the Christian life as such. The "where" of Christ's state of life was the will of the Father. The "where" of the Christian is the stand he takes in that will as it is revealed to him again and again in the call that comes through the Word of truth that is the Son. For Christ *and* the Christian, this "where" is the foundation of both his state and his life. ". . . I know that his commandment is everlasting life" (Jn 12:50). The command spoken to each individual and audible to him alone is for him the ultimate norm not only of his objective ministry [*Sein*], but also of his subjective commitment [*Sollen*]. But because it is the call of the living God, who as Person is always more than just an abstract commandment and a universally applicable principle, this call, which is spoken at this moment and at every moment, must also be heard at this moment and at every moment and must be obeyed because it is heard. In other words, there is no genuine doctrine of the Christian way and state of life that is distinct from or that ignores or excludes this concrete call.

For a long time, this truth was not sufficiently recognized. It was generally assumed that there was a universal concept of Christian striving for perfection that was independent of this call—a scale, as it were, of correct behavior, a course that had to be followed and that was plainly visible from the beginning even though it could be pursued only gradually. Almost the entire doctrine of Christian perfection in late antiquity and in the Middle Ages was built upon this concept of an "ascent to God". Not until St. Ignatius Loyola, in the *Spiritual Exercises*, looked once more to the Gospel itself was a new but definitive dimension revealed, a revolution effected, the value of which has not yet been fully recognized.

By going beyond the prevailing concept of the spiritual life, Ignatius characterized the contemplation of the life of Jesus as the contemplation of his call (*El llamamiento del Rey*, no. 91)[1] and built his image of Christ on this new concept. It was only logical, therefore, that he should require those who meditate on the life of Jesus to do so, not in theoretical contemplation, but in such a way that the concrete word of the Father be heard anew in every situation and that the grace to be desired be always and everywhere the grace "not to be deaf to his call, but prompt and diligent to accomplish his most holy will" (91). To this end, those who meditate shall "begin to investigate and ask in what kind of life or in what state (*vida o estado*) his Divine Majesty wishes to make use" of them and how they ought to "prepare [themselves] to arrive at perfection in whatever state or way of life God our Lord may grant [them] to choose" (135). In this way, the call that is heard individually and personally in attentive meditation on the word of God becomes the basis not only of the right direction of the Christian's progress, but also and explicitly of his "state", which Ignatius identifies with "[way of] life", thus distinguishing it from the general Christian state "within our Holy Mother, the hierarchical Church" (170), and equating it with the differentiated states of life—the priestly state, the state of the counsels, the married state (171)—and, even more narrowly, with the concrete situation in which each one finds himself in the here-and-now of the state he has chosen (172–74).

These three stages of the call—to a general state within the Church, to a particular state within the Church, and, finally, to a concrete situation within the particular state—are, in some way, analogous to the call by which the Christian is first summoned out of the world to be a Christian and then translated, by a unique second and later call, to a particular state so that, in this state, there may be bestowed upon him, through the concrete call that is

---

[1] Cf. *The Spiritual Exercises of St. Ignatius Loyola*, trans. Louis J. Puhl, S.J. (Chicago: Loyola University Press, 1951), p. 43, no. 91. Unless otherwise indicated, I have used this translation in part III. Further references to the *Spiritual Exercises* (henceforth *Sp Ex*) will be given in parentheses in the text, using the traditional paragraph numeration. [Tr]

spoken at this moment and at every moment, a Christian life that endures. The doctrine of the call must be regarded, then, as the indispensable complement of the doctrine of the Christian states of life. It may seem at first to be but the subjective side of the objective doctrine of the states of life. From what has been said above it is clear, however, that such a distinction is unjustified, for the call of God not only creates the "where" of the Christian's stand at any given moment, but is also the very substance of the stand he must take. By thus viewing the concept of state of life anew from the standpoint of the call, we discover a number of questions and aspects that have hitherto been given only slight attention, but that must now be given careful consideration because of their importance both in themselves and in their consequences.

1. THE DIVINE CALL

Christian revelation is primarily a revelation of hearing, not of seeing. Although the image of seeing is not excluded—for "we see now through a mirror in an obscure manner" (1 Cor 13:12); wisdom, when it appears, is the "mirror . . . and image" of the divine goodness (Wis 7:26); and Christ is "the image of the invisible God" (Col 1:15) so that, in seeing him, we also see the Father (cf. Jn 14:9)—nevertheless the comparison with hearing is the dominant one in revelation: The Second Person is heard primarily as "Word" (Jn 1:1) and faith in him comes by hearing (cf. Rom 10:17). The hearing of the Word is by no means a temporary substitute for the seeing that is wanting to us here below (as spiritual and mystical theology with its emphasis on seeing seemed to imply with varying degrees of emphasis in the centuries before Ignatius). On the contrary, it is the lasting proof that God never is and never will be a mere "object" of knowledge to us, but is rather the infinitely sovereign majesty of a Trinity of Persons that makes itself known in whatever way and to whomever it wills. That God speaks to us in his personal word is a greater grace than that we are allowed to see him: That we are deemed worthy of his word is the grace of graces that makes us partners in a divine, even a trinitarian, conversation. That the word of God is spoken to us is the highest revelation and honor the personal God can bestow upon us, for it presumes that God considers us capable of understanding his word through the gift of his grace and of possessing the Spirit who "searches all things, even the deep things of God, that we may know all things that have been given us by God" (1 Cor 2:10, 12). So tremendous is this grace that the creature thus addressed by God must forget its own wishes and desires, even its longing for "eternal happiness" and for the "vision of God" so that, trembling in the depths of its being, it may fall to the ground and hear his voice (cf. Acts 9:4) only to ask: "What shall I do, Lord?" (Acts 22:10).

But one who has been thrown to the ground by the impact of this compelling voice is also "set upon his feet" by it. When God speaks, he wants a partner. He wants one who is erect, who, hearing his voice, is yet able to stand upon his feet and answer: ". . . I fell upon my face, and I heard the voice of one that spoke. And he said to me: Son of man, stand upon thy feet, and I will speak to thee. And the Spirit entered into me after that he spoke to me, and he set me upon my feet; and I heard him speaking to me . . ." (Ezek 2:1–2). When God speaks personally, he wants to be understood personally; when he utters his personal word into the world, he wants that word to be returned to him, not as a dead echo, but as a personal response from his creature in an exchange that is genuinely a dialogue even though it can be conducted only in the unity of the divine Word that mediates between the Father and us. But just as that divine Word proceeds from the Father, yet is not the Father, but only declares the Father, so the creature can give back to the Father this word it has received by uttering itself in it—or better, by letting itself be uttered by it.

The Father spoke for the first time when he created the world. For he created it solely "through" the Word (Jn 1:3), in him, and for him (cf. Col 1:16). He created it by a sevenfold word that was spoken six times, but whose seventh utterance was silence (Gen 1:1–2:4). Within this word that "calls things that are not as

though they were" (Rom 4:17), every creature becomes what it is
by being called by name. Thus God calls the heavens (Is 48:13);
he calls the earth (Ps 50:1); he calls the waters (Amos 5:8); he calls
the stars (Ps 147:4); he calls the light, "and it obeyeth him with
trembling" (Bar 3:33). Creation is the first ἐκκλησία, the first
calling out of nothingness and chaos into being of that which has
no being. He upholds "all things by the word of his power" (Heb
1:3). "For God made not death, neither hath he pleasure in the
destruction of the living. For he created all things that they might
be; and he made the nations of the earth for health . . ." (Wis
1:13–14). But they possess being and health only in the word
of wisdom that "reacheth . . . from end to end mightily, and
ordereth all things sweetly" (Wis 8:1). "Let all thy creatures serve
thee, because thou hast spoken, and they were made. Thou didst
send forth thy Spirit, and they were created, and there is no one
that can resist thy voice" (Judith 16:17). This voice is first of all
the voice of creation; its effects are the existence and laws of the
natural world. "By the words of the Lord are his works" (Sir
42:15). This word does not have to separate itself from God in
order to call the world into being. "Remaining in herself the
same, she [wisdom] reneweth all things" (Wis 7:27); it requires only a proper discernment to know the Creator through
the work of his hands. "For by the greatness of the beauty and of
the creature, the creator of them may be seen, so as to be known
thereby" (Wis 13:5).

The word of God went forth a second time *when God turned
personally* to his intelligent creature, to man, speaking his word
internally within him. In a new act of boundless love, God chose
to share with man his personal and divine attributes; the divine
word entered through supernatural grace into the creature itself
in a holy exchange that exceeds all the perfections of creation.
"For if one be perfect among the children of men, yet if thy
wisdom be not with him, he shall be not regarded" (Wis 9:6).
Only through prayer can the creature attain this wisdom: ". . .
Give me wisdom, that sitteth by thy throne, and cast me not off

from among thy children" (Wis 9:4). ". . . In each generation
she passes into holy souls, she makes them friends of God and
prophets" (Wis 7:27; quoted from the Jerusalem Bible [Tr]).
For the creature, this new state of being spoken to by God
represents at one and the same time a free election, the grace
of friendship, and a prophetic mission. So free, indeed, is this
election that the new act of God is completely independent of
all that is natural in man—neither the existence nor the nature of
the new call can be determined or evaluated on purely natural
premises. Far from being a necessary precondition for this grace-
filled call, the creature's whole nature is, in fact, inconsequential
to it. Two men may have the same natural characteristics, and one
will be chosen, and one will not. "Then two men will be in the
field; one will be taken, and one will be left. Two women will be
grinding at the millstone; one will be taken, and one will be left"
(Mt 24:40–41). "So then there is question not of him who wills
nor of him who runs, but of God showing mercy" (Rom 9:16),
". . . as it is written, 'Jacob I have loved, but Esau I have hated' "
(Rom 9:13). There are no psychological tests for predicting who
will hear and follow the divine call. By nature, Peter was a reed
shaken by the wind; from an analysis of his character, no one
could have predicted that he was called to be the rock of the
Church. But Jesus bestowed upon him a new calling and with it a
new name—a new nature and a new aptitude: "Thou art Simon,
son of John; thou shalt be called Cephas (which is interpreted
Peter [rock])" (Jn 1:42). It is not by inquiring into his own
aptitudes and inclinations that the Christian—or, indeed, anyone
else—comes to know the personal and loving will of God in his
regard or the mission God has decreed for him. In the last
analysis, his fate is determined by the "holy calling" (2 Tim
1:9) that God utters to every person from the depths of his own
freedom, and that every person is obliged to serve with all his
strength as soon as he becomes aware of it. Sometimes, as if
by accident, God's call corresponds to the personal inclinations
and expectations of the one who receives it. But it can also
happen that, in some or in all respects, it will run counter to his

inclinations and expectations; that it will be at cross-purposes with his nature; that, like most of the prophets, he will shrink from his mission because he knows he has no aptitude for such an undertaking. After all, who has ever had a natural aptitude for the Cross?

Moses was called by a voice from the burning bush and answered: "Here I am." By his answer he bound himself to enter upon the sacred sphere of mission: "Come, now! I will send you to Pharaoh to lead my people, the Israelites, out of Egypt." Astounded, Moses queried: "Who am I that I should go to Pharaoh and lead the Israelites out of Egypt?" But the Lord replied: "I will be with you." And the Lord affirmed his words with the promise of signs and with the revelation of his holy name. When Moses demanded further reassurance, he was given three more signs: the staff that became a serpent and then a staff again; his hand that became leprous and was cured; the water that would become blood on dry land. But Moses was so convinced of his own inability that he persisted in his refusal: "If you please, Lord, I have never been eloquent, neither in the past, nor recently, nor now that you have spoken to your servant; but I am slow of speech and tongue." The Lord answered: "Who gives one man speech and makes another deaf and dumb? Or who gives sight to one and makes another blind? Is it not I, the Lord? Go, then! It is I who will assist you in speaking and will teach you what you are to say." But Moses responded: "If you please, Lord, send someone else!" At this persistent refusal, "the Lord became angry" and made Aaron his spokesman to the people instead of Moses (Ex 3–4, passim). For thus reflecting on his own ability or inability, Moses had to yield a part of his mission to his brother, just as later, for reflecting on the limits of God's mercy, he lost the privilege of concluding his mission and leading the people into the Promised Land. If he was, nonetheless, a "born leader", it was because wisdom "entered into the soul of the servant of God" and "opened the mouth of the dumb, and made the tongues of infants eloquent" (Wis 10:16, 21), as the Book of Wisdom expressly relates of Moses.

The same discrepancy between nature and mission is found again in the calling of the prophets. When Jeremiah hears the call to mission, he begins to stammer like a child: "Ah, ah, ah, Lord God! Behold, I cannot speak, for I am a child." And the Lord rebukes him: "Say not: I am a child; for thou shalt go to all that I shall send thee, and whatsoever I shall command thee, thou shalt speak. Be not afraid of their presence, for I am with thee to deliver thee" (Jer 1:6–8). And when Amaziah expresses doubts as to Amos' qualifications for the role of prophet, Amos agrees with him: "I am not a prophet, nor am I the son of a prophet, but I am a herdsman plucking wild figs. And the Lord took me when I followed the flock, and the Lord said to me: Go, prophesy to my people Israel" (Amos 7:14–15). God's call and election are never predictable. Samuel was slow to understand that it was really God who called him (1 Sam 3); Saul found a kingdom while he was searching for his father's lost asses (1 Sam 9); David was taken from his flock to be anointed king (1 Sam 16:11). Elijah cast a mantle over the unsuspecting Elisha as he was plowing a field (1 Kings 19:19). Precisely in the case of his most important calls to mission, God is careful to make plainly visible not only the general unworthiness, but also the natural ineptitude of the one called. He chooses whom he will; if the one he has chosen accepts the mission, he becomes, as it were, a new creation called by the Lord out of nothingness.

The higher the mission to which one is called by God, the more imperative it is that one *consent to the call*. For there is question here of the transferral to a human recipient of the personal word of God himself. But this word can be received only if one is prepared to accept full responsibility for it. It makes no difference whether the answer is given with repugnance, as Moses gave it; or generously and freely, as Isaiah gave it ("And I heard the voice of the Lord saying: Whom shall I send? And who shall go for us? And I said: Lo, here am I. Send me" [Is 6:8]); or reluctantly, as Jeremiah gave it, the "yes" of God's chosen one must be given before the office is laid upon his shoulders as the "burden of

God". But it is also possible to flee from God's call: "Now the word of the Lord came to Jonah, the son of Amittai, saying: Arise, and go to Nineveh the great city, and preach in it. . . . And Jonah rose up to flee into Tarshish from the face of the Lord, and he went down to Joppa, and found a ship going to Tarshish. And he paid the fare thereof, and went down into it, to go with them to Tarshish from the face of the Lord" (Jonah 1:1–3). Only after the Lord's call had delivered him into the hell of the whale's belly, thereby forcing him to recognize the inevitableness of God's election, did Jonah utter his "yes" and receive in a second call the confirmation of the first: "And the word of the Lord came to Jonah the second time, saying: Arise, and go to Nineveh the great city, and preach in it the preaching that I bid thee. And Jonah arose and went to Nineveh, according to the word of the Lord" (Jonah 3:1–3). For the one who receives it, the acceptance of God's mission can become a vicarious stewardship: "Son of man, I have made thee a watchman to the house of Israel; and thou shalt hear the word out of my mouth, and shalt tell it [to] them from me. If, when I say to the wicked: Thou shalt surely die, thou declare it not to him, nor speak to him, that he may be converted from his wicked way, and live, the same wicked man shall die in his iniquity, but I shall require his blood at thy hand" (Ezek 3:17–18). So, too, the heavy hand of the Lord weighed upon the apostle Paul: "For woe to me if I do not preach the Gospel! If I do this willingly, I have a reward. But if unwillingly, it is a stewardship that has been entrusted to me. What then is my reward?" (1 Cor 9:16–18).

Mission, then, requires man's "yes"—an act not less important than the act by which God calls his chosen one. For man's response to the call of God must be no less decisive and unlimited than the call itself. And yet the two words—God's word and man's word—are not to be regarded as equal. On the contrary, man's word is but the acceptance of God's call and mission—his simple cooperation in the eternal "yes" of God. His answer must be so absorbed into and enveloped by the word of his calling that it forms an indissoluble union with it. The act by which man chooses a vocation is but the acknowledgment of the choice God has made of him. Only in this sense could Ignatius Loyola speak of election (*elección*) without feeling obliged to divide the one act into its divine and human components. His only concern was that man should choose what God chooses for him; that he be ready to recognize the divine choice and to accept it when he has recognized it. For Ignatius, in other words, human "perfection" is not a theme in itself; it is comprised entirely of the two concepts of disposition (*Sp Ex*, 1, 20, and elsewhere) and indifference (ibid., 23, 179, and elsewhere), which together express the untroubled readiness of the soul to receive the divine will in whatever form it may make itself known.

The surrender of man's will to God's elective will means the sacrifice of his personal freedom insofar as it is regarded or exists as an entity distinct from the divine will ("Take, Lord, and receive all my liberty . . ." [*Sp Ex*, 234]), so that man's will may live from the divine will and may have no other object than the divine freedom of choice itself. In the renunciation of every desire to realize the possibility of human freedom as an autonomous freedom independent of God and in the perfect binding of oneself, in obedience, to God's call, his grace and his mission, Ignatius sees man's highest opportunity of sharing the absolute freedom that is in God. The identification of one's own self with the mission received from God is an act of perfect faith and, as such, is the union of our work with the work of God in us (Jn 6:28–29). It is, at the same time, that which the Lord called "truth" and equated with true freedom: "If you abide in my word, you shall be my disciples indeed, and you shall know the truth, and the truth shall make you free" (Jn 8:31–32). Just as the truth of Christ lies in the fact that he did not seek himself, but the glory of him who sent him (" . . . He who seeks the glory of the one who sent him is truthful, and there is no injustice in him" [Jn 7:18]), so the freedom of Christ lies in the fact that he shares by obedience in the omnipotence and freedom of the Father: ". . . Whatever [the Father] does, this the Son does also in like manner" (Jn 5:19). And whoever shares, *by his obedience to mission*, in this truth and freedom of God *shares also in the choice*, the plans and the providence of God himself. He no longer meets God as one who lays before him petitions of his own designing; his petitions and desires are included in the decrees of God. The making and the granting of a request no longer confront one another as human and divine words; rather, the granting is already foreseen in the making of the request since it is encompassed in the one will of God (Mk 11:24; 1 Jn 5:15). By God's elective will in Christ, the human word is included in the trinitarian dialogue between Father and Son in the Holy Spirit: "Father, I give thee thanks that thou hast heard me. Yet I know that thou always hearest me . . ." (Jn 11:41–42). "And whatever you ask in my name, that I will do, in order that the Father may be glorified in the Son. If you ask anything in my name, I will do it" (Jn 14:13–14).

But precisely here it becomes apparent that the surrender of human choice in favor of the divine call is by no means identical with the extinction of the creature's function in favor of the divine function. The creature's act of obedience is not a quietistic renunciation of its own nature, nor is God's act of love a suppression of the autonomy of the one loved. If it is true that God "is all" (Sir 43:29), that he must become "all in all" (1 Cor 15:28), that, consequently, all freedom must enter into the divine freedom, all choice must be a cooperation with the divine choice, then there is no deeper human freedom than this choice, no greater autonomy than participation in the divine autonomy. Nothing makes the human individual more autonomous than the divine mission that he accepts in free obedience and with full responsibility. "The nearer a nature is to God, the more closely the divine excellence is portrayed in it. But it belongs to the divine excellence that it moves and inclines and leads all things, but is itself not moved or inclined or led by another. It follows, then, that the nearer a nature is to God, the less it is inclined by another and the more it is able to incline itself" (Thomas Aquinas, *De ver*, q. 22, a. 4 responsio). The paradox of this autonomy within the divine election is ultimately resolved only in the mystery of the trinitarian love between Father and Son, which, in the genuine mutuality of an exchange that does not destroy the personal freedom of the Son (although the Father is the archetype of the Son and the Son is the image of the Father), allows the unity of the divine will to exist and have its origin in the unity of the Holy Spirit. For just as the Son chooses what the Father chooses and "can do nothing of himself, but only what he sees the Father doing" (Jn 5:19), so the Father is moved by this loving obedience to such an extent that he, in his turn, chooses what the Son chooses and always hears the Son (Jn 11:42) when the Son utters his "I will" (Jn 17:24). The mystery of this mutual deference of Father and Son in the Holy Spirit is explainable only in terms of love; it has nothing to do with the neo-Platonic theory of the assimilation of the contingent and finite will to the unchangeable decree of the "absolute being". This pre-Christian philosophical solution is satisfying only so long as one believes that the finite is nothing more than a resigned "letting happen" of what has been unalterably decreed from all eternity. At this level, the only recourse seems to be a pantheistic mysticism in which the finite being sacrifices its own will in order to submerge itself in the abyss of a godhead that has no particular definable attributes or will. Much of this philosophical concept of man's relation to God has been incorporated, though certainly not intentionally, into the history of Christian spirituality. Nor will it be exorcised until we have come to realize, through the trinitarian mission of the Son, that the essential unity of the divine will is not incompatible with the autonomy of the Persons who possess it. Election, calling and mission on the part of the Father; obedience and acceptance of mission on the part of the Son— these are, in God, an eternal process that has its beginning, its execution and its end in the unity of their intellect and will. But this unity does not prevent the accomplishment of their mission of love from taking place in the eternal "now" that is perpetuated whenever anyone in the world is chosen, called and missioned by God in Christ. For this reason, the Christian's obedience in faith continues to be, at the "height of mysticism" and in the highest union of the creature's will with the divine will, an always living and dramatic dialogue: God's loving call and the creature's loving response—a response made possible, it is true, by the strength and love of the call itself, but not for that reason excluding the genuine and lasting participation of the creature in all its freedom both in the answer itself and in the accomplishment of the mission it has accepted. Only thus can the creature attain the fullness of its Christian truth.

As the annunciation of the creature's election by God, the call never loses its character of an event that is happening in the here-and-now; hence it never loses its historically determinable place in Christian life. It is not a general, diffused sound, not a music of the spheres that the creature may fail to recognize as an actual occurrence; on the contrary, it makes itself known with all the marks of an historical event. It comes to the prophets as they are guarding their flocks, to the apostles as they are mending their nets, to Levi as he is collecting taxes. Even though it proclaims God's election as it was in the beginning and will be for all ages to come, it has its own precise location in time and place. This historical call, moreover, can itself be divided into a series of historical acts that, taken together, reveal the whole history of a vocation: the act by which one to be called later is objectively elected upon entrance into the world; perhaps the act of a "fore-call", of an as yet indeterminable sense of election; the act by which one called is separated from the world for the mission he is to receive; the act of mission itself, by which the call becomes a vocation accepted; and, finally, the new calls that occur even after the mission has been accepted and that serve as guides at certain turning points and junctures of its accomplishment.

Those sent by God have been chosen and predestined by him "before the foundation of the world" (Eph 1:4–5), "and those whom he has predestined, he has also called" (Rom 8:30). This eternal predestination takes place in time as an election and separation (*segregatio*) from the world *even from the womb*. It can be a purely divine and invisible act like that by which Jeremiah was sanctified before he came "forth out of the womb . . . and [was] made . . . a prophet unto the nations" (Jer 1:5), or like that by which Paul "from [his] mother's womb [was] set apart and called . . . by [God's] grace" (Gal 1:15). Or it can be an act proclaimed from the beginning by signs, as was the birth of Jacob (Gen 25:24–26) or that of John the Baptist, who was "filled with the Holy Spirit even from his mother's womb" (Lk 1:15), where he leaped for joy (Lk 1:44). Thus Christ, too, was "called . . . from the womb" (Is 49:1, 5) and foreordained as Messiah by the sign of the virgin birth: ". . . Therefore the Holy One to be born [of thee] shall be called the Son of God" (Lk 1:35). But it can also be accomplished through the instrumentality of those who, in a prophetic union of their own election with God's eternal election, consecrate the child that is to come for a particular vocation, as Samson was "consecrated to God from [his] mother's womb" (Jg 16:17), and as Anna consecrated her future son, Samuel, "to the Lord [for] all the days of his life" (1 Sam 1:11). This *incorporation of human election into God's eternal act of election* continues to be reflected in the Christian Church not only in the action of pious parents who consecrate to the service of God the child they hope to have, but even more especially in the prayers and sacrifices of parents and grandparents, or of relatives in the priestly or religious life, who, invisibly to the eyes of the world, but visibly enough to the eyes of faith, have been influential, from the beginning, in the fostering of a vocation. From this partially discernible mystery, it is possible to obtain a deeper insight into the more hidden mystery of the Church's own role, by virtue of its dedication, prayers and sacrifices, in fostering the vocations that occur within it. The community of those who adhere to God and who have united their wills with the will of God is transferred, in a manner incomprehensible to us, to the very source of the ways and elections of God and allowed to share in the wisdom that was created by God "from the beginning, and before the world, . . . and unto the world to come . . . shall not cease to be" (Sir 24:14), and in the word that "came out of the mouth of the Most High" (Sir 24:5).

The first intimation of the call is not necessarily the moment of definitive mission. It can happen that a young man will be many times awakened from "sleep", as was the youth Samuel, but will come only gradually, perhaps through the instruction of one who has already heard the call, to know how he must answer the Lord when he calls. Thus Samuel was instructed by Eli: "Go, and sleep; and if he shall call thee any more, thou shalt say: Speak, Lord, for thy servant heareth" (1 Sam 3:9). The anointing of the first kings of Israel did not take place at the moment when they assumed office; the apostles were first initiated into the Lord's company before they were gradually made acquainted with their mission. On the road to Damascus, Paul encountered the call of God in unmistakable fashion, but the call contained only the promise of his later mission, not the mission itself. Struck by the personal call of the Lord, Paul asked: "Lord, what wilt thou have me to do?" (Acts 9:6), only to be referred to the Church: "Arise and go into the city, and it will be told thee what thou must do" (Acts 9:7). Between Paul's "yes" to the call of God and his "yes" to his mission there stretched a long road, marked by his efforts to reflect on what he had experienced, to identify himself with the Church's tradition (Acts 9:26), to gain the Church's approval of his mission (Gal 2:2)—a road of stillness and recollection: ". . . Without going up to Jerusalem to those who were appointed apostles before me, I retired into Arabia, and again returned to Damascus . . . [for] three years" (Gal 1:17–18). The hour of mission did not sound for him until, in the church at Antioch where the prophets and teachers "were ministering to the Lord and fasting", the Holy Spirit spoke, saying: "Set apart for me Saul and Barnabas unto the work to which I have called them" (Acts 13:1–2). Only then did Paul's mission to the Gentiles become a mission both from God and from the Church. The meeting at Damascus was a meeting with the Son of God, corresponding to the association of the other apostles with the Lord: "And last of all, as by one born out of due time, he was seen also by me" (1 Cor 15:8). But the mission at Antioch was an investiture by the Holy Spirit, by whom alone all missions are conferred. It should be noted here that even the Lord, whose election to mission and whose "yes" to that mission were from all eternity, was entrusted with his mission only when the designated historical moment of his earthly existence had arrived: not at the age of twelve when he demonstrated that his election was known to him, but at his baptism in the Jordan when the Spirit of the Father descended upon him so that, from then on, he might pursue his mission "full of the Holy Spirit" (Lk 4:1). Only after his Passion and Resurrection, when the Holy Spirit had begun to go forth from him (" . . . If I do not go, the Advocate will not come to you" [Jn 16:7]), do the apostles receive their definitive mission: "As the Father has sent me, I also send you. . . . 'Receive the Holy Spirit . . .' " (Jn 20:21–22). In the future, every mission, every installation in a particular state or way of life within the Church will be the work of this same Spirit (cf. 1 Cor 12:4–11; 2 Tim 1:6–14).

But the conferring of mission, which occurs at a particular historical moment in the life of the one called, is but the starting-point of what will be thereafter a constant *being-led by the Holy Spirit*. Whatever such a one undertakes in the accomplishment of his mission must be an expression of that mission and must therefore be undertaken under the guidance and with the counsel of the Holy Spirit. So it was in the Old Testament: "And who shall know thy thought, except thou give wisdom, and send thy Holy Spirit from above" (Wis 9:17). And so it is in the New Testament: "So they, sent forth by the Holy Spirit, went to Seleucia and from there sailed to Cyprus" (Acts 13:4). "Passing through Phrygia and the Galatian country, they were forbidden by the Holy Spirit to speak the word in the province of Asia" (Acts 16:6). It was this same Spirit that led Paul into tribulation and suffering, only intimating to him what lay before him: "And now, behold, I am going to Jerusalem, compelled by the Spirit, not knowing what will happen to me there; except that in every city the Holy Spirit warns me, saying that imprisonment and persecution are awaiting me" (Acts 20:22–23). And although some of his disciples "told Paul through the Spirit not to go to Jerusalem" (Acts 21:4), he did not let himself be dissuaded from the course revealed to him personally by the Spirit, which required that he seal his mission by uniting his own sacrifice with that of the Lord.

When one has given one's full "yes" to the call he has received, the Holy Spirit does not let him fail. *It is as if God himself assumed the responsibility for the one he has called.* There can scarcely be a call that does not seem at many moments and perhaps for long periods of time to be too heavy for human shoulders to bear, that does not seem to place exorbitant demands on the one who hears it. It may be the mission of a Job, who came close to blasphemy in his night of suffering: "I am leveled with the dust and ashes. . . . You turn upon me without mercy . . ." (Job 30:19, 21), yet who, because he had spoken his "yes" at the beginning, could not abandon his mission in that long night, and who, in the end, was praised by God: "And let my servant Job pray for you, . . . for you have not spoken rightly concerning me, as has my servant Job" (Job 42:8). It may be the mission of a Jeremiah, who, in his night of bitterness and abandonment railed at God: ". . . Thou hast filled me with threats. Why is my sorrow become perpetual, and my wound desperate so as to refuse to be healed? It is become to me as the falsehood of deceitful waters that cannot be trusted" (Jer 15:18), but whom the Lord led with gentle reproof back to his rightful service: "If thou wilt be converted, I will convert thee" (Jer 15:19). It may be the weariness and repugnance of an Elijah, who sat under a juniper tree in the desert and "requested for his soul that he might die, and said: 'It is enough for me, Lord. Take away my soul, for I am no better than my fathers' ", but who by morning, "in the strength of [the] food" sent him by the Lord, was able to walk "forty days and forty nights, unto the mount of God, Horeb" (1 Kings 19:4, 8). Or it may be the uncertainty of the "friend of the Bridegroom" who, in the night of his prison cell, was no longer sure of his own mission: "Art thou he who is to come, or shall we look for another?" (Mt 11:3), and whose question the Lord answered by praising him before the multitude as "more than a prophet" (Mt 11:9). All these have their place in the mystery of that dark night of mission into which even the Son of God was sent by his Father: "Father, if it is possible, let this cup pass away from me" (Mt 26:39)—that night that is but the nadir of mission; that trembling "no" that is but the other side of the fearless "yes" that the God who calls has accepted and has in his safekeeping so that, in the breaking of the human vessel, no harm may befall the mission itself. Once the one called by God has uttered his elective "yes" to the mission entrusted to him, he moves into a final state within that mission from which God will not allow him to fall—unless he himself chooses to do so: "And I give them everlasting life; and they shall never perish, neither shall anyone snatch them out of my hand. What my Father has given me is greater than all; and no one is able to snatch anything out of the hand of my Father. I and the Father are one" (Jn 10:28–30).

As he makes his choice, the one chosen by God enters into this unity between Father and Son. It is clear, then, that while the Son "calls his own sheep by name" (Jn 10:3), while he makes himself their "way" (Jn 14:6) and "leads them forth" (Jn 10:3) so that "no one comes to the Father except through" him (Jn 14:6), the sheep he calls are, nevertheless, always the Father's sheep; it is the Father who has given them to the Son (Jn 10:29). In like manner, every mission, every qualitative calling within the Church, proceeds *from the Father*: "No one can come to me unless the Father who sent me draw him" (Jn 6:44); "No one can come to me unless he is enabled to do so by my Father" (Jn 6:66). When the Son calls the apostles to himself, he is, as he always is, the one mediator of the Father's call; when he calls "men of his own choosing" (Mk 3:13), he is the revelation of the free and elective will of the Father. The will of the Son is not the will of a commander-in-chief who disposes his troops as he thinks best for the campaign he is planning; it is an obedient will, satisfied with whatever the Father has decided, and concerned about those who have been entrusted to him: "They were thine, and thou hast given them to me, and they have kept thy word. . . . Not for the world do I pray, but for those whom thou hast given me, because they are thine" (Jn 17:6, 9). The care that the Son, the Good Shepherd, exercises in regard to his sheep is a vicarious one: "While I was with them, I kept them in thy name" (Jn 17:12). When his suffering is about to begin, the Son restores them to the Father for safekeeping during the Passion: "But now I am coming to thee; . . . I do not pray that thou takest them out of the world, but that thou keep them from evil" (Jn 17:13, 15). Only when the Son has accomplished the redemption that is itself the will and command of the Father (2 Cor 5:19) can he share his glory with those who have been given him: "Father, I will that where I am, they also whom thou hast given me may be with me; in order that they may behold my glory" (Jn 17:24). And just as it is not the Son's prerogative to assign the privilege of sitting at his right or left hand (cf. Mt 20:23), since it belongs "to those for whom it has been prepared by [the] Father" (Mt 20:23), so it is not his prerogative to claim more workers than the Father has allotted him. On the contrary, when he sees the shortage of laborers called to the harvest, he recommends prayer to the Father: "The harvest indeed is great, but the laborers are few. Pray therefore the Lord of the harvest to send forth laborers into his harvest" (Mt 9:37–38). This prayer corresponds to the care the Father himself has for the harvest, for "the Father also seeks such to worship him . . . in spirit and truth" (Jn 4:23–24); but it is clear that he seeks them in order to lead them to the one true worshipper, the Son. The call proceeds from the Father and *leads the one called to the Son*, who has been called from all eternity by the Father. When the Son calls the elect who are in the world, he does so in his role as mediator of the Father's call. The Father introduces the one called into the unity of the one and eternal call that has its source in the loving choice with which he chooses the Son. This choice is confirmed when the Father sends the dove down upon the Son at his baptism by John, in which descent everyone who is sent receives his mission. And when the one called seeks in the same Spirit to imitate the Son's work in the world, when he receives the Spirit breathed out upon him by the

Son and goes forth as one sent ("Behold, I am sending you forth
. . ." [Mt 10:16]), then this missioning by the Son *in the Holy
Spirit* is a participation in the mystery of the *filioque* in which the
Son breathes back his Spirit to the Father: "Father, into thy hands
I commend my Spirit" (Lk 23:46); "and . . . he gave up his
Spirit" (Jn 19:30). If the way by which the Son leaves the world
and goes to the Father (cf. Jn 17:28) leads through the midst of
"wolves" (Mt 10:16), and even "into the bottom of the deep"
(Sir 24:8) and to ultimate abandonment by the Father (Mt 27:46),
it is, nonetheless, the Son's way to the Father as determined by
the Father alone and trodden by the Son under the guidance of
the Holy Spirit: "No one takes [my life] from me, but I lay it
down of myself. . . . Such is the command I have received from
my Father" (Jn 10:18). But it is also the way that must be trodden
fearlessly in the Father's Spirit by those called to follow the Son:
"But when they deliver you up, do not be anxious how you are to
speak; for what you are to speak will be given you in that hour.
For it is not you who are speaking, but the Spirit of your Father,
who speaks through you" (Mt 10:19–20). Once the Son has
returned to the Father, however, it is as true to say that the Son
confers missions within the Church (Eph 4:11) as to say that the
Father does so (Rom 12:3–8); in either case, it is always in the
Spirit "who allots to everyone according to his will" (1 Cor
12:11). The call is a trinitarian one that not only calls the elect,
but continues to call in the very call by which they are called.

2. THE STAGES OF THE CALL

In addition to the vertical analogy of election and vocation, in
which the creature's election and answer are absorbed into the
absolute word of God's choice, there is also, as we have seen
above, a horizontal analogy of the call, since God does not elect
and call all men in the same way, but sends forth his call in
varying degrees of intensity and urgency. To the extent that
every call is a personal one, it raises the one called out of a
world that is not affected by it, whose inhabitants perhaps, like

the companions of Daniel, did not see the vision, but were over-come by "an exceeding great terror . . . and fled away, and hid themselves" (Dan 10:7); or who, like the companions of Paul, were present at the event, "hearing indeed the voice, but seeing no one" (Acts 9:7), or who "saw indeed the light, but . . . did not hear the voice" (Acts 22:9) and "all fell to the ground" (Acts 26:14) although the call was not intended for or addressed to them; a world that hears the voice of the Father, as did those who stood around the Lord at his baptism, but hears it as though it were thunder or an angel speaking to him (Jn 12:29), so that they have an indirect knowledge of the call in its objectivity and are thus unwilling witnesses to its occurrence, but have no inner understanding of what they have heard. This process can be repeated in ever-narrowing selectivity, so that at first a whole nation is separated from the nations that have not been called; then, within this nation, smaller communities receive a more specific call; and finally, within these smaller communities, cer-tain individuals are privileged to hear a call that is both intimate and personal. In such cases, those called in the first sense may well seem to those called in the second sense to be relatively "uncalled" and, consequently, lacking in understanding; or those called in the first sense may believe, on the basis of this first, general call, that they are obliged in good faith to protest against the more particular call of a given individual. That there is no confusion in the resultant analogy, or hierarchy, of calls is due solely to the fact that the one God "who works all things in all" (1 Cor 12:6) remains Lord of all calls.

Basically, to be sure, the elective call is a sign of grace and, therefore, of predilection. From the beginning, however, God has forbidden man to regard his predilection for one as a sign of his prejudice against another. As grace, his selective call is simultaneously a mission—a mission to those who have not been given the grace of receiving the call so directly. No one, then, has the right to see in the fact that another has not been chosen a sign of reproach. It is clear from the parable of the workers in the vineyard that those not called at one time may yet be called at a later hour and will not suffer thereby: "Take what is thine and go; I choose to give to this last even as to thee. Have I not a right to do what I choose?" (Mt 20:14–15). Indeed, if we think seriously about mission and, in particular, about its representative character, that is, about the fact that those who have been called are called for the sake of others and work so that others may reap the benefit of their labors, then the last words of this parable will have a special meaning for us: "Even so the last shall be first, and the first last, for many are called, but few are chosen" (Mt 20:16; cf. 22:14). The mystery of God's election is revealed in the way he treats those whom he has chosen: "Why doth one day excel another and one light another, and one year another year, when all come of the sun? By the knowledge of the Lord were they distinguished. . . . Some of them God made high and great days, and some of them he put in the number of ordinary days. And all men are from the ground. . . . With much knowledge the Lord hath divided them and diversified their ways" (Sir 33:7–8, 10–11). His election is wisdom as regards the whole: For inasmuch as he sets "all [his] works, two and two, and one against another" (Sir 33:15), he is the God who does all things well.

In the Old Testament, the call went forth to Abraham, whom it singled out from among the nations (cf. Wis 10:5): "Leave your country, your kinsfolk and your father's home" (Gen 12:1), and all his descendants shared in his obedience to the call—first his physical descendants, the Jewish nation; then, because his election was also representative and symbolical, "all the nations of the earth" (Gen 12:3). Thus, the people of Israel became the chosen people: ". . . The Lord, your God, . . . has chosen you from all the nations on the face of the earth to be a people peculiarly his own. It was not because you are the largest of all nations that the Lord set his heart on you and chose you, for you are really the smallest of all nations. It was because the Lord loved you and because of his fidelity to the oath he had sworn to your fathers . . ." (Dt 7:7–8). "But thou, Israel, art my servant, Jacob whom I have chosen, the seed of Abraham my friend, in whom I have taken thee from the ends of the earth, and from the remote parts thereof have called thee, and said to thee: Thou art my servant: I have chosen thee, and have not cast thee away" (Is 41:8–9). By this election, Israel became a "just people", even a "blameless" people (Wis 10:15), that it might declare God's "wonderful works" (Tob 13:4) and make them known among those not called. God's holiness was made manifest in it so that, like "a city set on a mountain" (Mt 5:14), it might draw to itself the gaze of all the nations that had not been called: ". . . And all nations shall flow into it . . . and say: Come and let us go up to the mountain of the Lord, and to the house of the God of Jacob, and he will teach us his ways, and we will walk in his paths" (Is 2:2–3). Because God does not repent of his call or withdraw his election (Ps 89:31–38; Rom 11:29), the finality of this call to Israel is not changed even when he abandons the Israelites for a time because of their disobedience to their mission, for it is precisely "by their offense [that] salvation has come to the Gentiles, that they may be jealous of them" (Rom 11:11). If this is the result of Israel's offense, Paul concludes, then its true and lasting mission for the election and salvation of the whole world will be accomplished in even greater measure: "Now if their offense is the riches of the world, and their decline the riches of the Gentiles, how much more their full number! . . . For if the rejection of them is the reconciliation of the world, what will the reception of them be but life from the dead? Now if the first handful of dough is holy, so also is the lump of dough; and if the root is holy, so also are the branches" (Rom 11:12, 15–16).

Thus all Israel will be saved (Rom 11:26), and, through Israel, the multitude of the Gentiles will be sanctified; in the election of Israel, "all the nations of the earth" (Gen 12:3) are included and invisibly forechosen. But Israel's election, though real and final, is also earthly and exemplary: "Now all these things happened to them as a type . . . for our correction, upon whom the final age of the world has come" (1 Cor 10:11) so that, at last, the "intervening wall" will be broken down (Eph 2:14) and the Gentiles, too, will be incorporated into the general election.

On the other hand, Israel itself was the recipient of a general call and thus, by contrast with those within it who had received God's special call, was as one "not called". Of the twelve tribes, it was only the one tribe of Levi that was separated from the rest for the special service of the Lord. "From among the Israelites have your brother Aaron, together with his sons . . . , brought to you that they may be my priests" (Ex 28:1). A complete ceremony of ordination marked the beginning of their service (Lev 8), thus distinguishing it from every secular service by the people. But this election and separation of the Levites was also representative: "It is I who have chosen the Levites from the Israelites in place of every first-born that opens the womb among the Israelites. The Levites, therefore, are mine, because every first-born is mine" (Nb 3:12–13). Thus the representation here is a double one: The one tribe of Levi represents the twelve tribes, and the individual Levite represents the individual first-born among all the tribes of Israel; for every first-born among the tribes in excess of the number of Levites a ransom of "five shekels" was required (Nb 3:47). The vicarious election to the priestly state was thus both generic and particular. And if the whole nation was called out of heathen lands by a call that was symbolical because it was concerned with one land as opposed to other lands, then in the more specialized election to the priesthood the symbolism of the call had to be even stronger and more prophetic, for the tribe of Levi "shall not have any heritage in the land of the Israelites nor hold any position among them", for "I will be your portion and your heritage among them", says the Lord (Nb 18:20).

But whereas the calling of priests and Levites stood midway between a general and a personal call, yet was closer to being a general call since they owed their calling to their membership in a tribe, the calling of judges, kings and prophets was always a totally personal call. That the full freedom of God's call might be made manifest, moreover, these latter were called, not out of the tribe of Levi (as it were, as the "most called" among those who were "more called"), but, without discrimination, out of all tribes, classes, professions and ages—by which God would have us see the relativity of the call of Israel itself, since he can call prophets and wise men even from among the Gentiles, as he did in the case of Balaam and Job. The special calls are the most vicarious. Their recipients have less meaning in and for themselves than does the existence of a specially chosen people, for they exist only as a mission to the people. "Thou, therefore, . . . arise and speak to them all that I command thee" (Jer 1:17). Their deeds and sufferings are symbolical; they are living charades that the people must decipher, living statements of God's promises—whether of good things or of bad—to his people. Nor are they at fault if their preaching goes unheeded, if Jerusalem kills the prophets and stones those who are sent to it (cf. Mt 23:37), if their prophecies echo unheard and their warnings are scattered on the winds. For it is by this means that they become prototypes of the chosen Son of God, whose mission foundered in fruitlessness and destruction: "And I said: I have labored in vain, I have spent my strength without cause and in vain" (Is 49:4). But precisely through this prodigal spending of his precious strength, this shedding of his most pure blood, was his mission fulfilled beyond his greatest expectation: "It is a small thing that thou shouldst be my servant to raise up the tribes of Jacob, and to convert the dregs of Israel. Behold, I have given thee to be the light of the Gentiles, that thou mayest be my salvation even to the farthest part of the earth" (Is 49:6).

For those called by God, *the Old Testament yields to the New Testament* and the old forms of the call are translated into new ones. The formal structure remains: The chosen people called out of their sinfulness are now the Church, the assembly of those called to holiness, to communion with Christ, to the glory of the redemption (1 Pet 1:15; 2 Pet 1:3; Gal 5:8; 1 Th 2:12; and elsewhere). From its concentration in Christ's priesthood, the Levitical priesthood, to which one had to be "called by God, as Aaron was" (Heb 5:4), expands anew in the hierarchy of the Church, which has the same medial position between the general ecclesial form of the call and its personal form; the calling of the prophets is transferred to the apostles and those who come after them as a personal call to the personal following of Christ in the state of the counsels. And while it is true that Israel's symbolical function is fulfilled in the "truth" of the Church, the Church continues, nevertheless, to exist on earth as the suffering body of Christ, representing with its head the coming of the kingdom, the "everlasting Gospel" (Rev 14:6) that has been foretold, for "the end comes when he delivers the kingdom to his Father" (1 Cor 15:24). Just as "Israel is holy to the Lord, the first-fruits of his increase" (Jer 2:3), and just as, in the naming of the first-fruits, the whole fullness of the harvest is likewise to be understood, so Christ, the Redeemer of all, "has risen from the dead, the first-fruits of those who have fallen asleep" (1 Cor 15:20) and heads the company of those whose mission it is to be his representatives. Those who are redeemed in the Church are "the first-fruits of his creatures" (James 1:18), whom they are to represent and to bring to salvation by their sacrifices and prayers. Virgins, especially, are "purchased from among men, first-fruits unto God and unto the Lamb" (Rev 14:4). It is possible to discern three stages in Christ's delivery of all creation to the Father. ". . . Each in his own turn, Christ as first-fruits, then they who are Christ's, who have believed, at his coming. Then comes the end . . . when all things are made subject to him" (1 Cor 15:23–24, 28). But the Holy Spirit is the first-fruits given to us (cf. Rom 8:23). He is bestowed with every mission and, in the hearts of the children of men, pleads with unspeakable groanings for the fullness of redemption, implanting the groaning of creation in those children of God who are already redeemed and who, as the representatives of creation, will carry its groaning before the throne of God (Rom 8:21, 23, 26).

As the Church represents the world, so the priest represents the community in his official capacity, and the "apostle" represents it in his own person. As the representative of all, it is the priest's function to offer the Lord's sacrifice—to fill up in his flesh "what is lacking of the sufferings of Christ . . . for his body, which is the Church" (Col 1:24) and, still in his representative role, to fill up even in his spirit what it is given him to share of the Lord's spiritual sufferings: "I speak the truth in Christ, I do not lie, my conscience bearing me witness in the Holy Spirit, . . . for I could wish to be anathema myself from Christ for the sake of my brethren" (Rom 9:1, 3). In this respect, the call to holiness as it was in the Old Testament is not changed in the New Testament: It is a call in grace to share in the distribution of grace and, therefore, a call to a vicarious bearing of the guilt of all. It is the summons to an effective sharing of Christ's mission.

And yet, between the Old and the New Testament, the nature of the call underwent a noticeable change. It did not become more personal with the appearance of the incarnate Son, but rather more community-oriented. As a call to a visible nation, which had to manifest its unique calling and holiness by distinguishing itself sharply (even to the point of relentless warfare) from the pagan nations around it, the call to the Jews placed greater emphasis on the negative character of their mission, while the positive was reserved for the promised messianic era when, at last, the nation's exalted mission to the pagan world would be accomplished and the ultimate meaning of God's predilection for Israel would be revealed. In view of their visibility, it was only natural, therefore, that the representative role of priests and Levites should be concentrated almost entirely on the legal accomplishment of their service while the inmost meaning of the sacrifice they offered should remain veiled in the hiddenness of the promised sacrifice of Jesus Christ. The call and mission of the prophets exhausted itself in a definite and clearly defined task: The words the prophet was to utter and the deeds he was to accomplish were described in material terms; his mission acquired thereby a manageable finiteness that corresponded to the relationship between God, the Lord, and his human servants in the Old Testament. Because the Mediator had not yet come, they—the Lord who gave the commands and the servant who obeyed them—stood face to face with no one to mediate between them. There was as yet no possibility that the one chosen might share in the shaping of his mission, no personal training for mission, no possibility that the one sent might, on his own mature responsibility, be able to formulate this mission in the Holy Spirit. There was as yet no Holy Eucharist through which the Son's own mission might reside in the one sent. There was as yet no possibility of seeing in one's neighbor the very Son of God and thus of equating one's surrender to the divine mission with one's surrender to the human "thou". There was as yet no outpouring into men's hearts of the love of God that would enable them to experience the call itself as an unprecedented invitation to share in the work of that love that poured itself out "to the end" (Jn 13:1) and obedience to the call as the spending of oneself with Christ in the service of that same love. Everything was still held, as it were, in abeyance; was revealed, as it were, in outline and under a veil. And yet everything that was needed was already present; obedience to the divine call could have been as radical among the people and priests and prophets of the Old Testament as it was later to be among the Christians and saints of the New Testament. For that reason, there is ultimately no gradation between the two Covenants, as there was none among the twenty-four elders of Revelation (Rev 4:4), who were chosen in equal numbers from both Testaments so that they might sing not only the ancient canticle that Isaiah had heard (Rev 4:8), but also the "new canticle" (Rev 5:9) to the Lamb that was slain.

The gradations of the call as they have thus far been described take place explicitly *within the order of grace*. They are, in every instance, gradations of the call of the God of Abraham, Isaac and Jacob, who is also the God of Jesus Christ; they are in no way identifiable with the calls of the Creator God as such as he reveals himself indirectly in the orders of creation. The choice of human ways of life within the purely natural orders and "vocations"— the choice of a career in medicine or architecture, for instance, but also the choice of the married state and of a particular spouse —cannot be regarded as objects of divine election and vocation in the same way as can the forms of election we have discussed above. The call to a divine mission is an act of the personal elective love of God, an act of unique and singular predilection that fits into no secular category, although, looked at from without, it has this in common with natural selection—that it is, in analogous stages, the basis of a state of life. Events in the natural sphere are undoubtedly subject to divine providence, and what the Christian and everyone else who is open to grace experience therein can reveal to them at every step the loving care of the divine Father. If they remain in close touch with God in prayer and receive with obedience and gratitude whatever God may choose to send them, they will accept their secular vocation and their marital partners as special signs of God's love for them and, in making this or that choice, will fulfill the will of God in their lives, which they will live daily under the guidance of his grace. It is nonetheless true, however, that what is properly designated as the call of God is always far removed from a sphere in which the call is not heard; and the sphere from which the most general call of God—that which places the individual in the Christian state as such—is far removed is precisely the natural order.

This is not to say that there are not, within this order, phenomena that bear an analogy to the divine call. There are, for instance, forms of poetic inspiration, of rapture, that are not without similarity to the forms of supernatural inspiration or mystical experience of God within a genuine mission. But these phenomena have their source in the powers and constellations of nature, the "mother of all" (Sir 40:1). There are cases in which the meeting with a particular woman seems so fraught with destiny that it takes on the character of an eternal predestination and seems almost to presume a common preexistence; but marriages written in heaven and destinies readable from the stars are always but a reflection of the decrees of God that no horoscope, no knowledge of cosmic relationships, no intimations of parapsychological events can comprehend, but that are made known by God in the inscrutable transcendence of his revelation in Christ. This, then, is the "mystery of his will according to his good pleasure. And this is his good pleasure he purposed in him [Christ]" (Eph 1:9), which was revealed to Paul (Eph 3:3).

That is why the Fathers of the Church were so adamantly opposed
—before Thomas Aquinas conceded that astrology and, consequently, recognition of the cosmic determinants of man's fate
were admissible within certain limits—to the association of these
determinants with eternal revelation and refused to regard the star
of Bethlehem as an astrological phenomenon: God's election and
vocation had first to be recognized in their full freedom from
the determinants inherent in the natural order before it could be
admitted, on a second level, that God's free choice can also make
use of natural determinants and can become incarnate in them, not
from inner obligation, but by virtue of his sovereign pleasure.

If we pursue this thought to its ultimate conclusion, there is no
reason why we should not regard all natural providence—as God
allows it to act through secondary causes, through planetary,
historico-traditional and hereditary influences—as being actually
in the service of God's will. For just as God, Creator and Redeemer, is but one God, and just as the Old Covenant of the
Father and the New Covenant of the Son are together but one
eternal covenant of the triune God with mankind, so natural and
supernatural providence form a unity in which "for those who
love God all things work together unto good, for those who,
according to his purpose, are saints through his call" (Rom 8:28).
For such as these, all natural providence becomes a transparent
revelation of the call of God, which is operative in all things, even
in the details of their daily lives. And yet the nature of the call is
not changed thereby. It continues to be a call to leave the world
and to enter the Church, to leave the community and to enter the
priesthood or religious life. As a call to enter the Church, it is
basically a call to Christian life and will be operative in the whole
structure of the Christian's career and marriage. It will be the
magnet that gives the natural orders their Christian polarization
in his life. It will be the Christian concept of mission that gives
meaning and discrimination to his choice of secular ways and
means. But it will not itself be a call to any secular order.

Strictly speaking, the Christian's choice of a state of life should
not be described as an obligation to determine whether God is

calling him to the married state or to the priesthood or religious life. His choice is not between two equivalent calls. From the Christian standpoint, it is between the either-or of the general call to the Christian way of life (of which the decision to marry is usually a consequence) and the special call to the priesthood or religious life. If he is *not* the recipient of such a special call, he may yet be called to the married state. In his Rules for Thinking with the Church, Ignatius makes a clear distinction: "We must praise highly religious life, virginity and continence; and matrimony ought not be praised as much as any of these. We should praise vows of religion, obedience, poverty, chastity and vows to perform other works of supererogation conducive to perfection. However, it must be remembered that a vow deals with matters that lead us closer to evangelical perfection. Hence whatever tends to withdraw one from perfection may not be made the object of a vow, for example, a business career, the married state, and so forth" (*Sp Ex*, 356–57). What may seem harsh in this theoretical formulation becomes simple and clear when we look at actual practice in the Christian way of life. No sound and balanced Christian will ever say of himself that he chose marriage by virtue of a divine election, an election comparable to the election and vocation experienced or even only perceived by those called to the priesthood or to the personal following of Christ in religious life. One who chooses marriage simply has *not* experienced that special election in his soul; he does so, therefore, with the best conscience in the world and without imputing to himself any imperfection, but he does not, for that reason, claim that he is following a way specially chosen for him by God. He is but obeying God's general will for his creatures: "My son, . . . search the whole plain for a fertile field, sow your seed there, trusting in your own good stock."[2]

---

[2] Many Greek manuscripts as well as the Old Latin text of the book of Sirach (Ecclesiasticus) contain additional noncanonical verses. For the verse quoted here (Sir 26:20), which is one of the verses (19–27) added between 26:18 and 26:19 of the canonical text, I have used the translation to be found in the Jerusalem Bible, p. 1071, note f. [Tr]

It is more conceivable that an artist who feels within himself a truly "divine" calling should point to the example of Bezalel, of whom God said to Moses: "See, I have chosen Bezalel . . . and I have filled him with a divine spirit of skill and understanding and knowledge in every craft: in the production of embroidery, in making things of gold, silver or bronze, in cutting and mounting precious stones, in carving wood and in every other craft. As his assistant, I have appointed Oholiab. . . . I have also endowed all the experts with the necessary skill to make all the things I have ordered you to make . . ." (Ex 31:2–6). We could certainly argue that there is question here of God's unique appropriation of secular skills for the building of his holy Tabernacle and even that his choosing of those possessed of these skills for the building of an earthly sanctuary belongs exclusively to the Old Testament, since the Tabernacle of the Old Testament was not, in fact, a "true tabernacle", but only "a shadow of things heavenly" (Heb 8:2, 5) and would eventually yield to the true worship of God "in spirit and truth" (Jn 4:23). But such an answer is not totally satisfying. In the calling of Bezalel something doubtless makes its appearance that, within the chosen people and therefore within the Church, can be understood only as an analogous representation of the actual call that is the basis of a state of life. For if everything that happens to one chosen for the priesthood or the religious life happens, not for himself, but to provide a model for the community and the individual believer in it, then the call itself must also be, not for the one who receives it, but to provide a model for the community. The gift of "a divine spirit of skill and understanding" in the Old Testament corresponds to that Christian reality that Paul calls *charism* and that can be the perfecting by grace and the appropriating for the service of God of man's natural talents and abilities. There is no abyss between the secular orders and the grace of redemption; on the contrary, each of man's secular potentialities can be perfected from above by God for the good of the Church and the redeemed world. Thus the wisdom of Solomon is not a purely transcendent wisdom, but a wisdom that is passed "in each generation . . . into holy souls" (Wis 7:27); that "pervades and permeates all things" (Wis 7:24; quoted from the Jerusalem Bible [Tr]); that can adapt all the laws of nature to its every mood (Wis 16:20–26; 19:18–19); a wisdom that is incarnate not only in the proverbs of everyday life on earth, but even in natural science itself: "For he hath given me the true knowledge of the things that are: To know the disposition of the whole world, and the virtues of the elements, the beginning, and ending, and midst of all times, and alterations of their courses, and the changes of seasons, the revolutions of the year, and the dispositions of the stars, the natures of living creatures, and the rage of wild beasts, the force of winds, and reasonings of men, the diversities of plants, and the virtues of roots, and all such things as are hid and not foreseen, I have learned, for wisdom, which is the worker of all things, taught me" (Wis 7:17–21). Proper to revelation, then, is a supernatural, theological penetration of all earthly sciences without exception: cosmology and astronomy, physics, biology, pharmacology, botany and zoology, history, psychology and other intellectual disciplines. As natural sciences, these sciences are not sufficient unto themselves; they are permeated by divine wisdom, which "reaches everywhere by reason of her purity", which is "a vapor of the power of God, and a certain pure emanation of the glory of the almighty God", "the brightness of eternal light", the "unspotted mirror of God's majesty, and the image of his goodness" (Wis 7:24–26); a spirit that is bestowed only on those who are humble and who pray; that is a fore-shadowing of God's Son, whose advent is near and "in whom are hidden all the treasures of wisdom and knowledge" (Col 2:3). "For in him were created all things in the heavens and on the earth, things visible and things invisible . . ." (Col 1:16).

It is not surprising, therefore, but rather to be expected, that every earthly discipline and skill that is closed upon itself and re-fuses to open itself to supernatural wisdom—which, like "every good gift and every perfect gift" (James 1:17), comes down from above—leads ultimately to folly; for there is, for every natural gift bestowed on man by God, a grace-filled charism that marks its perfection. Since God decided to establish creation in the reconciliation wrought by Christ, this perfection belongs, by a kind of necessity, to man's natural heritage, which will be forever incomplete without it. Nor will God refuse to perfect the earthly work of anyone who prays for it: "I wished, and understanding was given me; and I called upon God, and the spirit of wisdom came upon me" (Wis 7:7). Thus Jew and Christian pray together: ". . . Prosper the work of our hands for us! Prosper the work of our hands" (Ps 90:17).

This grace-filled perfecting and appropriating of secular skills by God can manifest itself in a variety of forms and degrees. It can be a restrained and, as it were, indirect irradiation of a person's lifework on earth by the blessing of grace, as, for instance, in the case of a pure scientist; it can be the external employment of one in a secular profession to accomplish the work of God's kingdom, as in the case of a doctor, a lawyer, or a journalist; but it can also be an interior laying claim to an individual's whole natural ability, as it was in the case of Bezalel, who is here the prototype of all those called to greatness in the realm of Christian art. In appropriations such as these, which possess the individual in a kind of holy madness, which consume his whole life and all his senses in the service of an art that is itself a service of God— so that the individual may remain unmarried, and the ordinary routine of his life may become a chain of unbearable situations and sufferings—in such "vocations", which undoubtedly have their origin in a natural gift, but which develop manifestly and inevitably under the guidance of "divine wisdom", no one will fail to see a genuine analogy to vocations to the priesthood or the religious life within the Church.

This is all the more true because, as we have seen, even the priesthood has a natural anchorage in man's life in the community; it is not a delusion, therefore, to believe that there can exist a kind of natural endowment or *typical aptitude for the priest-hood*, in which case the priestly state would reveal itself once again as a kind of center and point of intersection between a purely, or at least preponderantly, natural talent, such as those for the secular professions, and a purely grace-inspired vocation that does not have its source in human nature, as in the call to follow Christ in the evangelical state. From the perspective of human nature, such a vocation to the priesthood could be regarded as an upper boundary: The combination of natural aptitude and inclination with a general Christian and ecclesial piety would—so far as the subject was concerned—be sufficient for a priestly vocation. From the normal perspective of the priestly vocation, however, such an upper boundary would be but the lowest admissible boundary, for there would usually be added to this natural disposition the clearly understood call of God's grace that corresponds to the engracement of the priestly state in both the Old and the New Testaments. Certainly, as we shall see, the call itself can take on such a multiplicity of forms and degrees of intensity that no one type can be regarded as normative for it. It is from this fact that the priesthood acquires that pendulous middle position that embodies both the analogy and the gradations of the call.

There are two ways, then, in which the call of God may appear to be complex. On the one hand, a vocation may come into existence from the concurrence of a number of elements: a natural component of native endowment, inclination and the impulse to develop one's natural gifts and powers; the purely supernatural component of a direct call from God; and, between the two, a concatenation of secondary components: help or hindrance from one's surroundings and the external conditions of one's life; evaluation and, in the case of the priesthood or religious life, acceptance or rejection by Church authorities. This complex of elements does not, of course, obviate the possibility that the simple and pure will of God can and must manifest itself in an individual life through and in a constellation of elements. For, in the ordinary course of events, God's will does not reveal itself in the abstract; it is incorporated into and incarnate in a multiplicity of secular factors. It is clear, moreover, from the tension between the "pure" and the secularly "mediated" and incarnate call of God that there are many difficult questions and conflicts to be resolved in this area. In whatever manner they may be resolved, it is certain that every call of God to a decision affecting one's whole life, whether that call be incarnate or pure, must be understood with absolute certainty before one undertakes to make such a decision. On this subject, Ignatius has formulated a rule that cannot be misunderstood: Every call from God to a state of life "is always pure and undefiled, uninfluenced by the flesh or any inordinate attachment". But, he says, many deceive themselves in this respect, for "they make a divine call out of a perverse and wicked choice" (*Sp Ex*, 172). Together, the totality of the components that determine one's choice—character, milieu, Church, God—must enable one to recognize the clear and unmistakable will of God.

On the other hand, this will, in all its clarity and unmistakableness, can itself assume a variety of forms that are quite independent of the complexities we have just discussed. God's ways with men are so countlessly manifold and so unique and personal that the forms his call may take can also be ever new and different. If the complexity of the call as we have first described it can be compared to a circle composed of many segments, yet in such a way that the whole circle reveals the whole will of God, the second kind of complexity might be envisioned by picturing to oneself the whole circle arrayed in constantly changing colors. We shall speak first of this second differentiation of what is always God's call as a whole, for it continues to be operative in every constellation of different elements.

3. THE FORMS OF THE CALL

Every call of God is a proclamation of the eternal election by which he "chose us in [Christ] before the foundation of the world, that we should be holy and without blemish in his sight in love"; by which he "predestined us to be adopted through Jesus Christ as his sons" (Eph 1:4–5). It is an act of love, and its goal is the holiness that is always a form of love. Because it has been formed and shaped by the laws of love, it can be comprehended only in terms of love.

We have already seen, in our study of the assumptions on which the concept of "state" is based, that no sharp distinction can be drawn between precept and counsel, between what a Christian must do and what he may do. By requiring that we love God with our whole heart and soul and mind and with all our strength, the commandment of love proceeds, without clearly defined boundaries, from the prohibition of mortal sin to the avoidance of venial sin and imperfection and, ultimately, to those heights of perfection that are unattainable by man in his purely human condition. It is a command given to all Christians, but given in a qualitatively special form to one chosen for the special following of the Lord in a special state of life. For the call directs the attention of one chosen for the evangelical life not so much to the counsels themselves in their material and practical aspects as to the greater love that is now required of him and that makes him aware for the first time of the possibility of binding himself by vow.

It follows that God can issue the commandment of love, which is the essential content of every genuine call, in varying degrees of urgency and clarity. For many, its sound is dissipated; they regard it as something to be taken for granted, as something that does not require their special attention. Of course God demands love; of course there is such a thing as a first and greatest commandment; of course every Christian is called to obey it, whether well or badly, to the best of his ability. And God will help our weakness and, we hope, forgive our failings. So far as its content is concerned, the commandment of love sounds plainly enough, but it strikes no answering chord in the one who hears it. It compels him to no conclusions that could force him out of the rut he is in. It is like a pillar whose base and lower segments are illuminated and draw attention to themselves while the upper segments and capital are so hidden in shadows that one is only vaguely aware of their existence. One knows, certainly, that they are there, but it never occurs to one to observe them more closely. Though they are linked to the segments one can see by the shaft of the pillar, one does not feel obliged, or "called", to search out their secrets.

This attitude, which is that of many Christians, has a twofold aspect. Undoubtedly it is the expression of a certain indifference toward the love of God, of the desire "to be left in peace" that is, to some extent, common to all those marked by original sin and that was ultimately the reason why even the chosen apostles fell asleep on the Mount of Olives. Persons in this category will always experience a certain sense of guilt before the ever-increasing demands of the commandment of love. But whereas, in the case of those genuinely called, this guilt will be translated into a fundamental change of attitude, into an impulse to give themselves wholly to the following of Christ, it will continue to be for others no more than a remote and static background. Many of them are aware that "something should be done", but "the hour of death comes, and they have not made use of any means" (*Sp Ex*, 153). After all, their inactivity can always be explained away with the excuse that they have not received a special call. Because some are called to more than others are, those not so called may feel that they are less called. Whereas it is God's nature to be always oriented toward a "more" that is not to be interpreted in terms of a "less", but is itself already a "yet more" (Sir 43:30), it is man's nature to define this "more" precisely in terms of a corresponding "less". Thus, while God exceeds the human norm by his call for "more", man—for whom the opening thus afforded presents a first glimpse of the distinction between "more" and "yet more"—becomes for the first time properly aware that such a distinction exists.

The call to a "yet more" of love of God makes this "yet more" not only visible, but also accessible to man. Light illumines the upper regions for him, revealing both the whole horizon of love as it stretches into infinity and its distinctively divine form. Love no longer appears to be something unattainable; the impossibility of fulfilling its demands no longer appears to be a sad, but regrettably unalterable, fact. Love is rather a flame that enters the heart of him who hears its call so that, casting aside with a light heart all that is finite, he is able to nourish love's unquenchable fire and fan it into full blaze. From the very boundlessness of the divine command as it has been made known to him he comes to know also the boundlessness of the answer he can give—an answer in which the barriers have disappeared between obligation and choice, between precept and counsel. The manifold expressions of love no longer seem to be a "work of supererogation", but an integral part of the "one thing necessary". The sign of contradiction—the fact that absolute love, which *must* be loved, *is* not loved—is of the world. One who has been touched by love will not rest until he has done all in his power to gain the victory for love. His whole ethic is subsumed under the sign of this one commandment: Only that is good and permissible that can meet God's call for more love; and, even though it be a thousand times approved by the world as good and proper, only that is bad that cannot meet this test. He looks past all established norms to fix his gaze on the boundlessness of infinite love and cannot forget what he sees there. One who has ventured to look upon this love can perhaps act as though he has seen nothing, has heard nothing. He can hide behind the dictates of official morality and believe himself safe among men and perhaps even safe before God. But he deceives himself, for he will always be of the number of those who have said "no"; of those on whom Jesus has looked in sorrow.

The call to love God boundlessly is always, at the same time, God's offering of his own love to the one thus called. Because this is so, the call bears in itself the possibility not only of understanding, but also of responding to the love to which it calls. Indeed, every special form of the divine call contains also the special form and grace of the response. From this perspective, it is possible to comprehend the otherwise incomprehensible stages described by St. Ignatius in the meditation on the Three Kinds of

Humility. The first kind "consists in this, that as far as possible I so subject myself as to obey the law of God our Lord in all things, so that not even . . . to save my life here on earth would I consent to violate a commandment . . . that binds me under pain of mortal sin" (*Sp Ex*, 165). The second kind so purifies this responsive readiness that one awaits God's good pleasure in total indifference as to what he may command so that "not for all creation, nor to save my life, would I consent to commit a venial sin" (*Sp Ex*, 166). As Ignatius describes it, one would think that there could not possibly be another degree of humility beyond this absolute readiness. Nevertheless, there is, for Ignatius, a third "most perfect" kind of humility: "If we suppose the first and second kind attained, then whenever the praise and glory of the Divine Majesty would be equally served, in order to imitate and be in reality more like Christ our Lord, I desire to choose poverty with Christ poor, rather than riches; insults with Christ loaded with them, rather than honors; I desire to be accounted as worthless and a fool for Christ, rather than to be esteemed as wise and prudent in this world. So Christ was treated before me" (*Sp Ex*, 167). Except in answer to the clearly expressed—or at least directly or indirectly implied—will of God for one in a position to regard the third kind of humility as a valid option, the choice of this kind of humility, which goes beyond pure indifference, would be an anticipation of the divine call and, as such, a nullification of the whole foundation of the Spiritual Exercises. Even the ability to contemplate such a course of action, which is the way of those beloved of God, is a grace bestowed only in consequence of God's special invitation. Certainly no Christian life can be lived in total unawareness of the mystery of sharing Christ's suffering, for "all who want to live piously in Christ Jesus will suffer persecution" (2 Tim 3:12); but it is given to only a few to understand this mystery as the norm of their lives. That is why so many to whom God offers such a grace either wilfully ignore it or, by their way of life, make it impossible for him to utter the call he had intended for them.

All forms of God's special call—and that is basically what we are considering here—are forms of love and, for that reason, different from the mere command that a master might issue to his servant. Nevertheless, the manner and *the very sound of God's voice can be different* depending on whether the call is to the priestly state or to the state of the counsels. The priesthood is primarily an ecclesiastical function, hence the call to it will also have something official about it and will have, to a certain extent, the character of a *command*. It is closer to the categorical "follow me" that Christ spoke to his apostles, thereby summoning them from their secular way of life in order to give them a new position; it is like a muster roll in which each one is called by name and must step forward (Mk 3:13). Peter is taken by surprise when his name is suddenly changed and he is claimed for office; Nathanael's hesitation is overcome by the astounding revelation of the omniscience of him who calls him (Jn 1:42, 48). The call to the evangelical life is somewhat different. Because it is a call to personal discipleship and, therefore, much more in need of a freely given personal response, it is more like an *invitation*. To the young man who perceived in himself a yearning for wholeness the Lord opened a door and showed him the possibility of entering by it: "*If* thou wilt enter into life, keep the commandments." And then: "*If* thou wilt be perfect, go, sell what thou hast . . . , and come, follow me" (Mt 19:17, 21). In this way, too, as we have already seen, the calling of the beloved disciple differed from the calling of Peter to the ministry. Drawn by the Lord's love, John was already seeking him. When the Lord turned and asked: "What is it you seek?" the answering question: "Rabbi . . . , where dwellest thou?" elicited the welcoming invitation: "Come and see" (Jn 1:38–39).

In other words, the refusal to heed the "command" to office is like the ignoring of a precept, while the refusal to hear the "invitation" to personal discipleship touches something more personal; it is not precisely the breaking of a commandment (for there is a question here "only" of a counsel), but it wounds the Lord's love in a way that is far more intense and intimate. Jesus loved the young man who desired greater perfection (Mk 10:21).

When the youth "went away sad, for he had great possessions" (Mk 10:22), his sadness was slight compared with that of the Lord who watched his departure.

The word "counsel" is not fully adequate to convey the personal love of God that is reflected in the invitation to personal discipleship. Even when there is question of "good counsel", a counsel is still something that issues from an uninvolved source. If it is not followed, the one giving it suffers no loss thereby. The predilection with which God calls man and offers him the grace of insight into and participation in the deeper mysteries of divine love is affected differently by the discourtesy of a rejection than by disobedience to a formally expressed "commandment". But this also means that the change by which a call that is predominantly one of command becomes predominantly one of invitation is by no means to be understood as a lessening of its urgency. On the contrary, the more God's love is revealed in a call, the less this call can arm itself with genuine sanctions. The more such a call is the expression of God's defenseless love in search of man's cooperation and able to offer no other inducement to discipleship than the hope that man will understand the requirements of love, the more compelling—if the call is addressed to one who loves—will become the necessity of answering it. The urgency becomes so strong that every command, every precept of law, seems but an echo of this necessity: that God, who loves boundlessly, must be loved boundlessly in return. It was in this that John saw the whole of Christianity: "He who says that he abides in him, *ought* himself also to walk just as he walked" (1 Jn 2:6); "In this we have come to know his love, that he laid down his life for us; and we likewise *ought* to lay down our life for the brethren" (1 Jn 3:16); "Beloved, if God has so loved us, we also *ought* to love one another" (1 Jn 4:11). In the New Testament, this necessity is the foundation of every other necessity of laws that henceforth exist, not of themselves, but in dependence (cf. Mt 22:40) on the law of love in which "the whole law is fulfilled" (Gal 5:14) and even "all prophecy", whereas the law that is not regarded as an expression of love "is not made for the just, but for the unjust and rebellious, for the ungodly and sinners . . ." (1 Tim 1:9).

Nevertheless, it would be false to assume, at this point, that the two forms the call may take are diametrically opposed, for there are, in fact, points of contact between them. On the one hand, the state of election forms, as we have seen, an analogous unity so that what is initially a call to the priestly state can lead its recipient to ever greater personal discipleship, to a concomitant observance of the counsels, whether actually or in spirit. On the other hand, the priesthood can develop, like a hidden inner fruit, from what is initially a call to the state of the counsels. At the very least, we can say that every special call that comes in the form of a command has, at the same time, the form of an invitation, though not every form of invitation has also the form of a command.

Indeed, there are within the invitations of God *all possible gradations between a clearly expressed wish*, which can be the equivalent of a command for one who loves, *and the offering of a possibility*, the realization of which depends almost entirely on man's good will. In reflecting on his state of life, many a youth comes close to the region of God's special call; the call itself does not follow, yet he knows that nothing prevents him from drawing closer to that region in which the call is possibly or even probably to be heard. But he turns aside too soon and thus never hears the call. Or God charts the life of a young person in such a way that, when he reaches this or that turning point in his growth to maturity, he will, without knowing it, be brought face to face with the call. But he hides himself in the bushes, perhaps even as a child, and the road mapped out for him remains untraveled. Or it can be that he actually reaches the region of God's qualitatively higher call, comes "within calling distance" of God's voice, but the call—by reason of its objective form rather than the imperfect manner in which it is heard—allows him the choice of following it or not following it. On the one hand, he knows quite clearly that there is an ordinary way of life that it is not forbidden him to follow. On the other hand, the form in which the call comes to him lacks the magnetic appeal by which other forms are able to exert such an irresistible attraction. Just as the mystery of the divine freedom of grace gives free play to God's election, so this same divine grace gives free play also to the response of human freedom. The incomprehensible vicissitudes of the relationship of love between God and man are not less tender and manifold than are those between lovers before the door of the married state closes. There is room for many a reflection, many a consideration; and if, for some, loving hearts beat so irresistibly for one another that marriage seems to be the only answer, for others, love can require, perhaps for years and precisely for the sake of love, that the utmost discretion be exercised and that the partner be allowed to reach a decision in freedom.

Like every relationship of love between human beings, so every call of God has its own history and its own development. Only rarely is one who has not been called from earliest youth set on the path of vocation. As a child, one hears the voice of God, either urgently or at irregular intervals, or like a steady reminder and invitation that are not yet clearly defined and so are not necessarily understood by the child in the sense of a call to a state of life. Generally, it becomes clear only in retrospect and from the perspective of the call that the whole course of one's childhood has been a time of guidance, of protection and of planned preparation for the task later to be assumed. Neither in this regard nor in the call itself are there universally valid norms: Every form the call may take is a new and never-to-be-repeated love story. Only one thing is certain: Whoever follows the light of this call and remains true to the divine guidance will not be abandoned by God, but will be led to the clarity of absolute choice. It is uncertain, on the other hand, how long God's patience will endure for one who resists and closes himself to the call. Undoubtedly there are cases, like that of Jonah, in which God overtakes one who is fleeing before him and, by his supreme power, establishes such a one in his mission; cases, too, in which God tolerates for decades one pretending to be deaf to the call only to address him with the irony of love when at last he lies defeated on the ground: "It is hard for thee to kick against the goad" (Acts 26:14). Yet the other case, the case of the rich young man, is surely the more frequent one: God extends his invitation once, perhaps more than once, but finally ceases to call the soul that rejects his friendship. When this happens, God's wooing of this soul is essentially at an end. This does not mean that such a one's salvation is in doubt, for he will always receive the grace necessary to save his soul. But it does mean that he has lost forever the opportunity of becoming a chosen friend of God. God does not twice bestow a qualitatively special call. He may wait, it is true, until an individual is finally ready to make the definitive choice; but if the choice is negative, no later repentance will restore the opportunity that has been lost.

The forms of the call are always unique; they can neither be repeated nor assigned by casuistry to already existing categories. Yet these forms are the forms of every Christian life, and all casuistry relates to the law of God's personal guidance, which is always new. Every "system" of spirituality, of "asceticism and mysticism", is an attempt to understand and describe the forms of God's call, whether they lead to the Church's call of grace or to special vocations within the Church. The most important act of Christian life is, however, the personal hearing of every call directed to oneself and the ability to understand it. No one else can hear my call for me. No knowledge of God and his ways can replace an attentive and obedient ear. The essence of being a Christian is to be open daily and hourly to the call of God and to let oneself be touched and guided by it. "Take heed, brethren, lest perhaps there be in any of you an evil, unbelieving heart that would turn away from the living God. But exhort one another every day, while it is still Today, that none of you be hardened by the deceitfulness of sin. . . . Today if you shall hear his voice, do not harden your hearts . . ." (Heb 3:12–13, 15).

The differences in the form of the call not only affect the prehistory of God's election, but are revealed also, *even after the election* and in the undertaking of mission, in the differences that exist among those who are called. One called by God to become a priest will retain, in the nature of his missionary activity, something of the form of this call. His attitude toward God and neighbor, his way of looking at Christian life, of judging virtue and sin, even of administering the sacraments and of serving his congregation, will reveal certain traits that will distinguish him from the typical recipient of a vocation to the religious life. He will be "closer to nature"; however supernatural his motives, he will never lose sight of the natural aspect, but will be inclined to understand the guilty or those in need of instruction from the standpoint of character and morality and to instruct them with this in mind; he will preserve an inner sensitivity to family, state and social milieu. The religious priest, on the other hand, who has taken his place by the Cross at the invitation of the Crucified One, will see and judge everything from the perspective of the Cross, will sometimes show himself insensitive to and ignorant of the world in what pertains to the natural order, will solve problems of conscience from the supernatural perspective of the love of God and of Jesus Christ, will always view others in terms of their grace-filled mission, and will guide them on these terms.

In the case of explicit personal calls to discipleship, there are also considerable differences in the form such calls may take—differences, for instance, between those who are, to a certain degree, compelled by God to undertake a great personal mission and those who have been drawn into a particular state of life by the Lord's gentle embrace. Paul belongs to the first group; John to the second. Paul, who went up to Damascus "breathing threats of slaughter against the disciples of the Lord" (Acts 9:1), was thrown from the saddle by a call that was like a flash of lightning. Everything about his call was harsh: the light that shone around him and literally blinded him; the Lord's almost mocking victory over the strong-spirited man who lay on the ground "trembling and amazed" (Acts 9:6) before him; the brusque command: "Arise and go into the city, and it will be told thee what thou must do" (Acts 9:6); the merciless prophecy of the difficulties attendant upon his mission: ". . . This man is a chosen vessel to me. . . . I will show him how much he must suffer for my name" (Acts 9:15–16). Like a trembling ox, he was branded with the stamp of his vocation. No one asked his consent; it seemed to have been swallowed up by the enormity of the revelation of the mystery that was entrusted to him (cf. Eph 3:1–4). It was not expressed in words. Indeed, something of the violence of the grace that overpowered him at his calling remained so strongly in Paul's consciousness that he experienced his apostolate as a stewardship forced upon him even though he willingly accepted and performed it: "For even if I preach the Gospel, I have therein no ground for boasting, since I am under constraint. For woe to me if I do not preach the Gospel! If I do this willingly, I have a reward. But if unwillingly, it is a stewardship that has been entrusted to me. What then is my reward?" (1 Cor 9:16–18). Even when he received the most exalted revelations and sang the most glowing hymns about the love of God, Paul never forgot the image of the "ox that treads out the grain" ("Is it for the oxen that God has care? Or does he say this simply for our sakes?" [1 Cor 9:9–10]). Later, he felt again the goad against which he kicked: "And lest the greatness of the revelations should puff me up, there was given me a thorn for the flesh, a messenger of Satan, to buffet me" (2 Cor 12:7).

If it was the Lord's "feet like fine brass, as in a glowing furnace" (Rev 1:15) that shaped Paul for mission, it was the Lord's "eyes like to a flame of fire" (Rev 2:18) that did so for John. The Lord had no need to overpower him in order to win his allegiance. From the moment he caught sight of the Lord and heard his voice, John was drawn out of himself and into the pure seeing, hearing and touching of the love that was revealed to him: "I write of what was from the beginning, what we have heard, what we have seen with our eyes, what we have looked upon and our hands have handled: of the Word of Life. . . . What we have seen and have heard we announce to you, in order that you also may have fellowship with us" (1 Jn 1:1, 3). When John emerged from this experience to announce what he had seen and heard, shedding, as it were, streams of grace, he could proclaim only the wonder of the Lord's love. Whereas Paul's individuality projected itself precisely for the sake of his mission and drew all eyes to itself ("Brethren, be imitators of me" [Phil 3:17]), John's individuality was, as it were, extinguished, its outline erased; his whole being became, as it were, transparent so that the one light of the Lord's life might shine through it. Thus the forms of the call leave their mark on the forms to which they call. Nor is it permitted to say that one of these forms is better than another. They are all best when they correspond exactly to the call addressed to them, for "there are varieties of gifts, but the same Spirit; and there are varieties of ministries, but the same Lord; and there are varieties of workings, but the same God, who works all things in all" (1 Cor 12:4–6).

4. THE ELEMENTS OF THE CALL

Until now, we have been considering the call of God as an indivisible reality, an expression of the unity of God's will for the one called, the exact nature of which will differ according to the form and tone it may assume. We have seen, too, that this unity of God's call and will can be composed of many elements, all of which must be taken into account if we are to realize and understand the unambiguousness of the call. So long as we are in this world, we do not see God face to face even in the most exalted contemplation. Nor do we hear his voice except as it is mediated through the veil of creation. Christ himself, who is God, lets us see his divinity only through the veil of his humanity, and even the most intimate inspirations and impulses of the Holy Spirit in our soul, which, psychologically speaking, seem absolutely unmediated, are, by their very nature, transmitted through the medium of creation. This is true also of the divine call. We should not assume, however, that the call is necessarily weakened by being thus mediated or that it becomes thereby less unambiguous or less comprehensible. For just as Christ's word from the Father, though transmitted by created means, retains for the believer its absolute clarity and full strength of impact, so the call he transmits by secular means is equally unmistakable. But "their ears are uncircumcised, and they cannot hear" (Jer 6:10).

Two kinds of factors are operative in the mediation of God's voice: *subjective factors* that mediate the call through personal inner experiences, events and insights; and *objective factors* that make it known from without, above all through the ministers and elements of the objective ecclesiastical order of God's salvation. St. Thomas tells us that "God calls both exteriorly and interiorly". But since every call of God is addressed personally to a human spirit and since the Christian is destined by the Church and his mission within the Church to execute it either as an ecclesiastical office or as a charism, every call must somehow be transmitted both subjectively and objectively. It is impossible that God's call should come to an individual *only* from without so that the Church could, for instance, ordain as priest one who feels himself in no way inwardly called to the priesthood and such a one, by virtue of his ordination alone (which, of course, would be valid if he gave his consent to it), would become as one genuinely called. But it is just as impossible that God's call should come to an individual *only* from within so that it may or must be carried out apart from or even against the Church. On the other hand, it is quite possible that a personal call may not be immediately recognized as such by the Church and that one called will, in consequence, be obliged to carry out his mission against strong opposition even though he seeks to the best of his ability to do so in accordance with the mind of the Church. Despite the Church's resistance, such a mission will be as truly an ecclesiastical one as were the missions of those called to initiate great reforms within the Church, for they, too, had to overcome harsh opposition with the help of God's grace before at last—whether during their lifetime or after it—receiving ecclesiastical recognition.

The relationship between subjectivity and objectivity plays a role also in the graduated analogy of the call. If we assume the usual practice of baptizing children, then the objective call so obviously precedes the subjective in the general call by which Christians are called out of the world and into the Church that the individual's subjective answer is always second in time, a confirmation of the grace of baptism already objectively received through the Church. By reason of this sacramental grace, the Holy Spirit lives in the soul of the one baptized, uttering there his "Abba! Father!" (Rom 8:15) and inviting the spirit of one who has received his grace to do likewise. "The Spirit himself gives testimony to our spirit that we are the sons of God" (Rom 8:16). The objective confirmation of God's call by the Church is so much more prominent than the subjective that it seems initially to be the only element present, for the subjective consent to God's call is, for the time being, made vicariously by the godparents.

In the case of a conversion or a call to the priesthood, the two factors—subjective and objective—achieve a kind of balance. In a *conversion*, God's subjective call takes the initiative, leading one who has first surrendered himself wholly to the "kindly guiding light" (Newman) in his soul step by step into the Church. Feeling his way, the convert comes gradually to know the objective components and criteria of the call and of God's order of salvation as it is embodied in the Church, while the Church, for its part, comes to recognize a genuine call of God in the candidate for baptism. It is a mutual recognition of the genuineness of God's sign—by the convert, who learns to test the genuineness of what is subjective and experiential by subjecting it to an objective authority and a sacramental order; and by the Church, which places its ministerial function at the service of God's subjective way of grace for this soul.

Something similar occurs in the case of a call to the *priesthood*. Here, too, a subjective certainty of being called coincides with an objective acceptance and recognition on the part of the Church. But the constitutive elements of this mutuality are not always the same. On the one hand, an individual with a strong inner light and consciousness of mission may have to struggle for a long time before gaining ecclesiastical recognition; on the other hand, the eye of the Church may perceive an individual's vocation and his aptitude for it more quickly than he does himself and it may be his acceptance by the Church that confers on him the inner confidence and certainty he had hitherto lacked. Because the official Church plays so significant a role in the case of a priestly vocation—more significant than in the case of acceptance into the Church, the objective confirmation of the call and, with it, the indispensable admission to ministry is particularly important.

In the case of a vocation to explicit personal discipleship in the *state of the counsels* or to an explicit personal mission as such, as in the case of Joan of Arc, for instance, or the Curé of Ars, the balance falls unequivocally on the side of the subjective. Recognition by a superior is not an adequate complement or substitution for one's own lack of certainty about one's vocation. By the same token, a mission can actually exist even if it is not always recognized by the objective authority of a religious order or of the ecclesiastical hierarchy. For just as the Church, as an objective ministerial institution, has authority in all that pertains to the sacramental conferral of grace, to decisions in matters of dogma, to preaching and to the governing and guiding of the faithful, so God reserves to himself the right of personal access to souls in order that he may work in them and accomplish in them his good pleasure. The fact that all grace is bestowed through the communion of saints does not mean that it must, for this reason, be bestowed directly through the Church as an external institution. Nor does the experiential fact that the Church must exercise care in evaluating both subjective inner inspirations and ecclesiastical missions contradict the other fact that all calls to the personal following of the Lord and, indeed, all great and unique missions within the Church come, in the last analysis, purely from God and, psychologically speaking, are made known directly to the one called. The same Ignatius who, in his Rules for Thinking with the Church, was so insistent that "we must put aside all judgment of our own, and keep the mind ever ready and prompt to obey in all things the true spouse of Christ our Lord, our Holy Mother, the hierarchical Church" (*Sp Ex*, 353), was just as insistent that "God can give consolation to the soul without any previous cause [that is, without the obstructive mediation of creatures]", for "it belongs solely to the Creator to come into a soul, to leave it, to act upon it, to draw it wholly to the love of his Divine Majesty" (*Sp Ex*, 330). For this same reason, he advised that during the Exercises, which have as their sole purpose the hearing of the call to personal discipleship, "the director of the Exercises, as a balance at equilibrium, without leaning to one side or the other, should permit the Creator to deal directly with the creature, and the creature directly with his Creator and Lord" (*Sp Ex*, 15).

Whereas the ecclesiastical ministry plays a significant role in the secular priest's call to vocation, the superior of a religious order has a much lesser role with regard to the unity of the call. He is authorized and obliged to test whether the interior call is genuine, but he would fail not only against love, but also against the Holy Spirit if he rejected one seeking admission in cases where the call is genuine and there are no obstacles to or reservations about following it. It would be wrong to conclude from this, however, that such a one has an actual right to be admitted to a particular religious order or monastery, for this right can be established only by Church law. Nevertheless, it is the prerogative of the Holy Spirit to have his demands and inspirations accepted and followed by the Church as a whole. If God "calls both exteriorly and interiorly", as Thomas says, then it is his will that these two aspects work together to establish unity between vocation and mission. So, too, in other instances, the different aspects of a single grace work together to produce a fruitful unity: The grace of confession, for instance, achieves unity when subjective repentance is joined to objective absolution by a priest.

A quick glance at some recent studies of the concept of vocation will help to make this point clear.[3] A heated controversy on the

---

[3] Cf. Joseph Brandenburger, "Vocatio Sacerdotalis", *Zeitschrift für katholische Theologie* 38 (1914), 63–74; Wilhelm Stockums, "Der theologische Beruf nach den neuesten kirchlichen Bestimmungen", *Theologie und Glaube* 14 (1922), 193–212; Franz Hürth, "Zur Frage nach dem Wesen des Berufes", *Scholastik* 3 (1928), 94–102; Raoul Plus, "Vocation", *Dictionnaire apologétique de la foi catholique* IV

subject centered around the theses of the Sulpician, L. Brancherau,[4] who argued that the inner attraction, the strong subjective inclination to the priesthood, is the most significant criterion of a genuine vocation, and those of Canon Lahitton,[5] who, in several works in which his thought continued to develop, maintained above all that the priestly vocation has its source in the official Church, in the bishop, and requires of the subject only that he have "an aptitude" (*idonéité*) for such a vocation, which meant basically that he be suited to priestly service in the diocese.

In the first edition of his work, Lahitton defended the view that external calling by the bishop is a manifestation of God's eternal election; later he taught that the whole power of election is transferred from God to the Church in such a way that God actually divests himself of his power to elect in order to confer it on the Church, which already has the power of ordination.[6] The bishop, he said, creates (*crée*) the vocation—a view he tried to support by referring to Thomas' theological teaching that the bishop chooses his assistants just as a king chooses his ministers (*Suppl*, q. 38 a. 1) and, in consequence, always ordains his priests validly if not always licitly, since a certain "*vocabilité*" (aptitude) is, in any event, necessary. We find here, in a quite different setting, the same teaching about the states of life that we found in the works of Mercier and his followers. Brandenburger, in his caustic description of the controversy, points out—not without justice—that it was fundamentally a debate between secular and religious clergy. Servites, Dominicans, Capuchins—all reached for the pen to refute Lahitton's exaggerations. The most comprehensive effort was that of F. J. Hurtaud.[7] Nevertheless, a commission formed by Pius X decided, on all essential points, in favor of Lahitton's thesis, stating

(Paris: Beauchesne, 1928), cols. 1891–924. [Further references to the articles by Brandenburger and Hürth are given in parentheses in the text. Tr.]

[4] Louis Brancherau, *De la Vocation sacerdotale* (Paris: Vic et Amat, 1896).

[5] It is the first edition of Lahitton's work, published in 1909, to which von Balthasar is here referring and from which, I assume, he subsequently quotes. I have been unable to locate a copy of this first edition, but the substance, when not the actual wording, of the passages he quotes may be found also in the 6th edition (Paris: Beauchesne, 1922), 23, 24, 38, 90, 123–24, 144–46, and elsewhere. [Tr]

[6] Lahitton, *Deux conceptions divergentes de la vocation sacerdotale* (Paris: Letheilleux, 1910), 237.

[7] F. J. Hurtaud, *La Vocation au sacerdoce* (Paris: Gabalda, 1911).

that: 1. No one has the right to priestly ordination prior to the free choice of the bishop. 2. What is required of the candidate, the so-called *vocatio sacerdotalis*, does not consist—or at least does not consist necessarily and *de lege ordinaria*—in a certain aspiration on the part of the subject, or in an invitation of the Holy Spirit to enter upon the priestly office. 3. On the contrary, nothing more is required of the candidate that he may be licitly called by the bishop than the proper intention together with the necessary aptitude (*idoneitas*), which has its source in the candidate's gifts of grace and nature and is demonstrated by an upright life and sufficient knowledge so that there is a justifiable expectation that he will be able properly to carry out the duties of the priesthood and holily to fulfill its obligations.[8]

In this decision, which refers primarily to candidates for the priesthood and only indirectly to those seeking admission to the evangelical life of the counsels, the paramount importance of the external call in the case of a priestly vocation is very clear. Brandenburger correctly calls attention to the fact that the priesthood is primarily a social function (71) and that the place the priest will take in the diocese is an important factor in his acceptance. The bishop is under no obligation whatever to ordain a candidate simply because the latter feels himself called to the priesthood. In view of this decision from Rome, one might, in fact, wonder if there actually is such a thing as a direct inner calling to the priesthood as such, that is, to the pure function independently of the subjective following of Christ as it is purely incorporated into the state of the counsels; whether, perhaps, the *interna aspiratio*, the invitation of the Holy Spirit, is not directed wholly to this personal discipleship and is merely *interpreted* by many who experience it to be an invitation to the (secular) priesthood. No one disputed the fact that there can be no *purely* external vocation and, therefore, no priestly function in the absence of an inner acceptance and readiness to meet the demands of that function. This was admitted even by Lahitton, who, on the one hand, interpreted *vocabilité* as a *vocation intérieure*

---

[8] See letter written at Rome, July 2, 1912, by Merry Cardinal del Val, in which he informs Monsignor de Cormont, Bishop of Aire, that Pope Pius X had, "at an audience on June 26 [1912]", approved the findings of the commission appointed to study Lahitton's two books on vocation (*Acta Apostolicae Sedis, Commentarium Officiale*, annus IV, vol. IV [Rome: Typis Polyglottis Vaticanis, 1912], 485).

dispositive and, on the other hand, was obliged to acknowledge that the validity of an ordination depends, in the last analysis, on the free consent of the candidate: "The Church places the ultimate responsibility for the vocation he has received definitively on the subject. . . . This vocation (by the bishop) is itself conditional and subordinate to the free consent of the one called."

It is clear today that the commission's decision was not intended to question the existence of an inner calling (as Lahitton did with his exaggerated views), but only to affirm that the "feeling" of being called carried with it no right to *ordination* so far as the Church was concerned and that this subjective feeling was not necessary for a valid and licit ordination. "It would have been strange indeed if Rome had so bluntly condemned the language employed for centuries by ascetics, theologians, Roman Congregations, and even popes, including Leo XIII and Pius X" (Brandenburger, 72). "The Church receives those leaders whom the Holy Spirit has prepared" (Leo the Great). Ultimately, what Lahitton succeeded in doing with his theories was to establish the minimum requirement that must be present in a priestly vocation if ordination is to be validly and licitly conferred: the requirement, namely, that the inner vocation be represented at the very least by the candidate's *vocabilitas*, that is, by such a general natural and supernatural aptitude and disposition that the priestly function can be performed properly and worthily.

If this is true of a vocation to the priesthood insofar as it is an ecclesiastical function, it is not necessarily also true of a vocation to the evangelical state. The findings of the commission appointed by Pius X are simply not applicable to this state, for there is no question here of the Church's call to participation in an ecclesiastical function. The balance between interior and exterior elements has undergone a total change. If this fact had been remembered when the commission's findings were being discussed, things would have been much simpler. In his stimulating work on vocations,[9] Jean Baptiste Raus, C.SS.R, was concerned chiefly with the vocation to the *religious life*. He had no difficulty in showing that both Alphonsus and Thomas put the emphasis on the inner call. Thomas speaks clearly of an *instinctus* or *impetus* of the Holy Spirit, of a hearing of Christ's counsels.[10] Hürth, who was inclined to apply the commission's findings also to vocations to the religious life, did

[9] J. B. Raus, *La Doctrine de S. Alphonse sur la vocation et la grâce en regard l'enseignement de S. Thomas et des prescriptions du Code* (Lyons-Paris: E. Vitte, 1926

[10] "Contra Pestiferam Doctrinam Retrahentium Homines a Religionis

not question this fact in his critique of Raus' work, but attempted to limit the statement in two ways. On the one hand, he did not agree that the vocation and election that Raus required for both the priestly and the religious state must actually be *special* in nature and were not reducible to those ordinary graces of divine providence that are bestowed also on Christians in the lay state. Are there not special graces for the married state and can they not be placed under the same ordinary law of grace? Must it really be assumed, as Raus assumes with Vermeersch, that those not called to the state of election "are 'left' in the ordinary state rather than elected to it?" (98). Is it not possible even in the state of the counsels—and this is the other side of Hürth's argument—that the inner vocation can be limited simply to God's conferring on an individual such gifts and inclinations as would make the choice of the evangelical state *possible*, but not *necessary*? God's pre-election can, certainly, be assumed in many instances of a vocation to the religious life, but it must not be postulated as necessary in every instance in which an individual validly chooses the state of the counsels. On the contrary, God can give man, or "at least some men" (99), an aptitude that suffices for various vocations and, for the rest, leave it to the individual's free judgment to make the final decision.

It will be obvious that Hürth touches here on a possibility that we envisioned when we said that God extends his invitation to many individuals in a way that leaves them free to choose their state of life. In such a case, the subjective call would be limited to the minimum requirements of right intention and aptitude and would be the lowest level of a vocation to the religious life. In other words, Hürth does not interpret the commission's findings as a denial "that an inner invitation of the Holy Spirit . . . can be and often is present", but rather as a rejection of "the contention . . . that it is certain that one in whom it is not present does not have a 'vocation' " (99–100). To the extent, then, that a subjective element is necessary in the case of every vocation, it must be reflected in the conditions required of the candidate by the findings of the commission appointed by Pope Pius X (and by canon 1353 of the *Codex Iuris Canonici*).[11]

---

gressu", chap. IX, *Opuscula Theologica* in *Opera Omnia*, vol. XXIX (Paris: Ludovicus Vivès, 1876), 172.

[11] See canon 1353, *Codex Iuris Canonici* (Westminster: Newman, 1946), 462. This canon reads as follows: "Priests, and especially pastors, should exert them-

Paul Vigné[12] reduced the original controversy to two processes, of which the first characterizes a direct call, the second an indirect call. According to Lahitton, a vocation would follow the course: God, Church, subject; according to others: God, subject, Church. In the first process, the Church mediates or creates the vocation; in the second, it confirms it. In the first process, the priestly vocation is made known by the Church alone; in the second, it is differentiated from other vocations only by its object. In the first process, the candidate needs only to meet the criterion of aptitude; in the second, he must demonstrate genuine signs of a vocation conferred by God. We shall see that these two processes are but the principal manifestations of a single fundamental form of vocation, the first of which is more appropriate to the priestly vocation, the second to a vocation to the religious life. But intermediate forms are also possible, and the more clearly defined a (genuine and proven) inner vocation may be, the more the Church will have to consider this fact in calling and accepting the individual. The statement that no one has the right to ordination or to acceptance into a monastery contains, then, a certain inner analogy. It is absolutely true of ordination to the priesthood, but only sometimes true of personal vocations, for there are vocations that demand an absolute obedience and, when they have been tested and shown to be genuine, demand obedience also from all those without whom the vocation cannot be carried out. The findings of the commission appointed by Pius X, which provided a certain objective guiding principle for the priestly vocation, also fostered a certain minimalism that was entirely foreign to the clerical tendency of Mercier's thought. If carried to its logical conclusion, the overemphasis on the ontologically sacramental aspect, by reason of which the priesthood was ranked unequivocally above the evangelical state, ends in an alienation of the concept of vocation and thus of priestly holiness. Precisely in those instances in which vocation is being considered not individualistically but as a charism or ministry

selves to guard with special care from the contagions of the world boys who exhibit signs of an ecclesiastical vocation, to train them to piety, to instruct them in elementary studies and to foster in them the seed of the divine vocation." See also T. Lincoln Bouscaren, *The Canon Law Digest: Officially Published Documents Affecting the Code of Canon Law 1917–1933* (Milwaukee: Bruce, 1934), 643–55. [Tr]

[12] Paul Vigné, *Le Camus: La Vocation religieuse* (Paris: 1913).

within the Church must one be careful to keep in mind the possibility of personal election to the specific following of Christ.

What is true of the evangelical life is true in even greater measure of every *clearly defined qualitative mission within the Church*. If it is genuine, such a mission has the right to be tested by the Church; if its genuineness is confirmed, the Church has the obligation of acknowledging it. For while it is true that the individual Christian has his place under the shepherd's staff of the Church, the Church as a whole has its place under the staff of the Divine Shepherd, who can pasture both the Church and the hierarchy as he pleases. Those extraordinary missions that God confers on the Church and its hierarchy through a given individual demand of the whole Church an obedience that is not left to its discretion. Thus the Church has recognized the "finger of God" in the founding of all great religious orders, to name but one example, and has allowed itself to be formed and leavened by their new spirit, which is a direct gift of the Holy Spirit. It has also, after appropriate testing, which must itself be undertaken in the spirit of obedience, recognized the existence and right of a subjective vocation that stems, not from the Church, but from God. The bearer of such a mission continues to be, both before and after such recognition, an ordinary Christian who, as such, owes obedience to the Church; he will prove the authenticity of his Catholic vocation as opposed to every vocation that is not authentic by demonstrating first in his own obedience to the Church the spirit of loving obedience that he is called to renew within the Church. He will endure conflicts that necessarily arise out of these two demands for obedience—particularly among sinners, which all of us are—with the patience of one ready, certainly, to give his life for his mission, but also to confide to the Divine Spirit the guiding of that mission. God himself cannot permit an ineradicable contradiction between the Church and one's personal mission, for we "must be convinced that in Christ our Lord, the Bridegroom, and in his spouse, the Church, only one Spirit holds sway, which governs and rules for the salvation of souls. For it is by the same Spirit and Lord who gave the Ten Commandments that our Holy Mother Church is ruled and governed" (*Sp Ex*, 365). Admittedly, however, a mission sometimes develops only after the death of the one to whom it was entrusted—sometimes even long after, as in the case of Angela Merici, for instance, or Mary Ward.

It is clear from what has been said that conflict exists only by way of exception; it is normal for the subjective and objective components of a vocation to function together. This collaboration can have a multiplicity of nuances: It can progress from the complete preponderance of the objective (as in the baptism of children) to a kind of balance—as when the call is sounded not only interiorly in the one called, but simultaneously also by the ecclesiastical authority that mediates it and chooses its recipient—and ultimately to a preponderance of the subjective, in which case, however, dependence on the objective for affirmation and confirmation cannot be entirely lacking. For a vocation to the religious life is normally inspired by a priest or other individual in the state of election who guides its progress from a latent to an active state, offering advice and support to the one who wrestles with it. God uses men to lead men, not only in the course of "ordinary pastoral care", but also and especially in the course of extraordinary vocations. It is not true that the more interior and subjectively unmediated a call may be, the more independently it can be accepted, understood and accomplished by the one who receives it. Precisely the most subtle forms of the call are most in need of objective guidance and interpretation. In fact, the Catholic will recognize the form of God's call as authentic in such cases only if it demands, by its very nature, the supplementary objective interpretation and guidance of the priest and if the will to obey God expresses itself without inner conflict in a simple obedience to the Church. Far from seeking thereby to escape responsibility, the one called is but obeying the voice of God himself, which can never be a solitary voice isolated from the community and the Church. God himself decrees that his call should have these two components—objectivity and subjectivity

—because his work of creation and redemption is also twofold in form. If even natural ethics locates the norm of God's will in the tension between personal conscience and objective law, and if conscience, which is admittedly the ultimate norm of practical behavior, must let itself be guided and in certain cases even changed by objective norms, then this vital interaction in the realm of grace is perfected when the "will of God" takes the form of a personal call, an intelligible revelation. In practice, then, the touchstone of a genuine subjective call is one's readiness to submit oneself to the objective interpretation and guidance of a director "called" by the Church. Only in this way will the subjective mission be effectively united with the realm of the objective mission upon which it is later to exert its influence. If this does not happen, it is certain that the mission will degenerate, for the one called to it will have no choice, in his now rudderless subjectivity, but to thematize and aggrandize himself and his mission—but therein lies the beginning of all heresy.

Where there is question of explicitly subjective mandates, as in the case of mysticism, which, however, is to be regarded as genuine and intrinsically Catholic only when the experiences and "states" that are bestowed are not an end in themselves, but are fruitful for the community of the Church, God ordains a special union between one to whom he reveals his mysteries and one able to interpret them objectively; often he calls two by two those whom he has chosen so that there are no longer two persons with separate vocations, but "two in one vocation". Such unions can have the same necessity and urgency as the call itself. What has been written about the union established by God in the natural order can also be said of them: "What therefore God has joined together, let no man put asunder" (Mt 19:6). The model for such unions, which are the counterpart, on the level of the counsels and the vows, of the sacrament of matrimony, is the union ordained and, as it were, consecrated between Mary and John.

Thus far, we have been discussing the interaction between the subjective and objective aspects of God's will only as they relate to the intrinsically supernatural realm of the Church. But because God's voice, which is what we are discussing here, is always transmitted through the medium of created things, we must turn our attention also to *secular factors*. On the subjective side, these factors include all that belongs to one's nature—one's intellectual composition: will, understanding, disposition, character, talents, inclinations; and one's physical composition: health, physical strength and capabilities, the subconscious, latent or dominant elements of inheritance, and the like. On the objective side, they include, in addition to the Church, one's whole natural environment, one's manifold family relationships, the demands of the state, the whole historical constellation of the age, the special demands on contemporary man, and so forth.

Each of these factors can be a medium through which God's call can make itself heard. Each of them can—perhaps even must—be taken into consideration in the testing of a vocation, in the choosing of a vocation. Each of them can contribute in a greater or lesser degree to the rounding out of the sum which, taken in its entirety, expresses the unity of God's will.

There are many ways in which this will can become incarnate in secular media. Its divine character can shine through the secular medium in a manner so clear and "unmediated" that, outshining and displacing all things secular, it manifests itself in a way that is unmistakable. The one called is so overwhelmed by this evidence that it does not occur to him to doubt it or to put it to what could only be a superfluous test. He has heard and understood; he has only to obey. But it can also happen that the supernatural call, which is always present, is shrouded in a more or less opaque and changing veil through which it speaks, and must be separated from the various secular components by a careful weighing of its spiritual significance. The transition from the first, psychologically unmediated, form of the call to the second, which is mediated through the secular order, can be a gradual one. Ignatius recognizes this fact when, in his teaching on the Three Times When a Correct and Good Choice May Be Made, he includes a second time that serves as a transition from the first time to the third.

"FIRST TIME. When God our Lord so moves and attracts the will that a devout soul without hesitation, or the possibility of hesitation, follows what has been manifested to it. St. Paul and St. Matthew acted thus in following Christ our Lord.

"SECOND TIME. When much light and understanding are derived through experience of desolations and consolations and discernment of diverse spirits.

"THIRD TIME. This is a time of tranquility . . . that is, a time when the soul is not agitated by different spirits, and has free and peaceful use of its natural powers. If a choice of a way of life has not been made in the first and second time . . . , [it must be made] in the third time" (Sp Ex, 175–78).

In the first time, the will of God reveals itself in so elementary a fashion that hesitation and doubt are not even possible. In the second, it reveals itself, suddenly or gradually like the sun through the mist, as the mature consequence of inner experience, impressions, insights, inspirations, certainties. The sphere in which clarification occurs in this second time is the sphere of "discernment of diverse spirits", that is, the sphere in which the personal and supernatural powers of good and evil manifest themselves in the natural powers of the soul—for, even as "infused virtues", faith, hope and charity continue to be personal acts, and supernatural grace cannot fail to affect and influence one's conscious life. In the individual, then, the sphere of "discernment of diverse spirits"—which Ignatius, following the tradition of the Church, treats thoroughly in his Rules for the Discernment of Spirits (Sp Ex, 313–36)—stands on the boundary line between nature and grace. It is the sphere in which the light of grace, without actually becoming mysticism, permeates the normal intellectual life of the Christian through the phenomena of consciousness; the sphere in which the life of the soul is distinguished, even in the order of consciousness, from every purely natural consciousness. In this transitional state, the personal, grace-filled call of God makes itself known through the natural powers of the spirit. In particular, that which we call the natural "conscience", the power of deciding rationally what should be done in a given situation, becomes attentive to the personal voice and guidance of the Holy Spirit. But just as, on its upper boundary, this "second time" can flow uninterruptedly into the shining evidence of the "first time", so, on its lower boundary, it can flow uninterruptedly into the darkness of the "third time", in which the mediated character of the call has become also a psychological "mediatedness". The one called knows *that* there is a call of God, but he knows, too, that it must reveal itself through the natural order. Whereas, in the first time, the pure light of certainty presents itself to the eye in a blinding whiteness, and in the second time restores itself to an undifferentiated whiteness by reassembling gradually and unaided the scattered colors of the spectrum, in the third time, it is only the individual colors of the prism that present themselves to the eye of the beholder; he must combine them by his own effort until at last he too achieves the simplicity of whiteness.[13]

[13] We will be well-advised not to equate—or, at least, not necessarily to equate—the subjective obscurity of a call that requires a greater investment of intellectual activity, as in the case of the "third time", with a weakening of the call itself, as Franz Hürth (98–99) is inclined to do. Raus (32) expresses the teaching of St. Alphonsus in the following words: "The decision to enter a religious order presumes a choice, an election. But this considered and sincere choice of the state of spiritual perfection in the service of God can be the result only of a grace given from above, of divine assistance, of an inner invitation or inspiration of Christ acting upon the human will." Hürth interprets this passage to mean that "if someone has a sincere conviction that he has the necessary disposition and gifts for a vocation to the religious or priestly state . . . and if he then decides for the proper reasons to embrace this vocation, . . . the mere fact of such reflection and such a decision [is] the sign of the necessary inner disposition, of a divine vocation; and this is so even if, for the subjective consciousness of the one concerned, *every* (not merely every extraordinary) *spontaneous* inclination of the will toward one of these vocations is lacking, and both the reflection and the decision are based on a tranquil exercise of the intellect and purely practical reasons and have been carried out in the full awareness that such a one might *just as well* and with equally valid reasons have decided for another state" (99). But this interpretation of the "third time" seems to demand too much—or too little—of it. Raus has correctly described inner election as an essentially supernatural act and so has been careful

The apparent fragmentation of God's call into the various elements that reveal its natural components must not lead us to think that God's will is not one or that it cannot be discovered in its unity. Ignatius gives the ways and means of detaching oneself from the multiplicity of this "third time" in order to heed the simple call of God. Under no circumstances are the natural components to be viewed in their natural isolation or allowed to determine one's course of action. To do so would be to follow an inordinate inclination—and that is to be regarded as inordinate which would allow a partial motive or a partial decision to serve as the expression of the total will of God. One who sees must first regard all that is natural as a pure transparency, a mere instrument for the expression of God's will. He must dissociate himself from it and allow himself to be guided by it only insofar as it makes known to him the call of God himself. Ignatius calls this attitude indifference and defines it as the determination to be attentive, despite all natural motives and "calls", to the one grace-filled will of God that descends from above: "First Rule: The love that moves and causes one to choose must descend from above, that is, from the love of God, so that before one chooses he should perceive that the greater or less attachment for the object of his choice is solely because of his Creator and Lord" (Sp Ex, 184). Once this complete relativization of all natural and secular view-points and inclinations has been accomplished and the search for the pure will and call of God himself has been chosen as the only absolute, there is no longer a danger that the choice, even when

---

to distinguish it from natural "feelings" and "enthusiasms". It is an experience of *faith*; its laws can and must transcend those of purely natural consciousness, but without thereby becoming mystical experiences. And if Ignatius assumes no actual consciousness of these diverse spirits (Sp Ex, 177) even in the "third time", which he describes as a time of tranquility, nevertheless for him, too, "rational reflection" assumes the form of a "perception" that, in view of the indifference he presupposes, makes its choice in terms of the greater love of God (ibid., 179, 184). The apparent "rationality" of the third time is not sufficient justification for the assumption that God's choice, which is what one chooses during this time, is not distinguished interiorly from his "usual" guidance of all mankind by grace.

it has been made with what seem to be the purely natural powers of intellect and will, has been guided by anything other than the elective will of God himself. The "incarnations" of this will in subjective and objective secular situations are not a justification for regarding it as anything but "pure and undefiled" (*Sp Ex*, 172). This is the time to "consider which alternative appears more reasonable . . . [and to] come to a decision in the matter under deliberation because of weightier motives presented to my reason, and not because of any sensual inclination" (*Sp Ex*, 182). Because it is indifferent in a Christian—not a Stoic—sense, the "reason" that makes its choice here uninfluenced by "sensuality" is, despite the absence of perceptible inspiration, a spirit "led by the Spirit of God" (Rom 8:14), while the sensuality to which it is opposed is, although it seems to be purely psychological in nature, "the flesh [whose] inclination . . . is death" and whose "wisdom . . . is hostile to God" (Rom 8:6–7). Thus, what seems to be a natural choice is, at the same time, united with the divine election: "After such a choice or decision, the one who has made it must turn with great diligence to prayer and the presence of God our Lord and offer him his choice that the Divine Majesty may deign to accept and confirm it, if it is for his greater service and praise" (*Sp Ex*, 183).

The more or less total obscurity of the call behind its secular components is, then, by no means an indication that it has withdrawn to a distance, that it has become weaker or less clear or so fragmented that one called can no longer restore it to its original unity. Such obscurity is, rather, the normal condition of God's call in the world, even in the Christian world. The first and second "times" of choosing a way of life continue to be exceptions. In the usual course of events in the world, nothing more is required for the hearing of God's call than a pure and simple disposition of faith: "By faith he who is called Abraham obeyed the call of God" (Heb 11:8). "But the word that was heard did not profit them [the Jews in the desert], since they had no faith in what they heard" (Heb 4:2). For "faith is the substance of things to be hoped for, the evidence of things that are not seen"

(Heb 11:1). It is the possibility of seeing the divine reality through the medium of what is visible in the world, of hearing the voice and the eloquent silence of God in the often strident voice of worldly events. Faith, then, is movement, not static objectivity; it penetrates the questionable and questioning world around it to inquire into the will of God that is both in and above the things of earth: "Here I am; for thou didst call me" (1 Sam 3:9). "What shall I do, Lord?" (Acts 22:10). It is not content with what suits the desires of sensual man; rather, it has no rest until it knows what God wants of it even if his will is directly counter to its own desires.

For the most part, the call to the priesthood and the religious life will correspond to the first or second "time", while the general call to the lay state will have more in common with the third. If there is no special call that overwhelms the chosen one with its direct evidence or that evolves gradually into certainty, the natural components become more prominent. In the case of vocations to the priestly or religious life, more often than not, they present obstacles that must be courageously overcome, whereas, for the lay Christian, the force of the historical situation and the impetus of personal inclinations or aptitudes are decisive factors in the choice of a way of life. If he does not feel himself called to the priestly or religious state, he is justified in seeking and finding the will of God in the circumstances of his life; the general character of the call leaves to the freedom of the individual greater scope in the shaping of his own life. This does not mean that the will of God is uncertain or vague in such cases or that the individual must of necessity look more to his own resources and personal wishes than to God. Rather, God gives him a "longer lead", allows him more freedom of initiative in following the divine will.

As we have seen, God's call does not always reveal itself in the same manner. But the manner of its revelation can never be other than relative. It can happen, for instance, that the situation in his immediate milieu—a parish, perhaps, in which there is inadequate spiritual care—or in his country or in the world at large may so convince a young person of the need to dedicate himself wholly to its alleviation that he subsequently decides to enter the priesthood or an active or contemplative religious order. He is brought to this decision by the realization that all other forms of self-giving fall short of the actual need he perceives. Nothing short of his whole life can breach the gap. The circumstances cry too loudly for help to allow him to consider his own wishes and comfort. They compel him to indifference in the Ignatian sense, but leave him no time for its gradual acquisition. In a war or catastrophe, many a man becomes a hero who was not one in everyday life. But the world as a whole may seem to a young person to be in a constant state of war or catastrophe, and he is immediately aware that the remedies the world has to offer are not sufficient. At this point, he may decide on a life in Carmel (or an analogous form of total surrender to God) so that the depth of his response may be commensurate with the depth of the need. In the inevitability and irremediableness of human need, there makes itself heard the voice of the God who suffered and was abandoned: "I was . . . naked and you did not clothe me; sick, and in prison, and you did not visit me" (Mt 25:43). Or, if he does not express his sympathy in contemplation, he will do so in action—ideally, not by precipitating himself without adequate preparation into the first situation that presents itself, but by devoting years, if necessary, to preparing himself to act competently.

In this regard, the new forms of vocation to "secular institutes" are especially relevant today. Beyond a doubt, the call to such a vocation comes from the state of a world that is crying for help; but the one crying is he whom the world crucified, and the answer he demands must be as radical as that of the Cross. The strength and absoluteness of the call actually eradicate the differences in the "times" of the choice as Ignatius describes them; it issues from the "third time" with all the strength of the "first", thus giving the one called the strength to build and maintain a bridge between the evangelical life and the life of the world.

For one who seeks only the will of God, the elements of the call *combine inevitably to form a unity*. Many of those who claim not to have discovered this unity have been negligent in their search for it. They have refused to accept the element of renunciation that would have led to unity. There is no call of God in which this element is lacking. Renunciation is a constant ingredient of every choice. For a choice always points to *one* way, thus necessitating the renunciation of all other—and even of all other possible— ways. It is, moreover, a sign of the genuineness of every mode of Christian life, which must merit the fruitfulness of its vocation by accepting its share in the sufferings of Christ. Renunciation and sacrifice may well be, in fact, the principal components of a vocation—the price at which grace, fruitfulness and even visible success are to be purchased for countless other members of the "communion of saints". One called to such a vocation must be prepared to renounce, either entirely or in great part, the privilege even of seeing the fruit he has made possible.

The multiplicity of elements in which the call of God can and, in fact, most frequently does, reveal itself can sometimes lead to *conflicts* and questions of priority. Which duty takes precedence? In which of two apparently necessary ways does God's will lie? The indecision is resolved only when the one seeking to know the Father's will has made his way in faith and prayer through the initial confusion to a gentle awareness of what is required of him. Conflicts are inevitable in a world that has fallen and never ceases to fall away from God. Far from avoiding this form of "sinful flesh" (Rom 8:3), however, God's redemption deliberately became incarnate in it. Indeed, perplexity can itself be a form of the Passion and night of agony into which Christ was led by sin and to which he voluntarily surrendered himself. It is most acute when a genuine call of God's grace is crossed by extraneous elements and becomes impossible to fulfill. A young woman, for example, may experience a genuine and compelling call to the contemplative life, but may be prevented from following it by external circumstances and duties. She has no choice but to attempt the impossible—to try to fulfill both the call and her external duties. Or a young man may have a true vocation to the priesthood, but his natural capabilities either are insufficient or are judged to be so by the proper ecclesiastical authority. It would be premature to conclude from this that his call was not a genuine one and that it was the deeper will of God that he remain in the world. Beyond a doubt, there are genuine calls of God that, through no fault of the one called, are impossible to fulfill.[14] The call as an unmediated whole seems here to be no longer identical with the call as the sum of its components and parts. Nor is it possible to reduce either of the two parts to its counterpart. By entering into the "likeness of sinful flesh", the call itself takes on the form of crossed beams. It becomes a call to the Cross and is itself a crucified and suffering call. As we have said above, it is not necessarily the fault of the one to whom it is addressed that the call must assume this form. Nevertheless, the fault—whether collective, anonymous or attributable to a specific source—is extrinsic to the call and can be identified. God's ways in the world are not only mysterious and hidden, they are often in-comprehensible, as when the Father did not hesitate to lead his Son into the incomprehensibility of separation from him and even into the inevitable condition of death—of a death from which there was no visible escape and in which all was dark-ness. And yet, in a way we cannot understand, the Father's mission remains whole and untouched by this cataclysm; indeed,

---

[14] "Often the Holy Spirit gives the desire for something, the accomplishment of which he does not will; thus [he gave] David the desire to build a temple and Abraham the intention of sacrificing his son, but he did not accept from them the execution of their purpose. For the Holy Spirit sometimes sends such a desire for the good of the individual and for his merit, even though it is not to come to execution, and it is not expedient that it should do so. And for this reason, although it is morally clear to a religious order that an individual has been moved by the Holy Spirit to request the habit, if the individual is not suitable for the order, it cannot rightly receive such a one" (Francisco Suárez, "Opus de Religione", pars secunda, "De Statu Perfectionis et Religionis", bk. V, chap. VIII, sec. 3, Opera Omnia XV [Paris: Ludovicus Vivès, 1859], 331).

it becomes thereby forever whole and untouched: The Father has the power to let his call echo into the darkness of the nether world and to create a way of escape where there is no escape: "Thou leadest down to hell, and bringest up again" (Tob 13:2; cf. also Dt 32:39; 1 Sam 2:6). "For it was neither herb, nor mollifying plaster that healed them, but thy word, O Lord, which healeth all things. For it is thou, O Lord, that hast power of life and death, and leadest down to the gates of death, and bringest back again" (Wis 16:12–13).

We must not conclude, from the broken and crucified form of a particular call, that it is not, from God's point of view, a true and unified call, for its unity is, in fact, actually achieved in and through the form of the Cross, acquiring thereby, in a way we cannot understand, a share in the integral wholeness of Christ's call as it exists in the Father. And if the course of one so called seems to lead through all the perils of this world to a "place outside" every classical concept of a state of life; if such a one is compelled by circumstances and complexities beyond his control to take his stand where, to the human eye, there is no place to stand, then the Lord himself, who came to take his stand in that total "outside" that is beyond all states, will understand this non-state, too, as a true discipleship (Heb 13:11–14). "By faith Moses, when he was grown up, denied that he was a son of Pharaoh's daughter, . . . esteeming the reproach of Christ greater riches than the treasures of the Egyptians; for he was looking to the reward; . . . he persevered as if seeing him who cannot be seen" (Heb 11:24, 26–27).

The unity of the call, whether clearly recognizable or visible only to a blind faith that believes more in God than in itself, demands always *the unity of the answer* as well. For it is from the unity of the call that human life derives its ultimate unity, and this unity is guaranteed when man's answer is complete and unreserved, when he stakes all—literally all—that he is and has on his belief in God's call. For to believe in God's call means to renounce even the desire to control the design, content or course of one's life.

To believe in God's call means to surrender and sacrifice all one is, all one's hopes and desires, for the accomplishment of a mission one can never fully comprehend. Belief of this kind demands no guarantee for the event that the mission may fail and one may be left to one's own devices. To believe means to create an empty space in one's inmost being and to reserve it so that the word of God may reign there and may direct one's path. "By faith Abraham, when he was put to the test, offered Isaac; and he who had received the promises (to whom it had been said, 'In Isaac thy seed shall be called') was about to offer up his only-begotten son, reasoning that God has power to raise up even from the dead. . . . By faith they passed through the Red Sea, as through dry land" (Heb 11:17, 29). For when "it is no longer I that live, but Christ lives in me, and the life that I now live in the flesh, I live in the faith of the Son of God . . ." (Gal 2:20), then "I can do all things in him who strengthens me" (Phil 4:13). There is question here of a mutual sharing that involves not only the surface, but even the very essence of one's being, that is an exchange of one's own spirit, which is thereby commended into the Father's hands, for the Spirit of God, who henceforth takes the place of one's own self-determination. Thus Ignatius concludes his reflections on the choice of a state of life with the words: "For everyone must keep in mind that in all that concerns the spiritual life his progress will be in proportion to his surrender of self-love and of his own will and interests" (Sp Ex, 189). He gives this "mutual sharing" (Sp Ex, 231) the name of love: "Take, Lord, and receive all my liberty, my memory, my understanding, and my entire will, all that I have and possess. Thou hast given all to me. To thee, O Lord, I return it. All is thine, dispose of it wholly according to thy will. Give me thy love and thy grace, for this is sufficient for me" (Sp Ex, 234).

CHAPTER TWO

THE HISTORICAL ACTUALITY
OF THE CALL

1. THE CALL IS MADE KNOWN

Until now we have been considering the call as it is in itself
—its origin in God and its effect and demands upon the one
who receives it. In what follows we shall consider it in its
historical reality—as a call directed to and understood by man
and subsequently accepted or rejected by him. Our primary
concern will be, once again, with the qualitatively higher call
to the priesthood and the evangelical state, which, however,
contains in itself the idea and model of every other vocation
within the Church.

The call in its historical actuality is a meeting with the living
God, to whose nature it belongs to be actually present in history.
But if it would be one-sided to define the whole truth of the
Divine Being or of any being in terms of such actuality and so
to equate it with the pure dynamism of the merely historical in
which God and man meet only in the here-and-now of call and
answer, if to do so would be to negate the eternity of God as
well as the nature of the Church and the sacramental order and to
reduce what is Catholic to pure dialectic, to a nervous succession
of momentary events, it is nonetheless true that God as an
absolutely free and pure Spirit—indeed, as a trinitarian Spirit—
is ever and always the absolute historical actuality and that the
intelligent creature made in the likeness of this God is called into
existence for the historical actuality of meeting with him. The
historical actuality that is as characteristic of the divine as of the
human being is not something added secondarily, modally and
accidentally to the Divine Being; it is proper to the Divine Being
as such. It is only in the ever new meeting with the living God

that man experiences and knows that God is the Absolute Being who exists from all eternity.

The eternal actuality that is God is not continually present to man in this life; it is translated into the language of earth in such a way that God's essential freedom shines forth at unpredictable moments, revealing itself by its call. Hence those whom God visited in the Old Testament were surprised by Yahweh's ever new "descent" among them; hence, too, the light shining in Christ is not an ever-present light, subject to man's whim and lethargy, but a light that is always just now "passing by" (Lk 18:37), just now shining forth, just now ready to be used: "Walk while you have the light, that darkness may not overtake you" (Jn 12:35). "Behold, now is the acceptable time; behold, now is the day of salvation" (2 Cor 6:2)—". . . while it is still Today" (Heb 3:13).

This meeting with God that takes place in the now of any given moment does not nullify his eternity, his faithfulness or his patience. But the reverse is also true. God's eternally promised grace does not nullify the "now" of this meeting for which tomorrow will be too late. If these two moments were not simultaneous yet distinct from one another, God would be neither eternal majesty nor eternal love. His glory could not allow itself to be mocked by the notion that everything will be all right in the end, nor could his love reveal itself as love "to the end" (Jn 13:1) if it were not a love that is both offered in the now of this moment and lavishly bestowed at every moment. The fact that God is "the Savior of all men" does not alter the incomprehensible fact that he is, by grace, the Savior "especially of believers" (1 Tim 4:10). And the fact that he has called all believers "into his marvelous light" (1 Pet 2:9) alters even less the incomprehensibility of the personal and unique call by which he has set even me apart "from my mother's womb . . . and called me by his grace to reveal his Son in me . . ." (Gal 1:15–16).

God never ceases to make known to men the here-and-now quality of his grace, not only by recommending vigilance since he comes "at an hour that you do not expect" (Mt 24:44) and no amount of calculation can reveal "at what hour your Lord is to come" (Mt 24:42), but even more drastically by depicting the fearful possibility that one may be asleep when the call comes (Mt 25:5) and may thus fail to know, until it is too late, the mission to which one has been called (Mt 25:12). Such a failure becomes increasingly tragic in proportion to the uniqueness of God's call and of the grace that is offered. In the ordinary course of Christian life, there is a superabundance of divine patience, for God has obliged himself by grace to forgive again and again as often as man appeals to him: ". . . Everyone that shall call upon the name of the Lord shall be saved" (Joel 2:32). *But for one on whom a special mission has been conferred*—a mission that pertains not only to his salvation in the life to come, but also to the whole course of his life on earth; a mission he must hear, accept, initiate and accomplish—*there is but a single moment of decision*. Once that moment has passed, *the mission is lost forever*. Such a one sinks back into the crowd and is swallowed up by it. He cannot exchange his unique mission for another—perhaps a second-best—one. What is at stake is the meaning or lack of meaning of his whole existence. And God will not fail to make this clear to one who has let his mission pass him by.

Who is called? There is but one answer to this question: those ". . . of his [the Lord's] own choosing" (Mk 3:13), ". . . that the selective purpose of God might stand, depending not on deeds, but on him who calls" (Rom 9:11–12). For the world, the only certainty about vocations is the mysterious fact that God incorporates the prayer and sacrifices of Christians into his "selective purpose" that they may thereby become productive of new vocations. It is meaningful, therefore, to offer prayers and sacrifices for priestly and religious vocations. Credit for their increase must also be given to the Church, but the Church's role is so totally hidden in God that it can never be properly evaluated.

How many are called? To this question, too, revelation offers but one answer: many more than actually follow the call. As evidence of this, we have the often repeated word of the Lord: "For many are called, but few are chosen" (Mt 20:16; 22:14), and the parables that explicate it. The parable of the sower divides the scattered seed, which is "the word" (Mk 4:14), into four categories: The seeds that fall by the wayside are those "in whom the word is sown, [but] as soon as they have heard, Satan at once comes and takes away the word that has been sown in their hearts"; the seeds that fall on rocky ground are those "who, when they have heard the word, receive it immediately with joy, and they have no roots in themselves, but continue only for a time; then, when trouble and persecution come because of the word, they at once fall away"; the seeds sown among the thorns are those "who listen to the word; but the cares of the world, and the deceitfulness of riches, and the desires about other things, entering in, choke the word, and it is made fruitless"; and, finally, the seeds that fall upon good ground are those "who hear the word, and welcome it, and yield fruit, one thirty, another sixty, and another a hundredfold" (Mk 4:14–20; cf. Mt 13:3–9, 18–23).

If we may judge by the parable, only one-fourth of the seed produces fruit. In terms of success, it matters little, then, whether the failure of the other three-fourths occurs at the beginning or only in the course of growth; whether he who hears the word does not understand it at all; or understands it, but is unable to keep it; or understands and receives it, but subsequently turns away from it.

In the parable of the great supper, which opens with the king's invitation: "Come, everything is ready!", the call is at first unheeded. Then "they all with one accord began to excuse themselves. The first said to him, 'I have bought a farm. . . .' And another said, 'I have bought five yoke of oxen. . . .' And another said, 'I have married a wife, and therefore I cannot come' " (Lk 14:18–20). Only when the invitation is repeated—this time to "the poor, the crippled and the lame" (Lk 14:21, 23)—does it meet with success.

The parables refer primarily, of course, to Israel—and, after Easter, to the Church as a whole. Within the Church, however, the relationship between the Old and New Testaments, as well as between the world and the Church, is so intensified that levels of meaning are revealed in everything the Lord has said (see previous chapters) about the call: On one level, the parables distinguish Christians from non-Christians; on another, they distinguish the apostles, by reason of their special call, from the multitude of those not so called. To apply them to special vocations is not, therefore, to interpret them allegorically, but to give them a meaning explicitly intended by the Word of God who first uttered them. It is the same Word who sends his call to Christians in general and to the elect in particular; and the elect know that they cannot justify a rejection of God's particular call by pleading acceptance of his general one.

It would be futile to attempt, on the basis of these parables, to determine even approximately the number of those who are called. On the other hand, we cannot attach too much importance to the fact that only one-fourth of the seed in the first parable falls on good ground or that so many of those in the second parable "made light of [the call] and went off" (Mt 22:5). There is always waste product when God shapes and chisels—not because he is an imperfect craftsman, but because the material he is trying to shape so often eludes his grasp. "How often would I . . . , but thou wouldst not" (Mt 23:37). This is not to say that the "waste product" of God's special vocation and election does not remain within the Church. Leaving aside for the moment the question of the existence and attribution of guilt for this suppression of the divine voice, we may assume that *the number of Christians* invited to a personal following of Christ in the evangelical or priestly state *is far greater* than the number of those who actually accept the call. Even among his holy people, God's call is more likely to meet with resistance and rejection than with open ears and willing hearts. "Why did I find no one when I came? Why did no one answer when I called?" (Is 50:2; Jerusalem Bible); ". . . they elect to follow their own ways . . . for I called and no one would answer, I spoke and they would not listen" (Is 66:3–4; Jerusalem Bible). ". . . I have spoken to you rising up early, and speaking, and you have not heard; and I have called to you, and you have not answered" (Jer 7:13). "But the more I called to them, the further away they went from me" (Hos 11:2; Jerusalem Bible). The voice of the prophets, the bearers of God's word, falls also upon emptiness: "And thou shalt speak to them all these words, but they will not hearken to thee; and thou shalt call them, but they will not answer thee" (Jer 7:27). In its stubbornness, Jerusalem is a visible symbol of all those who have turned away from God's call: "Now all these things happened to them as a type, and they were written for our correction . . ." (1 Cor 10:11). "For to us also it has been declared, just as to them" (Heb 4:2). "For I have no one [else] so likeminded [as Timothy]. . . . For they all seek their own interests, not those of Jesus Christ" (Phil 2:20–21). "No one came to my support, but all forsook me" (2 Tim 4:16).

The hearing of God's elective call is the concern not only of those who are called, *but also of the whole Church*, whose responsibility it is to make this hearing possible. As we have seen above, God's call has both a subjective and an objective component: He urges it gently in the depths of the soul, but he expects his ministers to interpret and clarify it, to alert and guide those to whom it is addressed. "I have planted, Apollos watered, but God has given the growth. . . . For we are God's helpers . . ." (1 Cor 3:5, 9). Granted, these helpers are but "the servants of him whom you have believed"; granted, "neither he who plants is anything, nor he who waters, but God who gives the growth" (1 Cor 3:5, 7); nevertheless, "in Jesus Christ, through the Gospel, did I beget you" (1 Cor 4:15); ". . . I am in labor again, until Christ is formed in you" (Gal 4:19). The role of these "helpers"—who are not mere Socratic "midwives", but true "nurses" ("as if a nurse were cherishing her own children, so we . . . would gladly have imparted to you . . . our own souls" [1 Th 2:7–8])—is so important that in its absence the vast majority of vocations founder. Part of the fruitfulness promised those in the state of election is their vital role in inspiring and fostering new generations of priests and religious. Only in exceptional circumstances have lay catechists shown the ability—or the desire—to replace priests in this work. This has been the experience of the Church throughout all the centuries of its existence. Without good example and the careful cultivation of God's gentle call in souls, it is impossible for incipient vocations to take root and thrive.

We must admit that many of the sociological reasons advanced to explain why there are so many fewer priestly and religious vocations today than in the medieval and baroque periods indicate fairly clearly that not everyone who pursued a clerical vocation or "was put" into a monastery in those earlier days actually had a true vocation in the evangelical sense of the word. On the other hand, we cannot deny that a genuine call would have difficulty in making itself heard in the atmosphere in which today's youth is growing to maturity. Nor should we fail to mention the decreased understanding of such vocations within the religious orders themselves; the human respect that prevents those in the state of election from encouraging even those vocations they know to exist; and the discouragement with regard to emergency measures taken by the Church which come to be regarded as the normal state of affairs.

The imperative need for persons engaged in pastoral care sheds light, moreover, on one of the basic premises of this book: that the priestly ministry develops most fruitfully only in inner conjunction with the evangelical state, and that an increased understanding of every kind of religious life—the contemplative as well as that of active orders and congregations and secular institutes—is consequently an indirect, but nonetheless fundamental, condition for the renewal of the clergy. For confirmation, we need only recall the great difficulties experienced by priests in isolated parishes today, especially if they are unable to find housekeepers; the general ineffectiveness of supplementary regional meetings, which of necessity occur away from these parishes; and the fact that the fewest difficulties seem to be experienced by priests in religious life, who are bound together by common ideals, common training and a common way of life—especially if their ministries are in adjacent districts so that they are able to meet with some degree of frequency.

In the course of their preaching and catechetical work, priests who live the life of the evangelical counsels often have many natural opportunities for explaining their way of life to the people and stressing its absolute necessity. The Christian people themselves, moreover, if they have not been indoctrinated with false views, have an innate awareness that their well-being depends on the flourishing of evangelical life within the Church; that the "angels of the churches" (cf. Rev 2–3) will justly be held responsible for their spiritual welfare. Only priests who are also religious can form a living bulwark against the growing influence of press and mass media, which often denigrate the life of the counsels by their outspoken cynicism and denounce the Church itself as an institutional specter.

The "lay apostolate" is still the subject of much discussion, but the specialized movements of "Catholic Action" have had their day and could, in any event, flourish only so long as the individual groups were sustained by persons wholly dedicated to a particular apostolate. The need for such persons must also be impressed upon the youth of today, who are inclined to believe that the idealistic motivation of their formative years will also suffice for their later professional lives. Parents, too, who have long since learned to recognize the insufficiency of such an illusion, must come anew to the realization that their criticism of Church, clergy and religious orders is unseasonable so long as they do not encourage at least one of their children to be attentive to the call of Christ.

The balance among the ecclesial states of life should be so preserved or restored as to foster among them a genuinely co-operative interrelationship and mutual enrichment analogous to the relationship of the sexes in natural (secular) communities. Thus Christian families should be in contact with the rectory and with nearby religious institutions while these, in turn, should remain in contact with families so that, acting with and through one another, they may work together to build up the many-membered body of the Lord: "I hope you will always understand, even as you have understood us in part, that we are your boast, as you will also be ours, in the day of our Lord Jesus Christ" (2 Cor 1:13–14).

How is the call made known? We have already discussed this subject in the section on the nature of the call. Both the fact of the call and the particular manner in which it is made known are freely determined by God, whose voice is perceived differently not only by each of those to whom it is subjectively addressed, but also in each of its objective manifestations. It can be a gentle invitation or a compelling challenge. It can extend over years like a slowly waxing dawn or it can strike suddenly like a searing flash of lightning. Rare, indeed, is the call that has not already made itself known in childhood. Rarely, indeed, will the call awaken the elect from sleep as it awakened Samuel, or mark him as God's possession, as it clearly marked the Mother of God, bidding him hold himself in readiness for a mission that is only later to be revealed. One elected, but not yet called, by God will know that he must wait, that he must make no final decision about the direction or course his life will take because God may have definite plans for him. His knowledge will not be based on an awareness of personal endowments as is that of the genius, who must often make superhuman efforts to inaugurate the work he is destined to accomplish. On the other hand, no feeling of unworthiness or hesitation must prevent God's chosen one from holding himself in readiness for the call. In his time of waiting, he will live a kind of supernatural pre-existence, guarded by the angels of God. The dreams of such a one will be different from those of ordinary sleepers. At decisive turning points in his youth, he will experience unusual signs of God's providence; inexplicable warnings about matters that might otherwise have tempted his pride or his sensuality; meetings with persons whose existence or words are chance indications, warnings or confirmations of insights he would have been unable to articulate for himself. Perhaps he will become aware of this chain of events only from the vantage point of an awakened vocation and it will offer him the key to his whole past life, which will then be attracted to this new center as pieces of iron are attracted to a magnet. Once he has made his choice, he will understand not only the objective fact of God's continual guidance of his life, but also, and with equal clarity, the lifelong feeling that has exerted its mysterious influence on all the years of his growth to maturity.

When does the call make itself heard? The more usual time is in the years of adolescence, that is, between the ages of fourteen and twenty. But if the development of an individual's Christian awareness has not kept pace with the rest of his education, he may well be between the ages of twenty and thirty before he is truly receptive to the call—assuming, of course, that he still possesses the openness and readiness to hear it. Unquestionably, God is free to call men later if he so chooses. He can expose them to disappointments—perhaps the death of a spouse or other loved one—in order to make them realize the emptiness of their lives and so to draw them to himself. Or he can let them complete their training for a secular profession only to discover that it falls short of their expectations, that the narrow framework of worldly occupations and cares toward which their chosen study is oriented can only rob them of the best of which they have dreamed. Such experiences, whether happy or unhappy, will help the individual who hears God's call later in life to a more conscious sacrifice and a more fruitful apostolate. In fact, this longer time spent in the world can prove advantageous for those entering active (as opposed to contemplative) religious orders or secular institutes, where they will have to live the life of Christ amid the turmoil of the world. It can be particularly advantageous if it was, besides, a time of hard work and deprivation, not only because such a one will long more eagerly for the true source of salvation, but also because he will be able to accept with greater equanimity and understanding than those who had not had this experience the sacrifices and hardships that will be required of him in the priesthood or the religious life. God's call can make itself heard at any time, even in the eleventh hour. It is important, therefore, that those in the lay state remain attentive to the end. Vocations like that of Brother Klaus[15] are, admittedly,

---

[15] The reference is to St. Nicholas of Flüe (1417–1487), popularly known in his native Switzerland as "Brother Klaus". He was married and the father of ten children. During the last nineteen years of his life, which he spent as a hermit, the Holy Eucharist was his sole nourishment. His wise counsel is credited with having saved the Swiss Confederacy during the Diet of Stans (1481), at which he was not

infrequent. But one does not always have to await the death of a spouse before listening more attentively to a call one has always heard more or less distinctly. If lay persons listened more attentively, it might well be that, once their children were grown and the duties of their first state had been fulfilled, more of them would, like the Lord's Mother, enter upon a second state of life in which their natural fruitfulness would be transformed into a supernatural one. ". . . At an hour that you do not expect, the Son of Man will come" (Mt 24:44). "They were eating and drinking; they were marrying and giving in marriage; . . . they were buying and selling; they were planting and building . . ." (Lk 17:27–28), but when Noah entered the ark, "the flood came and destroyed them all" (Lk 17:27). So will it be at the coming of the Son of Man. "For as the lightning when it lightens flashes from one end of the sky to the other, so will the Son of Man be in his day" (Lk 17:24). If, instead of burying themselves in their business pursuits, men lived in readiness "to pray always and not to cease praying", then Jesus would not have had to utter the bitter words: ". . . When the Son of Man comes, will he find, do you think, faith on earth?" (Lk 18:8). It is never too late to wait for him unless one's "too late" has already been transformed into a "no". Young people possess an inner receptivity to every form of idealism and, in consequence, a kind of natural readiness to respond generously to God's call for generosity. Their natural talent is, as it were, a grace bestowed upon them for the exercise of a supernatural readiness that must last a lifetime. This spiritualization of their youthful idealism, this transformation of their natural readiness into a supernatural one, must take place while they are between the ages of twenty and thirty. If it does not, the adult will come to regard the time of his youth as a pleasant, if somewhat foolish, illusion whose "truth" is but the nostalgically agreeable memory of school days that are gone forever. To

---

himself present. He was beatified in 1669 and canonized by Pope Pius XII in 1947. For further information about Brother Klaus, see T. Boos, "Nicholas of Flüe, St.", *The New Catholic Encyclopedia* (New York: McGraw-Hill, 1967), vol. X, p. 453. [Tr]

turn the clock back to the "good old student days", the wise philistine may, from time to time, share a beer with the younger generation, but he will regard it as a duty to initiate them into the mysteries of the disillusionment that awaits them. For how can wonder dawn in him who is determined to close the door on wonder? Never again will he experience the mystery of a great awakening to God. When a young person decides to give himself wholly to God, the philistines of this world "look on and sneer" (Wis 4:18; Jerusalem Bible). "Yet people look on, uncomprehending; it does not enter their heads that grace and mercy await the chosen of the Lord, and protection, his holy ones" (Wis 4:14–15; Jerusalem Bible).

2. RECOGNITION OF THE CALL

One who has been called must be aware of God's call and must understand its nature before he can respond to it. This does not mean that there is a clearly defined interval between the moment when the intellect becomes aware of the call and the moment when the will responds to it. There may even be cases in which an unambiguous awareness of being called is met with an a priori "no" on the part of him who is called. More frequently, however, intellect and will cooperate in making the call clear, and a conscious *willingness* to hear it prepares the way for an ever deeper insight into it. Nevertheless, the decisive "yes" that is, in every instance, required of one called to a special vocation must be preceded by the clear knowledge that one is indeed called. Hence not only the person who is called, but also those entrusted with his spiritual guidance, must be well-versed in the signs of God's election.

Much has already been said on this subject, especially as it relates to the difference between a vocation to the priesthood and one to the religious life. At the lowest level, a kind of general piety and an inclination to and aptitude for the priestly ministry are all that are required for the priesthood, provided only that they be supplemented and confirmed by the Church's acceptance of the candidate. Between this lowest level and the unambiguous call to personal discipleship, the call makes itself known in varying degrees of clarity and with more or less discernible signs that can never be totally lacking in any genuine vocation to the priestly or religious state. If one questions the candidates about the motives that have led them to this state, one receives a variety of answers. Some have very explicit reasons—an attraction to the pastoral ministry, for instance, which is often directed to a particular form of this apostolate, such as missionary work, the education of youth, and so on; others stress the sacrifice they want to offer to God and that they believe God demands of them; still others become embarrassed and find nothing to say but "I felt I had to." It need hardly be said that the ability to formulate one's motives with more or less clarity is not a valid criterion of the certainty of a vocation. A feeling one cannot express can be more definitive than the compulsion to engage in some specific religious activity. It might even be said that such a compulsion can be the sign of a genuine vocation only if it has its source in a general and unqualified openness to God's call. For, without exception, the "yes" God demands of his elect is, above all, the "yes" of indifference, of that trusting gift of self that, "in every state and way of life", wants and chooses only what God wants and chooses. This "yes", which is the hallmark of the elect and which is always unconditional, encompasses even a return to the lay state if such should be the clearly revealed will of God. In particular, a "yes" to the evangelical life is, at least at first, an implicit acceptance of every form of this state, even when an inclination to one or other communal form of religious life soon makes itself known. Even after the candidate has particularized his vocation in terms of a specific religious order or congregation, Ignatius demands that he remain in indifference as to whether he is to be accepted as a lay brother or a priest.

Since the only response to God's special call to personal discipleship is an unqualified assent, this assent must have its source in an a priori absence of qualifying conditions in the intellect—an absence that persists in spite of and preserves its independence in relation to every qualifying motive and predisposition. On the other hand, this same assent must be made in full awareness that one is committed thereby to indifference not only in the abstract and in the absence of qualifying conditions, but also in reference to a specific mission and task that will be chosen not by oneself, but by a representative of that Church in which one wants to serve God.

The result is a center that can be approached from two different directions.

The first way of approach begins with the realization that there are concrete situations or relationships in the world that must be changed at any price. No one else seems to worry about them; no one else looks deeply enough into them. So one decides to do something oneself. Subjectively, one feels that one has placed everything one has at the service of a cause that seems to belong—and may actually belong—to the kingdom of God. As long as no further step is required, however, this is basically an undertaking for the lay state. Certain social structures are to be changed: To do so requires experienced sociologists; certain pedagogical methods are to be improved: To do so requires expert educators. But no one becomes a priest on the condition that he will be appointed pastor in a certain town. Peter received no promise that he would become a fisher of men in Bethsaida. Between the urge to do something and the "yes" of the Church there occurs the moment of universalization. One who would be the Lord's disciple must first leave his nets and follow Jesus, "not knowing where he [is] going" (Heb 11:8). And "another will gird thee, and lead thee where thou wouldst not" (Jn 21:18). The candidate may reveal to his superior or bishop the specific motive that led him to his "yes", and this motive may be taken into consideration when his mission is being assigned—but it need not be. If his assent cannot be separated from the particular purpose that gave rise to it, it is not universal, not Catholic; it is not directed wholly to Jesus Christ, but to a cause of which no one can say with certainty that it is the task God has decreed for me for the sake of the kingdom. No one decides for himself what his charism will be. It is the Lord who decides. And when the Church acts in the Lord's name, the bishop or superior must respect the decrees of the Lord, for they are the touchstone against which he will test the candidate's motives; but both the bishop or superior and the candidate himself must accept with indifference whatever the Lord may decree. In addition, the needs of the diocese or order must also be given precedence over the wishes of the subject. One who does not attain this indifference must not delude himself that he is imitating Christ's attitude toward the will of the Father. Christ himself did not determine the means of salvation by which the Father chose to remedy the ills of the world; but when the time came to put these means into practice, he was obedient to them even to death on the Cross. The "yes" to Christ's call is always associated with a death that gives actual expression to one's "being buried together with Christ" in baptism and from which one is awakened, not by his own power, but by the Church, which acts in God's name.

The second way of approach begins as a conscious retreat from the world, a retreat about which one is not yet certain whether it is distinctively Christian and Catholic. One understands the words of "the Preacher": "For all his toil, his toil under the sun, what does man gain by it? . . . All things are wearisome. No man can say that eyes have not had enough of seeing, ears their fill of hearing" (Qo 1:3, 8). One has, perhaps, had the same experience as the Preacher: "I said in my heart: I will go, and abound with delights, and enjoy good things. And I saw that this also was vanity. . . . And when I turned myself to all the works which my hands had wrought, and to the labors wherein I had labored in vain, I saw in all things vanity and vexation of mind, and that nothing was lasting under the sun" (Qo 2:1, 11; New Catholic Edition). One's retreat may seem to be an all-encompassing indifference: "A time to be born and a time to die. . . . A time to kill, and a time to heal; a time to destroy, and a time to build . . ." (Qo 3:2–3). But it is not yet clear whether the way one is taking leads one with Buddha away from the "wheel of rebirths" or whether it is the way imprinted upon the world by God himself:

". . . I will see and consider the Three Divine Persons seated on the royal dais or throne of the Divine Majesty. They look down upon the whole surface of the earth, and behold all nations in great blindness . . . [and] those on the face of the earth, in such great diversity in dress and in manner of acting. Some are white, some black; some at peace, and some at war; some weeping, some laughing; some well, some sick; some coming into the world, and some dying . . ." (*Sp Ex*, 160). To see the world in this way is to see it with the eyes of God. The negative moment of retreat and the indifference it presupposes can—and must if the vocation is a genuine one—have as its foundation the positive attitude of the heavenly state. One called by God is, in a special way that permeates his consciousness, "not of the world" (Jn 17:14). He has "died" and his "life is hidden with Christ in God" (Col 3:3); therefore, he seeks "the things that are above, where Christ is seated at the right hand of God" (Col 3:1); he is "known by God" even before he himself knows God (Gal 4:9); like Paul, he can say that through Christ "the world is crucified" to him, and he to the world (Gal 6:14). For God's election is an eternal act. It draws him who has been chosen into eternity, but only that he may there be incorporated into God's eternal decrees and be sent with Christ into the world. If he survives—indeed, if he has existence at all—it is in the strength of his calling and the fire of his mission, which have their source in the city of the living God. Perhaps he will always consider himself a stranger in this world, for his "citizenship is in heaven" (Phil 3:20). But this does not mean that his task on earth does not burn more brightly—with a fire that has its source in heaven—than do those of his fellow men, who are of this world.

This supernatural orientation is very different from the motives that a free-thinking psychology often ascribes to those called by God: lack of concern about the world and society; uncontrolled emotional complexes; even fear of life itself. Such motives —especially those feelings of inferiority that are part of almost every young life that has not yet come to an awareness of its own worth—may, of course, make themselves felt also, and even especially, in the case of those called by God, and may forge apparently unbreakable bonds with precisely the supernatural element of such a call. When this happens, one must examine one's motivation in prayer and, with the help of a wise director, distinguish between the two sets of motives in order to discover which is dominant. If the vocation is genuine, it is usually not advisable to postpone one's acceptance of it until all the natural hesitancies that every adolescent experiences in one way or another and often supposes are peculiar to himself have been surmounted. What matters is that they not be allowed to determine the outcome of one's choice, though it may, at the time, be impossible to exclude them completely from one's mind. In this connection, Ignatius quotes to good purpose the words addressed by St. Bernard to the demon: "I did not undertake this [work] because of you, and I am not going to relinquish it because of you" (*Sp Ex*, 351). Once one has recognized that the call transcends all one's uncertainties, there is no better way of putting an end to these uncertainties than to respond with a courageous "yes" to the God who calls.

The two ways converge, then, on a common center. In the first way, the individual is called to a particular and possible mission, but must let himself be purified to the point of indifference. In the second way, the indifference he already possesses must be subjected to the rules for the discernment of spirits (*Sp Ex*, 313–36) and must prove itself truly Christian by its willingness to let itself be specified in terms of a particular mission. Such a mission finds its inspiration in the need, injustice and sinfulness of the world; but it must learn that there is only one remedy for this: the Cross. There is no Christian liberation that is not also a redemption. God's elect stands here at the divine source of all missions, but he has still to learn this truth: The nearer he will be to God, the more deeply he must let himself be used and consumed for the advancement of God's plans for the world.

Recognition of a genuinely present call to the special following of Christ can be *endangered* and, at least for the moment, made impossible by the absence of either its subjective or its objective component. Unwillingness or inability to hear the call are subjective obstacles. It is difficult to know with certainty to what extent a special call can be totally silenced if one does not follow it in youth, but culpably postpones it until later. The relevant factor here is one's unwillingness to hear a call one has already begun to hear. One retreats from it, and the seed of the word falls on ground that bears no fruit. If the call then ceases to make itself heard and he who has rejected it is left "in peace", he can only pretend to excuse himself on a plea of innocence; at a particular point on his journey through life, he has made it impossible for God's voice to be heard by him again; hence his failure is culpable. This is not, of course, to deny the possibility that certain individuals may indeed be genuinely and through no fault of their own unable to hear God's call. They hear what may be a call, but they do not know how to interpret it: "When anyone hears the word of the kingdom, but does not understand it, the wicked one comes and snatches away what has been sown in his heart" (Mt 13:19). Such a possibility, if it is to be truly without blame, presumes an objective lack of clarity in the call itself. The objective component may, in fact, still be lacking; the call may not as yet have been fully articulated by God. God's calls are not rigid and mechanical; they are infinitely varied and dynamic, if for no other reason than that he has made them dependent on man's cooperation and on the active vigilance of his Church. Both he who hears the call and he who guides such a person have a role to play. Others—those who pray and those who sacrifice— also share in making the divine call an endeavor of the whole communion of saints. Thus there is generally a stage at which the call is still objectively weak: a gentle knock, a first intimation of God's love for an individual. It can be God's will that the person respond only gradually. He can let his call shine like a ray of sun through the mist, visible perhaps only as a brightening of the clouds that are not fully dispersed. He can let the mist thicken again so that it is only in the recollection of that hour of brightness that one is inspired to pray and seek further. At such a time, the role of the spiritual director is especially important. It is he who must explain and clarify. He must be tactful so as not to frighten timid souls by demands that are too sudden, but must rather disclose to them gradually and, as it were, incidentally, the excellence of the state of election. The dialogue can remain at this stage for years. It is usually better for the one who is called to come to the knowledge of the call by his own efforts than for someone else to make him aware of it. Tactless zeal does more harm than good, and one who has once been frightened by it will be slow to risk thinking again in terms of a vocation. Nothing, finally, is more likely to arouse young people to resistance than the suspicion that someone is trying to "persuade" them by guile or coercion.

Insofar as it depends on God, it is, of course, impossible that the first gentle knocking, the first vague intimation of God's special election, will not eventually reveal itself as an unambiguous call. If there is no disobedience on the part of him who is called or of those (parents, teachers, priests) who direct him, God will let the call sound so clearly that it cannot fail to elicit the proper response. If, on the other hand, the call reflects God's will or wish for one in the lay state, it may perhaps never lose its unobtrusive and enigmatic character. For while many things are prescribed by God's commandments, there are also many things that are not prescribed—things that would cause an individual to advance with giant steps along the way of perfection if he heeded God's invitation, but to which God's graciousness will not compel him. For the lay person, there is no question of the existence or nonexistence of a mission, as there is for those called to the priestly or religious state, where everything must be subordinated to the mission they are to receive, that is, to a "yes" that presumes, in any event, that they have understood God's call in its full clarity. In such cases, the priestly and religious states are as important as the individual who consecrates himself to them. One who chooses the married state, on the other hand, does not assume that this state will be enriched by his entry into it. Hence everything about his life and his relationship to God retains a more personal character than can be the case for one called to a special mission in which the person is completely subordinated to his office or his solemn promise.

Where there is question of a special mission to which insurmountable obstacles are likely to arise either from the character of the one called or from his external circumstances, it can be the part of mercy not to force such a person to a full awareness of his vocation. Yet there can also be instances in which, despite the obvious impossibility of an external following of God's call, the individual's full awareness of it is willed by God and intended to serve a useful purpose. Perhaps he is to know what God has decreed for him so that he can make this unattainable ideal the rule of his life. Perhaps it is God's will that he go through life with a "thorn in his flesh"—in a holy dissatisfaction with the pedestrian environment in which he is doomed to live.

Once the initially indistinct call has begun to reveal itself as a form of election, the young person is faced with a difficult question: *priesthood or religious life?* He must seek his answer in the nature of the call itself. As we have said above, the call to the priesthood is primarily a call to ministry; that to the religious life is primarily a call to personal discipleship. If both motives are present, he must determine which is uppermost. A vocation to the secular priesthood usually manifests itself in an explicit attraction to the priestly function as such—to preaching and instruction, to administering the sacraments and to the pastoral care of those in need. A vocation to the religious life manifests itself in the desire to give oneself wholly to God and, in the case of a clear vocation to life in a monastery or convent, in the desire to submerge one's whole person in the anonymity of life under a rule that gives primary emphasis to one or other of the vows. But even this desire for complete self-surrender must have an ecclesiastical and apostolic stamp of which the one called may not at first be aware, but that he will soon come to understand in its totality if his vocation is genuine. He must realize that it is not for his personal benefit or spiritual advancement that he has been permitted to choose this way of life. On the contrary, if he holds fast to the ideal of "self-perfection", he must understand it only as a means to an end—to the glorification of God and the service of his kingdom. Between the priestly and the religious states, there are, in fact, many transitional forms that the spiritual director may as easily interpret as belonging to one of these states as to the other. God himself can bestow a temporary vocation to the priestly state and only later clarify his will by a call to closer discipleship in the life of the vows; he can bestow a vocation to the religious life, and only later enlarge it to include the priesthood; he can even, as we have seen, call one to a secular priesthood that embodies all that is essential in the evangelical life.

Finally, one called to the observance of the counsels must also make the narrower choice *of a particular religious community*. Here, too, one may hear the divine voice clearly from the beginning, and with it the voice of the spirit and founder of a particular religious order. This should not surprise us. In the process of establishing a religious order, the founder acquires a special role as mediator of the graces reserved for his spiritual children. Just as the Lord's mother is the mediatrix of all graces, so every saint who has laid the foundation of a religious order and impressed upon it his own personal spirit continues to guide its growth so that it may be imbued with new strength and permeated in the deepest and most effective way possible with the spirit that gave it birth. In choosing a religious community, a candidate nearly always experiences in prayer a lively attraction to the saint whose community he would like to enter. From this attraction, which is like an imprint upon his soul, he is able to discover which saint has placed his mark upon him. If this is not immediately apparent to him, he will seek to familiarize himself with each religious community in turn until he finds the objective counterpart of his vocation. There is little danger that he will, in the process, fall prey to an inordinate attraction, for it is rare indeed that one ready to surrender his whole life is found wanting in generosity precisely in the matter of choosing a religious community. The pupils of a school conducted by a particular religious order will be drawn in great numbers precisely to that order; the zealous canvassing of an area by a missionary community will not be without success. Indeed, there will always be a great number of what we might call "neutral" vocations that owe their existence solely to the external influence of the Church. Nevertheless, a distinction is in order here between the first example and the second: Years spent in the formative atmosphere of a school under the auspices of a religious community may, without the slightest external "pressure", give the young soul a lasting and genuine understanding of religious life, whereas the mere "rounding up" of candidates for a mission workshop is less likely to inspire them with a genuinely spiritual motivation. An individual who is convincing, who consumes himself wholly in the service of his mission, in whom there is no perceptible vanity, who always and in all ways reflects the spirit of his community—in the ordinary course of events, only such a one can awaken new vocations. To meet a person of this kind can be more meaningful for the aspirant to the priesthood or the religious life than any number of books about a particular state of life or religious community, for in him the aspirant experiences the living reality of that for which he is sincerely seeking. He knows that his seeking has been understood, for he sees in such a person, as in a mirror that is both objective and personal, the actual living of the rule. If the person truly leads men to God, he will not—or at least not for any length of time—allow free rein to the power of personal attraction. Rather, he will become as quickly as possible a pure transparency of the Lord who calls, who is the true and only leader. "Again the next day John was standing there, and two of his disciples. And looking upon Jesus as he walked by, he said, 'Behold the lamb of God!' And the two disciples heard him speak, and they followed Jesus" (Jn 1:35–37). "You yourselves bear me witness that I said, 'I am not the Christ. . . .' He who has the bride is the bridegroom. . . . He must increase, but I must decrease" (Jn 3:28–30).

3. ACCEPTANCE OF THE CALL

Recognition of the call is followed by an act that either accepts or rejects it. There is no third alternative, for even a nonacceptance that simply ignores the call or constantly postpones a decision regarding it to a time of one's own choosing is a form of rejection. This is true because God's word as such, and especially when it is personally extended to an individual in the act of election, has the character of an utterance that, of its very nature, both requires an answer and bestows the grace and strength necessary to make it. Acceptance of a call to a particular state of life is, therefore, subject to the law that every divine grace must be freely accepted by him to whom it is offered, just as one must assent to the grace of justification if one is to be inwardly sanctified by it. Here, too, the central act in which man utters his "yes" to God's redemptive and sanctifying grace is preceded by a more or less lengthy preparatory process in which God acts upon man's intellect and will. During this time, God causes the soul to open gradually; he enlightens and strengthens it by his helping grace, and the soul cooperates by opposing no final "no" to his action upon it. It listens to his word, lets itself be enlightened and warmed by it, and taught "all truth" (Jn 16:13) until it is ready, in cooperation with God the Father, to bring forth the unconditional "yes" that will ensure its active participation in the "yes" of eternal life. "He who believes in the Son has everlasting life; he who is unbelieving towards the Son shall not see life . . ." (Jn 3:36). "Amen, amen, I say to you, he who believes in me has life everlasting" (Jn 6:47). Thus the proclamation of the truth of eternal life is transformed into a demand for its acceptance in faith: ". . . He who believes in me . . . shall live and . . . shall never die. Dost thou believe this?" (Jn 11:25–26). The initial act of justification, which bestows a living faith, is thus the model of all further acts in that continual exchange between God and man that is but the always living union of the word by which God chooses man and the response by which man chooses God. It is also the inner form of that highest act of choosing that takes place in the light of sanctifying grace: the act of choosing one's vocation, in which God reveals to the Christian and, if the latter so wills, bestows upon him the special way of life in which he is to "take his stand" with Christ. Since every Christian is called to a particular state of life, it follows that every Christian must eventually find himself in a situation that requires him to make a choice, not only the first choice of justification by which he chooses to take his stand within the Church itself, but more especially also the second choice—the choice of a special state of life within the Church—by which he is assured a permanent place within that Church. He must, therefore, consciously ask himself whether or not God's special call has been addressed to him and he must remain attentive, but indifferent, until it is made clear to him what he is to do. Neglect of this requirement that is placed upon all Christians is a principal reason why so few of God's calls are heard and accepted today. Most Christians believe—and are all too frequently strengthened in their belief by the attitude of those around them—that there is, in their case, no possibility of a special call; that, if there were, God would have made it known to them long ago in a manner that was unmistakable. Strictly speaking, however, one should enter upon the lay state only after one has stood, consciously and in full readiness to comply with God's will, before the either-or of the elective states of life. And one should be aware, in the process, that Christian life in the world is usually more difficult than life under vows. This is why St. Ignatius lays down the following rule for one who, in the course of the Spiritual Exercises, is about to choose a state of life: "He must be fully indifferent as to whether he will follow the way of the counsels or the way of the commandments. So far as he himself is concerned, he should be more inclined to the way of the counsels if thereby he will serve God better. Without doubt, it requires more obvious signs to determine that God's will would have us remain in a state of life that demands only the observance of the commandments than that it would have us enter upon the way of the counsels; for the Lord clearly exhorts us to the keeping of the counsels, whereas of the other state of life he says only that it is fraught with great dangers."[16]

As in the act of justification, so it is possible to distinguish, in the act of choosing a state of life, the time before the act, the actual time of the act and the time after the act. This succession of times is not to be understood as a process of "perfecting", as though the individual who has not yet been chosen is less perfect than one who is in the act of choosing or one who has already made his choice. Mary was perfect even before her meeting with the angel, for she was just as obedient to the will of God then as later. God's ways with man constitute a history in which it is impossible to measure the various stages against a moment that is outside or beyond time. It is enough if we give to each moment its fullness of meaning—that is, if we strive at every moment to know and to do the will of God.

From this perspective, *the time before the choice* is a time of preparation. Just as all the Old Testament was a time of preparation for and instruction about Christ (Gal 3:24) and, as such, is indispensable for an understanding of Christ and the New Testament, so, for the Christian, the waiting-time of youth is indispensable as a time of training for his meeting with the Lord. And just as the holiness of the saints of the Old Testament consisted in living in expectation of a redemption to come that was comprehensible to them only in faith and present only in promise, and in making this promise the sole substance of their lives (Heb 11), so the life of a Christian before the act of choosing must be shaped by faith in his coming encounter with God. This means, above all, that he must take no action before that time that would in any way preempt God's freedom of decision. Such an action would not only be a conscious and a priori rejection of any call God might subsequently make to the priesthood or religious

---

[16] "Exercitia Spiritualia Sancti Patris Ignatii de Loyola et Eorum Directoria", *Monumenta Ignatiana*, series secunda, tomus unicus, caput 23, 4, in *Monumenta Historica Societatis Jesu* (Madrid, 1919). Further references to the *Directory* (henceforth *Dir*) will be given in parentheses in the text.

life; it might also create hindrances that would make it impossible for the one called to enter into either of these states. Indeed, a young person who has even a remote and dreamlike intimation that he may be one of God's chosen ones and who must, therefore, wait with double attentiveness for the call of God, should so shape and monitor his life that God can take possession of it at any moment. Above all, he must foster his intellectual powers of perception and keep them alert; he must join to them both a desire to know everything, whether secular or spiritual, that might impinge upon his destiny and a generosity that is ready for all the adventures of life. Even when he is sorely tried by sexual temptations, he must avoid—and must instinctively avoid—all that might dull him prematurely, that might teach him to be content with cheap sensual pleasures. "Insofar as it is a sin", Thomas Aquinas says, "folly arises from the fact that one's spiritual sense has been blunted and is thus unfit to judge things that are spiritual. But man's senses are most immersed in earthly things by lust, which concerns those very strong desires by which the soul is greatly captivated" (2a 2ae 46, 3 responsio). We mention this here only in reference to the preparation for a choice of vocation, not in reference to the practice of spiritual direction in seminaries and novitiates.

The time of waiting must be spent in the patience depicted in the Gospels: a patience that is the direct opposite of inactivity even though no external activity is visible; a patience that is rather the exercise of an always growing preparedness, of an active warring against the obstacles to indifference, of an unceasing longing for the coming of the Lord. He will wait in vain who sleeps during the time of waiting in the hope that he will be awakened by a miracle. One must await the day of the Lord in prayer and fasting, with loins girt and a lamp burning in one's hand (Lk 12:35). What is true of the act of justification is true also of this time of waiting: The more the soul prepares itself in advance by enlightenment and purification, the more the motives and wishes of the self will recede into the background and the more one's spirit will be filled with the thought of God alone. It would be wrong, therefore, to compare the choice of vocation with the trying-on of various states of life as one might try on various styles of clothing to see which of them "looks best", which is most "satisfactory" and "becoming". Such a concept is generally the product of a youthful vanity that wants to play a role in life, that wants to gain recognition for itself. But the best way of assimilating oneself to the will of God is to exclude all such egotistic points of view. This is usually a gradual process. Even when it has no obvious connection with one's choice of vocation, every small act of obedience to God is a step toward the great and decisive act that can take place only when one has learned to obey. If he who obeys is one of those called by God's special election, God will not leave him in doubt: He will demonstrate to him again and again that every act of obedience will be rewarded with an increase of light in his soul.

The act of choice itself can be experienced as the unique moment of identity between divine and human choice, as an unparalleled *kairos*, the luminosity of which was not equaled in the past and will not be equaled in the future. Before this moment, one's life, like that of the disciples who had their roots in the Old Testament, was a life of unillumined waiting, of longing and often of failure. After this moment, it will be a life of mission in which human effort will never be commensurate with the absoluteness and breadth of what is demanded of it, a life of constant striving adequately to fulfill the task to which one is called. Between these moments lies the indivisible point of inter-section where seeking becomes finding and finding has not yet become again an "endless seeking" in the immensity of love.[17] "We have found him of whom Moses in the law and the prophets wrote, Jesus the son of Joseph of Nazareth" (Jn 1:45). This grace is reserved for those who receive God's special call, but it is not without analogies in the ordinary life of the Christian: in those hours of meeting with God that require the "yes" of fidelity and

---

[17] Cf. St. Augustine, "In Joannis Evangelium Tractatus CXXIV", tractatus LXIII, sec. 1, PL 35, col. 1803.

that stamp and consecrate one's life for years, perhaps forever; in those hours of conversion in adulthood in which the act of justification in baptism forms a single whole with the act of personal election and vocation; or in those keen-sighted hours of decision that, by the power of God's love, are able to bestow on a past full of meaninglessness and guilt a meaning that will be productive of unexpected fruit in the years ahead.

This does not mean that there will be such distinctive hours in the history of every vocation. The time of preparation can also flow *almost imperceptibly* into the time of fulfillment. In such instances, the light of knowledge keeps pace from early youth with the light of assent; the certainty of being called, perhaps to a particular religious community, is so eminently present (as it was in the case of St. Thérèse of Lisieux) that it matures from childhood along with one's intellectual development, but without ever clearly revealing itself. The obedience of the child ripens automatically into the obedience of the adult. Such an election has been, from the beginning, a part of God's eternal act of election; the individual's assent is given, as it were, "before the foundation of the world" (Eph 1:14), so that, when at last it enters the soul with the grace of baptism, it takes possession of it and begins to grow there. Between this and the first mode of choosing there are also many transitional stages that require a gradual or even an intermittent choice.

But if he who is called must await with indifference the hour of God's definitive call, he must also remind himself that he is always slower and more laggard with his answer than God is with his word and question. It is possible, therefore, that God may already have indicated the time of choice even while the one he calls is still waiting for him to do so. God always accommodates himself, moreover, to the ecclesiastical powers that assist and cooperate with him. We can understand, then, why Ignatius was so convinced that *the time of the Spiritual Exercises*, which are ordered principally to the choice of a state of life, is a time of decision. He firmly believed that an individual faced with the necessity of such a decision would be ready, if he had been converted by the Spiritual Exercises to a state of total indifference and had received proper ecclesiastical guidance, to hear and respond appropriately and with a kind of grace-given infallibility to the voice of God's election. Admittedly, "experience shows that those who make the Exercises in a state of conflict are able to recognize the truth more easily later when the Exercises are over—and to recognize it for the very reasons that were advanced during the Exercises" (*Dir*, chap. 33, 3). But Ignatius intended this later gloss to refer only to exceptional cases. He was convinced that God would never reject one who knocked if only because God himself has to knock so long before man hears and opens to him (cf. Rev 3:20). The movement of the "different spirits" that Ignatius assumes will be experienced by everyone who makes the Exercises with a proper intention (*Sp Ex*, 6–10) is at once God's infallible preparation of the individual for the choice he is to make and an interior training of the soul for the act of choice itself, which is always an actual historical event. Ignatius gives strict instructions as to how the spiritual director is to conduct himself: If, in the time before the choice, he is permitted to urge recognition of the gradually emerging will of God regarding the choice that must be made, he may not in any way share in the act of choice itself, but like "a balance at equilibrium, without leaning to one side or the other, [must] permit the Creator to deal directly with the creature and the creature directly with his Creator and Lord" (*Sp Ex*, 15), and must even expressly "admonish [the exercitant] not to be inconsiderate or hasty in making any promise or vow" (*Sp Ex*, 14). The unmediatedness of the relationship between God and the soul during the act of choice must be distinguished from the time of ecclesiastical mediation that precedes and follows it; all secondary causes are intended only to assist the mystery of the unmediated oneness of word and answer. When the ministerial function of the Church yields thus to the unmediatedness of the act of choice, the Spiritual Exercises reveal their kinship with mysticism, which Ignatius also expressly envisions as unmediated (*Sp Ex*, 329, 336), but with this difference: Of the mystical unmediatedness of the union of divine and human experience (or contemplation) and of divine and human will, only the second is presented as a paradigm universally binding on every Christian who is called. Whereas the unmediatedness of experience—or contemplation—belongs properly to those things that are *gratiae gratis datae* and that man can, therefore, acquire neither by effort nor by training, the unmediatedness of the will is attainable by every Christian with the help of God's grace—at least to the extent that nothing more is required of him in this ecstasy of the will than that he surrender his total liberty to the elective will of the God who calls him (*Sp Ex*, 234). On the other hand, this unmediated union of the will of the individual Christian with the will of God is not something that transcends or exceeds the ecclesiastical sphere. The required suspension of ecclesiastical guidance does not mean that the soul is now to proceed under its own guidance to its meeting with God. That the opposite is true is clear from what we have said above: that every election within the Church is to a mission for the Church. If the Church founded on Peter has now fulfilled its ministry and must yield its place, it is only to make room at a deeper level for the Church by which it is totally encompassed, the Church founded on Mary. For nowhere is the faithful Christian more clearly assimilated to the primitive act of the Church itself—to the "yes" by which Mary made possible the incarnation of "head" and "body"—than in the answer he makes to the call that lays claim to his entire life.

God does not hesitate to compress the whole meaning of the life of his elect into this single hour of choice. It would be unworthy of him to try to force his decree upon the elect or to offer it again once it has been rejected. Like the meeting between lovers who have chosen one another for life, the meeting between God and his elect must be completely free and unhampered. This is the honor God bestows on man—that he accepts him as a partner. God's hour of choice will not take man by surprise, like the favorable or unfavorable contingencies of an examination that can have incalculable repercussions on one's life and state. Rather, one "taught of God" (Jn 6:45) will be well known to his teacher when he comes to the final examination; his conduct through the years may, perhaps, already have indicated the answer he will give. God calls no one to come unprepared to the choice of a way of life. If the pupil fails, it will be because he has long ago begun to say "no"; if he passes, it will be because he has long ago learned to say "yes". "See that you do not refuse him who speaks. For if they did not escape who rejected him upon earth, much more shall we not escape who turn away from him who speaks to us from heaven" (Heb 12:25).

Once the choice has been made, the moment of acceptance is a starting-point for all that is to follow. The mission one thereby accepts becomes henceforth the content of one's existence. The Christian is no longer just one chosen by God, but also one called by God, and from this fact he derives all the strength he needs to fulfill his task. As long as he lives in this strength, he will be as safe from pusillanimity and irresoluteness as from presumption, for "we are [not] sufficient of ourselves to think anything, as from ourselves, but our sufficiency is from God" (2 Cor 3:5). "But by the grace of God I am what I am, and his grace in me has not been fruitless—in fact I have labored more than any of them, yet not I, but the grace of God with me" (1 Cor 15:10).

4. REJECTION OF THE CALL

Rejection of the call is not to be confused with the impossibility of following it for external reasons, although, as we have seen, this latter complication does arise, if only because God's personal call is, in the last analysis, free and independent of all secondary causes that may further or hinder it. God is also free, if he so wills, to let an individual know that he is, in fact, one of the elect even though worldly obstacles may conspire to obstruct his vocation. Such obstacles may be external in nature: rejection of the candidate (whether with or without cause) by the bishop of the diocese or the superior of a religious community, family obligations of a spiritual or material nature, sickness, and the like. They may also be internal, having their source in the candidate's character: instability and a kind of natural weakness (Mt 13:21) that prevent him from letting God's seed take root and grow within him; deficiency of spiritual strength (*de poco subjecto*, *Sp Ex*, 18) that makes him unable to bear, even for a brief moment of trial, the "yoke of God" that is laid upon him. Even after he has begun his training for the priesthood or religious life, such a person can, without fault, be released from it or leave it of his own accord even though his vocation is a genuine one.

Actual rejection of the call has its roots in a lack of indifference, of that inner and ever-greater "humbling" of oneself before the will of God that lays claim to one's whole being (*Sp Ex*, 165–68). Such rejection may be deeply hidden in the soul of one who does not acknowledge its existence even to himself, but forces it into the "unconscious" by choosing self instead of God. Instead of placing the meaning and shaping of his life entirely in the will of God who calls him, he holds fast to his determination to shape his life according to his own good pleasure. The more specious his reasons, the more strongly will he be tempted to do so: The more talent and intellectual ability he possesses, the more urgently these gifts demand their own natural development and, in doing so, hold out the false promise of a natural mission and foster in him a corresponding awareness of such a mission; the more distinction he enjoys by reason of his natural endowments, the greater will be his temptation to say "no" to God's call and the deeper will be the loss he incurs with the loss of his divine calling and mission. It belongs to the nature of sin always to present evil under the appearance of good, and to the nature of scandal to omit the one thing necessary under the pretext of a second-best that must also be considered and done. He who rejects God's call will always be ready with an excuse that seems unassailable to himself and to the world. He will point to the great things he will be able to accomplish if he stays "in the world", to the scarcity of outstanding Catholic lay persons, to statements of the Church's hierarchy about the need to train such lay persons, to the greater likelihood that he, as a lay person, will be able to penetrate those alienated groups to which others no longer have access. He will be eloquent in praising the theological excellence of the married state and in quoting scriptural texts to support his contentions. In a word, he will repeat most of the excuses with which the guests of the parable rejected the king's invitation to his banquet table. Since of themselves all these actions are completely praiseworthy, and since they are also the actions of most of his fellow men, the world will acclaim his "realism" and wisdom in not involving himself in esoteric ventures—in a relic of the Middle Ages. Today's Church, they will argue, needs persons who are more practical, who have a courageous grasp of the difficult problems of contemporary society: It would seem, therefore, to be the special obligation of today's Christian to concentrate his efforts on strengthening the position of lay Catholics in the world.

It need not always be egoism that stirs such thoughts in the minds of the elect; it may also be fear of placing oneself wholly at the mercy of God, of having to renounce not only one's external possessions, for most of today's youth are ready to do that, but also and especially the internal "personal ideal" one has formed for oneself. It may be fear of existence in a state of pure mission that slows the steps of God's elect and causes many a one to take refuge in sickness or neurosis—that fear that often attacks those in the priesthood or religious life retroactively when the time comes to leave the protective atmosphere of the place of formation and go out "like sheep among wolves". It may be fear of a single prescription that one does not believe one can fulfill—fear of celibacy, for instance, or of obedience, or of the possibility of being placed in this or that position or sent to this or that ministry. It may be fear of the call itself—fear of being exposed to that unpredictable voice that cuts through the already considerable commandments of God and the Church with its demand for what is more than or different from what one is ready to do. Finally, it may be fear of God, whose manifestation of himself one is unable to endure and whom one seeks in embarrassment to clothe in the garb of conventional religion. At the root of all these forms of a reflection unable to transcend itself lies lack of faith; for faith is that childlikeness that casts itself into the arms of God and expects from him all its strength and help: "Amen I say to you, whoever does not accept the kingdom of God as a little child will not enter into it" (Mk 10:15).

Depending on the nature of the call itself, man's rejection of it can assume *many different forms*—from the clear and conscious rejection of a call that is unmistakable to a rejection that is disoriented and lost in the mists of half-awareness in which a call that reveals itself only gradually demands at each stage of its revelation a corresponding response on the part of him who is called. Undoubtedly there is truth in the maxim that the weaker the call, the more easily it will be suppressed. But there is truth, too, in that other maxim: that every genuine call *to a qualitatively higher mission* can, at any given moment, make itself so comprehensible that rejection of it is a fully responsible spiritual act. This is not to say that the actual guilt for such rejection may not lie with one who chokes the tender seed of vocation in the soul of a child by word or deed, by leading him astray or by a cynical word that, like a hailstorm, destroys God's planting: "But whoever causes one of these little ones who believe in me to sin, it were better for him to have a great millstone hung around his neck, and to be drowned in the depths of the sea" (Mt 18:6). How many persons grow to adulthood in an atmosphere of unbelief or of lukewarm and liberal Catholicism without ever being exposed to the concept of a closer following of Christ. One thinks of Kierkegaard, for instance, who felt obliged to eschew marriage, but could find in Protestantism no state that corresponded to such a way of life. One thinks, too, of the many Catholics who are in almost the same situation within the Church. It is impossible to blame them. But what a loss for the kingdom of God!

Theologians disagree as to whether one can reject God's special call without incurring sin. Most of them would agree, however, that rejection of a "counsel", which does not bind under pain of sin, cannot itself be a sin, but can be made sinful by such attitudes toward God's call as apathy, heedlessness, sensuality or contempt. The matter can best be discussed in terms of the various kinds or degrees of the call. Some calls are never properly comprehended as such because those to whom they are addressed do not have the necessary spiritual acumen to do so. Such persons do not sin. It is conceivable also that some calls may be hardly more than a permission to follow this or that way of life. If indeed such calls exist, they, too, may be ignored without sin. Closely related to these latter calls are those calls to the secular priesthood that are almost entirely external in character and that depend for their genuineness on the decision of ecclesiastical authority. If Lahitton is right, it is no more sinful for one who has received such a call not to advance to ordination than it would be for the Christian who has received no call at all. Once we leave this lowest level of vocation, however, and begin to consider those —traditionally most numerous—vocations in which God reveals to a soul his personal election, we find that other laws—the laws of love—have begun to play a significant role. One must be very cautious in such cases about claiming that only the "commandments" bind under pain of sin, that one can heedlessly ignore the wishes, invitations and intimations of God's love. Is it not God's will to offer his best gifts—even his most important ones—in such a way that he seems rather to ask than to command? And cannot the rejection of God's gifts in such a case be detrimental to, and perhaps even render impossible, the accomplishment of the plans fashioned by God's love?

Love has its own laws—laws that are gentler than the laws of fear or of minimalist ethics, for they express the glowing center of life where God and the soul meet in eternity. "For I say to you that unless your justice exceeds that of the Scribes and Pharisees, you shall not enter the kingdom of heaven" (Mt 5:20). A "personal" invitation can sound more urgently than an "official" command. And the magnitude of one's failure to respond will be in proportion to the greatness of the mission to which one is called. Such a mission is never without its social implications. If one had accepted God's call, a vast multitude of one's fellow men might have gained access to the Lord; many who will now remain forever in their sins might have been drawn to confession; many who will now be left in ignorance might have accepted the word of God; many who will now be forever cold might have been inflamed by the fire of faith, hope and charity. As it is, a part of God's field will be forever uncultivated. The few workers in the Lord's vineyard will be even more overwhelmed by the task that confronts them and, in consequence, will perform it less carefully and will be all the sooner exhausted. He causes untold harm who rejects God's call because his "no" affects not only himself, but also all those who depend on his mission. And, in the end, he will be called to account not only for himself alone, but also for all the graces that have been withheld from the world by reason of his "no". Every qualitatively higher mission bears within itself the promise of supernatural fruitfulness: thirtyfold, sixtyfold, a hundredfold (Mt 13:8). But all this fruit depends on the "yes" of those sent by God; it can be destroyed if even one of them says "no". If no sin is purely private in nature because, as a sin against love, it involves the whole communion of saints in its misery, this is even more true of the rejection of mission.

We have already said that God does not send a second mission to one who has rejected his call to a first one. For such missions are personal. God does not utter the word he has reserved for one individual indiscriminately to another. Rather, the reverse is true. Acceptance of a call is fruitful; its fruit can even contain the seed of God's further calls to his elect. Rejection of a call, on the other hand, is the essence of unfruitfulness. Neither in the Church nor in the world can it become the source of a fruitfulness that is alien to it. Missions are by nature irreplaceable, and the more personal and distinctive they are, the more irreplaceable they become. If the ordinary Christian falls out of grace, he can regain it by repentance and conversion; but a qualitatively higher mission once lost is *lost forever*. No amount of tears will suffice to recover it. "Take heed lest anyone be wanting in the grace of God; lest any root of bitterness springing up cause trouble and by it the many be defiled; lest there be any immoral or profane person, such as

Esau, who for one meal sold his birthright. For know that even afterwards, when he desired to inherit the blessing, he was rejected; for he found no opportunity for repentance, although he had sought after it with tears" (Heb 12:15–17).

The greater the mission, the more unique it is. For him who is called to do great things for the Lord, it is a question of all or nothing. If he rejects his mission, he can neither demand nor expect it to be replaced by one that is second-best. If he is too comfortable to make the whole sacrifice that is required of him, he cannot demand that God offer him another, less demanding one. *Every qualitatively higher mission is indivisible*, and it is precisely here that the incisive word of the Lord becomes most incisive: "He who is not with me is against me" (Mt 12:30). Guilt increases in proportion to one's awareness of what one is rejecting: "But that servant who knew his master's will, and did not make ready for him and did not act according to his will, will be beaten with many stripes. . . . But of everyone to whom much has been given, much will be required; and of him to whom they have entrusted much, they will demand much" (Lk 12:47–48). The Jews, who knew the will of God, but were unwilling to accept it, are a perpetual warning to all who are called. Every parable that depicts Israel's refusal ends with the retraction of its national mission: "Therefore I say to you, that the kingdom of God will be taken away from you . . ." (Mt 21:43). ". . . The king . . . was angry; and he sent his armies, destroyed those murderers, and burnt their city" (Mt 22:7). "For I tell you that none of those who were invited shall taste of my supper" (Lk 14:24). And that the relationship may be clear between this withdrawal of the promise from Israel and the possibility that one's mission may be retracted even under the New Testament, the Lord proceeds to speak first of discipleship, of the carrying of the cross, of the abandonment of all things, and only then of what he demands of those whom he calls: "So, therefore, every one of you who does not renounce all that he possesses, cannot be my disciple. . . . If even the salt loses its strength, what shall it be seasoned with? It is fit neither for the land nor the manure heap, but must be thrown out. He who has ears to hear, let him hear" (Lk 14:33–35).

One who has been called to season the kingdom of God, but is unwilling to do so, cannot expect that he himself will be seasoned by the kingdom. God would have been prodigal with him if he had been prodigal with God. But he is like the niggardly and calculating Pharisee "to whom little is forgiven" because he "loves little" (Lk 7:47). Just as an aborted fetus cannot be restored to the womb that should have borne it, so a rejected mission cannot be restored to the spirit that has refused to bear it. Since that moment of identity between the divine and the human "yes" that should be the central source of meaning for the life of God's elect is lacking in his case, the life of one who has refused to hear God's call remains of necessity an unfulfilled and empty longing for that which will not come to pass again, like the life of a young woman who has been unhappy in love and whose whole future is already contained in her past.

The fate of him who rejects God's call is determined by this absence of meaning, the form of which depends on the degree of consciousness with which the rejection has been made and the degree of guilt that is thereby entailed. If his rejection lies on the borderline of unconsciousness, and hence of guiltlessness, it may happen that, for reasons incomprehensible even to himself, his life will be forever unfulfilled. He will be pursued by misfortune. He would, perhaps, like to marry, but the engagement is broken; his fiancée withdraws her consent, but he does not know why. He tries again, and is again unsuccessful. None of his undertakings flourishes. Either he has no children or those he has die at an early age. He is not able, as others are, to put his affairs on a firm footing and to establish himself in a life free from care. The malaise that possesses him has its source rather in his destiny than in his character. He remains a stranger among men and feels himself such. No one will explain to him the true reason for his unsettled condition; no one wants to rob him of hope. Perhaps God will have pity on him and grant him repose.

There are also those who have rejected God's call in full consciousness of what they are doing. Of them the word was spoken: "If anyone does not abide in me, he shall be cast outside as the branch and wither; and they shall gather them up and cast them into the fire, and they shall burn" (Jn 15:6). This withering and burning can assume various aspects. There are those who are on fire all their lives. Day by day they know and feel that they have lost their true life, that their existence is sterile and vain. They try to give the appearance of convinced Stoics, smiling philosophers of worldly wisdom, or hardened cynics, but the mask is thin. Through the openings, one can see their burning and despairing spirit. Perhaps, if they are fortunate, their whole soul is in revolt; they are constantly aware of the sword of what might have been; a hundred times over, they would gladly cast the pieces of silver onto the temple floor. They are branches that have been "broken off" as an example to others not to be "high-minded", but to fear (Rom 11:19–20). The fact that they have been "broken off" and are condemned to burn does not mean, however, that they are doomed for all eternity, but only that they have missed their role on earth. It will be best for them now to accept as a fire of purification the flame that burns them and to place it, in a spirit of reconciliation, at the disposal of the Church and of God's new elect.

If the mission intended for them was a great one, they would have been capable of a great "yes". In all too many instances, their awareness of this fact becomes their license for a "no" of like proportions. They substitute themselves for their mission and try to match the proportions of their lost mission by the inflation of their own ego. They are known by their self-centeredness. They try to attract followers, to draw disciples to themselves, to become the center of a "group". They recognize each other from afar and make agreements among themselves in order to strengthen themselves in their alienation. They have a compulsive desire for frequent association with what they have rejected. They cannot refrain from searching out the secrets of grace in themselves and others only to destroy them anew by the acid of their rejection. They are attracted to whatever is new and interesting, especially to whatever is sensational in the field of religion, for they find therein a substitute for the simple greatness of the life of mission. Unable to drink from the vessel they have drained, they wallow in its dregs.

To these must be added those especially tragic figures who accept their mission and live it faithfully, perhaps even for a long time, but later slip slowly and imperceptibly away from its restraining hold, distorting the clear picture they have hitherto presented to the Church and the world and letting their infidelity be known at last to their friends and become a scandal to many of the faithful. Was this person not a lighthouse by which one could orient oneself—but what is he now? It is scarcely believable that one who seemed to incorporate in himself something of the infallibility of the Church could fall so miserably. The form of his mission, which was a pure gift of God, has become for him, all unnoticed because he no longer prays with sufficient humility, the form of his own ego; the trancelike self-assurance with which Peter walked on the waters and by which he himself has thus far felt himself to be supported is transformed into a caricature of self-assurance in which he no longer perceives the mistakes he is making. If he is a theologian, he constructs a superdogma, a superchurch; he magnanimously allows all those who find it no longer necessary to observe the restrictions of the Church that is yesterday, today and forever the same to have their own superfaith. The old faith has become tasteless for him; he needs stronger and stronger condiments until at last only the condiments seem to have meaning for him. But the condiments consume him inwardly and—saddest of all!—destroy the fruitfulness of his previous achievements. Because he no longer builds on the foundation that is Christ, "the fire will assay the quality of [his] work: . . . if his work burns he will lose his reward, but he himself will be saved, yet so as through fire" (1 Cor 3:13, 15).

Finally, there are those—and theirs are usually the less significant missions—in whom the missioning word of God does not burn, but withers; or, more correctly, in whom rejection of the word provokes a withering of the spirit. Their faith could have become a living faith if only it had placed itself courageously at the service of God's work on earth, as the body places itself at the service of the soul: "For just as the body without the spirit is dead, so faith also without works is dead" (James 2:26). In their Christian and personal lives they dispense with the soul and become, in consequence, but empty hulls. If they deceive themselves for a time that they can substitute an important position in the world and a corresponding influence as a lay apostle for the divine mission they have rejected, they are compelled in the end to acknowledge that their lives have withered and—worst of all punishments!—lost their meaningfulness. Granted, they try, in the beginning, to do more than others do; "but the cares of the world, and the deceitfulness of riches, and the desires about other things, entering in, choke [their self-devised apostolate], and it is made fruitless" (Mk 4:19). Their profession, their business, their family keep them so occupied that they have little time for what was once their chief concern. If God had destined them for the lay state, they would have borne, in that state of life, the hidden but living fruit that God expected of them. As it is, they squander their lives and consume them in unproductive criticism, especially of the Church, but without contributing anything to its betterment. Even after they have confessed it as a sin and received absolution for it, the fundamental "no" with which they once responded to the mission decreed for them remains behind as an emptiness in their soul and leads them to many a guilty action that would otherwise have been left undone.

It is not impossible that the activities of Catholic lay persons often remain unfruitful because, among lay apostles who are genuinely such, there are also many who are not—those, namely, who lacked courage for the total sacrifice to which they were called and whose outwardly well-intentioned seed does not have the benefit of the fruitful rain of grace that was reserved for their true mission. They prevent the healthy flow of blood in the arteries of the Church, causing thereby more damage than appears on the surface. The Church is strengthened by persecution from without. Its very life is threatened by persecution from within.

This does not mean that one entrusted with the care of souls should not be concerned about those of his flock who have said "no" to God's call. On the contrary, he must seek them out and console and support them in the flames in which they are consumed. He must do all in his power to see that they are "gathered up" (cf. Jn 15:6), not into a community based on their "no", but into a communion of repentance for sin that, despite everything and in a way we cannot understand, will be able to become, by the power of God's grace, the beginning of a new fruitfulness.

KEY TO ABBREVIATIONS

ACW	*Ancient Christian Writers*
Ante-Nicene	*The Ante-Nicene Fathers*
Con haer	"Contra Haereses Libri Quinque"
De civ Dei	"De Civitate Dei"
De Gen c Man	"De Genesi contra Manichaeos"
de Leg	"Tractatus de Legibus et Legislatore Deo"
De Off	"De Officiis Ministrorum"
De perf	"De Perfectione Vitae Spiritualis"
De statu perf	"De Statu Perfectionis et Religionis"
De ver	"De Veritate"
Dir	*Directory*
Eccl Hier	*Ecclesiastical Hierarchy*
Etym	"Etymologiarum Libri XX"; *Etymologies*
Fathers	*The Fathers of the Church*
In Luc	"Expositionis in Evangelium secundum Lucam Libri X"
Kanoniker	"Kanoniker, Augustinerregel und Augustinerorden"
LG	*Lumen Gentium*
LTK	*Lexikon für Theologie und Kirche*
Nicene	*A Select Library of the Nicene and Post-Nicene Fathers of the Christian Church*, Series 1.
PG	*Patrologiae Cursus Completus*, Series Graeca
PL	*Patrologiae Cursus Completus*, Series Latina

Post-Nicene	*A Select Library of the Nicene and Post-Nicene Fathers of the Christian Church*, Series 2
PO	*Presbyterorum Ordinis*
Professio	"Die Professio der Kleriker und die Entstehung der drei Gelübde"
Quaes Disp	*Quaestiones Disputatae*
Quodlib	*Quaestiones Quodlibetales*
Reg Past	"Liber Regulae Pastoralis"
Sp Ex	*Spiritual Exercises*
ST	*Summa Theologiae*
Summa Aurea	*Summa Aurea in Quatuor Libros Sententiarum*
Suppl	*Supplementum Tertiae Partis*